UPROOTING THE DIASPORA

THE MODERN JEWISH EXPERIENCE

Deborah Dash Moore and Marsha L. Rozenblit, editors

Paula Hyman, founding coeditor

SARAH A. CRAMSEY

UPROOTING THE DIASPORA

Jewish Belonging and the "Ethnic Revolution" in Poland and Czechoslovakia, 1936–1946

INDIANA UNIVERSITY PRESS

This book is a publication of

Indiana University Press
Office of Scholarly Publishing
Herman B Wells Library 350
1320 East 10th Street
Bloomington, Indiana 47405 USA

iupress.org

Manufactured in the United States of America

First printing 2023

Library of Congress Cataloging-in-Publication Data

Names: Cramsey, Sarah A., author.
Title: Uprooting the diaspora : Jewish belonging and the "ethnic revolution" in Poland and Czechoslovakia, 1936-1946 / Sarah A. Cramsey.
Other titles: Jewish belonging and the "ethnic revolution" in Poland and Czechoslovakia, 1936-1946
Description: Bloomington : Indiana University Press, 2023. | Series: The modern jewish experience | Includes bibliographical references and index.
Identifiers: LCCN 2022042853 (print) | LCCN 2022042854 (ebook) | ISBN 9780253064950 (hardback) | ISBN 9780253064967 (paperback) | ISBN 9780253064974 (ebook)
Subjects: LCSH: Jews—Poland—History—20th century. | Jews—Czechoslovakia—History—20th century. | Jews—Poland—Identity. | Jews—Czechoslovakia—Identity. | Jews—Migrations—History—20th century. | Jewish nationalism—Europe—History—20th century. | Jewish diaspora. | World Jewish Congress. | BISAC: HISTORY / Jewish | HISTORY / Modern / 20th Century / Holocaust
Classification: LCC DS143 .C73 2023 (print) | LCC DS143 (ebook) | DDC 305.892/4—dc23/eng/20221221
LC record available at https://lccn.loc.gov/2022042853
LC ebook record available at https://lccn.loc.gov/2022042854

For the "Chief"

. . . Whatever else we might think of this world—
it is astonishing.
But "astonishing" is an epithet concealing a logical trap.
We're astonished, after all, by things that deviate
from some well-known and universally acknowledged norm,
from an obviousness we've grown accustomed to.
Now the point is, there is no such obvious world.

—WISŁAWA SZYMBORSKA (1923–2012)

CONTENTS

ACKNOWLEDGMENTS

I HAVE SOMETHING TO SAY.

It has been percolating for a while. Some of the questions that I explore in the following pages began coalescing two decades ago during my undergraduate work in history and religious studies at the College of William & Mary in Virginia. Others matured across multiple years in places such as Prague, Oxford, Cincinnati, Warsaw, Kraków, Náchod, New York, Haifa, Vienna, and Szczecin where I learned languages, tracked down archival documents, and lived vigorously with support from the US Department of Defense's National Security Education Program Boren Fellowship, the Oxford Center for Hebrew and Jewish Studies, the Polish and Czech Fulbright Commissions, the Rabbi T. Levy Tribute Fellowship at the American Jewish Archives, numerous Foreign Language and Area Studies awards, the Andrew Mellon Foundation, the American Council of Learned Societies, the Carol Lavin Bernick Faculty Grant, and the Vienna Wiesenthal Institute.

My first attempts at explaining the processes behind the uprooting of the east central European Jewish diaspora were collected in a dissertation that I wrote as a doctoral student in the History Department at the University of California, Berkeley. That exercise initiated a flow of words that continued to erupt in New Orleans, in Brussels, and, finally, at Leiden University, where I have found the most incredible colleagues and a vivacious academic home. At Indiana University Press, three anonymous reviewers as well as Marsha Rozenblit and Deborah Dash Moore (the editors of the Modern Jewish Experience series) helped mold my unpolished manuscript into an articulate monograph. The roots of this book are deep and far-reaching. And so is my gratitude.

So many others have helped me find the words I offer here. At conferences, in seminar rooms, and, if I was lucky, across tables laden with food and drink, I learned from Yehuda Bauer, Wolf Gruner, Eliot Nidam, Michael Brenner, Marion Kaplan, David Sorkin, David Engel, Norman Naimark, James Sheehan, Mustafa Abu Sway, Steve Weitzman, Holly Case, Chad Bryant, Jindřinch Toman, Raz Segal, Petr Bílek, Petr Brod, Jan Láníček, Malena Chinski, Katarzyna Person, Meghan Forbes, Alice Lovejoy, Krista Hegburg, Lisa Peschel, Itay Zutra, Hugh Agnew, Tara Zahra, Bill Eddleston, Winson Chu, Martin Putna, Jacob Labendz, Konstanty Gebert, Angela Botelho, Deena Aranoff, Jay Espovich, Laura Brade, Tony Anemone, Molly Pucci, Natalia Aleksiun, Katrin Steffen, Jonathan Skowron, Madhavi Nevader, Martin Goodman, Joanna Weinberg, Alison Salvesen, Bill Hagen, Marc Lee Raphael, Emily Greble, Atina Grossmann, Kyrill Kunakhovich, Brian Horowitz, Jon Deak, Shaina Hammerman, Martin Weiss, Norma Feldman, Rachel Rothstein, Anna Cichopek-Gajraj, Mark Lewis, Edith Raim, Irina Marin, Kateřina Čapková, Kenneth Bertrams, Corey Williams, and Ab de Jong.

All questing souls should find themselves in a community like the University of California, Berkeley. So many people there have given me their time. Mabel Lee, Zachary Kelly, Solomon Lefler, and Gina Farales-Blanco provided me with much more than administrative support. Professors such as Margaret Lavinia Anderson, Carla Hesse, John Efron, Tom Laqueur, Yuri Slezkine, David Frick, Martin Jay, and (last but absolutely not least) Jason Wittenberg enabled me to see the past more clearly. Jeff Pennington at the Institute for Slavic, East European, and Eurasian Studies and Ned Walker at the Berkeley Program in Eurasian and East European Studies offered me scholarships, guidance, and counsel during my time in California. At frequent meetings of the Kroužek (Berkeley's Working Group for the Culture and History of Central Europe), my extraordinary colleagues made my questions sharper, my knowledge deeper, and my bar tab longer. Thanks are due to Michael Dean, William Jenkins, Mark Keck-Szajbel, Jacob Mikanowski, Jakub Beneš, Andrew Kornbluth, Terry Renaud, Lisa Jakelski, Daniela Blei, Udi Greenberg, Andrej Milivojevic, and Sheer Ganor.

Some of my friends and colleagues read significant portions of this book and offered their insights. I am exceedingly grateful to Dylan Siegel, Pieter Lagrou, Pierre Purseigle, Gunter Bischof, Chad Bryant, David Rechter, Maurits Berger, Terry Renaud, Ula Madej-Krupitski, and Stephen Christopher Russell. Michał Grochowski, Mary Fraser Kirsh, and Dariusz Stola read the entire manuscript and offered invaluable comments on nearly every page. Alison Panelas organized my footnotes and bibliography. Daniela Blei created the index.

Miriam Schultz, Michał Grochowski, Kamila Šatrová, Andrea Semancová, and Ula Madej-Krupitski made my translations more accurate. Courtney Strickland and Jan Burzlaff helped me obtain important documents when I could not travel myself. Finally, I could not have done this research without the help of librarians and interlibrary loan departments at the University of California, Berkeley, and Tulane University. Paul Hamburg, Elissa Mondschein, and Eric Wedig deserve special recognition.

Other friends and family members supported this book by caring for the author and, after 2018, her daughters. I must thank Stacie and Jeff Stanley, Padma and Mandyam Srinivasa, Veena Srinivasa, Louisa Morgan, Mary Slonina, Kate Powers, Christine Forsthoefel, Alanna Rosenberg, Nina Hartog, Kamila Šatrová, Andrea Semancová, Larissa Gassmann, Sydney Daniels, my grandparents, Diane and George Cramsey, Bill and Bunny Cramsey, Joan and John Holets, Nick and Rebecca Cramsey, Molly Cramsey and Zac Coleman, Annette Toierow, Annette Makowski, Marie-France Villatte, Alison DeJongh, Rachel Dieter, Olivia Rastatter, my couslings (Makensie, Mercedes, Cassandra, and Josh), and my nieces (Emmy, Anna, Lina, and Brynn).

This book uprooted the lives and routines of my own precious family. To my daughters, Salomé Rose and Orly Deborah, I hope that one day you both learn the joys and tribulations that accompany the strange phenomenon of inspiration. As your names have promised, you have brought peace and light to my life. The experience of carrying you, bearing you, and becoming your mother has fundamentally changed my understandings of time, the past, and what matters. I must apologize to my husband, partner, and most adamant supporter, Ilan Tojerow. I still have not found unique words in any of my languages to thank you for everything that you have given me and how fiercely you love me. In awe of you, I grasp for words from others such as Wisława Szymborska: "And so it happened that I'm here with you. And I see really nothing usual in that."

And after all of this, I still have two more debts.

I respect my *doktorvater* John Connelly as a scholar, as a writer, as a mentor, and, above all, as a *mensch*. For fifteen years, he has devoted a staggering amount of time to me, countless letters of recommendation, and, finally, a word-by-word reworking of much of this book. I appreciate his wonderful family, his generosity, his humor, our shared love of eastern Pennsylvanian culture, and, above all, his sharp, honest criticism. He made this book possible.

Finally, Laurie "the Chief" Koloski made my existence as a historian plausible. In the first month of the year 2000, I stumbled into her freshman seminar entitled "Stories about Communism" barely able to find "east central Europe" on a map. After a few months of reading Kundera, Hrabal, Miłosz, Kovály, and

Andrzejewski under her encouraging influence, I became captivated by the languages, literatures, histories, and humanity contained within the modern experience of this special region. I took numerous courses with her, traveled with her and a team of undergraduate students to complete an oral history project in Kazimierz, and learned time and again that the hardest question to answer is "So what?" Over a generation, she has remained a constant in my life, buying me pierogi at Jadłodajnia U Stasi, welcoming me into the home she shares with her husband, Dave, and guffawing with me over histories both distant and intimate. This book emerged from conversations we began during the first class I took with her more than two decades ago. And so, I dedicate this work to her with deep, deep gratitude.

UPROOTING THE DIASPORA

INTRODUCTION

IN THIS BEGINNING AND TO THIS PARTICULAR END

Uprooted from his Polish home, Ignacy Schwarzbart sat down at a borrowed desk in London to write yet another report in November 1940. As a one-time newspaper editor and prewar Sejm representative, as well as a current member of the Polish government-in-exile, Schwarzbart expressed his opinions with a mix of journalistic precision and political authority. Upon completion, the report traveled by post and secretarial hands to the offices of the World Jewish Congress (WJC) in Geneva, London, and New York City. Besides his high-profile job in Prime Minister Władysław Sikorski's exiled government, Schwarzbart served as a representative to the WJC (a transnational organization established in 1936 to represent "all" Jews living throughout the diaspora), and he sometimes submitted reports to their headquarters.[1] Written thirteen months into the massive European conflict that became known as the Second World War, this report contains some of the earliest wartime ideas that Schwarzbart sent to his WJC colleagues. At a time when Nazi occupation authorities were just sealing the Warsaw Ghetto, Schwarzbart could imagine only one eventuality for the Polish Jewish collective to which he himself belonged. Even if Zionist-inspired plans for Jewish settlement in Palestine developed in the "most" favorable direction, signficant numbers of Jews, Schwarzbart acknowledged, would continue to live in "postwar" Poland and in Europe more generally.[2]

No one could predict the shape of plans for Jewish migration out of east central Europe, whether British authorities would increase emigration into Mandate Palestine, or how the war might uproot Jews and others, but such uncertainties did not concern Schwarzbart. In fact, he called attention to only "one danger" at this historic moment, a danger that surprisingly originated from within the Jewish people themselves: "the theory of liquidating the *golus*."[3] By using a Yiddish word for the "diaspora," Schwarzbart was referring to a broader idea that had percolated among Jewish nationalists for generations and had roots stemming from much older Jewish traditions. Essentially, modern and ancient supporters of this theory called for the coming together, or "ingathering," of (presumably) "dispersed" Jews to the lands within and around Jerusalem as well as that city's Temple complex.

Such a mass movement toward the eastern part of the Mediterranean would dramatically impact the peoples living in the space between Salzburg and St. Petersburg, where a majority of the world's Jews lived by the time of Schwarzbart's birth in the Austrian Galician town of Chrzanów in 1888. At the age of fifty-two and living through his second global war, Schwarzbart used his report in November 1940 to "oppose" those who wanted to "negate" the Polish Jewish diaspora. Instead, he wanted to guarantee "the development of Jewish culture" amid "the nations among whom [the Jews] live." For this exiled Polish Jew and many of his generation, the Jewish diaspora would clearly remain rooted in east central Europe after the current war and occupation. Thoughts supporting the alternative were, in his opinion, "dangerous."

A mere seven years later, the danger had shifted starkly: the drastically diminished Jewish diaspora remaining in east central Europe had *itself* become dangerous. Support for that diaspora's continued existence imperiled the building up of a Jewish state on the territory of Mandate Palestine. By June 1947, much had changed. First, the great majority of a diverse and numerous *goles* had been violently uprooted, dehumanized, and killed during the Shoah. Second, widely accepted ideas about minority rights had been replaced with Allied-endorsed plans for population transfers meant to cause political and ethnic boundaries in east central Europe to coincide. Third, Jewish and non-Jewish supporters of the "diaspora" now imagined that the displaced Jews of east central Europe would belong to a Jewish polity in the Middle East and could be transferred there with the support of the United Nations as part of the unmixing of ethnic populations in places such as Poland and Czechoslovakia. This collection of revolutionary ideas had, in the two years since Victory-in-Europe Day, accrued acceptance throughout the Allied universe of diplomats, statesmen, nongovernmental officials, and caretakers within the United Nations Relief and Rehabilitation Administration (UNRRA).

Ignacy Schwarzbart shared in this acceptance. By June 1947, permanently uprooted from his Polish home, he worked full-time in New York City as the head of the Organization Department for the World Jewish Congress. The exiled Polish government still existed, but few states recognized it. Schwarzbart's erstwhile "dogma" about the future rootedness of the Jewish diaspora in east central Europe had become unrecognizable. In fact, now the WJC wanted the surviving Jewish diaspora remaining on the European continent to be diminished even further.

Or so it was written in a memorandum submitted by the World Jewish Congress to Dr. Victor Hoo, the secretary of the United Nations Special Committee on Palestine. Schwarzbart's employer believed that it had become "impossible for many Jews" to live in places such as Poland, Slovakia, Hungary, Austria, and Romania and that "Jewish survivors in the region" had to "seek a new life elsewhere."[4] That elsewhere had already been determined. The "inexorable logic of facts" pushed "every objective observer" to the "conclusion that only Palestine can provide an answer for the Jewish masses who must emigrate from the lands in which normal life is no longer possible." And since Palestine could absorb "all the Jews who desire to settle there," there was no need for the WJC to suggest contingency plans. After centuries of persecution that culminated with Nazi policies of "uproot[ing]," murder, and the destruction of a "culture and way of life," the pre–World War II world, the one that Schwarzbart clung to at that desk in England, "no longer existed." In sum, the WJC urged the United Nations Special Committee on Palestine to agree that the movement of Jews away from Europe had become "inevitable."

The development of the argument casting the displaced Jews in postwar Europe as the ideal citizens of a Palestine-based Jewish polity was not inevitable.[5] The negation of a significant slice of the postwar Jewish diaspora in the wake of the Second World War and the Holocaust was not necessarily self-evident. And although a majority of survivors and those who cared for them increasing saw the reestablishment of Jewish life throughout much of postwar Europe as untenable, the process by which this agreement emerged cannot be perceived as automatic. What, in 1947, the World Jewish Congress described as "inevitable" was in fact the opposite. The process by which east central Europeans of both Jewish and non-Jewish backgrounds as well as powerful Allied personalities sprinkled throughout Europe and North America came to the conclusion that the Jewish diaspora belonged "elsewhere" and should be transported there with the theoretical and financial support of a broader international community required a revolution in thinking about Jewish belonging, a sweeping change in international norms, and accelerated, deliberate work.[6]

In detailing this drastic change, this book contributes a late chapter to an older story about Jewish belonging in Europe. Especially since the

Enlightenment, intellectuals, diplomats, and statesmen of both Jewish and Christian heritage debated how Jews might synthesize their particular identities or supposed "otherness" with the rising modern notions of citizenship.[7] In the nineteenth and twentieth centuries, a "Jewish question" emerged that was posed with increasing intensity as new states arose—Germany, Romania, and then Czechoslovakia and Poland.[8] Debates raged across generations, but at a certain point during the Second World War, a consensus formed among unlikely actors that promised to resolve the tensions of Jewish life in east central Europe swiftly and decisively.

To capture the coalescence of this consensus, *Uprooting the Diaspora* studies roughly a dozen people working in identifiable institutions such as east central European governments-in-exile, government bureaucracies in postwar Poland and Czechoslovakia, UNRRA, and the WJC. Together, they engineered new conceptions of Jewish territorial belonging, initiated a shift away from minority rights, and demanded that the overall unmixing of ethnicities within east central Europe include the endorsement of an "empirical Zionism" that equated those European Jews uprooted by war, occupation, genocide, and postwar events with Jewish displaced persons bound for old-new homes in the Middle East. All three of these significant interlaced transformations became part of an event that I call the "ethnic revolution," which (at least according to Edvard Beneš) had roots in Nazi-era policies of demographic engineering, increasingly gained adherents within non-Jewish and Jewish Allied audiences across a very short period during and after the Second World War, and exploded with the willing support of important actors across the region in the wake of liberation.[9]

None of the actors in this book anticipated how their ideas about the nationalization of space, their opinions about an "empirical" form of Zionism, or their positions vis-à-vis the European Jewish question would change between 1936 and 1946. As their contemporary Stefan Zweig reminds us, "it remains an irrefragable law of history that contemporaries are denied a recognition of the early beginnings of the great movements which determine their times."[10] While some of those covered on these pages seemed more prescient than others as the 1940s unfolded, Zweig's observation (written during his own exile in early 1940s Brazil) stands almost without exception. This history of a particular decade-long conversation among non-Jewish and Jewish east central Europeans—such as Ignacy Schwarzbart, Edvard Beneš, Nahum Goldmann, Jan Masaryk, Arieh Tartakower, Joel Cang, Zorach Warhaftig, Aryeh Leon Kubowitzki, Yitzhak Zuckerman, and Jakob Apenszlak—reveals how definite ideas linking people to land eclipsed other ideas of ethnic and religious coexistence going back

Mothers and their children enjoy Krasiński Garden in the Jewish quarter of interwar Warsaw. Courtesy YIVO Digital Archive on Jewish Life in Poland.

centuries.[11] It all happened in a very short time, during and after the Second World War. Much of the story defies common expectations. For example, far from diminishing the intensity of nationalism, the Holocaust hardened senses of ethnicity. What seems evident to many observers in our day, that after World War II and the Shoah a Jewish political entity on Palestinian territory should exist and be populated by European Jews en masse, only became evident to the east central Europeans and observers of east central Europe studied here in an unpredictable and uneven way.

TIME, AUDIENCE, SPACE, AND LANGUAGE

I begin with a few words on time, audience, space, and language before I clarify three key concepts—the ethnic revolution, empirical Zionism, and the diaspora—that have already crisscrossed this introduction and will run like thin red lines through this narrative.

Chapter 1 begins in August 1936 at the first meeting of the World Jewish Congress in Geneva. The narrative continues more or less chronologically and extends simultaneously to the end of 1946 across both chapters 4 and 5. By the end of that year, language regarding the "Jewish origin" of some displaced persons entered drafts of what would soon become the constitution of the International Refugee Organization, and the flow of uprooted Polish Jews (most of whom had survived the 1940s in the Soviet Union) passing through Czechoslovakia toward other destinations slowed considerably. These events coincided with others to bring the ethnic revolution to a point of no return. While a noticeable piece of the Jewish diaspora that survived World War II and the Holocaust remained in Poland and Czechoslovakia at the end of 1946, a majority of Jewish survivors had sought new lives elsewhere (and not necessarily in Palestine). Before and after the decade stretching from 1936 to 1946, this narrative includes some excavations of documents and personalities from the early 1930s (especially in chapter 1), and at other points its focus extends forward, such as when it covers Jan Masaryk's address at the United Nations meeting in Lake Success during the fall of 1947 (as in chapter 5), the WJC memorandum sent to the United Nations Special Committee on Palestine in the summer of that same year (as in this introduction), or the long-term consequences of the ethnic revolution in the conclusion.

Uprooting the Diaspora contributes to several historical literatures. First, this book (especially the first three chapters of it) offers a new institutional history of the World Jewish Congress and personalities therein from its establishment in 1936 throughout the Second World War and the immediate postwar era.[12] Second, by aligning a change of international norms regarding population transfers with plans for unprecedented levels of Jewish emigration away from this region and plans for the forced movement of other east central European minorities, including millions classified as "ethnic Germans," I embed this Jewish story more firmly in an east central European one.[13] Third, this narrative illuminates how wartime thinking about Jewish belonging more generally collided with an awareness of the Shoah, other wartime horrors, and postwar circumstances and then translated (messily at times) into concrete policies impacting Jews who had citizenship in interwar Poland and Czechoslovakia and the possibilities for their movement away from the region.[14] Finally, *Uprooting the Diaspora* can be situated alongside other studies that explore Jewish nationalisms and the complex "Zionist movement" in east central Europe from the second half of the nineteenth century through the 1930s and the 1940s.[15]

At its core, however, this is a book about a particular generation born in the late 1800s or early 1900s that came of age before empires dissolved during the Great War and intimately experienced life in one of two "new," ethnically heterogenous post–World War I states: Poland and Czechoslovakia.[16] For the most part, these particular men (and they were, mainly, men) took the rootedness of Jewish communities in east central Europe (a region that can extend beyond the borders of interwar Czechoslovakia and the Second Polish Republic but is centered in the footprint of those particular states) for granted—that is, until another, more exclusive way of linking ethnicity and territory became willingly and abruptly normalized during the first few years of the 1940s.

Now I would like to propose some general thoughts on language and its relation to the telling of the Jewish experience. Conversations about rootedness, uprootedness, and the consequences of both unfolded in settings replete with Jewish east central Europeans, non-Jewish east central Europeans, and observers of the region from a variety of different religious, ethnic, and cultural backgrounds. The languages used in these conversations varied according to the participants, of course, but readers will notice that my archival searches across three continents privileged more documents written in Polish, Czech, and English than in Hebrew, Yiddish, or German. For instance, English dominates the documents drawn from the United Nations, other international organizations active in the 1940s, my survey of *Foreign Affairs* as well as the foreign correspondent's desk of the *Manchester Guardian*, and the archive of the World Jewish Congress. The largely unexplored émigré newspaper *Nasza Trybuna* (hereafter *NT*), which showcases a more personal side of important figures in our narrative such as Ignacy Schwarzbart, WJC leader Arieh Tartakower, and editor-journalist Jakob Apenszlak, among others, was published mainly in Polish beginning in 1940 but used some English-language editions to reach a broader American audience. Descriptions of cultural events from Polish Jewish citizens that spread across the wartime Soviet Union, new ideas coalescing within east central European exiled governments, and policies crafted in postwar Poland and Czechoslovakia are preserved in Polish and Czech for the most part.[17] And while authors exploring similar topics prioritize sources written in other Jewish languages (composed at the time and afterward), I am writing a different book.[18] This is a story about the Jewish experience rooted in east central Europe until, at a certain point in the 1940s, important regional and international actors decided that this centuries-old status quo should irrevocably change. Coming from both Jewish and non-Jewish backgrounds, they communicated this change with each other and to their audiences largely in English, Czech, and Polish.

In a larger sense—and here I consider the telling of Jewish history both in general and in this instance specifically—it is (almost) impossible to write about the Jewish experience without exploring how "Jews" interacted with "non-Jews." It is essentially within these interactions that the Jewish experience assumes a larger and more transformative meaning. Take, for instance, the interaction between Czechoslovak president-in-exile Edvard Beneš and Vladimir Jabotinsky as detailed on the first pages of chapter 2, which brings the collision of vocabularies justifying population transfers into sharper focus. Or consider the range of interactions between young and growing Polish Jewish families who survived the Second World War in Soviet Central Asia alongside "local" populations and other evacuees. This significant "surviving remnant," their wartime experience, and their encounters with former "neighbors" who welcomed or cursed their eventual return "home" in 1946 are discussed in chapter 5. And finally, as I consider in chapters 2 and 3, important discussions ensued between both Jewish and non-Jewish east central Europeans living in exile that reveal the difference between what they collectively "knew" about the complex web of regional and local events that tragically added up to the genocidal Holocaust and what they "accepted" as reality at specific moments. The merging of Jewish voices and the Jewish experience with broader east central European narratives about wartime intelligence, diplomatic consensus or disagreement, and societal coexistence or the tragic breakdown of communal relations results in a history that more closely resembles lived, contingent reality.

THE ETHNIC REVOLUTION

I am not the first historian of east central Europe to write about the ethnic revolution of the 1940s. Over the past generation, historians of the Habsburg Empire and its successor states have found inspiration in the work of sociologist Rogers Brubaker and have introduced the category of "national indifference" into the telling of the past. Observers of the European past, Brubaker contends, should not assume that "nations" are timeless and existing entities, thereby reducing a "category of practice" to "category of analysis."[19] Brubaker casts "groupness" not as inevitable but as a special event deserving of its own chronology. Furthermore, the work of "nationalist activists" throughout east central Europe demonstrates the extent to which nationalism as a movement demanded hard work, especially among populations that did not necessarily have a "national consciousness" or that inhabited more than one linguistic universe. As acolytes of Brubaker tell the story, nationally "indifferent" peoples (those who celebrated their Czech-German bilingualism or those who felt local or regional identities instead of national ones, for example) became targets of national propaganda and pageantry in the second half of the nineteenth century and the first few decades of the twentieth century.[20] The climax of these studies often aligns with the post–World War II expulsion of "ethnic" Germans (or the Volksdeutsche) from the territories of Czechoslovakia, Poland, and beyond. Close readings of these studies reveal how often our telling of the past bends toward a chronology that nationalists (be they Polish, Czech, or Jewish) create to justify both their political movement and their idealized ethnicized polity. When scholars understand "national indifference" as a viable category of analysis, historian Tara Zahra suggests, they can better problematize the rise of the ethnically defined nation-state.[21]

What I hope to contribute is a combined emphasis on Jewish belonging, on the speed at which decisions about Jewish territoriality were made, and on the willingness of those involved to distance themselves from their former beliefs.

Notably, the Jewish and the German Jewish dimensions of the east central European ethnic revolution in the 1940s remain underexplored. Questions about "Jewish belonging" in the region hinge on two separate but interlaced elements: the parameters of the "Jewish people" (what could be called "national indifference") and the boundaries of their "presumed" homeland (what could be called "territorial indifference"). As we will see in chapter 3, members of the World Jewish Congress who joined the so-called American Emergency Committee for Zionist Affairs in 1942 could not agree which "ties" bound together "the Jewish people" even in the abstract, nor could they agree where "those" Jews belonged geographically, although many in attendance paid shekalim to indicate their membership in the World Zionist Organization.[22] I return to this tension when I define "empirical Zionism" next, but in closing on this point, let me suggest that the uprootedness that Jewish populations in this region experienced during the Second World War and in the immediate postwar period necessitated drastic new answers for modern questions related to national and territorial indifference vis-à-vis the Jews.[23] Accepting the movement of ethnically or nationally defined Jews away from Europe to a "new" homeland far away represented the pinnacle of the ethnic revolution just as the granting of citizenship to Jews represented the pinnacle of the French Revolution.[24]

Besides illuminating the Jewish underpinnings of the ethnic revolution, *Uprooting the Diaspora* emphasizes two underappreciated aspects of this event: the speed of this revolutionary change and the willingness of those Jewish and non-Jewish actors who contributed to it. The following narrative extends from 1936 to 1946, but the ethnic revolution intensified twice within this decade: from the end of 1943 to the end of 1944 and again across just a few months during the second and third quarters of 1946. Both of these periods coincided with indecision within UNRRA related to a specific category of displaced persons or those "displaced persons unsuccessfully repatriated" to their prewar homes, be those homes in the former Czechoslovak region of Subcarpathian Rus', the parts of eastern Poland ceded to the Ukrainian and Belarusian Soviet Socialist Republics, or cities, shtetlach, and villages made unlivable by war, occupation, uprising, or genocide. Essentially, over only a score of months, important voices in the Allied wartime and postwar universe (including some east central Europeans, some non-Jews previously committed to minority rights, and some Jews previously committed to preserving diaspora lives) made arguments, plans, and decisions to further uproot a significant portion of the remaining Jewish diaspora from communities where Jews had lived for many centuries. Since the transfer of populations realigned the demographics of east central Europe, wartime shifts in ideas about ethnic belonging greatly influenced the eventual course of postwar socialist revolutions in the region as well.[25] The change in thought and policy was swift, brutal, and yet, surprisingly, acceptable to other decision-makers (some very far from east central Europe) with a stake in the outcome.[26] If the "ethnic revolution" required "hard work" from self-described nationalists, John Connelly reminds us that "plenty of people were willing to do it."[27]

EMPIRICAL ZIONISM

Plenty of people, including those strongly committed to the Jewish diaspora in the region until the early 1940s and those in positions of Allied authority, became increasingly willing to definitively uproot that same diaspora when offered a new form of Zionism that made logistical sense. Out of the diverse and complex Zionist movement native to modern east central Europe, an empirical form of Zionism emerged by the mid-1940s.[28] And while I technically named this concept, actors at the time definitively outlined the details of it.[29] Adherents of empirical Zionism equated the displaced Jews unable to return to their prewar homes with the ideal candidates for a "transfer" away from continental Europe and to an old-new homeland in Palestine. Their formula depended on three broader developments: the inability of UNRRA to offer viable solutions to specific Jewish aspects of the overwhelming displaced persons problem at that organization's earliest meetings, the quick acceptance among east central European leaders such as Czechoslovak president-in-exile Edvard Beneš of population transfers to solve minority issues (and mainly the "German" minority issue) after the Second World War, and the tragic scale of the Shoah, which meant that the numbers of uprooted European Jews could be reasonably absorbed in the Palestinian Mandate. Given altered international norms, the breakdown of east central European societies along ethnic lines, and the sharp reduction in Jewish populations, empirical Zionism seemed like a logical response to the postwar Jewish question.

When faced with this confluence of events and the logic inherent in empirical Zionism, even statesmen and diplomats without Jewish roots, those with documented prewar Zionist sensitivities, or those inextricably tied to the diaspora began to consider a novel iteration of Zionism that seemed reasonable given the vastly changed circumstances. And notably, many who metamorphosized into empirical Zionists throughout this decade did so without consulting the surviving Jewish masses (most of whom survived the 1940s in the Soviet Union) that they claimed to represent. In many ways, this book charts how various actors imagined the future of Jews in east central Europe rather than the actual experience of the men, women, and children uprooted by their visions and actions. And while these actors worked at a time marked by extreme urgency, chaos, and trauma, they imposed their own drastic visions on others nevertheless.

I tread carefully around the word *Zionism*, even as I place the word *empirical* in front of it and historicize its emergence. Like other modern "isms," this word is historically contingent and often too blunt when used in the abstract. Especially in the late nineteenth and early twentieth centuries, Zionism refers to a diverse and changing movement, not one static way of looking at the Jewish world. Throughout the Austrian Empire, for instance, "Zionists" and "Jewish nationalists" sometimes operated as distinct entities or political parties and sometimes did not, depending on circumstance and context.[30] In Habsburg Galicia, where Schwarzbart was born and raised, the "Zionist" movement focused on two tracks: the "nationalization (of) Jewish identity and securing national rights in the Diaspora" very early.[31] Moving forward, throughout the Great War, the interwar period, and the early 1940s, the "Zionism" rooted in east central Europe "served a range of local functions—ones that, at first glance, might appear at odds with post-Holocaust conceptions of what Zionist activism entailed."[32] In Czechoslovakia, for instance, Zionism became a "vehicle for integration and cultural survival."[33] In Poland, "Zionist groups" took on distinctly Polish characteristics, as I explore more fully in chapter 1.[34] Far from "simple and carefree," the Zionism explored in this book is "hard and complicated."[35]

The histories of the World Zionist Organization and more extreme groups such as the New Zionist Organization (also known as the Revisionists) that splintered off from it contain decades-long and heated discussions about where a "perceived" Jewish nation could feel at home, who belonged to that nation, and how migration between the present and future should unfold. Of course, these discussions did not yield easy, dichotomous answers. The idea that Jews would continue to live in the European diaspora even after the consolidation of a Jewish polity somewhere else, as my first chapter shows, inspired even the most vocal Palestine-centric Zionists to continue "work in the diaspora" or *Gegenwartsarbeit*.[36] In fact, this urge for more globally organized work in the places where Jews lived unleashed an organizing committee that eventually led to the creation of the World Jewish Congress, and some representatives within this organization attended World Zionist Organization meetings while they built up the WJC platform.[37] And so, as Joshua Shanes has demonstrated, the "conventional distinction" between self-described "Zionists" and other Jewish nationalists falls apart on closer inspection.[38]

The elision of this distinction impacts the way I perceive the causal power of ideology more generally and an ideology dedicated to a transcendent nation-statism (be it Zionist, Czech, or Polish) more specifically. Ideology obviously matters when we talk about actors in this past (as well as any other past). *Uprooting the Diaspora* shows, however, that specifics of Zionist ideology, especially with regard to the position of a Jewish nation-state within that ideology, were in great flux during the short period covered in this book. It remains difficult, I think, to pinpoint something that is changing and attribute causality to that entity. Furthermore, an over-intensive focus on ideology, especially an ideology filtered through the narrow "prism of the nation-state," conceals at least two things, according to Dmitry Shumsky: "the long and continuous series of political alternatives to the nation-state" that animated the political imagination of the Zionist movement and "specific changes" in the Zionist consciousness that prioritized an "ethnically Jewish" nation-state in Palestine.[39] My goal is to chart how more general ideas about empirical Zionism, the rootedness of east central European Jews, and the viability of population transfers in this "hopelessly mixed" region changed swiftly and significantly during the particular decade in question. Some writings composed after events unfolded in 1948 and the labels of "Zionist," "non-Zionist," and "anti-Zionist" can obscure more than they clarify. We cannot excise these categorizations or ideologically driven histories composed after the establishment of Israel from our studies, but they need to be used with nuance. By challenging the inevitability of nation-state-focused ideology, my analysis "emphasizes the interconnectedness and fluidity" of Jewish thinking and seemingly distinctive political movements.[40] And by following the acceptance of this highly contingent empirical Zionism beyond predominantly Jewish circles, my analysis also does something else.

My exploration of the east central European context and conversations encircling empirical Zionism in the 1940s reveals clear connections between the future of this European region and the future political belonging of Jews who were once rooted within it. Empirical Zionism is deeply imbricated within the broader ethnic revolution in east central Europe, and it is difficult to extract this form of Zionism from this particular time and, for the most part, this particular place. The success of this formula was contingent on east central Europeans realizing (and Edvard Beneš realized this sooner than almost everyone, as we see in chapter 2) that the demographic unmixing of their region after the Second World War demanded the simultaneous embrace of Palestine as an ethno-territorial state that mirrored new ethnicized iterations of postwar Polish, Czechoslovak, and German body politics. Going even further, this book ventures beyond diplomatic memos and boardroom conversations to offer, in chapter 5, an alternative reading of the postwar *bricha*, or the semilegal movement of European Jews away from their European homes, often with stopovers in the postwar displaced persons camps.

THE DIASPORA AND ITS "NEGATION"

"Diaspora," historian Erich Gruen observes, "lies deeply rooted in the Jewish consciousness."[41] Perhaps more than any other concept, it cuts across all the chronologies, geographies, and peoples that constitute Jewish civilization. Arguably, there is not one Jewish diaspora but many.[42] Those who tell the Jewish experience across millennia must devote time to Egypt, Babylon, the Iberian Peninsula, the Caribbean Islands, New York City, and the so-called Pale of Settlement as well as the hills, valleys, and deserts encircling Jerusalem. When cast against a Jewish backdrop, the word *diaspora* has a variety of connotations, from the biblical, eschatological, and liturgical to the rabbinic, spatial, and national. While *Uprooting the Diaspora* focuses mostly on the last two adjectives on that list, it is helpful to tease apart the idea of the "diaspora" before discovering how the east central European manifestation of it was definitively uprooted. And finally, during this excavation of both the word and the concept, let us not necessarily produce what we "describe or designate."[43] Like the concept of "nation," the idea of the diaspora is "used to make claims, to articulate projects, to formulate expectations, to mobilize energies, to appeal to loyalties." It is a category of analysis, to use Brubaker's phrasing, that "does not so much describe the world as seek to remake it."[44] To put it another way, Ignacy Schwarzbart assumed that the diaspora was a real entity existing in his world and on a defined historical timeline.[45] Only with this awareness can we historically analyze what was obvious to him and so many of his colleagues.

Etymologically, *diaspora* is a Greek word that appears thirteen times in the Septuagint, a translation of the Hebrew bible for Hellenized readers dating from the third and second centuries BCE.[46] Those translators used *diaspora* to represent a few Hebrew words but never to represent the Hebrew words *galuth* (displaced, against one's will, from one's home) and *golah* (residing in a foreign country).[47] These two words in Hebrew almost always refer in a negative sense to the so-called Babylonian exile during the sixth century BCE. The word *diaspora* in the Septuagint has a few connotations. For example, God uses this word to threaten Jews who are not respecting his commandments, and thus this word often connotes a "potential" dispersion related to divine power.[48] As used in other Greek-language texts from the ancient world, the word *diaspora* does not necessarily carry a negative inflection. The Alexandrian Jewish philosopher

Philo understood *diaspora*, for example, as referring to familial origins when he wrote in the first century CE. For Philo, all the Jews (or *Ioudaioi*) living in Egypt possessed both a "metropolis" or a mother city and a "fatherland." Thus, Philo and other Jews in Alexandria were descendants of their mother, Jerusalem, and of their father, "the country where [their] ancestors had chosen to live."[49] Theirs was a voluntary emigration and not a forced exile.

Place and context changed the meanings of *diaspora* and *galuth* over time until eventually these words were used interchangeably in the modern era. The destruction of the Second Temple in 70 CE and the failure of the Bar Kochba Revolt in 135 CE initiated a new dispersion of people who followed evolving Jewish law away from Jerusalem and its environs. The Jewish sages writing in the first and second centuries CE increasingly used Hebrew (not Greek), and thus the word *diaspora* "gradually disappeared from Jewish thought and the meaning of *galuth* expanded" from only referencing historical exile to also absorbing the more neutral Septuagint meaning of dispersion. Both concepts were often cast in negative terms to connote loss, nakedness, and exile from the land "imposed by God."[50] The idea of "the diaspora" also took on liturgical meaning in rabbinic texts and later the *Talmudim* whereby rituals performed "outside" of the historic biblical lands assumed different rules at times.[51] Finally, up through the modern period, diaspora and galuth assumed eschatological importance for some Jews who imagined that the messianic age would bring them and the bodies of their dead loved ones back to Jerusalem and its surroundings.[52]

Like other nationalists in east central Europe, Jewish nationalist activists would draw on this multilayered and historical concept of "diaspora" as a way to strengthen their nation's claim to autonomy and eventually a specific land.[53] It is important to note that the concept of diaspora expanded beyond the Jewish experience and entered into lexicons indicating other examples as well.[54] Many Zionist-leaning Jewish nationalists spoke about diaspora and galuth/*goles* (in Hebrew and Yiddish, respectively) interchangeably as well as the so-called negation (or cancellation) of both as they designed their platforms and propaganda for the masses in the second half of the nineteenth century and afterward.[55] In an oversimplified way, negating the diaspora implied abandoning diasporic homes and returning Jews to the land emanating outward from Jerusalem. Diaspora, as this section has shown, does not necessarily assume a negative aspect. By the advent of the age of nationalisms in the long nineteenth century, however, diaspora had become something that "had to be overcome."[56]

Political disagreements among Jews living in the region between Berlin and Moscow quite often hinged on one's personal view of the diaspora, whether it should be negated, or how that negation should proceed. In 1909, for instance, the so-called "spiritual Zionist" Ahad Ha'am and "autonomist" Simon Dubnow exchanged articles directly challenging each other's views on this range of topics, despite Dubnow's contention that both men "stood together against those who completely negate[d] the diaspora."[57] Dubnow admitted, however, that his own embrace of the diaspora was due to "historical necessity." He suggested that both he and Ahad Ha'am would joyfully "transfer the entire Diaspora to a Jewish state" if they had the power to do so.[58] Regardless, the revival of the spiritual center in Palestine depended on the "quantity" of "healthy national material" that the diaspora could offer.[59] Other national leaders with Zionist leanings had much more pessimistic views of the diaspora despite the fact that Palestine could support only a fraction of the Jews rooted within it.[60] Chapter 1 confronts this reality explicitly. For now, we should note that Zionist activists such as Theodor Herzl, Aaron David Gordon, and others frequently cast the notion of "diaspora negation" as central to their political platforms demanding "human actions" such as migration and the creation of a Jewish polity in the Middle East.[61] Once views about the diaspora were weaponized politically, the common ground that Dubnow sought in 1909 became even more elusive. A century after some these texts were written, it remains important for the historian to negotiate between the rhetoric and the reality.[62] At times, the voices in this narrative use these words interchangeably, and the idea of diaspora is increasingly portrayed in gloomy shades as the chronology presented here moves forward. The description of diaspora provided here should help raise our consciousness when either occurs.

A SUCCINCT CHAPTER OUTLINE

Together, the five chapters of *Uprooting the Diaspora* detail the decade-long history of a transnational conversation about Jewish belonging that transpired between east central Europeans of both Jewish and non-Jewish backgrounds from a similar generation and other diplomats, politicians, and observers within the broader Allied universe. Chapter 1 draws on the work of sociologist Małgorzata Melchior and a collection of documents from the 1930s to explore the rootedness of Polish Jews during the interwar period, problematize calls for emigration away from Poland, and complicate terms such as *Zionist, anti-Zionist,* and *non-Zionist.* Chapter 2 begins in the 1940s and covers three years in "exile" as east central Europeans in the Polish government-in-exile, the Czech government-in-exile, and the World Jewish Congress debated plans for the postwar world. Using words from Edvard Beneš, a survey of the journal *Foreign Affairs,* the émigré Polish-language newspaper *NT,* and documents from the World Jewish Congress, this chapter explores how plans for population transfers and the regranting of minority rights clashed publicly and privately. It also describes how conflicting news regarding the Jewish tragedy circulated throughout the Allied universe. Chapter 3 covers the work and words emanating from the Office Committee of the World Jewish Congress across one calendar year. Between 1943 and 1944, the WJC reacted as the Allied powers failed to codify legal definitions for Jewish displaced persons at two UNRRA meetings, as the extent of the Jewish tragedy became more apparent, and as ideas casting displaced Jews within Europe as the ideal citizens for a Jewish polity in Palestine coalesced. Empirical Zionism emerged during the timeline of this chapter and helped shape the thinking of east central Europeans of both Jewish and non-Jewish backgrounds quickly and decisively.

In the final two chapters, the diplomatic history showcased in *Uprooting the Diaspora* merges with a social story about two different postwar contexts (Czechoslovakia and Poland) in the same period, from 1945 to the fall of 1946. These chapters consider the links between the expulsion of "ethnic" Germans and postwar Jewish movements, how the category "displaced persons unsuccessfully repatriated" and ideas about Jewishness entered international and national legal codes, how postwar antisemitism proved more violent than its prewar iteration, and how more than a hundred thousand Polish Jews who survived World War II and the Holocaust in the Soviet Union returned to Poland and joined the *bricha.* Finally, the short conclusion reflects on the so-called "ethnic revolution" and its consequences.

A peculiar travel document grows older in a gloomy archive deep within the maze of Prague's cobblestoned streets. On its dimpled leather cover, gold letters shine in contrast to the deep-blue skin surrounding them: "Temporary Passport of the Czechoslovak Republic."[63] Inside, a creased travel identity card reveals the target recipient: someone with "uncertain citizenship." Beginning in 1947, after revisions to passport laws came into effect at the end of 1946, the Ministry of the Interior gave "authority to the departure" of travelers with "uncertain citizenship temporarily staying in Czechoslovakia." The special page directs "controlling organs to facilitate the holder of this travel identity card in crossing the frontier on the described journey." Empty lines encourage the bearers to list their date of birth and their final destination. Unmarked boxes ask for descriptions of eye color, hair shade, and other distinguishing marks. Only clean versions of this passport remain in the dusty archival folders, marked with red and black pens alongside numbering systems that have outlived their necessity. Who were these European-born travelers without a European homeland, and how did their citizenship status become uncertain? Perhaps this study will help us understand who clutched these small documents and how their movement away from their prewar east central European homes became theoretically and logistically possible.

ONE

ROOTED

A Contingent Look at Polish Jews in the Late 1930s

LATE IN THE EVENING OF August 10, 1936, the Polish Jewish engineer Anselm Reiss read an unexpected declaration to the inaugural event of the World Jewish Congress in Geneva. This meeting, a networking opportunity full of welcome messages and self-congratulations for eight hundred delegates from all over the globe, included committee meetings and planned speeches, such as those from the high commissioner for refugees coming from Germany, Sir Neill Malcolm, and WJC leaders Stephen Wise, Nahum Goldman, and Maurice Perlzweig. But Reiss, the voice of some fifty Polish delegates from often-sparring political parties and more than three million Jews who had Polish citizenship, temporarily stole the show with a simple message: Polish Jews belonged in Poland.[1]

Poland had been built by Jews, he said, and Jews had shed their blood and grown as a community in Poland "for hundreds of years." Poland's Jews possessed the "unquestionable right like other citizens, under the protection of the state and the law, to life, to peace and to work freely," and despite vitriolic antisemitic political propaganda and discriminatory economic initiatives, they refused to be "terrorized" into leaving. To his colleagues from the rest of Europe, Reiss highlighted the ostensible unity of Polish Jewry, in whose struggle they expected to find support from the whole of Jewish people.

"Lively and long applause" coursed through the assembly. Afterward, Nahum Goldmann, a leader of the World Jewish Congress, congratulated Reiss and his Polish Jewish colleagues on their "unified political declaration."[2] Those "familiar with the internal Jewish situation in Poland," Goldmann said, would consider the first World Jewish Congress a success if it managed "to unite the various parties and currents of Polish Jewry."[3] Goldmann continued to speak in vague language. Despite being offered at a time of "diversity and strife," the Polish Jewish declaration signified a potential "commonality that transcended politics, class, gender and religious belief."[4]

WJC members assembled in Geneva were not the only listeners supportive of Reiss's declaration. Three days later, a regular contributor to the popular Polish-language Jewish daily *Nasz Przegląd*—"N.S."—championed Reiss's proclamation as a "blatant expression" of the "views which prevail among the widest masses of Polish Jewry."[5] N.S. contrasted the Geneva declaration to a statement from Yitzhak Grünbaum, a Zionist who had left Poland for Palestine in the early 1930s. At a press conference a month earlier, Grünbaum had said that "'the hour of exodus from Poland had struck,'" provoking a "barrage of criticism both from his political friends and foes" but echoing remarks by Revisionist Zionist leader Vladimir Jabotinsky.[6] Earlier that month, Jabotinsky had penned a missive to Polish foreign minister Józef Beck suggesting that Poland should urge British Mandate authorities in Palestine to adopt a constructive plan for the peaceful "exodus" of nearly seven hundred thousand "Polish Jewish immigrants to Palestine" as soon as possible in the name of "humanitarian principles and its own political interests."[7] The views of Jabotinsky, Beck, and Grünbaum were misleading, according to N.S. In his view, most Polish Jews subscribed to Reiss's protest against the mass emigration of Jews from Poland.

Inspired by this statement and others that seem to contradict it, I explore the "rootedness" of Polish Jews in interwar Poland and show how discussions casting emigration as a solution to Jewish, peasant, or economic "problems" in Poland in fact did not translate into viable plans.[8] I consider critically the claim that migration might have improved the lot of Polish Jews or others in the economically depressed Second Republic, as antisemites, Revisionists, and state demographers claimed in the 1920s and 1930s. In the end, members of the World Jewish Congress and the Jews whom they wanted to represent remained committed to the diaspora, despite the dire geopolitical context, despite calls to coordinate emigration opportunities away from homelands throughout east central Europe, and, for some, despite their broadly conceived commitment to Jewish settlement in Palestine.[9] Talk of "evacuation," Jabotinsky's demands for wide-scale exodus (from hundreds of thousands to millions) of Jews from Europe, or calls for the "negation of the diaspora" threatened the essence of the World Jewish Congress's platform and prompted officials working for the WJC to take action.

Drawing on sociologist Małgorzata Melchior's theory of "rootedness," I explore the writings of five men: Arieh Tartakower, a sociologist, activist, and member of the WJC Office Committee who lived in Poland for most of the interwar period; James McDonald, a diplomat who was appointed by the League of Nations as the first high commissioner for refugees (Jewish and others) from Germany; Jewish American Baruch Zuckerman, who took a WJC-led trip to Poland in 1937 and 1938; Jakob Apenszlak, an editor of and contributor to *Nasz Przegląd*; and, finally, Joel Cang, a Polish Jewish journalist who wrote about minority politics, his country, and the region around it for the uncensored, English-language presses. These five men, along with a few other personalities connected to the World Jewish Congress, help us understand the "ethnic revolution" traced throughout this book.

THE ROOTEDNESS OF POLISH JEWS IN THE LATE 1930S

The World Jewish Congress convened in Geneva to organize the Jewish diaspora throughout the world. Yet because many Jews could trace their lineage back many centuries, we need to examine the word *diaspora*.[10] Were not Polish Jews, in fact, "rooted" in interwar Poland?[11] This rootedness took multiple forms: local, regional, and national; familial and communal; political, linguistic, and cultural; and logistical and emotional.[12] As Melchior explains, a feeling of rootedness includes three essential attributes: an "awareness" of one's own place in the world, "specific references" from a shared past that create a "sense of continuation," and "knowledge" of origination, transmitted in social, historical, and cultural forms.[13] And while rootedness is "hard to define," observers such as Melchior and Simone Weil demand that we try. Being rooted, Weil wrote in the 1940s, "is perhaps the most important and least recognized need of the human soul."[14] This "need" for rootedness remained as the 1930s progressed despite charged political debates in the Sejm about calls for Jews to leave Poland, despite a growing sense of pessimism about the continued viability of minority rights in the Polish Jewish press, and despite more manifestations of antisemitism. From the late 1930s, a significant cross section of Polish Jews—from politicians to historians, from keepers of taverns to those staffing stalls on market days, and from self-described "Zionists" to acculturating teenagers—were rooted in both place and memory, in the complicated Polish present, and in plans for the foreseeable future.[15]

Before and after Anselm Reiss and his colleagues claimed to speak for the collective of Polish Jews in Geneva, scholars of this complex collective sought to understand it, attribute adjectives to it, and recognize the diversity within it. Observations from the late interwar period and literature from subsequent years argue that nearly every Jew territorially or historically rooted in the lands that became part of the Second Polish Republic had been "Polonized," linguistically or otherwise, by the second half of the 1930s.[16] And while some scholars have maintained that this was a population living in a "self-contained world within which it was possible, if one chose, to live almost without venturing into broader society," others have emphasized a richer interpretation.[17] Contemporary Polish Jewish historians and their recent chronicler Natalia Aleksiun assert that significant interaction took place beyond financial transactions, resulting in a "cultural cross-fertilization" of Jewish and non-Jewish groups.[18] In the Second Republic, linguistic, social, and cultural aspects of Polishness entered almost all Jewish spaces, from Hasidic prayer halls and observant homes to holiday resorts with kosher catering and the bustling coffeehouses frequented by Warsaw's Jewish intellectuals.[19] This embrace of Polish language and culture did not preclude separatism and the continuance of "Jewish difference," which sometimes cost Jews their livelihoods and lives.[20] Undoubtedly, the Polish Jews alive in the 1930s saw that antisemitism could be used as a political tool and contribute to systematic discrimination and the outbreak of everyday violence.[21] Nevertheless, Jews built autonomous institutions, as well as their own linguistic universes, and created unique forms of cultural belonging that permeated what was probably the most diverse community of Jews on the planet.[22]

Their belonging to Polish geography did not, of course, inhibit spiritual ties, dreams, or, in even rarer cases, concrete plans to leave Poland at some point in the immediate or vaguely distant future. Despite his rejection of Zionism, Avraham Mordechai Alter of Ger, the third rebbe in that Hasidic dynasty, "supported buying land in Palestine" and even encouraged his followers to go there and establish institutions in his name.[23] Some Polish youth imagined futures in Palestine and elsewhere in YIVO autobiography contests in 1932, 1934, and 1939.[24] Hasidim and Orthodox Jewish leaders and parents found varying ways to come to terms with the increasingly secularized youth, who abandoned "religion" for Zionist and socialist groups in unprecedented numbers.[25] Marci Shore tells us that, despite being atheists and of different political stripes, all of the children of the prominent Berman family (including Zionist Adolf and Stalinist Jakub) convened faithfully at their parents' Passover seder and promised to do the same "next year in Jerusalem" out of respect for their observant elders.[26] Jewish intellectuals took advantage of their abilities to travel extensively, live in France or the United States, or make aliyah when such possibilities existed.[27] Anselm Reiss attempted to begin a life in Palestine, yet like many of his peers, he returned to the country of his citizenship after a handful of years. The three-pronged concept of rootedness offered by Melchior does not preclude these actions, nor should a concession of rootedness diminish the reality of sympathies that might be classified as Zionist.

In fact, awareness of rootedness helps us better understand the different forms of Zionism that developed in Poland. Kamil Kijek has argued that the Polish patriotism that infused Polish Zionist culture as well as the school curriculum of the Zionist-supported Tarbut system "gave local Polish Zionism its own special flavor" that stood in contrast to Zionist cultures developing in Palestine or elsewhere.[28] Also in the 1930s, self-defined "Zionists" among public-facing Polish Jewish historians used their "understanding of Zionism as a form of diaspora nationalism" and their interpretation of the past "to envision a future in which Jews would be at home in Poland while maintaining a strong Jewish national identity and culture."[29] Directly before the Second World War, the Polish Jewish historian, rabbi, and Sejm member Mojżesz Schorr noticed that "even the most ardent Zionists are to some extent assimilated in the world of ideals [*ideowo zasymilowani*]. Not only are the Polish writing skills of many of them excellent, but they encounter Polish culture beginning in their school years and [continuing] throughout their lives, and it affects them in all aspects of their spirit, in the sciences, art, and literature."[30] All forms of Jewish nationalism active in interwar Poland took on striking Polish characteristics, even Palestine-centric forms of Zionism.[31]

Even the most revolutionary Zionists had to concede that a statistically significant diaspora would remain in Poland indefinitely. For example, when Vladimir Jabotinsky spoke at the Warsaw Society of Jewish Physicians and Engineers in late September 1936, the leader of Revisionist Zionism criticized those who suggested that his proposed evacuation scheme implied the transfer of all Polish Jews. Even if Mandate Palestine could absorb more than 50,000 Jews annually and the non-Jewish population within Poland increased naturally, the Polish Jewish diaspora would still number 2,792,000 ten years in the future.[32] Increasingly, geopolitical conditions further restricted short-term plans to settle sizeable numbers of east central European Jews as new restrictions imposed by British authorities came into effect during the late 1930s. Furthermore, on a fundamental level, even the so-labeled "Zionist masses" (in Poland, in east central Europe, or even in the United States) did not leave en masse, even when they had opportunities to do so.[33] Thus, although coverage of events in the Mandate permeated *Nasz Przegląd*, the topic of Jewish settlement in Palestine dominated conversations among WJC officials, and international officials focused on refugee issues, east central European Jewish nationalists were not necessarily territorially monogamous in 1936.

Around 3.1 million Polish citizens declared their allegiance to the Jewish faith in the official census taken in 1931.[34] Almost 400,000 of them listed Polish as their mother tongue.[35] The census did not register bilingual or trilingual capacities, but one must, by the 1930s, assume a widespread knowledge of Polish among those who listed Yiddish or Hebrew as their language of everyday use.[36] On top of this fact, responses to the question about "mother tongue" (*język ojczysty*) sometimes became political declarations, especially for those designating Hebrew for this answer. Since that 1931 census, the population had grown, and worldwide emigration away from Poland had stalled. This population was increasingly young: 43.1 percent of these Polish Jews were under the age of twenty at the end of the 1930s.[37] According to government data, more than 80 percent of Jewish school-age children in the upcoming 1937 school year planned to attend a state-run school.[38] By the end of the 1930s, then, nearly half of the roughly 3.3-million-strong Jewish population had lived almost their entire lives in a Polish state, around the Polish language, imbricated in a Polish legal system, and cognizant of particular cultural signifiers that marked their time and place. And yet, the religious, cultural, linguistic, political, and economic diversity of this collective should not be overlooked, despite the monolithic unity presented by Anselm Reiss at Geneva and by some historians who speak of unified "Jewries" but in doing so simplify the heterogeneity of human groups.

Collective experiences and memories did congeal, of course. Undoubtedly, the Jewish population in the Second Republic, their parents, and their grandparents had been collectively impacted by the uncertainty, brutality, and massive displacement that accompanied the Great War (particularly on the Eastern Front), two Russian "Revolutions" in 1917, and the conflicts that raged until the Treaty of Riga in 1921.[39] The initial advance of the Central Forces into the Russian Empire and Russian administration responses to this invasion, to cite at least one staggering statistic, initiated a (largely compulsory) mass movement of Jews, employees of evacuated factories, and other civilians that contributed to the registration of more than 3.1 million refugees in nonoccupied Russia in May 1916.[40] Others poured westward to Berlin and Prague or southward to Vienna. There, displaced, they learned about the 1917 Balfour Declaration, which stated that the British government looked with favor on "the establishment in Palestine of a national home for the Jewish people." This event infused the generation-old World Zionist Organization and its diverse constituents with new hope but also new questions.[41] In fact, Balfour's letter offered little certainty in an uncertain time. Joseph Roth observed that it was "terribly hard to be an eastern Jew; there [was] no harder lot than that of the eastern Jew newly arrived in Vienna."[42] Violence, displacement, and uncertainty continued long after the signing of peace treaties to end the Great War and the Polish-Soviet conflict.[43] A startling pogrom in Lwów/L'viv/Lemberg in November 1918 preceded a "catastrophic pogrom wave," which began in December 1918 in Ukraine and, by the end of 1919, had "claimed several tens of thousands of Jewish lives."[44] As Ezra Mendelsohn reminds us, physical violence was "part of the scene" and thus an "important phenomenon which should be understood in the context of economic decline, of psychological despair and, perhaps, also of strong acculturating tendencies among the youth."[45]

After the Great War, Poland emerged on the map of Europe for the first time in more than a century and brought together territory, railroads, and populations from three different empires. Military gains under Józef Piłsudski extended Poland's northeastern and eastern borders and resulted in the incorporation of a significant percentage of Ukrainians, Belarusians, Jews, and "local" inhabitants living under Polish governance. More than 30 percent of these new Polish citizens were not considered "Polish" according to two interwar censuses. The more than three million Jews who gained Polish citizenship belonged to different socioeconomic classes. They expressed their connection to Jewish law and Judaism in various ways. Interwar Poland brought together Hasidic leaders and their courts, which helped make the Orthodox population in this new state the largest in the region.[46] The Jews in the Second Republic also belonged to a dizzying panoply of political organizations and parties.[47] In Poland, "Zionists" and "Bundists" were not always in opposition, and an individual could claim allegiance to both "groups" simultaneously or over a political lifetime.[48] "Non-Zionists" and "anti-Zionists" agreed only to a certain extent. In voting booths, "Jewish willingness to back the Bezpartyjny Blok Współpracy z Rządem, or BBWR, in the 1928 elections as well as other 'Polish' parties in Polish-majority settlements open[ed] the tantalizing possibility that for Jews, the prospect of political assimilation was real and not simply theoretical."[49]

Interwar reality does not always align with preconceptions that we carry, either consciously or unconsciously. As a case in point, some of the most "conservative" groups in Polish Jewish society seemingly utilized revolutionary methods in their schooling for young women.[50] Supporters of Polish-language schooling also sent their children to summer camps run by Zionist-leaning parties, contributed to shekel membership drives, and even traveled to meetings of the World Zionist Organization.[51] The largest minority in interwar Poland were the Ukrainians, and irredentist groups within that population of more than five million waged a violent campaign marked by high-profile assassinations

Fig. 1.1. An archway in the Jewish quarter of interwar Warsaw.
Photo collection of Willem Van de Poll/Nationaal Archief of the Netherlands.

against the Polish government.[52] The "Ukrainian question" often trumped Poland's "Jewish question." Other minority groups, Germans, Belarusians, and those who described themselves as simply being from "here" (*tutejsi*) meant that debates about minority rights extended far beyond Jewish circles.[53] As usual, lived reality proved messy.

The Jewish population, like all populations in Poland, had experienced the effects of a massive depression in the 1920s and 1930s, which left 40 percent of the working population idle, reduced industrial production by 35 percent, halved wholesale prices, and substantially reduced fiscal revenue and foreign trade.[54] Unlike other populations in Poland, they encountered discrimination and antisemitism in their daily lives, from severe limitations imposed by anti-shehita laws and government officials calling for the emigration of "excess" Jews to the pervasive "ghetto benches" cordoned off for Jews at universities and the "Aryan paragraphs" that constricted membership in all different types of professional organizations.[55] The generation born in the wake of the Great War and their ancestors may have had relatives who had moved abroad, to the United States, South America, western Europe, or Palestine. And while the financially solvent "American cousin [remained] the last hope of every Eastern Jewish family," some of those relatives eventually came back.[56] For a majority of Jews in Poland, their *doykayt*, their sense of "here-ness," their rootedness, was practical, territorial, and temporal.[57] As much as Polish Jews could anticipate the route their life would take, a continued existence in Poland seemed well within the range of immediate possibilities. It was the only reasonable possibility for most.

HOW ARIEH TARTAKOWER AND JAMES MCDONALD BALANCED THE REALITY OF ROOTEDNESS WITH CALLS FOR MIGRATION

Some activists attentive to the rootedness of east central European Jews advocated for small-scale and organized migrations that would benefit both the Jews who left and those who stayed behind. The next section highlights two such voices, one from the Polish Jewish WJC activist and wartime "Office Committee member" Arieh Tartakower and the other from James McDonald, an American who served as the first high commissioner for refugees (Jewish and others) from Germany beginning in 1933 when the office was created until his resignation at the end of 1935. Both Tartakower and McDonald had unique vantage points on the tension between Jewish rootedness and political developments in east central Europe that attempted to cast Jews as nonindigenous "others." Because of their vastly different kinds of expertise, they would have different reasons for supporting controlled Jewish migration away from Europe, yet both conceded what this chapter has already suggested: while some emigration was possible, the future homes for most east central European Jews would remain in Europe.

Arieh Tartakower intimately knew about rootedness and the difficulties inherent in migration. Trained as a lawyer as well as a sociologist, by the late 1930s Tartakower had become a noted expert on Polish Jews and their migrations. He also knew that emigration did not always succeed. After serving in the Austrian army during the Great War, Tartakower finished his doctorate at the University of Vienna and settled in Łódź after a bout with malaria cut short a stay in Palestine.[58] There he began building a solid academic and political profile, serving in the city council and acting as chair of the Histadrut (a Zionist labor party).[59] In 1925, he and his wife, Malwina, welcomed their first and only son, Jochanan. Besides this work, he lectured at the Instytut Nauk Judaistycznych in Warsaw and published on demography, the structure of societies, and the complexities of migration across four languages.[60] His two-volume compilation *The Jews in Renewed Poland: Activities, Society, Economy, Education and Culture* remains one of if not "the best synthesis of Polish Jewish History."[61] He also was a delegate to the World Jewish Congress in 1936.

When during its second session on August 9, 1936, he spoke on "Emigration and the Politics of Jewish Emigration," Tartakower joined a pressing conversation to which he was already closely connected. Unlike Joseph Roth, who in 1937 could not summon "the grace and insight to suggest some way out of our present difficulties," Tartakower offered a solution: the World Jewish Congress would help manage emigration out of Europe to better preserve Jewish life in Europe.[62] Quoting numbers that drew from his own research, Tartakower told the audience that before the war, 150,000 Jews had emigrated from the Polish lands annually, yet now that number had declined by two-thirds, flowing mainly to Palestine in part due to restrictive American policies.[63] He recommended that the WJC develop publicity encouraging Jews to leave Europe, negotiate with governments to find emigration possibilities, and help Jews transfer assets, all in order to reduce a "surplus" of Jews and ameliorate economic consequences. A solution to the "question" of emigration would take many years but would unlock opportunities, securing "the possibility of a new and decent life for hundreds of thousands."[64] Instead of unlikely mass transfers of rooted populations, Tartakower and his colleague Jacob Lestschinsky spoke of controlled emigratory flows to alleviate overpopulation. They were not alone.

James McDonald, former chair of the Foreign Press Association, became high commissioner for refugees when Germany withdrew from the League of

Nations in 1933. His office was affiliated with (but not financially supported by) the League of Nations and included delegates from a handful of League member states, such as Poland, Czechoslovakia, the Netherlands, and Argentina.[65] To investigate the refugee issues plaguing Germany and east central Europe, McDonald traveled to the region in spring 1934 and embarked on a multi-city tour. While in Warsaw and other Polish towns, McDonald outlined a plan to assist the "thousands of German refugees scattered all over Europe" who became stateless and often lacked access to a valid passport once they left Germany and their former state canceled their citizenship. He offered surprisingly concrete details of this plan in an interview given to Polish Jewish journalist Joel Cang, who himself is the subject of the last section in this chapter.

Complicated problems demanded multiple solutions, and McDonald prioritized them for Cang and his readership. First, all refugees should acquire passports and temporary permits. Second, he wanted to ensure that the sixty-five thousand German refugees, 80 percent of whom were Jewish, would find work. Most were in France, but there were also significant populations in Belgium and the Netherlands and upward of six thousand in Poland. Third, McDonald envisioned the thrust of his work to involve "the settlement of as many as possible of the Jewish refugees in Palestine."[66] During the previous year (1933–1934), ten thousand German Jews had arrived in Palestine, and he expected nearly as many "to be settled there in the course of the next twelve months." With the help of donations from British and American Jews, "resettlement" should commence in "countries overseas whose governments have expressed willingness to admit a considerable number of skilled and professional refugees." His office could entreat governments about emigration outlets and could facilitate the transfer of property and assets held by evacuating Jews.[67] Recently, McDonald had proposed a loan of several million pounds to help the refugees at the League of Nations; this proposal drew inspiration from a similar loan "floated under the auspices of the League to help Greece resettle her nationals a few years ago." Cang reiterated McDonald's view at the end of his article. The main center for resettlement "must be Palestine."[68]

Like Arieh Tartakower speaking in Geneva two years later, James McDonald advocated a transnational institution to coordinate emigration activities (his office, not the WJC), planning for economic consequences, and making Palestine a viable destination for Jews. He differed from Tartakower in other registers, the first being scale. McDonald wanted as many Jewish refugees as possible to settle as quickly as possible in Palestine. To justify his plan, he cited the Greco-Turkish population exchange (interestingly, not in terms of the transfer of two populations, which it was, but as a resettlement of one ethno-religious group) in connection to his plan to have wealthy Jews in America and Britain subsidize the movement of German Jewish refugees away from Europe. Tartakower did not employ this example at this time. As chapter 2 shows, McDonald was in the minority. Diplomats, statesmen, and actors connected to the League of Nations rarely envisioned mass population transfers as an acceptable tool available to states or international organizations.

McDonald prioritized the Greek-Turkish case because it was a League-endorsed endeavor that he hoped could serve as a precedent. But his brief invocation ignored the reality that this event—the forced movement of 1.6 million people—was a "human catastrophe of hitherto unknown dimension" that unfolded amid brutality emerging out of the Greek-Turkish War.[69] McDonald did not, it should be noted, make reference to the treaty signed between Turkey and Bulgaria in Adrianopole in 1913, which was the first interstate treaty on the exchange of populations in modern history.[70] In the wake of the peace treaties that concluded the Great War, European states became, for the most part, imbricated in a system based on minority rights, not a system based on the rights of states to manage their minorities.[71] The international community, bulwarked by the League of Nations, did not sanction mass population transfers or mass expulsions.[72] In fact, the League of Nations was built, as McDonald himself argued convincingly elsewhere, on nearly three centuries of precedents protecting the rights of minorities to be rooted and protected within states.[73] Here McDonald was citing an extreme exception as he built a logistically untenable argument.

Of course, the situation facing McDonald and his commission was new and urgent but not necessarily unprecedented. On February 20, 1921, the International Red Cross approached the Council of the League of Nations with a request concerning the hundreds of thousands of Russian refugees who had, since the beginning of the Great War and the two Russian Revolutions, flooded into border countries and had lost Russian citizenship on Lenin's initiative in 1921. To ameliorate the situation, the International Red Cross Committee "proposed that the League should appoint a High Commissioner for Russian Refugees" to consider three main aspects: first, "the definition of the legal status of refugees; second, their repatriation to Russia, their emigration to other countries, or the organization of their employment in the countries where they were residing; and third, the co-ordination of the various efforts already being undertaken for the material relief of the refugees."[74] The council agreed to appoint a high commissioner with the understanding that the League was not responsible for the "organization or financing of relief and that its work should be considered temporary."[75]

On September 1, 1921, Dr. Fritdjof Nansen assumed the office of the high commissioner for Russian refugees, and by July 1922, Nansen had convened an Intergovernmental Conference that "accepted an arrangement for a certificate of identity which would be considered valid by adherent countries."[76] This certificate became known as a "Nansen passport."[77] In practice, citizens deprived of citizenship from their former state could, in exile, apply for a Nansen passport and thus have some semblance of official identity papers, travel privileges, and domicile status for a finite period.[78] Alongside his work creating, maintaining, and extending his namesake passport, Nansen helped in the evacuation of 156,000 Greek refugees from Asia Minor and of 10,000 Turkish refugees to Asia Minor. His work paved the way for the consequent movement of 650,000 Greek refugees, the movement of more than 125,000 Bulgarian refugees that had to be settled within Bulgaria, and the settlement of Armenians in Erivan. Nansen also "made himself the spokesman for the claims of the Ruthenians, the Montenegrins, refugees from Central Europe and Jewish refugees in Rumania [*sic*]" before his unexpected death in 1930.[79]

While McDonald could trace a lineage from Nansen's commission to his own, McDonald's interview with Cang as well as his extensive diary reveal an initiative quite different from the activity associated with Nansen's name. In part because of his friendships and financial partnerships with American Jewish groups and individuals such as Felix Warburg as well as contacts with politically influential Jews such as Chaim Weizmann, McDonald frequently pinpointed Palestine (and not, notably, America) as an ideal location for German Jewish refugees and suggested that wealthy Jews elsewhere should activate their bonds of solidarity through monetary donations or investments to ensure the passage of these refugees from their former countries to the Palestinian Mandate.

Tartakower also drew on refugee-related trajectories after the Great War to justify the role he proposed for the WJC in the mid-1930s, but his plans seemed much less ambitious than the ones offered by McDonald. The same year he spoke at the first meeting of the WJC in Geneva, Tartakower detailed how the WJC should respond to the contemporary emigration situation in a Yiddish-language brochure published in Paris. Across fifty pages, Tartakower described how "bitter and serious times" initiated after the Great War had narrowed the options for "hundreds of thousands who need to emigrate in order to save themselves from physical and spiritual destruction."[80] Organizations dedicated to helping Jewish immigrants had failed to offer "a certain idealism of national enthusiasm, which can only be achieved if the colonizing work is carried out by the organized people and not by separate institutions."[81] Ideally, when the WJC became a permanent institution (and it was more or less permanent by the end of 1936), Tartakower proposed, its executive branch should include an emigration department. This department would "function as the highest controlling body of all Jewish emigration associations: coordinating their activities, as well as their activities with those of other Jewish economic, and possibly also political, institutions, and issue certain orders."[82] Diplomatically, this department would have far-ranging influence, negotiating with "states and international corporations: and creating central institutions" like a "Jewish Emigration bank" and a "Jewish colonization fund."[83] Tartakower did not expect the WJC to eclipse existing emigration organizations. Rather, he thought the WJC could become an umbrella organization coordinating and improving their work. Finally, in terms of public opinion, the WJC had the capacity to lead an "awareness-raising campaign" and educate the Jewish masses about the interconnectedness of emigration and socioeconomic realities.[84]

Tartakower knew that the population of Poland was growing, and the elimination of emigration options, mainly to the United States and western Europe, meant that more people suffered in deteriorating economic conditions. In Tartakower's assessment, the natural growth of nearly thirty thousand Polish Jews annually increased "social pressure" and "pauperization."[85] According to his numbers, the non-Jewish population by the 1930s was growing naturally at double the rate of the Jewish population, and Jewish demographics were thus being diluted overall.[86] For Tartakower, this status quo was untenable. Higher populations strained an already struggling economic and social atmosphere. Besides this, he expressed concern for the "spiritual and moral decline" of Polish Jews as a whole and a lack of organized emigration options that could alleviate the population's strain on the faltering economy.[87] Grouping Polish Jews by size of settlement, Tartakower noted that in big cities the assimilation of the Jewish population had quickened, the marriage age for Jews had increased well beyond the norm for non-Jews, and the percentage of children born outside of marriage had drastically increased, sometimes at a rate more than three times higher than that of the non-Jewish population.

Elsewhere in his writings, Tartakower outlined his concern for the Jews as a people even more explicitly. In his 1938 publication *Zarys socjologii żydostwa* (*Outline of Jewish Sociology*), Tartakower considered the future of Polish Jewry from several angles, offering a vigorous and nuanced definition of Zionism that included an awareness of Arab populations and providing for settlement outside of Palestine as well as continued support for the continuation of diaspora life. He conceded that "only the creation of its own normal national existence may respond to the tragedies of Jewry [*tragedie żydostwa*]."[88] But accepting this fact did not preclude a future for Jews living in the countries of the *goles* or the reality of "Zionists" fighting for the future of this diaspora.[89] And while the creation of a Jewish state "would undoubtedly correspond to the will of the overwhelming majority of Jewish society on the whole globe," other forms of territorialism and colonialism should not necessarily be eliminated from short-term (this is undefined) plans. "Whether and in what form the proposed Jewish state will be implemented is," Tartakower admitted, "difficult to predict in the present transitional period."[90] Despite his ideological views on the need for separate national space, Tartakower remained a realist. Like others of his era, his view of Palestine-centric Zionism had an elastic quality, and his understanding of Polish Jewish rootedness was nuanced.[91]

McDonald saw the Jewish and Polish Jewish worlds in much starker colors. An article filed by Joel Cang in the *Jewish Chronicle* after McDonald's visit to Warsaw in 1934 revealed that the high commissioner had even more ambitious albeit vague plans for the Jews of Europe. McDonald wanted to consider not only "refugee" problems but "the Jewish problem as a whole."[92] Perhaps this urge led McDonald to have a "long conference" with Jabotinsky in Warsaw, where the "revisionist leader outlined his views on the possibility of settling an increasing number of Jews in Palestine."[93] McDonald did more than meet with Jabotinsky; he danced with him as well. The two spent an evening of food and music at the Adria restaurant, and McDonald was so intrigued by Jabotinsky, who "interrupted the dancing with brilliant and pungent phrases which bit like acid" about Weizmann and others opposed to the Revisionist cause, that he invited him for a luncheon the next day. His two talks with Jabotinsky "deeply impressed" him on several registers. McDonald's remarks about larger Jewish problems, however, were not solely related to his conversations with the Revisionist leader. Across three days in Warsaw in April 1934, McDonald encountered Jabotinsky twice, convened with a twenty-one-member committee "representing every faction and shade of Jewish opinion in Poland," and had tea at Dr. Mojżesz Schorr's house. It is possible, however, that McDonald's words to Cang were inspired by a day of traveling in and beyond Warsaw.

Throughout his eight-hundred-page diary covering the years 1933–1935, McDonald noted hundreds of memorable conversations and exceptional trips across Europe and the Americas. The day he spent traversing the Jewish quarter of Warsaw and two villages outside of town offered "impressions" that would "never be forgotten." Two things stood out: people's extreme poverty and their infatuation with Palestine. In Warsaw, the travelers entered "two hovels where whole families lived" in "wretched clothes and shoes that were eloquent proof of the wretchedness of the people."[94] In a larger unnamed village, McDonald and his entourage went to the market, the headquarters of the halutz, and the cooperative bank and en route got caught in a thick crowd of people alerted to his presence.[95] "How piteously," McDonald observed after just a few hours in these places, "the people look to Palestine! It is for them the solace now and the hope for the future. I can now begin to understand the powerful populist appeal which Weizmann, Jabotinsky and other Zionist leaders no matter how much they may differ as to methods make to the masses of the Polish and eastern Jews."[96] McDonald was struck by the perceived fractures cutting through Polish Jewish society. And it was obvious that the combined effects of time spent with Jabotinsky and an encounter with longings for Palestine in Poland's countryside had left deep impressions on a man already interested in linking the German Jewish refugees with emigration opportunities in Mandate Palestine. And yet, even if McDonald harbored his own Zionist visions of finding opportunities in Palestine for Poland's Jews, he provided no more specifics at this point than either Jabotinsky or even Weizmann.

Five days after McDonald's three-day trip to Poland, on April 25, 1934, Barent Litvinof of the *Jewish Chronicle* asked for clarification about McDonald's supposed claim that it was insufficient to simply consider the refugee problem; "one must consider the question of Jewish emigration as a whole." McDonald replied that he had "nothing more to say."[97] Throughout his appointment as high commissioner from the fall of 1933 to the end of 1935, McDonald did not reveal many specifics about the options his committee considered. His copious diary says nothing about his involvement in the Haavara agreement, although he did lobby the British to have Jews enter Palestine.[98] He spoke with colleagues about the foundation or expansion of Jewish settlements in Biro-Bidjan, Portuguese East Africa, French colonies, the United States, and South America. McDonald spent a dozen weeks in South America in 1935 but did not commit to facilitating large-scale German Jewish emigration.[99] On October 8, 1934, Weizmann refused to embark on a joint effort with McDonald's committee because he didn't want to be "married to a corpse" (McDonald had refused to travel to Palestine ahead of his trip to Brazil and Argentina). McDonald recognized that a diverse collection of Zionists, non-Zionists, and anti-Zionists held positions of power in British and American Jewish organizations and would not endorse a worldwide response to a problem they deemed associated only with displaced German Jews.[100]

Tartakower's vision had a broader scope, which involved more synthesis among actors and the marginal reduction of the diaspora. His writings and activities, however, hinged on an undeniable reality: even if the WJC could create new emigration outlets, millions of Jews would remain in Poland.[101] And this reality, the reality of the rootedness of Jews in Poland, was, in Tartakower's words, "uncheerful, often tragic but not necessarily hopeless." Reflecting on Jewish life in Poland near the end of 1938, just months after Poland's government revoked the citizenship of Polish citizens who had lived abroad continuously for more than five years, Tartakower described the moment as one when "it is difficult to play with prophecies because we do not know what the next day will bring." He remained conditionally, perhaps hesitantly, optimistic despite this. "But, if in the end," he wrote, "the nightmare of the current political and social relations passes" and "the Polish state overcomes the current economical issues and subjugates the hydra of anti-semitism, which is the threat not only to the Jews, but also undermines the foundations of the whole society, then better times will come also for the Jewish people."[102]

McDonald was less optimistic about the situation in Germany. A few months before resigning his position in December 1935, he wrote to Eleanor Roosevelt (and by way of her, the president) about the enormity of a situation that few seemed to grasp. "Unless present tendencies are sharply reversed," McDonald insisted, "the world will be faced in the near future with the problem of another great exodus of refugees from Germany." Furthermore, this man who had met Hitler in April 1933 believed that Reich leaders had "set for themselves a program of forcing gradually the Jews from Germany by creating conditions there which make life unbearable."[103] He had spent more than two years advocating for the stateless German Jews in neighboring countries and for the Jews of other nationalities who had been expelled from Germany and who either had been forced back to their former states or lived, like hundreds of Polish Jews in Antwerp, in circumstances of precarious legality.[104] Over time, McDonald had become frustrated with his lack of authority, the informal relationship his commission had with the League of Nations, and the lack of empathy shown by the so-called Christian world. Moreover, he had learned that it was difficult even for the German Jews and Jews of other nationalities within Germany who had been forcibly expelled to find new homes when few destinations were available to them in the 1930s.

And despite assertions from luminaries such as Louis Brandeis that Palestine could absorb between four and five million emigrants, or Chaim Weizmann that five hundred thousand Jews (not necessarily from Germany) could settle in Palestine before he died, McDonald could not unite enough powerbrokers from Jewish and British circles behind his hope to make Palestine the main center of resettlement.[105] Nonetheless, he did help make Palestine a favored destination among German Jews during and after his time as high commissioner. Interestingly, a *New York Times* article announcing the appointment of

McDonald's replacement, Sir Neill Malcolm, noted that future refugee work would benefit from a plan to expatriate one hundred thousand Jews from Germany over four years and settle half of them in Palestine.[106] Malcolm would travel to Geneva and address the first meeting of the World Jewish Congress five months into his term.

There, the optimism and declarations of unity infusing Tartakower's writings rang out frequently. Stephen Wise and Nahum Goldmann considered the meeting a turning point in Jewish life as the end of an era of "Jewish division and unconcerted action."[107] In a strange way, declarations from Tartakower, Reiss, Wise, and Goldmann as well as other Jewish observers of the late 1930s sometimes mimicked the demands of interwar historians of the European Jewish experience who expected solidarity when, for the most part, disunity reigned.[108] Disagreement riddled the conversations of WJC delegates. Berl Locker, for instance, who had journeyed to the meeting from Palestine, claimed that his peers in the Polish delegation were not elected democratically and represented certain political parties instead of a unified Polish Jewry.[109] American Louis Segal applied the same criticism to the US delegation, which did not include any representatives from the "Jewish plutocracy" or the "Jewish labor movement."[110] Moreover, several delegates expressed anxiety about how delegates to the WJC were selected in their own home countries.

The disharmony reached a pitch when the deliberations devolved into an argument over the preamble to the WJC constitution. On behalf of the so-called Executive Committee, Dr. Jacob Hellmann from Poland proposed that the wording "The World Jewish Congress is the representative body of the Jewish collectivity in matters relating to Jewish life in the diaspora" should be accepted by all constituents, thus provoking heated debate. More than ten years later, Aryeh Leon Kubowitzki recalled that "the American, English, Italian and Swiss delegations oppose[d] the wording because it [was] not a statement of fact, since it declare[d] the WJC to be the representative body which in their opinion it can only aspire to become." This objection stalled the adoption of the WJC preamble at the 1936 meeting, instead punting the issue back to "the executive with the understanding that the reference to the representative in charge of the congress is a goal to be reached rather than as a statement of fact."[111] Perhaps ironically, the delegates found it difficult to agree on the democratic process of delegate election and their constitution's preamble. In this way, the fundamental issues confronted at the first WJC meeting in 1936 reveal massive disunity despite calls for and promises of the opposite.

And yet, in spite of these impossible calls for unity and the harsh reality of disunity, a seemingly unified set of problems facing east and central European

Fig. 1.2. Muranowska Street in the heart of the Jewish quarter of interwar Warsaw. Courtesy YIVO Digital Archive on Jewish Life in Poland.

Jewry remained: the unexpected emigrations unleashed by the political rise of Adolf Hitler and his Nazi Party, the status of these now-stateless uncitizens, and the broader issue of minority rights throughout east central Europe. In Poland, Jews together faced "ghetto benches" and other forms of discrimination at universities, bans against the ritual slaughter of animals (shechita), and boycotts throughout the country that contributed to the further economic demoralization of Jews in Poland.[112] These remained key issues precisely because these Jewish populations were rooted (for better, for worse, and for the future) in east central Europe. Experts such as Tartakower provided statistical data, but to a certain extent the dire state of Polish Jewry became increasingly obvious to novice eyes despite further attempts by the Polish government to encourage emigration, often with charged antisemitic language. On Józef Beck's instructions, for example, the Polish delegate to the Economic Commission of the League of Nations "raised the question of Jewish emigration on 5 October 1936, claiming that the Jewish problem in Poland required rapid measures of relief."[113] Moreover, as Polish government officials continued to cultivate contacts with international Zionist organizations, a group of Polish government experts went to Paris in May 1937 to again discuss with the French opportunities for Jewish settlement in Madagascar. Even further, in 1938 a non-Zionist Jewish committee for colonization headed by Mojżesz Schorr (who had himself attended a meeting of the 1905 World Zionist Organization) was set up under ministerial patronage "to foster emigration to countries other than Palestine."[114] Despite these efforts, barely nine thousand Jews left Poland in 1937.[115] And so, it was in the interest of officials from the World Jewish Congress to organize Polish Jewry more systematically.

BARUCH ZUCKERMAN AND THE WJC'S FAILED MISSION TO POLAND, 1937–1938

"Only a Talmudist could possibly understand Polish Jewish politics," Nahum Sokolov lamented on his visit to Poland in 1933. While not a Talmudist himself, Baruch Zuckerman had developed an understanding of Polish Jewish politics after nearly a year in Poland. He learned that the language he used to discuss Jewish politics in the United States often proved redundant in Poland. By appointing Zuckerman to travel to Poland and compel Polish Jews to purchase ballots, cast votes, and create a national congress, which could become an affiliate member of the World Jewish Congress, executive members of the WJC hoped to diminish a paradox that was evident at the 1936 inaugural meeting of the WJC in Geneva: the unrepresentative nature of the World Jewish Congress delegation. To be more effective and have more international legitimacy, the WJC needed documented constituents, and where better to find them than in Poland, home of the largest Jewish population in Europe and the second largest in the world after the United States?[116]

The WJC's plan to convene a Congress of Polish Jews ultimately failed, but this failure is illuminating on at least three registers.[117] First, an exploration of Baruch Zuckerman's assignment to organize Polish Jewry into a constituent body of the larger World Jewish Congress helps us understand contemporary political descriptors in a more nuanced way. Zuckerman's report shows that the adjective *Zionist* had acquired a specific meaning in the Polish context by the late 1930s, and there were, in fact, a "bewildering number of Zionisms."[118] In 1939, by way of example, the World Zionist Organization counted three separate Zionist federations, each of which corresponded to past partitions of Poland and each of which was dedicated to improving daily lives of Jews in Polish spaces.[119] Second, Zuckerman's failure confirms how elusive "unity" was among Polish Jews at this time. Even when attempting to unite Jews around a supposedly "neutral" platform, Zuckerman and his colleagues spread out across the country found it impossible to synchronize this "hopelessly divided" community.[120] Third, and perhaps most importantly, the failure of Zuckerman's mission in 1937–1938 demonstrates the limits of the World Jewish Congress's power and authority, especially vis-à-vis Polish Jews. The World Jewish Congress had little mandate to speak or act on behalf of a population that refused to organize on the WJC's terms in the late 1930s.

In February 1938, slightly less than a year after his arrival in Poland, Zuckerman offered a report that detailed both his work rallying support for the WJC and the Congress of Polish Jews (later called the Congress of Jewish Self-Help in Poland) and his opinions about the reality of the present and plans for the future.[121] Even after eleven months in the country, Zuckerman remained shocked by what he observed. "The mutual hatred among Jewish parties in Poland," Zuckerman wrote, "and the mottos employed in their fights among each other are often simply unbelievable."[122] Even "in the face of the greatest catastrophes that have occurred recently," he continued, "it was impossible to organize a common defense front."[123] Entrusted by the WJC with "helping Polish Jewry to organize itself," he had spent months with its leaders, digested myriad newspapers, traveled across the country popularizing the WJC to Polish Jews, and sold voting cards to those interested in helping create a Polish Jewish Congress. His report shows that Polish Jewry in 1938 defied simple categorization. Zuckerman's reference point of American Jewish politics had proved a faulty prism through which to view the complexity of Polish Jewish experience.

In a country of more than three million Jews, Zuckerman estimated nearly as many different outlooks. He admitted, for instance, that "almost every thinking Jew has his own program and his own way of achieving the balance" of galuth.[124] Even familiar words such as *assimilationist* and *nationalist* could not be understood axiomatically because the division between those "supposed" groups had "long since lost its exactitude." To Zuckerman's surprise, even the word *Zionist* had acquired a new meaning. "Very often now," he admitted, "we meet Zionists of various shades who adopted the viewpoint that Jews are absolutely and eternally rooted in the soil of Poland."[125] This had changed since the Great War. Before 1914, "Zionists spoke very openly and clearly about exile from the *galuth*, now, however the situation is such that Zionists are afraid of such open talk." Changes in the "last few decades, especially in Poland, forced them to emphasize Jewish integrity in Poland and to fight against the emigrationist attempts of the Polish Government." The non-Zionists, Zuckerman explained, went even further and regarded "all talk about an emigration event to Palestine as a crime against the interest of the Jews of the Poland." Despite both fighting for the continued existence of Jews in Poland, an "enormous abyss" existed between Zionists and non-Zionists, "the like of which [did] not exist in any country in the world." And perplexingly, Polish Jews would switch from "party to party according to the type of election and issue at stake."[126] The political climate in Poland forced the recalibration of Zuckerman's basic political vocabulary, and debates over emigration had reshuffled the loyalties and beliefs of Polish Jews substantially.

Conversations across political parties and economic divides often returned to the intertwined issues of emigration, the status of Palestine, and the future of Jews in Poland. After first convening with the twenty or so Polish Jews who already had an affiliation with the WJC, Zuckerman expanded his network.[127] The Folkist (or People's) Party, led by party leader and newspaper editor Noach Pryłucki, who had attended the inaugural meeting of the WJC in Geneva, initially joined conversations with Zuckerman but later withdrew after conflicts developed. The main difference between the People's Parties and the Revisionists, Zuckerman noted, "was on the question of whether Palestine should find a place in the Congress or not."[128] The Revisionists insisted that Polish Jews as a group issue a "resolution which would in the name of Polish Jews demand that England and the League of Nations remain true to their obligations."[129] The People's Party could not accept this idea, nor could they accept the organization taking a stand on the problem of emigration. Once disconnected from the congress, Pryłucki began, in Zuckerman's evaluation, "an active campaign against the Congress." As the Joint Distribution Committee (JDC) and certain ministries in the Polish government also worked to "sabotage" the activities of the WJC, Zuckerman found himself increasingly surrounded by vocal enemies and unable to rescue the work of the congress from the internal and external issues plaguing it.[130]

Zuckerman and the organizing committee of the Congress of Polish Jews strove to create a democratically elected body that represented all Jews, regardless of gender, political party, or religious affiliation, living in Poland.[131] They failed partially because of the issues detailed in Zuckerman's 1938 report and mostly because their call for unity proved decidedly divisive. Nearly all voices in the Jewish press wrote with the censors in mind, some mocked the initiative, and others supported the efforts of the organizing committee as the process to select a countrywide Polish Jewish representative body crescendoed between December 1937 and March 1938.[132] On many occasions, organizers encountered aggressive resistance by state officials. Called at some moments the "Congress of Polish Jews" and at other moments the "Congress for Jewish Self-Help," the discussions around the campaign lacked emphasis on specific goals besides the oversimplified promise to offer a representative voice for Polish Jews. Like the Provisional Jewish National Council before it, which attempted in 1919 to convene a National Assembly that would be elected democratically by all adult, male Jews in Poland, the imagined congress was never elected because of the organizers' inability to resolve contested issues and simplify their initiative in a way that would interest multiple sectors of Polish Jews. Organizers and their helpers included men such as Moses Kleinbaum, Arieh Tartakower, Ignacy Schwarzbart, and Anselm Reiss.[133]

The coverage of the event in the Polish Jewish press diverges from Zuckerman's February 1938 report and shows the ways in which Zuckerman and his peers oversaw and facilitated a two-part process in 1937 and 1938 to bring the Congress of Polish Jews to fruition. First, delegates from across Poland bought voting cards with both Polish and Yiddish imprints to essentially register themselves as "democratic" members of the Polish Jewish masses.[134] Second, the delegates on these registration lists would elect representatives to speak on behalf of Polish Jews in a body that would convene in the near future. The planning for countrywide registration of all Polish Jews picked up in the fall of 1937 when the Central Organizing Committee announced plans to convene eleven regional conferences in places such as Łódź, Wilno, Równo, and Białystok on November 10.[135] To this end, all the offices of the Jewish Economic Committee, like the one in Łódź, would be transformed into offices for the Polish Jewish Congress in pursuit of a successful registration and later election.[136] By November 18, *Nasz Przegląd* reported that the Central Organizing Committee had ordered 1.25 million voting cards for purchase, each representing an individual's registration to vote for the congressional body. On the next day, Nahum Goldmann traveled to Łódź to give a speech on the initiative at WIZO. Another event in Łódź one month later failed to draw a large audience because authorities had restricted access to the planned meeting room. Two hundred delegates from fifty-two cities in the Łódź region moved to a room too small to accommodate everyone. Among the speakers at this event, Arieh Tartakower lamented that the largest Jewish communities in the Łódź region would not be represented at the conference.[137]

Despite these hurdles set up by state authorities, the campaign continued and gained momentum.[138] An advertisement in *Nasz Przegląd* on December 26, 1937, announced that one thousand volunteers would spend St. Stephen's Day selling election cards for the newly renamed "Jewish Self-Help Congress in Poland."[139] By the first week of January, there were organizing committees in more than five hundred towns, and the Central Organizing Committee had begun distributing questionnaires to assess the results of the election card campaign.[140] In Kraków, under the leadership of Rabbi M. J. Klieger, a meeting on January 5 passed "unanimously a resolution in which nonpartisan religious

Jewry declared its accession to the Congress of Polish Jews."[141] A few days later, on January 9, the Central Organizing Committee announced that district conferences in Białystok and the Wołyń region would take place and that representatives of the Jewish community and political parties would attend.[142] The Warsaw committee was organized around the same time.[143] By January 13, voting cards went on sale in Katowice.[144] Mayors in a few cities in Volhynia such as Kostopol and Berezna confiscated voting cards in mid-January, thwarting some efforts to rally support for the congress.[145] On January 16, representatives of the Organizing Committee held an event in Buczacz, while in Warsaw the congress opened, with nearly 250 different groups, organizations, and institutions participating.[146] Initial reports delivered at this event were optimistic. Two hundred thousand election cards had been sold in the Małopolska region, along with three hundred thousand in former Congress Poland (or Lesser Poland). Soon, the Central Organizing Committee in Warsaw decided that five hundred delegates would be elected from across three historic regions.[147]

As deadlines approached, a publicity campaign ran through the Jewish press. From late January through the first week of February, eight ads appeared in *Chwila*, including one on January 30 promising that the "Congress would fight for a better tomorrow for the Jews."[148] On January 30, a rally took place for academics devoted to the Jewish Congress in Poland. Dr. Moses Kleinbaum, Dr. Ch. Szoszkies, and lawyer Zorach Warhaftig, among others, helped stimulate interest in the initiative.[149] Kleinbaum also addressed a crowd a week later, this time with Anselm Reiss, who had announced the declaration of the unified Polish Jewish delegation at the 1936 Congress in Geneva.[150] In an editorial on February 3, Dr. Eliasz Markus drew an allusion between the congress and the Council of Four Lands, suggesting that Polish Jews had "remained broken down in individual groups, devoid of a common platform" and declaring that the time when one Jewish party played off another party to gain power had "passed."[151] This initiative, Markus declared, would produce a "dignified" and "serious" representation for the entire Jewish community. Still, people had to be reminded to get involved. A written appeal from the Central Organizing Committee of the Jewish Congress in Poland complemented two broad advertisements in *Nasz Przegląd* in the two days before the sale of electoral cards was scheduled to end on February 7, 1938.[152] The sales of the cards, however, passed beyond this initial deadline because the election campaign continued and garnered both supporters and opponents. On February 11, thirty-two different parts of the Jewish Craftsmen Union in Łódź agreed to "massively" participate in the campaign.[153] The Prezydium

Rady Naczelnej Kupiectwa Żydowskiego (Presidium of the General Council of Jewish Merchants) decided not to support the work of the Central Organizing Committee.[154] But thousands of others did, particularly those in medium and large cities.[155]

After the election campaign closed on February 27, 1938, the Central Organizing Committee began "preparatory work for elections," which they hoped to schedule for April 24.[156] A short update a few weeks later noted that Central Organizing Committee reports indicated a change in the date of the electoral calendar in response to a delay in negotiations with parties that were outside of the congressional sphere.[157] Despite all these preparations, after "exhaustive discussions" within the committee in early April, the decision was made to "postpone the congress indefinitely."[158] After months of press coverage, the plan for the democratically elected and unified congress of Polish Jews or the Congress for Jewish Self-Help in Poland "passed away without a trace."[159]

Opinion pages were not kind to the Organizing Committee. In November 1937, for example, famed editor and writer Hillel Zeitlin criticized the committee's partisan nature. The founders who demanded a congress, Zeitlin wrote, "remain[ed] faithful to their old party habits" instead.[160] In "proclaiming a general Jewish congress, they mean[t] the creation of a new Jewish nationalist council" where some "Zionist groups [would] be represented," other parties would be represented, and "non-party Jews [would] not be represented." Less representative than the Jewish representatives in the Sejm, this congress, Zeitlin concluded, would caricature Jewish representation and be recognized as authoritative by no one. Likewise, Jakob Apenszlak, editor at *Nasz Przegląd,* harbored doubts about how representative the congress would be. Addressing fifty-two delegates of the General Zionist Party, Apenszlak criticized the electoral structure as designed by the organizing committee. The Polish state, Apenszlak asserted, was more representative than this congress.[161] Though favoring a congress, Apenszlak disagreed with the methods by which its organizers strove toward democratic representation as well as their end goals. For Apenszlak, a self-help plan for Polish Jews should "normalize the life of the Jewish masses against various emigration theories."[162] As indicated by Zuckerman's report, Noach Pryłucki, who had attended the 1936 meeting in Geneva, became a vocal enemy of the congress not only because of the campaign's failure to emphasize Palestine-related or emigration issues.[163] Instead of being a congress of the Jewish people in Poland, this charade would be, in Pryłucki's assessment, "a Congress of a few Zionist parties."[164]

Concluding his eight-page report explaining the failure to hold a congress, Zuckerman returned to the issue of emigration, which by February 1938 had become an even more important node of Poland's Camp of National Unity platform. Citing a speech by Bronisław Wojciechowski during the Sejm's budget commission, Zuckerman linked discussions about Polish Jews to emigration.[165] In Wojciechowski's evaluation, "the responsibility of the Jewish problem in Poland does not rest with Poland but is international and . . . all nations must come together and find a solution to this problem." This solution "will come in the way of emigration."[166] And yet, Zuckerman feared that a disintegrated Polish Jewry would be ruined "more easily by this process of (economical and literal) uprooting." He hoped, however, that "an integrated Jewry would still be able to make a stand. We are still three million people in Poland and still 10% of the population. It will not be easy to uproot the 10% if they are organized." He envisioned the fate of Polish Jewry as wrapped up with the fate of world Jewry. In his concluding paragraphs, Zuckerman reflected on the WJC's failing effort to organize Polish Jewry. "Polish Jewry," he wrote, "spawned American and Palestinian migration" and "still is [a] rich and tremendous creative force. It represents a reservoir of cultural creativeness of the Jew for the entire world." In fact, "a normal healthy Polish Jewry is a national treasure of first magnitude."[167]

Two important tensions run through Zuckerman's report. First, questions about emigration infused discussions about Polish Jewry, and yet Poland's Jews remained rooted in Poland. And second, even though the population of more than three million Jews was fragmented by gendered, generational, religious, political, social, linguistic, and economic cleavages, there remained a tendency to expect a semblance of unity, especially in the face of a palpable danger. While Zuckerman's report remains a problematic source insofar as it is skewed toward explaining why his efforts to mobilize Polish Jews failed, his observations help us problematize foundational questions that cut through histories about the Polish Jewish experience during the interwar period and understand the political vocabulary of the 1930s.

JOEL CANG'S JOURNALISTIC EFFORTS TO CONTEXTUALIZE ROOTEDNESS

When Baruch Zuckerman filed his eight-page report at the end of February 1938, Joel Cang was also in Poland, the country of his citizenship, working on an article that would eventually be published in the second issue of *Jewish Social Studies* in 1939. We now turn to Cang's sociological research as well as his journalism to understand the rootedness of Polish Jews from two broader perspectives. First, as a Polish citizen writing for English-language audiences of the *Guardian*, the *News Chronicle*, and the *Jewish Chronicle* as well as scholarly journals, Cang related Jewish issues to minority questions in general and Polish state policies on the Ukrainian minority (the largest minority in the Second Republic) in particular.[168] Second, Cang relied on interviews he conducted with peasants and other "ordinary" Polish citizens. His writings reveal the rootedness of Jews as well as their Ukrainian, Belarusian, and Catholic neighbors, while showing once more why wide-scale plans for Jewish emigration failed. This perennial failure occurred as Hitler's government increased its legal, ideological, economic, cultural, and social assaults on Jews in Germany and, in late 1938, expelled thousands of Jews of Polish heritage from the growing Reich.

In his writings, Cang reveals programs advocating Jewish emigration as doubtful in reality yet potent as propaganda. Combining his expertise as a journalist with keen academic insight, Cang offered readers of *Jewish Social Studies* a nuanced look at the opposition parties in Poland and their views on the Jews' predicament more generally. As he surveyed the complicated political landscape of post-Piłsudski Poland, he covered parties known for their antisemitism, such as Roman Dmowski's National Democrats, the Conservative Party led by Prince Janusz Radziwiłł, and new parties including Mieczysław Michałowicz's Democratic Party and the Stronnictwo or "faction" of Ignacy Paderewski, along with the Socialists, the Peasant Party, and youth movements suspended in between. His message was clear: demands for the emigration of Poland's Jews had failed to capture political support from the Polish peasantry and had distracted Polish public opinion from real problems.

Drawing on published speeches, coverage in a variety of party-specific and more generalized papers, and his own reading of human psychology, Cang worked through analyses of antisemitism and proposals for mass emigration. There were three basic approaches. The National Democrats (or Endeks) and the Conservatives consistently demanded that Jews leave Poland, yet by doing so they diverted attention from the real problems plaguing Polish society. Peasant parties had exhibited more moderate views toward the Jewish minority. Finally, the Socialists, despite some antisemitic outliers, remained committed to an inclusive Poland that included Jewish citizens en masse. While conversations about Jewish issues dominated domestic and international coverage related to the Second Republic, land reform and conflicts emanating from the Ukrainian and German minorities were, in Cang's opinion, the largest problems facing the state.

Cang explained why, focusing on the suddenly caustic rhetoric of the Conservative Party vis-à-vis the Jews. At the birth of the Polish state in the early 1920s, 44 percent of the total land was in the hands of rich landowners, while sixteen million peasants, or 64 percent of the population, owned only about

10 percent of the arable land. Since then, "about three million hectares [were] divided out amongst the land-hungry peasants," but "three million Polish farmers [were] forced to maintain themselves and their families on less than two hectares of land." Polish nobles, Cang argues, staved off agrarian reforms that took place in other neighboring countries, and instead of making land available, they advised peasants to "'go to the town' and oust the Jews." And so the "desire to retain their vast holdings" in fact "determined the anti-semitic policy of the conservatives in Poland."[169]

Much as antisemitic language could divert attention from discussions of land reform, so could an inordinate emphasis on the Jewish minority disguise problems of integrating the German and, even more so, the Ukrainian minorities.[170] Throughout the 1920s and the 1930s, the government-sponsored newspaper *Gazeta Polska* detailed the deadly conflict that raged between "radical" Ukrainian nationalists and the Polish state. Writing elsewhere on the results of the state's pacification policy toward Ukrainian populations in Poland's east, Cang admitted that even though the "Polish Government ha[d] shown an honest desire to bring about some form of cooperation with some leaders of the Ukrainian minority," after three years of normalization "Polish Ukrainian relations ha[d] reached a bad stage."[171] And yet, despite the campaign waged by some Ukrainian radicals against the Polish state (which resulted in the assassinations of high-ranking government officials), a massive pacification campaign led by the Polish army against Ukrainian-dominated villages, and, later, official documents filed on behalf of Poland's German minority before the highest international body, *Gazeta Polska*'s journalists did not recommend compulsory evacuation or the forced migration of these decidedly more "problematic" minorities. The next chapter details how the idea of population transfers as a statecraft tool became more normative as the international community departed from an interwar system that supported, at least on paper, minority rights.[172]

When and why do ideas casting Jews as belonging elsewhere coalesce and become public?[173] It is helpful to consider the shifts within the Peasant Party and Cang's assessment of them to better understand how calls for Jewish emigration became popular at certain moments and served political ends.[174] In December 1935, for example, the Peasant Party issued a platform at the United Peasant Parties Conference that included something new: a call for Jewish emigration from Poland to Palestine and other places.[175] Yet this idea did not remain official policy for long. Soon afterward, the Peasant Party leader took down "the Jewish question from their time tables," deciding to either "ignore the problem altogether or make but slight reference to it." The individual peasant, Cang believed, had played a role in the elimination of this language. By

1937, the Jewish question was "not the most important problem in the country" for the Peasant Party.[176] The problem of democracy proved more urgent. Cang cited the August 1937 peasant strikes and riots as further proof of the Peasant Party's attitude toward the Jews. At a time when more than forty people were killed as a result of peasant violence, the Jewish population remained safe.[177] And yet despite this, Cang admitted that the "Polish Peasant Party does not conceal its view that if someone must emigrate to Madagascar it should be the Jew and not the Polish peasant."[178]

Cang observed that this particular political propaganda related to Jewish emigration had infiltrated even the inclusive Socialist Party (PPS) by the end of the 1930s.[179] Cang cautioned that this "new tendency which seeks the solution of the Jewish problem by Jewish emigration should not be considered representative of the official policy and attitude of the PPS." In fact, "the official party press has made it clear, in reply to objections by leaders of the Bund, that this view does not represent the party's stand." Ideas casting "integrated" Jews as the only Jews deserving of their roots in Poland should be seen, Cang reflected, as symptomatic "of the results which anti-Jewish propaganda has produced in influencing even some socialists to regard the mass of Jews as aliens and to consider mass emigration as the sole solution to the Jewish problem in Poland."[180]

It is clear that Cang considered calls for mass emigration as a distraction from more pressing issues and, for the most part, unlikely to improve the horrific economic and social situation of Polish life in the late 1930s. In his reporting on the 1937 World Zionist Organization Congress, Cang referenced a "plebiscite carried out by the anti-Jewish Warsaw afternoon paper *Goniec*." Regarding the situation in Mandate Palestine, the paper put a question to its readers: "Will an independent Palestine hasten Jewish emigration from Poland?"[181] In response to this question, 600 Poles and 978 Jews replied yes, and 16,272 Poles and 195 Jews said no. The vast majority of Polish Christians (albeit ones reading a known antisemitic paper) did not believe that Jewish emigration could be hastened even in the wake of such a drastic development. Arguably, a majority of Christian readers of an "anti-Jewish" paper realized how rooted Polish Jews were in Polish society. The situation of German Jews, Joel Cang realized during the course of his reporting, was a different story entirely.

By the end of the 1930s, German Jews and in fact all Jews living in the Third Reich encountered a violent uprooting. One of the "chief objectives of Nazi policies towards the Jews between 1935 and September 1939," Marion Kaplan writes, "had been to foster emigration, once called 'the territorial solution.'"[182] From the "Syrian" and "Ecuador" Projects to the "Madagascar Plan" and the "Haavara Transfer," from 1933 onward the Nazi government devised plans "to deposit Germany's unwanted Jews around the globe."[183] These statewide initiatives dovetailed with government support for individual emigration to create an atmosphere of forced expulsion. Even before they left Germany, thousands of German Jews found themselves on the move, often leaving smaller towns for the anonymity of the larger city. Cang traveled to Danzig in 1935 to witness this firsthand.[184] Between 270,000 and 300,000 Jews managed to flee Germany overall from 1933 to 1939, and 1933 and 1938 marked the years with the highest exit numbers.[185] The "first waves of refugees fled to neighboring countries, probably hoping to return home at some point or to continue abroad if necessary," and the "proportion of the total number of emigrations who fled overseas grew dramatically as the conditions in Europe worsened in the late 1930s" (especially after Kristallnacht).[186] Between 50,000 and 60,000 German Jews left Europe for the Palestinian Mandate in the 1930s.[187]

Soon, the experience of Polish Jews living inside and outside the borders of the Second Republic dovetailed with the uprootedness plaguing German Jews. Cang first alerted readers of the *Jewish Chronicle* to the difficult situation facing Polish Jews living abroad on March 26, 1938, about two weeks after the Anschluss, which had brought 200,000 Austrian Jews into the Reich. He noted that upward of "20,000 Polish Jews living abroad would soon find themselves without a country." Half a year later, after the Munich Agreement and just before Kristallnacht, Cang's horrifying prediction rang true when at the end of October 1938 the *Polenaktion* began. On the night of October 27–28, police authorities detained fifteen to seventeen thousand Jewish citizens of Poland; rescinded their German residence permits; transported the detained Jews, including children separated from their parents, to the German-Polish border; and unloaded them there, making them walk the rest of the way to the border.

Cang zoomed in on Zbąszyń, where the family of Herschel Grynszpan was caught in no-man's-land after being expelled from Hanover along with 481 other Jewish citizens of Poland.[188] From the end of October to the end of December 1938, Cang filed biweekly updates on the situation of Polish Jews within Germany as well as those expelled from there. Cang documented the brutal tactics utilized by the Germans, rumors of disease in the refugee camps, the high incidence of suicide among the deportees, and the slow deliberations between the Polish and German governments, which kept Jews confined to spaces in towns such as Zbąszyń for months on end.[189] Cang reached out to his editor at the *Manchester Guardian* that November to see if that paper could offer him some form of permanent employment if he and his family had to flee Poland themselves. They did not, but he was officially appointed as a foreign correspondent for the *Manchester Guardian* in 1938 after being denied such a status in 1932.[190] The journalist's professional rise coincided with more precarious circumstances for Polish Jews, inside, outside, and on the state's borders. In an increasing number of cases, rootedness had acquired both tragic and pessimistic undertones by 1938 and 1939.[191] It entailed severe implications for Polish Jews living outside Poland and increasingly demanded more coverage, and a new word pervaded Cang's writings by late 1938 and 1939: *expulsions*.

In less than a year, Joel Cang would learn about rootlessness himself. In September 1939, as his city of Warsaw fell to the Wehrmacht, he fled with his wife, Bela, and three-year-old son, Stefan, and traveled for ten days by train and foot until they arrived in Bucharest. From there, they traveled to England, where our story reconnects with him in 1946. In fact, many of the voices encountered in this chapter (Tartakower, Lestschinsky, Goldmann, Apenszlak, Perlzweig, Kubowitzki and others) experienced rootlessness at the end of the 1930s as well. As we move forward across this pivotal decade, we question how their own uprooting impacted their opinions of Jewish rootedness in Poland, east central Europe, and beyond.

CONCLUSION

By the end of 1938 and the beginning of 1939, even some Polish Jews living elsewhere found themselves inextricably tethered to Poland. The expulsion of thousands of "Polish" Jews from Germany made some Polish Jews already in Poland more aware of their commitment to their community and their country. Arieh Tartakower, who vigorously wrote and spoke in favor of Jewish emigration away from Poland, swore that Poland's Jews would "never" leave for political reasons alone, even if they were destined for Palestine.[192] A colleague who contributed to the three-volume history of the Jews in Poland that Tartakower had edited expressed similar sentiments. Emanuel Ringelblum, a young historian based in Warsaw, volunteered with the JDC to assist the evacuees in Zbąszyń and elsewhere in 1938 and 1939. His travels all over Poland "showed him the immense determination of Polish Jewry to hold and defend itself against economic anti-semitism."[193]

The same month that Ringelblum penned his letter, May 1939, Jabotinsky announced to Warsaw reporters covering his travels throughout eastern Europe that his "evacuation plan had failed."[194] Especially in the wake of the 1939 White Paper further restricting movement into Palestine, Polish Jews simply could not and, it appears, would not leave en masse for the Mandate or anywhere else. In 1938 and 1939, the United States did not even fill the immigration quota designated for Polish citizens. To make life in Poland even more palatable for those who might want to leave, the first few months of 1939 saw the "highest rates of industrial growth since the years of inflation in the early 1920s" and a decline in antisemitism as political tensions between Poland and Germany began to rise.[195] Even in August 1939 as the Wehrmacht's invasion of Poland loomed and a panicked flight of people in the western portions of the state began, Apolinary Hartglas, president of the General Zionist faction of the Zionist Organizations of Central and Eastern Poland, wrote that "to other than ideological motivated emigration to Palestine, we say no, never."[196]

And, finally, two days after Chaim Weizmann dismissed the 576 delegates from the 1939 meeting of the World Zionist Organization in Switzerland, Zorach Warhaftig traveled with his wife and his friends on a sealed train back to Poland so that he could help defend his city and the city of his wife's parents: Warsaw. We encountered Warhaftig briefly in this first chapter when he attended a meeting in advance of the WJC-sponsored campaign to elect representatives to speak on behalf of Polish Jews. He becomes an important personality in our story moving forward.

For now, we should note what he wrote about the summer of 1939 nearly six decades later. Warhaftig remembered that "only a few" members of the Polish delegation to the congress "opted to remain in Switzerland" rather than quickly return to a country soon to be invaded by the Wehrmacht. For Warhaftig, this was inconceivable. He recalled that "no such thought crossed my mind or that of my wife. We knew that we simply had to get back to our families in Warsaw and do our duty as loyal Polish citizens. At no time in the past had our Jewish and civil responsibilities coincided so harmoniously as they did [then], when . . . confronted with the menace of Hitler's Nazi hordes."[197]

Soon, however, the uprootedness that marked German Jews in the 1930s would reshape the lives of Polish Jews and millions of other Polish citizens. That story of displacement linked to war, occupation, flight, and genocide is well known. Another story of uprooting, a story about the intellectual uprooting of the Jewish diaspora native to Poland and the region around it, coincides with this more obvious physical one and continues next.

TWO

IN EXILE

Debating Postwar Plans during an Uprooted Present, 1940–1943

AS FAR AS THE ARCHIVAL record reveals, Edvard Beneš and Vladimir Jabotinsky met just once, privately, in March 1940. Jabotinsky came to Beneš seeking letters of introduction that would facilitate his upcoming public campaign to raise funds for a Jewish Legion in the United States.[1] Amid talk of practical matters, Beneš and Jabotinsky also shared a theoretical discussion concerning the unmixing of ethnicities in east central Europe. Beneš spoke of "transferred" ethnic Germans and Jabotinsky of a "voluntary evacuation" for European Jews, but, in essence, these very different men used similar vocabularies as they planned for the postwar world.

The topic came up naturally in the course of that discussion, aided by a map of Czechoslovakia that hung "prominently" on the wall of their meeting room at the former Czechoslovak Embassy in London. Jabotinsky pointed at the "shaded portions," and Beneš explained that the darkened hue "marked the minority populations" in the so-called Sudetenland, specifically the roughly three and a half million "ethnic" Germans who had possessed Czechoslovak citizenship at the time of the 1938 Munich Agreement.[2] Estimates indicated that roughly two-thirds of this population had supported Konrad Henlein and his right-wing, pro-Nazi Sudeten German Party in the parliamentary elections of 1935.[3] Beneš (and others) alleged that the policies of this particular minority population could be linked to the series of diplomatic, military, and political events that culminated in the (eventual) absorption of Czechoslovak territory into the Third Reich in March 1939.[4] With his finger extended, Jabotinsky asked Beneš, "'What do you propose to do with them?'" Beneš replied, "without a moment's hesitation, '*they will have to leave* [the notetaker included this emphasis in the original]. We shall have no more fifth column in our country. If an effective administration can be set up in my country soon enough after the end of the war, these Germans will be transferred smoothly; if not, then . . .' and he shrugged his shoulders significantly."[5] Keenly aware of his audience, Beneš next turned to the Jews of Czechoslovakia, asserting that recognizing them as a "national minority would open the way to similar demands by others in the State and could be employed by dangerous elements and movements for disintegrating" a reconstituted polity.[6] This was not the first time Beneš made this argument. As the leader of the Czechoslovak delegation to the Paris Peace Conference in 1919, Beneš had resolutely opposed minority protections requested by Jewish and German representatives.[7] Such conditions, Beneš surmised more than two decades before his conversation with Jabotinsky, would constitute a breach of state sovereignty. His basic thinking on this issue had not changed, but his advocacy for the transfer of over three million "ethnic" Germans represented a revolutionary intellectual shift.

Jabotinsky seemed to ignore Beneš's comments on national minorities and instead seized on his statement about the need for Germans with interwar Czechoslovak citizenship to "leave." Pivoting to the subject of Revisionist Zionism, Jabotinsky outlined his own hypothetical program for "voluntary evacuation" of east central European Jews to Palestine as well as his own reasons "for claiming assistance in realizing that plan."[8] He explained that a Jewish state in Palestine could be established on both sides of the Jordan River, how he planned to protect land and resources, and, finally, how an international loan could reinforce philanthropic funding offered by the Jewish people worldwide, but especially from Jewish donors in the United States and the United Kingdom. Beneš hesitated. Perhaps Jabotinsky had misinterpreted the earlier part of their conversation. In fact, Beneš "repudiated any idea wishing Jews away" from Czechoslovakia. As an "ordinary cultural or religious minority," Jews could live there happily. They could never, however, take the form of a "national minority again." With this clarification, Beneš was contradicting the Czechoslovak Constitution of February 29, 1920, which granted "equality to the country's minorities" and allowed Jews to declare their nationality as Jewish regardless of their mother tongue.[9]

While both Beneš and Jabotinsky envisioned the ethnic homogenization of east central Europe, they had different priorities within this overall plan. Jabotinsky spoke only about Jewish population movement in the form of evacuation. Beneš spoke mainly of the German minority on Czechoslovak territory and refused to explicitly support population transfers of Czechoslovak Jews at this particular moment. He remained adamant, however, that the status of Jews in postwar Czechoslovakia would change from what it had been between the wars.[10] In essence, both of these men dreamed similar dreams. According to Abraham Abrahams, Jabotinsky's assistant who witnessed the meeting between the two, the "closeness between the nationalist of the one nation and the other" was palpable. "There was," Abrahams recalled, "almost a complete accord between them."[11] From their very different positions, they agreed more quickly on measures treating populations according to ethnicity than almost all of their diplomatic peers in Zionist circles, Allied administrations, and those officials generally concerned with postwar relief and rehabilitation.

Only seven months into the Second World War, both Beneš and Jabotinsky considered population transfers (either when applied to an irredentist German minority in the Czechoslovak context or when attached to plans to shepherd Jews toward a Palestinian homeland) as viable and acceptable solutions recasting the heterogeneous, post–World War I nation-state in the region.[12] International norms protecting minority rights and discouraging the forced or voluntary movements of politically vulnerable human groups would thus shift, in this shared calculus, to encourage the ethnic reorganization of populations in east central Europe. Yet when applied to Jewish populations, this shift logically necessitated the simultaneous embrace of a Jewish polity in the Middle East. Jabotinsky could already envision this, of course, and while Beneš did not yet speak directly about this contingency, he would soon address it in strikingly absolute terms that would agitate officials in the World Jewish Congress.

At first glance, Beneš and Jabotinsky make strange bedfellows. In spite of the copious ink spilled about both, their trajectories rarely intersected as clearly as they do now in this narrative. The wider world knew Beneš for his realpolitik diplomacy, his vigorous embrace of the League of Nations' system, and his polished diplomat pedigree hewed during and after the Great War, when he and Tomáš Garrigue Masaryk engineered the creation and international recognition of the First Republic of Czechoslovakia.[13] He was head of state during the Sudeten crisis of 1938, after which he abdicated and went into exile. Despite his self-described humiliation over the Munich fiasco, Beneš remained a well-respected diplomatic personality and was appointed as a visiting professor at the University of Chicago in January 1939.[14] A few weeks later, after the Nazi occupation of the rump-state of Czechoslovakia in March 1939, he left academia in the hope of assembling a government-in-exile that would represent Czechoslovak interests in the anti-Hitler diplomatic universe. In contrast, Jabotinsky had neither the law degree nor the international experience nor the political power of Beneš; what he did have were thousands of committed followers who would pack auditoriums when he arrived in New York in the weeks after this meeting and attend his funeral when he died unexpectedly later that year.[15]

And yet, these two men with different pedigrees, professional statuses, and life expectancies could see the same future in early 1940, and that future included nation-states built on massive shifts of population.

By drawing closer to the ideas of WJC officials living in exile such as Maurice Perlzweig, Ignacy Schwarzbart, Arieh Tartakower, and Aryeh Leon Kubowitzki, we can explore how this small group of high-profile members (many on the World Jewish Congress's Office Committee) and other officials corresponding with them perceived Beneš's quick gravitation toward evacuationist language, a lessening of minority rights, and a Palestine-centric solution to the Jewish question. Indeed, Beneš embraced the drastic uprooting of east central European Jews and others much more quickly than east central European Jews did, many of whom had strong "Zionist" leanings. Our document trail, which draws on the journal *Foreign Affairs*, the émigré Polish-language newspaper *Nasza Trybuna*, and a multinational collection of archives, reveals that this group of Zionist-leaning thinkers felt threatened by Beneš's perceived embrace of radical, pseudo-evacuationist Zionism throughout 1940, 1941, 1942, and even 1943. I say this even as I concede that it is difficult to separate what Beneš actually thought from how WJC officials interpreted his thinking.

At times in this chapter, Beneš seems like an active shaper of policy; at other times, he appears to be a passive vessel refracting ideas back at his conversation partners; and at still other times, our documents paint him as a mixture of both or something entirely different. His expressed intent regarding Jewish belonging was slightly inconsistent over time, especially as he negotiated his broader views about population transfers and the German minority in Czechoslovakia in general against popular opinion emanating from his occupied homeland. And yet, WJC leaders maintained an almost monolithic reverence for Czechoslovakia as the "most hospitable environment" for Jews in interwar east central Europe and thus remained threatened by Beneš's transformation throughout 1943 even as they discovered contradictions in the Czechoslovak leader's thoughts.[16]

By intertwining three narratives—one about the perceived intellectual progression of Edvard Beneš away from the diaspora, another about the intellectual commitment of the WJC to the diaspora up until at least the end of 1943, and a third concerning awareness of the Jewish tragedy unfolding in occupied Europe—this chapter integrates three important historical threads that have not yet been synthesized. In the first few years of the Second World War, WJC members working in exile were jolted by language emanating from Czechoslovak leaders also in exile. Just as the utopian views of "evacuation" offered by Jabotinsky in the 1930s threatened those committed to the Jewish diaspora in

Fig. 2.1. Edvard Beneš, pictured in front of a map of Europe, signs the new constitution during a swearing-in ceremony of the new Czechoslovak government in London on July 23, 1940. Photo by Tovey/Popperfoto via Getty Images.

places such as interwar Poland, the views Beneš publicly and privately espoused about the erasure of minority rights, population transfers, and the idea of a Palestinian-based citizenship for "national" Jews stunned the leaders of the WJC and jeopardized the spirit of their institution on a fundamental level in the early 1940s. During this time, these European Jews remained solidly committed to the rootedness of Jewish life in Czechoslovakia and east central Europe overall and built this commitment into their contemporary and future plans even as they learned about the Shoah. As we learned in chapter 1, the adjective *Zionist* fails to capture the complexity of their individual pasts, shared present, and divergent futures.

EVACUATIONISM AND EXILED BENEŠ CIRCA 1940–1941: TWO GREAT THREATS FOR THE WORLD JEWISH CONGRESS

News of Edvard Beneš's evacuationist sympathies and disdain for the postwar reimplementation of the minority rights systems first surfaced in the internal correspondence of WJC officials on November 20, 1940. Seven months after his private meeting with Jabotinsky, Beneš and his National Liberation Committee had established operations in London, England, after the fall of France earlier that year. There, in the bustling expatriate universe of the wartime British capital, Ignacy Schwarzbart of the Polish government-in-exile alerted his WJC colleagues on both sides of the Atlantic to the demise of Czechoslovakia's exceptionally tolerant interwar policies toward her Jewish citizens. In a report on the current state of Polish Jewish affairs, Schwarzbart dramatically switched tone and cautioned his readers that "prominent and responsible politicians of one of the defeated states in central Europe" were considering future policies demanding that "Jews will either have to be part of the ruling population or get Palestinian citizenship, in which case they would be treated as foreigners."[17] These ideas originated from someone "considered to be 100% democratic" and could spread to other countries. "Now," Schwarzbart decided, "is the time to watch this danger-point."[18]

Like the interwar Czech political elite and his Czech Jewish colleagues, Schwarzbart continued to subscribe to the myth of Czechoslovakia as "a liberal and democratic island whose progressive, western Czech leaders held out against the anti-democratic and chauvinist nationalist forces that engulfed the rest of Central and Eastern Europe in the interwar period."[19] The historians Andrea Orzoff and Tatjana Lichtenstein have been chipping away at this myth, but their works confirm that portrayals of "Czech leaders as uniquely tolerant, democratic, and Western, indeed as friends of Jews," were widely shared by Czech nationalists, Czech Jews, and Czech Zionists alike.[20] And so, Schwarzbart's language, which might seem to opaque to us, necessarily targeted the one leader whose perceived shift portended a detrimental turn of events for the World Jewish Congress.

Five months later, another internal report of the WJC warned that Beneš and his views had become a persistent problem. When Czechoslovak citizen and WJC employee Dr. Lev Zelmanovits visited Beneš twice in March 1941, he found that the yet-to-be-recognized Czechoslovak leader had "firmly decided not to settle the Jewish problem until the whole minority problem in general is settled."[21] Seeking clarification, Zelmanovits pushed Beneš to concede that the Jews could not easily "be compared with other minorities." Eschewing nuance, Beneš tersely replied, "A minority is a minority."[22] One year after Beneš met with Jabotinsky, the views he had indicated privately had not changed. In a letter to Arieh Tartakower, Zelmanovits revealed more than in his official memo. Beneš was, in his assessment, "the biggest problem we face."[23] According to Zelmanovits, Beneš "had his own idea concerning the solution of the Jewish question in Europe . . . after the war, all countries should help in establishing a Jewish state. [Beneš] is certain it will be Palestine. After the

Jewish state is established all Jews will have to decide either to be absorbed in the Jewish nation, or in the nation of their homeland. In the first case, they will be citizens of the Jewish state, aliens in the other countries, and should be immediately transferred to a transit country."[24] With regard to minority rights, Beneš did not see these guarantees impacting Jewish populations, as minority right protections would be relevant only for populations with majorities in neighboring countries. Zelmanovits considered these views a "great danger" for all European Jews, and so he had tried to "dissuade" the president. His efforts had failed, however, and Beneš's views were echoing through the exiled government. Zelmanovits urged action upon Tartakower. "Our principle should be," he wrote, "to persuade Dr. Beneš that his conception is wrong." Officials at the WJC had now heard a second and more alarming siren about Beneš, one that resonated more clearly than Schwarzbart's earlier warning.[25]

On April 17, 1941, a triumvirate of WJC actors sat down with President Beneš to clarify his language regarding minorities, ask him why he had yet to appoint an official of Jewish background to the Czech National Council, and explain precisely how the Jews differed from the other, more threatening and identifiable, minorities in his state.[26] The impulse for the meeting with Beneš stemmed from his universalizing statement: "A minority is a minority." Noah Barou warned Beneš that "mutual enemies had already begun a whispering campaign informing the non-Jewish world that even the Czechs were changing their attitudes to the Jews" and that the Czechs had "abandoned" their former Jewish citizens as well as their influence and standing in the democratic world."[27] To this, Beneš responded with a reassurance that he had not "changed his principals."[28] He remained "the same Beneš who had always fought for Jewish rights and had always supported Jewish democratic and national claims."[29] Next, Beneš listed his most pressing problems: acquiring recognition from the Allies as the legitimate government of the Czechoslovak state, assembling that governing body out of a fragmented exiled body politic, and deciding whether he could trust Germans among the Czechoslovak émigrés. The high percentage of German-speaking Jews in London's Czechoslovak circles worried Beneš. After all, the German-speaking element within his state had proved to be the polity's undoing.

Beneš continued speaking until Sydney Silverman interrupted and asserted "that the Jewish minority question differed entirely from the German [one] as there was no territorial nation behind the Jews."[30] In response, Beneš "admitted the difference but insisted that as a matter of principle all the minority questions would have to be settled simultaneously on the principle of minority representation."[31] Just as he had with Jabotinsky more than a year earlier, Beneš referred to a map, this time pulling one out before his guests to demonstrate the vulnerable nature of the Czechoslovak state with regard to German-speaking populations. Beneš explained that a country such as Czechoslovakia could not exist if another national group, such as the Germans, laid claim to its territory. In response to Silverman's distinguishing between the Jews and the Germans, Beneš proposed "that the civilized world would find a reasonable settlement of the Jewish question after the war and that he and his government would do their best to facilitate this."[32] Silverman countered by reasserting "that he could not see that a parallel existed between the German and Jewish minorities."[33]

The dialogue between Beneš and Silverman showcases the limitations of an all-encompassing term such as *minority* and, like the other documents cited in this section, suggests that WJC officials did not fully grasp how "minority rights" had functioned for the Jews in interwar Czechoslovakia. Note that Silverman challenged Beneš on his imprecise comparison between the German minority in Czechoslovakia, which could offer loyalty to a specific nation-state, and the Jewish minority in Czechoslovakia, which had no geopolitical equivalent. To be a German national and a Czechoslovak citizen was not, Silverman implied, synonymous with being a Jewish national and a Czechoslovak citizen. He was correct to a certain extent. Jewish nationality was an exceptional category in interwar Czechoslovakia because it was, in the words of Rebekah Klein-Pejšová, the "only nationality in east central Europe unbound from language."[34]

The drafters of the 1921 Czechoslovak census determined that nationality would be assessed on the basis of "mother tongue" in all cases except one: individuals whose nationality differed from their mother tongue. Overwhelmingly, such individuals declared themselves to be of Jewish nationality.[35] Notably, the inclusion of Jewish nationality in this census and the subsequent one in the 1930s resulted in lower numbers of German and Hungarian nationals of the Jewish religion, especially in Slovakia and Subcarpathian Rus'. In other words, it benefited Czechoslovak state-builders to make such an arrangement. This census-related concession, however, was the only special right awarded to the so-called "Jewish minority" in Czechoslovakia. Czechoslovak Jews could declare Jewish nationality but did not have "full national rights" in the interwar period.[36] Like all interwar democracies, Tara Zahra reminds us, "Czech national democracy was rife with contradictions."[37] This nuance seemed lost on WJC officials as they responded to Beneš's threats to recalibrate "minority rights" for the Jews and others in the postwar Czechoslovak state.

Britain accorded de jure recognition to the Czechoslovak government-in-exile on July 18, 1941—directly after the Nazi invasion of the Soviet Union—and thus changed the alignment of Allied and Axis powers. The Soviets too recognized this government, and Beneš's views became even more problematic for the WJC.[38] His new authority put Beneš in a position to implement his ideas after the conflict. And so, despite being busy with relief activities, meetings with other Allied leaders in both the United States and the United Kingdom, and the day-to-day operations of maintaining an international organization, WJC leaders continued to devote ample energy to the Czechoslovak leader.

For example, in September 1941, Dr. Jacob Robinson, head of the Institute of Jewish Affairs of the WJC, produced a dozen-page memorandum on Beneš's "ideas on the Jewish problem."[39] Using institute resources, statements by Beneš, and interviews such as the two referenced above, Robinson challenged Beneš on at least two issues relevant to our discussion: the reestablishment of Jewish nationality in postwar Czechoslovakia and the probability of Palestine's political status and absorptive capacity. If, as Beneš desired, Czechoslovakia was restored to its pre-Munich frontiers, Robinson saw no reason why a special nationality status for Czechoslovak Jews could not be restored as well. In his assessment, the provision for Jewish nationality had been successful in interwar Czechoslovakia, especially in the easternmost Subcarpathian Rus'. As recently as three years before, Robinson recalled, the principle of "personal self-determination of nationality" was formulated by Beneš, and it remained protected by the June 26, 1935, Czechoslovak citizenship law.[40]

Robinson also challenged Beneš on the absoluteness of his claims. Even if the Jewish nation were to achieve statehood, it remained clear to Robinson that "not all Jews would immigrate to Palestine." Essentially, every Jew remaining in postwar Europe would face a cruel choice under Beneš's plan: "Either he accepts the idea of being evicted in 30–60 years and in the meantime he and his children and his children's children will live under the status of aliens, or he will receive full rights of citizenship for the price of renouncing any connection with Jewish life." Essentially, for full citizenship, Robinson interpreted that Beneš would make the Jews "pay a price never demanded by any government in the world."[41] Related to this point, Beneš and the postwar plans he articulated assumed the consolidation of a Jewish nation-state in Palestine and the logistical possibility of large-scale migration there. "We have no idea," Robinson asserted, "what kind of policy Dr. Beneš has reserved" for a postwar world that did not include these realities. And even if a Jewish state emerged out of postwar settlement, Robinson questioned how "this little Jewish state in Palestine would be in a position to give effective protection to millions of Jews in Europe."[42]

Arieh Tartakower evidently agreed. In the same week that Robinson finalized his report, Tartakower met with the Czechoslovak president to seek clarification. Since we last encountered him in Geneva, Warsaw, or Łódź in the late 1930s, Tartakower had relocated to New York City in 1939. There, in exile from Poland, he waited—for news about the land and the friends left behind; to see his wife, Malvina;[43] for the next Office Committee meeting, where his colleagues would discuss their work in the World Jewish Congress and look to him for leadership and guidance. He also waited for the next opportunity to exercise his editorial hand. Since arriving in America, Tartakower had created a Polish-language newspaper with his fellow editor Jakob Apenszlak called *NT*, assumed increasingly important positions in the WJC hierarchy, and served as the chair of the Department for Relief and Rehabilitation. We turn to this specific relief work of his department in the WJC and *NT* later, but our concern at this moment lies with Tartakower's response to the "new" ideas that Beneš circulated. Like his colleagues Schwarzbart, Silverman, Barou, Robinson, and Perlzweig, Tartakower did not approve of Beneš's wartime tone.

Tartakower spoke with Beneš during yet another meeting held between WJC officials and the Czechoslovak president-in-exile. In the midst of their conversation, "Dr. Beneš [had] expressed himself against granting the Czech Jews minority rights in the future Czech Republic" because he concluded that Jews who remained in Czechoslovakia should "assimilate themselves with the Czech population," thereby forsaking their right to group autonomy.[44] Moreover, Tartakower added, Beneš felt that "national Jews [those who selected Jewish as their nationality on the interwar census] should be deprived of Czech citizenship and should be induced to emigrate to Palestine as soon as possible."[45] In November 1940, Schwarzbart suggested a similar eventuality when he warned his colleagues at the WJC about an anonymous central European politician. Less than a year later, Tartakower broadcast the name of "the" politician to the leaders of his organization with an explicit caveat. In Tartakower's assessment, Beneš displayed "a very dangerous attitude which contrasts markedly with the former democratic traditions of Czechoslovakia and endangers the position of Jews in other countries."[46] Tartakower admitted that he and the "WJC tried to convince Dr. Beneš of the inadvisability of following such a policy" and continued to hope "that a change would occur."[47] Vocabulary espousing Jewish evacuationism had to be confronted directly.

When Tartakower raised concern that Beneš's ideas could destabilize the position of Jews in other countries, one particular state stood out in his mind: Poland. For instance, when Tartakower joined colleagues to draft a "Polish Jewish declaration" in September 1940, the small group reasoned that once the horrible war ended, Jews would not forsake their Polish home. The Jews, "as loyal citizens of Poland," should "constitute a permanent element and the attitude towards them as a national cultural group should leave no room for any plans about emigration or evacuation."[48] This declaration spoke directly to some representatives in the Polish government-in-exile who harbored sentiments similar to those stressed by former foreign minister Józef Beck, who once supported government-sponsored schemes to move Poland's Jews elsewhere in the late 1930s. It also spoke to rumors circulating in WJC circles about the shocking ideas of Edvard Beneš. Like other exiled east central Europeans in the WJC, the first years of Tartakower's wartime work included numerous vocalizations against the evacuation of Polish, Czech, and other Jewish communities away from Europe.

Take, for example, an incident in the fall of 1940. Even before Schwarzbart cabled the first intimations of Beneš shocking turn, the WJC learned that Jan Stańczyk, who served as minister of labor and social welfare in the Polish government-in-exile, had issued a statement concerning the future of Jewish life in Poland.[49] This unexpected declaration spurred the leaders of the WJC to assemble for a special meeting on November 18, 1940, to discuss two "grave objections." First, Stańczyk had made his statement without consulting the WJC, and second, while British and Free French leaders had issued statements guaranteeing attention to the Jewish plight in Europe, Stańczyk occupied a lower rung in the Polish government. To correct these errors, Tartakower suggested that the WJC "insist on a formal declaration issued by the Polish government concerning the rights of the Jewish people in the coming Polish State" and, furthermore, that "this declaration be delivered by the head of the Polish government to the authorized organs of the Jewish people."[50] The Office Committee agreed, and Tartakower lobbied Polish government-in-exile prime minister Władysław Sikorski in June 1941.[51] Thus, a year after a war began that threatened to uproot Polish Jews completely, Tartakower did not consider a mass evacuation from Poland a viable part of postwar plans. He had no reason to imagine otherwise at this point, nor could he have known that upward of 90 percent of all Polish Jews would be dead in just over two years.

Neither could Ignacy Schwarzbart, who remained committed to anti-evacuationism as well. Writing to Tartakower two months after he cabled the WJC about Beneš, Schwarzbart urged that "Jews must remain in Europe, as their transfer even in tens of years is impossible." For this reason, Schwarzbart felt it was their shared duty to "defend ourselves against evacuationism" and the duty of the Polish government "not to listen to bad . . . advice."[52] A few days later, Tartakower agreed with Schwarzbart: "You are right in warning against any possible revival of the negation of the diaspora."[53] While he did not think that the "danger" was as great as detailed in Schwarzbart's letter, Tartakower conceded that there might be some "fanatics among us who are ready to throw away the idea of our future life in Europe and even in other parts of the world." Therefore, Tartakower considered it a shared "duty to liquidate such views by a suitable explanation of our peace aims, not only to other peoples but also to" Jews.[54] He assured Schwarzbart that the WJC was currently working to thwart postwar solutions threatening both minority and individual rights in the Jewish diaspora. Tartakower recommended that Schwarzbart focus on securing a statement from the Polish government eliminating anti-Jewish laws.

This correspondence with Schwarzbart, some of the earliest in Tartakower's massive, polyglot paper trail, indicates two themes that align with the analysis presented in this chapter. First, the World Jewish Congress actively worked to secure diplomatic contacts in exile, focus the world's attention on the plight of European Jews, and thus fashion themselves a relevant nongovernmental actor. Second, Tartakower and his colleagues believed that when the war ended, Polish and European Jews would mostly continue to be rooted in their prewar homelands. Emigration toward the Palestinian Mandate was, of course, desirable. But a significant east central European diaspora would remain. Given what they knew at the time, this made perfect sense. Accordingly, Allied leaders such as Edvard Beneš who proposed the quick, postwar establishment of a Jewish nation-state in Palestine and a population transfer there for the unassimilated Jews as the best solution for Europe's Jewish problem elicited severe concern within WJC circles.

TRANSFER: HOW INTERNATIONAL NORMS SHIFTED IN *FOREIGN AFFAIRS* BETWEEN EDVARD BENEŠ'S TWO POLITICAL EXILES

Edvard Beneš's transformation into an advocate of population transfers and Palestinian citizenship for "nonassimilated" European Jews stunned WJC members in the early 1940s. But they were also astonished at the incipient transformation of international norms about minorities in general and the Jewish minority in particular. A survey of the journal *Foreign Affairs* as well as scholarship from a coterie of Beneš experts shows how sharply Beneš and the new vocabulary he invoked deviated from interwar iterations about minority rights and forced population movements.[55] Experts on this shift such as R. M. Douglas, Matthew Frank, and Chad Bryant have agreed in principle that Beneš stood at the forefront of this key change among the Allied powers. An article that Beneš wrote for *Foreign Affairs* in 1942 is often understood as a key turning point away from Czechoslovakia's broader support for minority rights in the region and more generally. That article represents this section's endpoint. To grasp and problematize its significance, our analysis begins nearly two decades before it was published.

Interwar Writings from Beneš

Beneš's English-language writings from the 1920s and 1930s confirm Bryant's statement that "the morality of shifting whole populations was a matter of debate and not a given."[56] Beneš himself gauged the strength of democracies in central Europe by their treatment of minorities. In an article for the *Slavonic and East European Review* in 1929, then–Czechoslovak foreign minister Beneš conceded that the political attitude of minorities in Czechoslovakia, Austria, Germany, and Hungary was at times "negative" and "irredentist" because these minorities claimed to have been incorporated in the new states against their wishes, "in violation of the principle of self-determination."[57] Yet now, almost a decade after Saint-Germain, Beneš claimed that "a very considerable change has been effected in these conditions."[58] The minorities' views had changed as the new states grew in strength and as "international consolidation" diminished hopes for regime change.[59] The minority groups, "and with them all practical politicians in Central Europe, are steadily becoming conscious of the fact that a complete carrying into effect of the right of self-determination is not feasible, in view of the intermixture of the various nationalities."[60] Still, Beneš conceded the importance of reckoning with the continued existence of national minorities and therefore "facilitating their cultural and economic development by a thorough application of democratic principles."[61]

The improved relations between national minorities and majorities in the new states proved that this would continue to be the prime register on which the strength of democracy would be measured. There was nothing temporary about the status quo in Beneš's thinking. He believed that the postwar order was a permanent system of states created by nations once oppressed by Austria-Hungary, national but at the same time mixed, with "fragments of other nations included on geographical or economic grounds."[62] A secure balance between minority self-determination and democratic institutions was, for Beneš, uniquely central European and necessary for the "stability of their international position."[63] Casting his gaze back on the previous decade, Beneš felt assured that "democracy found fruitful soil and struck firm roots in Central Europe."[64] Beneš seemed sure that the future would include minorities in central European states, even if he warned about legal precedents that cast minorities as personalities within international law.[65]

Beneš felt sure about other things as well. In a piece published three years after the conclusion of his first exile away from east central Europe, Beneš saw immense progress in a region once dominated by the Habsburg Empire. As a result of the cooperation in the Little Entente between officials in Prague, Bucharest, and Belgrade, central Europe had ceased "to be a center of political chaos" and had grown "into a firm structure along the lines laid down by the peace treaties." The impossibility of drawing exact borders between the nationalities had not resulted in "disorder."[66] The power of this new alliance as well as Czechoslovakia's treaty with France had created a looser transnational entity that, despite its young age, had played a role in managing conflicts within and between these new states.

Four years later, Beneš celebrated another component of the postwar settlement: the commitments to mutual assistance and disarmament enshrined in League-sponsored agreements and pacts. All states joining the League unconditionally submitted each of their international conflicts to an international tribunal for peaceful settlement.[67] Writing after the Locarno agreement that had brought Germany into the League of Nations, Beneš championed the treaty as the first time sovereign states had committed to settle disputes by peaceful methods. And so, immediately after Locarno, Beneš seemed increasingly optimistic. He did not anticipate war, unresolvable disputes among League members, or any readjustments in the populations or boundaries of European states in the near future.

In Beneš's telling, the League of Nations and its scaffolding had profoundly altered the status quo. Before the Great War, "the foreign policy of all countries was as a rule egoistic and self-centered."[68] In such a system, war was inevitable. The League thus contradicted hundreds of years of human behavior, embodying "a bold effort to safeguard peace and create a basis for developing international cooperation." It was a "voluntary social contract between civilized nations" that had transferred into the international sphere democratic principles previously known only to the domestic sphere.[69] Going further, Beneš posited that "the peaceful settlement of international disputes is becoming the official method of political procedure; it is becoming the normal rule, the recognized duty."[70] After a decade or so of existence, the League of Nations was, Beneš argued, "an integral part of international life" by 1930. "That in itself is a remarkable fact."[71] In just a few years, Beneš's declaration would appear somewhat stale as the League increasingly lost credibility and the support of individual states.

Minority Rights and Population Transfers Elsewhere in Foreign Affairs

Other observers writing in *Foreign Affairs* about east central Europe, the coalescing power of the League of Nations, and the inevitability of minorities within states in this region echoed the ideas Beneš espoused.[72] Even in a 1923 article critical of the post–Great War peace treaties, Hungarian sociologist and journalist Oszkár Jászi could not disregard one reality. It must be "admitted," he wrote, "that in central and eastern Europe it is often impossible to draw an absolutely equitable ethnographic line between different peoples, so inextricably are they intermingled." Thus, it was "inevitable" that "national minorities should be sacrificed to the principle of building up a national home for the homogenous majority of the population."[73] Zooming in on the Hungarian milieu, Harold Temperley analyzed the range of decisions available to the Allied Delimitation Commission. This commission made decisions that could be cast in ethnic terms, other times economic considerations reigned supreme, and at still other times the desire to penalize Hungary played a factor in decisions. The wording laid out in the Treaty of Trianon, which codified the Delimitation Commission's work, did not "authorize the Commissioners to consider areas at a distance from the frontier," nor did it grant the sanction of the "wholesale transfer of large populations or important towns."[74]

This mention of the "wholesale transfer of large populations" in Temperley's article marks the only time this concept appeared in an article focused on central Europe before the late 1930s and early 1940s, save one by Hamilton Fish Armstrong, who wrote about Hitler's policies in 1933.[75] In fact, few articles in *Foreign Affairs* written between its inception in 1922 and 1942 referenced or promoted population transfers as a viable, normative, and ordinary tool of statecraft, nor did these articles emphasize the localized minority transfer projects in colonial settings, such as British-occupied Iraq and French-occupied Syria.[76] And when contributors to *Foreign Affairs* did talk about exchanging populations or solving the minority question with movement instead of protections or treaties, they almost always spoke about populations far away from Prague, Warsaw, and Berlin in jurisdictions belonging to Turkey, Greece, and Palestine.

Articles mentioning the sixth convention of the Lausanne Treaty outlined the exchange of Greek and Turkish populations in at times positive, at times complicated, and always unique terms. Just a few months after the treaty was signed in 1923, Arnold Toynbee considered the League's decision to raise an international loan and "replant within the new Greek frontiers the three-quarters of a million of Greek refugees from Eastern Thrace and Anatolia" as an "event of importance."[77] Toynbee anticipated that the imposition of homogeneity on a mixture of Turks, Greeks, and Bulgars would increase regional stability. His analysis did not dive deep, however, into the details of the exchanges. If it had, he would have found the proverbial devil that Countess Waldeck discovered in her study fourteen years later. She emphasized the complexity of the task that demanded two special commissions, one in Athens (which operated from September 1923 to December 31, 1930) and one in Sofia (which operated from September 8, 1926, to early 1932), four international loans, and refugee resettlement activities that lasted upward of seven years.[78] And it is telling that neither Waldeck nor Toynbee described the population exchanges as violent or incomplete (despite both adjectives being justified) or emphasized the minority protections embedded in article 40 of the Lausanne Treaty. They both, however, contributed to the creation of what would soon become a "perceived" precedent.[79]

The 1937 Peel Commission Report, for example, cast the population exchanges within the Lausanne Treaty as an "instructive precedent" that could guide arrangements for planned population movements and territorial divisions within British-controlled Mandate Palestine.[80] Writing in *Foreign Affairs,* Viscount Herbert Samuel refused to accept the eventuality of population transfers as outlined in the commission findings. He pinpointed an irony in the Peel Commission report: "And how," he asked, "could compulsory removal of people whose families had been established in their present towns and villages often for a thousand years be reconciled with the 'strict guarantees for the protection of minorities'?"[81] Writing about the 1937 Royal Commission Report elsewhere very soon after it was published, Herbert Samuel noted that the possibility of population transfers was exceedingly doubtful.[82] In the wake of these misgivings, approval of the Peel Commission Report was delayed by amendments that Churchill and Lloyd George offered and, in early 1938, a "Palestine Partition Commission" convened to more carefully assess the Peel Commission's proposal. Even though the Peel Commission demanded land and population transfers to actualize a viable partition, entities in government and in the press considered this demand too extreme.[83] Just because the Treaty of Lausanne established an isolated precedent, it did not follow that population exchanges or compulsory movements would become acceptable solutions, even in a "faraway" place like Mandate Palestine. In fact, it was a revolutionary and controversial central European leader who dismantled the commitment to minority rights that had been percolating in the European diplomatic universe since the late nineteenth century.

Slowly and incrementally, coverage of Hitler's rise to power and his government's policies related to land conquest, population transfers, and demographic control within German spaces found coverage in *Foreign Affairs*. A 1932 article by Paul Scheffer, for example, indicated that Hitler and his Nazi Party would "only" make trouble for "immigrant Jews" who did not fit into German society. In the following year, now with Hitler installed as chancellor, Armstrong discussed how the ruling party had established "Race Offices," which were tasked with "separating the population into two groups which may not inter-marry," as well as an aggressive foreign policy. They wanted, Armstrong claimed, Anschluss with Austria, the corridor and Silesia back from Poland, Danzig, Northern Schleswig, Memel (or Klaipėda), Eupen, Malmedy, and their former colonies, among other territories understood to be "German."[84] Besides land, Armstrong indicated, the Nazis also wanted the exchange of people. Armstrong referenced Dr. Wilhelm Frick, the Nazi minister of the interior, who in May 1933 noted that "'a full third of Germans live outside the Reich'" and that "'the revolution will only be complete when the entire German world is inwardly and outwardly formed anew.'"[85] Such a revolution, R. W. Seton-Watson explained in 1938, would quickly become an extensive, pan-European operation, as twelve European states counted significant German minorities.[86]

Seton-Watson's words about a European-wide revolution to unite "German" people on "German" territory took on even more resonance as 1938 and 1939 progressed. The Munich Agreement of September 1938 included a clause that allowed for the transfer of two hundred thousand Czechs and "democratic" Germans.[87] The Italo-German Pact of May 1939 authorized the transfer of the Volksdeutsche, or people classified as being ethnically German, from Italy to German territory. Just days after World War II began in September 1939, Götz Aly writes, Hitler promised Reichstag members that his state would "'create a new ethnographic order'" and "*Lebensraum* would be ordered according to nationality."[88] On September 28, 1939, less than four weeks after the invasion of Poland commenced, Adolf Hitler gave a speech explaining how conquered eastern territories would be governed. Hitler declared that the "most important task" at present was to "establish a new order of ethnographical conditions, that is to say, resettlement of nationalities in such a manner that the process ultimately results in obtaining better dividing lines than is the case at present."[89] Soon after this public declaration, the German-Estonian protocol of October 1939 authorized transfers of Volksdeutsche from Estonia to an expanding Germany.[90] During that same month, Hitler made a personal decision to start the relocation of the Polish and Jewish population from Gdańsk, Gdynia, and Poznań.[91] As 1939 drew to a close, eighty-eight thousand Poles and Jews had been expelled to make room for Baltic Germans "returning to the Reich" and others (civilians, government officials, and POWs) who had been displaced more generally.[92] And in January 1940, Heinrich Himmler, head of the SS and in charge of the Volksdeutsche Mittelstelle (VoMi or the Ethnic German Liaison Office), staged a photo opportunity to capture the return of thousands of ethnic German peasants leaving the Soviet-occupied Polish Volhynia and crossing the San River to settle in evacuated homes throughout the Greater German Reich.[93]

Immediately before and during the Second World War, the articles in *Foreign Affairs* aligned with a reality marked by quick and decisive changes vis-à-vis minority rights and the viability of massive population transfers. Clearly, an ethnic revolution of sorts was underfoot, and the leadership of this revolution extended beyond Hitler and his associates. As early as February 1940, August Zaleski, the exiled Polish prime minister, responded to the Nazi-initiated population movements in his country by including plans for the deportation of Germans from the borders of prewar Poland and east Prussia as a Polish war aim. Beneš met with Jabotinsky one month later, in March 1940, to discuss their shared interest in demographic engineering. Around the same time, Nicola Politis, a prominent Greek diplomat and leading authority on international law, declared before French academics assembled at the Centre d'études de politique étrangère that the "system of minorities protection initiated in 1919" had failed, opinions had "evolved," and now Europe required a drastic "operation." There was no solution, Politis wrote, "more appropriate than the exchange, indeed the compulsory exchange, of populations."[94]

According to historian Matthew Frank, however, Politis's French colleagues did not necessarily embrace his ideas at this juncture.[95] Neither did the executive members of the World Jewish Congress respond positively when Beneš's endorsement of population transfers infiltrated their telegrams in 1940 and 1941. But the shift from shock about population transfers to curiosity about population transfers occurred quite quickly for others. Historian Phillipp Ther describes how British officials, while condemning Nazi population transfer policies, were simultaneously investigating how useful such policies might be in fashioning a new postwar order.[96] Such a postwar order would be built on a scaffolding of wartime displacement. From the outbreak of war in 1939 until early 1943, governments "transplanted more than 31 million people mostly from east central Europe."[97]

Writings on Population Transfers by Weizmann and Beneš in 1942

In the same issue of *Foreign Affairs* published in January 1942, Chaim Weizmann and Edvard Beneš employed the concept of population transfers in their own plans for the postwar future. Observers of both the president of the World Zionist Organization and the Czechoslovak president-in-exile pinpoint these articles as key nodes on a broader trajectory away from minority rights and toward the movement of minorities, so a closer look at these two articles is necessary. First, let us begin with Weizmann. He imagined two potential postwar population movements: that of the "vast masses" of European Jews who would "have to immigrate" away from their prewar homes and that of Arabs who would "not wish to remain in a Jewish state."[98] Six months after Operation Barbarossa, Weizmann knew that the reintegration of Jews after the current war would "present a peculiarly difficult problem," especially in eastern and central Europe. In Weizmann's assessment, "the experience of the past twenty years and the vexed problem of 'minorities' which has caused so much trouble in Europe, hardly give much ground for hope of a satisfactory solution on the spot." He conceded that "many Jews will return and re-adapt themselves to the new conditions," but these would represent the minority of the European Jewish minority. Instead, this "complex problem" demanded "courage, imagination and sympathy" in the abstract and emigration to Palestine specifically. He imagined that Palestine would "take care of very rapidly after the war" four hundred thousand families, or nearly two million souls, and thus relieve the misery engulfing postwar populations in Europe.[99]

If this estimate was not staggering enough, Weizmann suggested higher numbers in other settings. For example, in a conversation with Ivan Maisky, the Soviet ambassador to the Court of St. James, on February 3, 1941, Weizmann thought that four or five million east central European Jews, "and in the first place Polish Jewry," could be settled on land that was currently sustaining one million Arabs.[100] And so, Weizmann's organized population movement involved a substantial number of Jews who had been rooted in interwar Poland. Recall that three hundred thousand Jews left Europe for Palestine from 1920 to 1939. Not counting those that eventually returned (and in some years the net immigration hovered near zero), Weizmann anticipated that in one calendar year after the conflict ended, seven times more Jews would leave Europe than did across a generation. As detailed in chapter 1, Jabotinsky's 1930s plans for "evacuation" seem almost mild in comparison.

Turning back to his *Foreign Affairs* article, Weizmann does not mention who will pay for the reunion of Europe's Jews "with the soil of Palestine." He does, however, cast this reunion in inevitable terms. He writes that such settlement in Palestine would help "solve the Jewish problem—one of the most disturbing problems in the world." Jews who settled in Palestine would control their own immigration, achieve self-government in their own state, and "cease being a minority."[101] As the "new" minority, Arabs would "enjoy full autonomy in their own internal affairs," and if they did not wish to remain in a Jewish state, albeit one founded on "complete civil and political equality of rights for all citizens, without distinction of race or religion," there would be, Weizmann suggested, another option. If "any Arabs do not wish to remain in a Jewish state, every facility will be given to *transfer* [emphasis mine] to one of the many and vast Arab countries."[102] Weizmann labeled only one of the population movements he included in his postwar plans a "transfer." Essentially, however, he spoke about two.[103]

Unlike Weizmann, Beneš wrote about population transfers more generally in the January 1942 issue of *Foreign Affairs* as a way to secure peace throughout postwar Europe. From his position as president-in-exile, Beneš suggested that Germany must be decentralized, central Europe must be reorganized with a Czechoslovak-Polish Confederation at its core, a Balkan confederation must emerge, Soviet Russia should become more involved in European affairs, and the minority question must be dealt with, especially as it pertained to the German "colonists" and those century-old German populations that had, almost, an "autochthonous character."[104] Dealing with minority questions, for Beneš, meant forcing "Germans" to move.[105] Unlike after the last world war, future peacemakers would use transfers of populations to create linguistically and nationally homogenous states. The events at Munich had forced Beneš to declare that "it will be necessary after this war to carry out a transfer of population on a very much larger scale than after the last war." This transfer would carry conditions. It should be done humanely. It should be organized and financed on an international scale. And "human democratic rights," as opposed to national rights, would be protected.[106] An unanticipated logic prompted his change of thought. Beneš argued, "Hitler himself has transferred German minorities from the Baltic and from Bessarabia. Germany, therefore, cannot *a priori* regard it as an injury to her if other states adopt the same methods with regard to German minorities."[107]

Beneš did not mention Jews or Palestine in this January 1942 article. Jews, however, continued to be on his mind. Just a week or two before their articles in *Foreign Affairs* hit newsstands on both sides of the Atlantic, Beneš met with Weizmann in person. According to US secretary of state Cordell Hull, who witnessed the conversation, the Czechoslovak president-in-exile suggested to Weizmann that "when the war was over it might be necessary to 'dilute' the Jewish population of Czechoslovakia by a third." Weizmann allegedly responded that "Palestine could absorb them."[108] Just as Beneš found common ground with Jabotinsky in March 1940 on the erasure of the minority problem from east central Europe, he found agreement nearly two years later with Weizmann about the role that Palestine could play in determining the future of the Jewish minority in postwar east central Europe. Independent of the contemporary displacement wrought by Nazi invasion and occupation, which continued to uproot the Jews of east central Europe and beyond, Beneš and others made plans and promises for future displacements that served their own political ends.

Historians seeking to understand how Edvard Beneš evolved into an advocate of postwar population transfers and, eventually, a public negator of minority rights usually cite his January 1942 article in *Foreign Affairs* as an important node in those combined trajectories. They disagree, however, precisely when and why he decided that "transfer" was the best option. Frank contends that in public Beneš was more reluctant to speak in specific terms, which is why he wrote about population transfers more vaguely. Frank pinpoints two moments in 1940 to show how Beneš's ideas about transfers solidified.[109] Bryant suggests that the Czech Underground Movement pushed Beneš toward this more extreme solution in the summer of 1940.[110] Beneš did not, however, concede a "maximum solution" including pre-Munich borders and the complete expulsion of the Germans until the summer of 1941, after the Blitz had hardened British public opinion against the Nazis and Beneš's relationship with the exiled leader of the Sudetenland Social Democratic Party Wenzel Jaksch had "become strained."[111] R. M. Douglas also emphasizes Beneš's relationship with Jaksch to demonstrate how Beneš's ideas regarding population transfers changed. For Douglas, however, only at the end of 1941 did the president advocate for the postwar organization of Europe along ethnic lines when he no longer felt the need to work closely with Jaksch.[112] And finally, Norman Naimark prioritizes a sequence of meetings in Moscow on December 16, 1943, as the apex of Beneš's thought evolution.[113]

The timing of Beneš's thinking matters less, in my mind, than the drastic change in Beneš's thinking. In 1938, as the Sudeten Crisis began to escalate, then-president Beneš recognized "the moral right of Europe to take an interest in our minorities" and expressed Czechoslovakia's "readiness to make her contribution to a general settlement" of the issue despite the "purely internal character of the minority question."[114] By January 1942, basic ideas about what was permissible had undergone deep change in Beneš's mind, and the inevitability of ethnic heterogeneity in this region was no longer a given. His contribution to *Foreign Affairs* made all these views glaringly public and potentially confirmed for the leadership of the World Jewish Congress exactly what they feared most at that juncture.[115] Of course, Beneš did not provide dates for when the relocation trains would begin chugging, concrete numbers for the unscrambling of property ownership, or a step-by-step calculus determining which "Germans" would be relocated. He outlined, however, the preconditions for a "postwar" peace in east central Europe and, by default, the future existence of Czechoslovakia. To cite Bryant once again, "Without him the expulsions would not have happened as they did, if at all."[116]

REROOTING: THE EXILIC WORK OF THE WORLD JEWISH CONGRESS AND EXILIC WORDS FROM *NT*, 1940–1943

Beneš spent most of his first three years in exile laying the intellectual foundations for the massive uprooting of central European minorities, and in particular the Germans of Czechoslovakia. Members of the World Jewish Congress, conversely, spent most of their wartime exile preparing for the regrowth of collective Jewish life in this region. Few members of the Office Committee championed plans for the reestablishment of central European Jewish life as vigorously as Arieh Tartakower did in the early 1940s. While he exhibited deep concern for all the Jews stranded in occupied Europe, worked to secure visas from countries for those stripped of their citizenship throughout North and South America during the war, and lobbied for the establishment of a Jewish national home in Palestine as well as some migration there, Tartakower concentrated intensely on postwar plans for the country of his own interwar citizenship: Poland. So did his colleague and coeditor Jakob Apenszlak. Both made frequent editorial contributions to their Polish-language, New York–based newspaper *Nasza Trybuna* that demonstrate their devotion to rerooting Jewish life in postwar Poland, even as they simultaneously supported plans for Jewish settlement in the Middle East. Apenszlak and Tartakower began publishing *NT* in November 1940, and both remained editors and frequent contributors until the fall of 1946. In fact, the WJC subsidized the publishing of *NT*, which aimed to be a New York–based extension of Apenszlak's interwar newspaper *Nasz Przegląd*, the Polish-language Jewish daily that consistently enjoyed the highest circulation rate among the Polish-reading Jewish masses. As far as I can tell, it has not yet been sourced by historians seeking to understand the east central European exile universe or changing minds within this particular wartime diaspora of Polish Jews.

"Poland Is Also Us": Anti-evacuationism and Pro–Minority Rights

The "sword of history" was turning, and Arieh Tartakower had things to say about it.[117] In the inaugural issue of *NT*, which hit newsstands the same month that Schwarzbart sent his cryptic telegram in November 1940, Tartakower reinforced the rootedness of Jews in Poland. He and his fellow Polish Jews were "tied to the Polish land like animals were," and he did not "want anyone to question this fact." Surprisingly, Tartakower had found a way to rationalize the tragedy of war. "If the present war tragedy is to have any sense," he wrote, "then the *gehenna* of Jewish society in Poland will not be repeated." Tartakower thought, in fact, that postwar Jewish life in Poland would vastly improve on its prewar iteration. Polish Jews expected, he reasoned, "the recognition of our political and national rights, real equality in the field of economic life," and the "right to work in tandem with other citizens of the Republic of Poland." The path of "forced emigration or evacuation" would not impress the "just stewards [*sprawiedliwy wlodarz*] of the future Polish Republic." No one, be they Jewish or Christian, should "question our right to Polish soil, because Poland is also us. Polish Jews!" ("*Bo Polska, to również my. Polscy Żydy!*").[118] Opinions about the viability of rebuilding Jewish life in postwar Poland and in postwar Europe take on more complex tones when this newspaper is juxtaposed with a timeline of WJC official documents and epistolary exchanges. In the first three years of the 1940s, visions and plans for a dynamic Jewish future in Poland existed in *NT* and within the World Jewish Congress as well.

It follows, then, that articles in *NT* questioned other journalists who called for Jewish evacuation from Poland. In the final days of 1940, for example, Tartakower suggested that they write about other subjects, such as Jewish equality in Poland or the broader phenomenon of economic migration, instead of just Jewish migration. Journalists could, moreover, explain "that Palestine is a poor country which alone does not solve the Jewish questions and that is why some other territories are also needed."[119] Living in a period "where the stakes for what is said and written are a hundred times greater than in normal times," Tartakower urged journalists, especially his British peers, to do better. Regrettably, the false dream of evacuation continued to captivate both non-Jews and Jews alike. Those who cast evacuation as the only rescue for all Polish ills, according to Tartakower, did not use reason as they built their arguments. Instead, they used anger and a "lot of nerve."[120] Furthermore, Tartakower was ashamed to say, some Jews themselves continued to support this evacuation dream. Tartakower dismissed these arguments and accused pro-evacuationists of "undermining" and "betraying" the state of Poland.[121] Of course, as a dynamic Zionist-leaning politician active in Poland during the 1920s and the 1930s as well as a former *oleh* himself, Tartakower was not against voluntary or controlled migration toward Palestine. Here, however, he protested large-scale and impractical plans that dichotomized the diaspora from the perceived "center" and negated the possibility of postwar Jewish life in Poland.

Tartakower continued to display his contempt of pro-evacuationists in 1941 and 1942 as well. While criticizing an article in *Jestem Polakiem* that argued for the necessity of evacuating Jews from Poland by drawing on revisionist arguments, Tartakower wrote with force midway through 1941. "In the case of such open betrayal of Jewish interests and in the face of this united front with anti-Semites," he observed, "it is worth knowing that as far as Jewish society is concerned this small group of blind people represent a minority and do not realize how they degrade the dignity of Jewish society through their behavior."[122] The stakes in this argument against evacuation were quite high, in Tartakower's opinion. In fact, he believed that "there will be no free Jewish people if there is no free and strong European Jewry, and among them a numerous and powerful Polish Jewry."[123] In his assault on pleas for evacuation, Tartakower was not afraid to dabble, slightly, in hyperbole. His vivid language should not distract us, however, from his underlying message: mandatory Jewish migration away from Poland and Europe would be detrimental across many registers and imperil Jewish life throughout the entire world. And so, one year later he wrote that "we do not need evacuation debates on the Polish national council" or in the company of American Jews.[124]

Apenszlak clearly agreed. Why, he asked, is a solution of emigration only "acceptable when it comes to Jewish citizens?"[125] The government would never promote discussions concerning the emigration of workers, peasants, or the Polish intelligentsia. In fact, applying "emigration to any group within the Polish population would be proof of the bankruptcy of a government that wants to send its citizens abroad. Such ideas would be unacceptable in a public discussion."[126] Talks about the postwar relationship between Polish Jews and others in Poland should concern only "the equality of all citizens in Poland, how the Jewish community forces work together to provide Jews with conditions for the development of national and cultural life in Poland itself."[127] Success would ensue only if discussions about "Jewish outflow outside the borders of the Polish Republic" were excluded.

Words against evacuation frequently became words about minority rights and how minorities would have national, cultural, linguistic, and political protection in postwar Europe. A few months after *NT* emerged in print, the Joint Committee on Polish Jewish Affairs met to discuss the current state of affairs with the exiled Polish government. This assortment of leaders from the American Jewish Congress and the WJC had much to consider.[128] Nahum Goldmann and Stephan Wise submitted their evaluation of a disappointing visit with the Polish ambassador to the United States, Jan Ciechanowski. The ambassador thought that the minority treaties forced on Poland were the "real cause of all the trouble" in the 1930s, as they "prevented the Polish government from doing anything for the benefit of the Jewish population."[129] Those in attendance were concerned by Ciechanowski's thoughts. Near the end of the meeting, Tartakower warned against "dangers which he saw in the present discussion."[130] The important decisions about the future of Polish Jews, he argued, would be reached in America, especially since the war situation relegated Palestine to an even more remote geopolitical position. Polish authorities, however, could not be cast aside as irrelevant even if these authorities misunderstood the basic concept of national minorities. Writing in response to articles published in the government-in-exile-sponsored journal *Dziennik Polska* after Stańczyk's declaration on Jewish rights in November 1940, Tartakower was shocked by the absence of words about "national minorities in general and about Jews in particular." He continued, "You read these articles once and twice, and ask: for the love of God, did these people fall from Mars? Do you not know that there will be millions of Jews in post-war Poland?"[131]

One month later, Apenszlak was confused not by Polish authorities but by Jewish Americans, of Polish and other backgrounds. When he spoke about the adjective *polsko-żydowskiego* (Polish Jewish) in America, Apenszlak received "strange pushback."[132] It seemed that some Jews were too Polish for American Jews. Did Polish Jews, Apenszlak asked, "not have the right to preserve their nationality and to preserve their own cult and customs?" Were the Polish Jews in exile to "give up their relationship with the Polish Nation?" Obviously not, Apenszlak surmised. Suppose that "someone dared American Poles to perform such a task." That instigator would be condemned "rightly from the position of true democracy and progress. And yet it is required of Polish Jews." In American society, he deduced, people were constantly searching for the "proper definition of the Jews." Both Apenszlak and Tartakower realized that sharing vocabulary with government officials or with American Jews did not necessarily guarantee a shared awareness of what constituted a minority, minority rights, or Polish Jewry.[133]

Celebrated Polish Jewish poet Julian Tuwim had his own ideas about national minorities, and he admitted that these ideas had evolved over time. Soon after he arrived in New York from South America, Tuwim sat down for an interview with Apenszlak, which then graced the pages of *NT*. The two thousand subscribers would have easily recognized possibly the most famous poet from interwar Warsaw. His journey from Europe to New York via a stay in

South America spoke to one of the key leitmotifs of the paper. With frequent dispatches from around the globe, from places such as Palestine, Africa, Santo Domingo, Tehran, and Shanghai, *NT* became an intellectual meeting point for a new global, literate diaspora, one that found comfort in their belonging to a unique and temporary Polish Jewish civilization. Speaking to this new diaspora about the problem of Polish-Jewish coexistence, Tuwim was, after twenty years of meditation, convinced that "Jews are a nation, not just a religion."[134] And thus, like other nations, Jews had the right to their "own culture and language as other nations" did. So then, if Tuwim as a "poet of Polish Jewish origin" demanded national rights, he concluded that he must grant Polish Jews these national rights "in full as well." Nearly two years into the war, the concept of national minorities, especially Jewish ones in Poland and elsewhere, remained both real and relevant for contributors to these newspaper pages.

Reactions to Diplomatic Alignments, Future Federations, and Relief Needs

The initiation of the largest land invasion in recorded history, Operation Barbarossa, on June 22, 1941, changed the configuration of powers at war in Europe while also expediting the series of events that came to be known as the Holocaust. Now, in addition to the revocation of citizenship, the uprooting of peoples, the establishment of governing structures such as the *Judenrat*, the delineation of ghettos, the robbery of property, starvation plans, and slave labor schemes, Jews living under Nazi occupation came to face a brutal mass-murder campaign on an unprecedented scale. Radio Berlin broadcast news about multiple shootings of Jews in Białystok, and bloody pogroms by Hitler's forces settled on the pages of *NT* as early as July 1941. On July 31, 1941, Hermann Göring wrote to Reinhard Heydrich instructing him to make a new "overall plan showing the preliminary organizational, substantive, and financial measures for the execution of the intended final solution [*Endlösung*] of the Jewish question."[135] Nazi policies encouraging emigration, evacuation, and uprooting had now evolved into something more explicitly genocidal as Nazi soldiers pushed eastward.[136] In the vacuum of power left by retreating Soviet officials and with the consent of incoming Nazi command, local militias, hooligans, and (in many instances) Polish Christian, Ukrainian, Lithuanian, Latvian, Romania, and (to a much lesser extent) Belarusian neighbors slaughtered hundreds of thousands of Polish Jews in places such as Jedwabne and elsewhere in the summer of 1941.[137] In the wake of Wehrmacht troops, infiltrating *Einsatzgruppen* units began mass killings later in the summer and fall of 1941.

Deportation continued in other areas of Nazi-occupied eastern Europe (such as eastern Galicia), but these policies of uprooting existed alongside policies of mass murder. Plans for the construction of killing centers (Bełżec, Sobibór, and Treblinka) under Operation Reinhard commenced in October 1941.[138] Mass-gassing operations began at Chełmno on December 8, 1941.

And just as Operation Barbarossa and the changes it unleashed altered the landscape between the eastern boundary of the Generalgouvernment and the western reaches of the Soviet state, so too did it reconfigure other dynamics elsewhere. One other shocking piece of news accompanied the reports of the Białystok shootings in *NT*. The 1941 Polish-Soviet Agreement, signed after the Soviet Union declared war on Nazi Germany and ostensibly switched sides, included a promise on behalf of the Soviet government to send tens of thousands of Polish citizens evacuated to places such as the Ural Mountains and Kazakhstan to Palestine, where they could join fighting units on the Allied side. But even as reports of heavy Jewish civilian losses in east central Europe and reports detailing the movement of some Polish Jews away from Soviet captivity toward Jerusalem flowed into the paper's office on West Thirty-Fourth Street, a commitment to planning for Jewish life in postwar Europe remained.

Apenszlak welcomed the development codified in the Polish-Soviet Agreement. He equated justice with "saving the Jewish people from the clan of homelessness" and "assuring their own and free homeland."[139] Tartakower maintained similar thoughts. "The highest postulate of justice," he wrote in the same issue, "is to save the Jewish people from the clique of homelessness and to grant it their own native homeland."[140] But welcoming the changes that unfolded as the Soviets joined the Allied cause did not negate visions of postwar Polish futures in their diasporic homeland. In an article gesturing toward the future a few months later, Tartakower predicted that in the "first moments after the war," reconstruction of the destroyed country would begin, and it "will be necessary to resume the epic of cultural creation in conditions that will probably be better and more worthy."[141] *NT* remained replete with visions of postwar Jewish life in Poland. And the Poland of their 1941 dreams would be, it seemed quite certain at that point, part of a new and exciting central European federation.

Representatives of Czech and Polish Jews living in the United States convened a meeting on September 25, 1941, to "inaugurate a state of cooperation" and to "secure their civil rights and national rights in their respective countries."[142] Those gathered noted a contemporary irony. In the past, "the situation of the Czech Jews was much better than the Polish Jews," but now it "seemed that the situation had changed somewhat."[143] While the Polish government-in-exile had "evidenced in a series of declarations made during the last months" an unbiased attitude toward the individual and national rights of their Jewish citizens, "difficulties ha[d] arisen unexpectedly in Czech government circles in regard to Jewish minority rights."[144] The committee hoped that a union between Czech and Polish Jews in North America would "ensure the legal position of the Polish Jews" already expressed by the Polish leader while "inducing" the Czech government to change its present attitude. According to Tartakower, the chair of the meeting, the committee was "directed towards securing the civil and national rights of both the Czech and Polish Jews" and creating a precedent for cooperation between Poland and Czechoslovakia in the future.[145] The work of this small coterie mirrored larger initiatives undertaken by Polish and Czech diplomats in London. Between 1940 and the summer of 1942, officials-in-exile from Prague and Warsaw assembled to lay the groundwork for a postwar Polish-Czechoslovak federation.[146] As the only two central European countries counted in the Allied universe, Poland and Czechoslovakia naturally took the regional lead in preparing for the postwar future.[147]

In 1942, Tartakower's correspondence and committee work include constant reference to the Polish-Czechoslovak Confederation as well as other subjects related to rescue, relief, and reconstruction. Tartakower monitored the movement of food, medicine, and money toward those Polish Jews living in the Generalgouvernment or the estimated six hundred thousand Polish Jews scattered throughout the Soviet Union.[148] A memorandum Maurice Perlzweig sent to Tartakower and the rest of the WJC Office Committee revealed the daunting logistical problems that relief providers encountered. In the same month that Beneš wrote about population transfers in *Foreign Affairs*, Perlzweig conceded that "the time has obviously come for a change in our strategy in regard to the problem of Polish Jewry."[149] Talks with South American representatives to the WJC and higher-ups in the British government had convinced Perlzweig that the "difficulty" faced by the WJC stemmed from "London" and not the United States. Simply put, the British needed to do more to ensure that Polish Jews in occupied Europe obtained more support. And so, Perlzweig lobbied his fellow WJC colleagues to "put pressure on the Polish government to act on our behalf pressing for modification of the British position."[150] The main goal, according to Perlzweig, remained the expansion of shipping opportunities so that more supplies could reach Polish Jews behind enemy lines.

As 1942 progressed, preparing for the administration of postwar relief became almost as important as extending contemporary relief to Polish Jews for both the WJC in general and Tartakower specifically. In a report summarizing three years of relief work and the organization's current relief agenda, Tartakower highlighted the efforts directed toward Polish Jewry. Since the relief department of the WJC had been established in Geneva in 1939, employees had worked to "establish contact with the Polish Jewish refugees scattered in all countries around Poland and enabled them to communicate with their relatives in the US and in other overseas countries."[151] For Tartakower, the time was ripe to alter the circumstances of Polish Jews living in the Generalgouvernment and elsewhere as well as consider the future of Polish Jewry. First, the WJC should work to "salvage the European Jews from destruction."[152] Tartakower and his colleagues understood "that the problem of helping Polish Jews is only a part of the broader task of saving the entire European Jewry which is enslaved at the present by Nazi Germany and is being systematically destroyed."[153] To do so, the WJC should continue negotiations with Allied governments, especially those of Great Britain and the US, to provide aid. Tartakower and his committee also directed attention to the postwar world. "Millions of people" would survive this war, he predicted.[154] Apenszlak agreed. "Thinking about tomorrow," Apenszlak wrote, "we are consoled in our faith steeped in the inexhaustible power of European Jews and in a prime position the millions of Polish Jews who have always been the main generator of our energy and national initiative."[155] For both editors of *NT,* a continued Jewish diaspora in Poland and elsewhere remained an incontrovertible fact midway through 1942.

The Clash between Perceptions, Hopes, and Realities

Apenszlak and Tartakower were not alone in these thoughts. Across the fragmented political spectrum of Polish Jews in London, New York, and spaces in between, a consensus of rootedness remained even among those from different patches of the political spectrum. Take, for example, Labor-Zionist Ignacy Schwarzbart and Bundist Szmuel Zygielbojm, the two Jewish members on the Polish National Council. A few weeks after Zygielbojm's nomination to the council in early 1942, Tartakower commented on a divide between the two men.[156] In an official address to the council, Zygielbojm stated that "Polish Jews are not interested in any emigration from Poland, neither to Palestine nor to any country."[157] In response to this statement, Tartakower relayed, Schwarzbart "answered very sharply, stressing the deep connections between Polish Jewry to Palestine which is, however, in no way a contradiction of their Polish patriotism."[158] While Schwarzbart and Zygielbojm disagreed publicly regarding how many Polish Jews wanted to leave Poland, these two men hypothetically agreed that Poland would remain a home for Polish Jewry. Furthermore, we should not assume that their divergent political allegiances would necessarily preclude agreement under these specific circumstances. As Baruch Zuckerman learned in his visit to Poland and the end of the 1930s, labels such as "evacuationist," "Zionist," and "Bundist" could sometimes obfuscate more than they clarified. Despite this reality, both Tartakower and Apenszlak had things to say about people in these categories.

Contributors to *NT* directed wrath toward others besides the evacuationists. In early 1942, Tartakower confronted the Bundists. "They cannot work with the Zionists," he charged, "who propagate Jewish evacuation from Poland." And yet, in Tartakower's assessment, "the position of all responsible Zionists in the matter of evacuation is well known." Tartakower suggested that the public should know about the Bund's intransigence and realize that changing circumstances demanded "a new, vital and creative energy."[159] Maybe, he hoped, "the boundless tragedy of the present times has not passed without echo? Perhaps in the fires and in the blood of the Jews stranded across Poland and Romania and in the Slavs throughout Europe and on the world's land, a new, deeper consciousness has grown?"[160] Maybe, indeed. But Tartakower's criticism of the Bund, Revisionists, and oversimplified perceptions of both indicate how much he wished to move beyond prolonged interwar rivalries. Instead, he wanted to envision Jewish futures in Poland and in Palestine. Writing about plans to create Jewish units within Allied forces, Tartakower reiterated a familiar refrain: "We want to see Jews with rights not just on paper in the future Europe," and "we want to have our own free, national home."[161] Two weeks later in an article devoted to the "Building of a Jewish State," Tartakower reiterated a similar desire. Two historical goals, he writes, "are at the moment in front of the Jewish people: rights for Jews as individuals, as people belonging to a national society and the proclamation of a Jewish state in Palestine."[162] The diaspora and the center would exist together. It was not always easy, however, to maintain this balance in postwar dreams and during wartime nightmares.

Like the pages of his paper, Arieh Tartakower's office space came to reflect the transnational crisis that had absorbed all displaced Polish Jews. Every day, letters and telegrams piled on his desk. From Toulouse, Casablanca, and Martinique and from Syria, Lisbon, and French Sudan, uprooted European Jews provided accounts of tragedies. "Dante's Inferno," he admitted, "seems playful in comparison to what is happening in these places."[163] The newspapers flowing into his office gave him little comfort. "Day in and day out," he lamented, "the heart tears when we open the newspapers not only because of the news from the battlefield, but because of other notes found on the middle and back pages."[164]

The litany of updates was depressing. "The Portuguese Government decided to prevent all incoming refugees by May 1 1941, the Japanese government decided to deport refugees to internment camps in Shanghai, the French Government arrests refugees and forces them into labor in the Sahara and the German police catch Jews like wild dogs on the street and sends them to the General Gouvernment."[165] These letters and newspapers inspired his daily work. "I would like to see," he wrote, "the responsible man who does not realize that our main task is not to help but to take care of the refugee's future and to look after hundreds of thousands of those who are already refugees and those who might become refugees in the next few years."[166] And for Polish Jewish refugees in particular, Tartakower had a special message: "Let faith in a free and just Poland grow in our hearts together with faith in the free and worthy future of the Jewish people."[167] In March 1942, Tartakower promised that "we will never lose faith in Poland, Mickiewicz and Żeromski because they belong to us and we are in the same measure as Polish citizens responsible for her freedom, dignity and happiness."[168]

Apenszlak had even larger hopes. Despite the horrific reports of Polish Jewish losses crossing his desk in the fall of 1943, Apenszlak declared that "the greatest Jewish concentration" would "remain in the Polish lands after all."[169] These Jews would be strengthened with "the supply of funds from victorious democracies," and the "population potential of Jews in Poland" could be increased "in the repatriation movement of refugees who managed to survive the war in the countries of asylum." With this reality in mind, Apenszlak wanted to emphasize that the "general rehabilitation process after the war" might overlook "Polish problems" if "Jewish and non-Jewish communities do not realize them." "Who," Apenszlak wondered, "is to fill this gap in the general framework if not Polish Jews?" He saw "an urgent need for a congress of Polish Jews in America, including both American Jews of Polish descent and those of Polish nationals who are in this country."[170] Furthermore, those Jews returning to Poland "should have the freedom to express their influence on the program decisively" so that "the Jewish refugee can obtain a representative office in Poland."

Elsewhere, anxieties riddled some of *NT*'s articles. Tartakower realized, at the end of 1942, that demands of equality were insufficient. "The enormity of the misfortune that has fallen on Polish Jews," Tartakower argued, "cannot be compared to the misery of the Polish population." While "the Poles lost a lot," the Jews "lost everything: they were displaced from all positions, robbed of their belongings, expelled from their homes, they were even deprived of health and physical strength under the pressure of hunger and inhuman labor," and thus the rebuilding of Jewish life in Poland must start from scratch.[171] And, of course, there were other moments when the optimism showcased by *NT* for a rooted postwar Polish Jewry seemed to vanish completely. Tartakower's tone in the August 20, 1943, issue of *NT* was changed from just a few weeks earlier. Under a front-page announcement that one and a half million Jews had been killed, Tartakower's writing showed someone beginning to absorb the reality of the tragedy. In an article entitled "We Won't Give Up," Tartakower pleaded, "Where is justice here?" Playing on the concept of Poland as the "Christ of nations," Tartakower used strong language. The Jews, the "crucified nation is denied the most primitive right to its own land and after two thousand years of misery" endured a "horrific *Gehenna* under German thugs." By the end of his article, Tartakower conceded that "nothing or almost nothing will save European Jews." In response to this reality, he abruptly changed topic and ended his column by saying, "Jewish Palestine will not die. We will win it. For ourselves and others."[172]

As I have already suggested, ideas about building a Jewish national home in Palestine pervaded *NT* but rarely existed without a concomitant commitment to rebuilding life in Poland. This article in August 1943 represents perhaps the first clear instance when the Jewish future in Palestine took precedence over the Jewish future in Poland. For Tartakower a bit more than Apenszlak, this deemphasis on a renewed Jewish life in Poland would become, my next chapter reveals, normalized throughout 1944. As the calendar pages flipped forward in 1943, however, the idea that hundreds of thousands if not millions of European Jews would survive the war and return to their prewar homes remained tangible for Apenszlak, Tartakower, and other members of the World Jewish Congress. Sadly, this belief in the continued numerical strength of Polish Jews did not align with the horrific reality that these men, their families, and their peers could not fully know. Even those who received (what we now know to be) accurate intelligence reports about the Shoah could not fully realize what had been so quickly and brutally lost.

UNDERSTANDING THE "JEWISH TRAGEDY" IN EXILE: PLANNING FOR THE INCONCEIVABLE AND ACCEPTING THE UNBELIEVABLE

When did exiled members of the World Jewish Congress, readers of *NT*, and the broader Allied universe of diplomats and statesmen realize that Jewish populations in occupied Europe had been targeted for systematic and industrialized extermination?[173] Knowledge about the event that came to be called the Holocaust emerged in uneven waves, was not always credible, and was not always believable. Above, I mentioned that reports of mass shootings near Białystok were broadcast on Radio Berlin soon after Operation Barbarossa in July 1941. The estimate of six hundred thousand Polish Jews dead appeared a few times in *NT* from 1941 to 1942. Throughout the war, reports detailing the "extermination" of Polish Jews filtered into the World Jewish Congress and the exiled governments via underground reports, diplomatic channels, and risk-taking couriers. The extent of this extermination, however, remained hard to confirm in exile throughout 1941, 1942, and most of 1943. In May 1942, Szmuel Zygielbojm, newly appointed to the Polish government-in-exile, had received reports detailing an inconceivable extent of the Jewish loss in eastern Poland and announced these findings in a meeting of the Polish National Council. On July 23, 1942, the head of the Warsaw *Judenrat*, Adam Czerniaków, committed suicide. In the first week of August 1942, Janusz Korczak met his own death at Treblinka. Soon after, stories about both men and vivid details of the circumstances of their deaths filtered out of occupied Poland. And then, WJC official Gerhard Riegner transmitted his infamous telegram detailing heinous atrocities against Jewish populations in Europe from his office in Geneva to the WJC office in London on August 8, 1942.

In his communication, Riegner wrote that he had "received [an] alarming report stating that, in the Führer's Headquarters, a plan has been discussed, and is under consideration, according to which all Jews in countries occupied or controlled by Germany numbering 3.5 to 4 million should, after deportation and concentration in the East, be at one blow exterminated, in order to resolve, once and for all the Jewish question in Europe. Action is reported to be planned for autumn." Riegner continued, "We transmit this information with all the necessary reservation, as exactitude cannot be confirmed by us." Riegner noted that his source was "generally reliable" but did not comment further. According to Perlzweig, Riegner transmitted the telegram to the US State Department and the British. He received no direct reply from the Americans.[174] At first, according to historian Michael Fleming, the British Foreign Office held up the telegram, and only after consultation with British diplomats was Silverman able to communicate this news to WJC leader Stephen Wise in New York. Wise received the telegram on August 28 and consulted with his State Department colleagues, including Sumner Welles, in the days and weeks that followed. Ten weeks after Riegner first transmitted this news, Wise "was able to publicly reveal that Sumner Welles had authenticated the information received from Riegner. The authority of the State Department was thereby attached to the claims made in the Riegner telegram and subsequent reports."[175]

According to Maurice Perlzweig, the telegram had "what I can only describe as a shattering effect. Nobody here is disposed to doubt that the information is at least substantially correct." And yet in spite of this, Perlzweig continued, "it is desperately difficult to know what to do. We thought at first of publication, but then it occurred to us that when the news seeps through to Europe it will have a demoralizing effect on those who are marked as hopeless victims." Perlzweig and his colleagues instead relied on Wise and his contacts to help decide the best way forward. "We shall act," he promised in his note, which found its way to the London office of the WJC, "if act we can, as soon as the advice and aid we seek become available."[176] Receiving reports did not equate with accepting the reports or even publicizing the reports. Those of us with the advantage of hindsight must cultivate a more delicate understanding of how information about the Shoah first came to light and spread. Nearly four decades later, while reflecting on the fact that nearly the entire Polish delegation to the 1939 WZO meeting in Geneva returned to Poland, and at a time when war was increasingly inevitable that August, Perlzweig said, "We don't believe in reality unless it hits us in the face."[177]

Consider that on September 24, 1942, *NT* published other reports from the WJC office in Geneva. According to these documents, eight hundred thousand Polish Jews had been scattered all over the globe, two million had experienced the war in Poland, and between three and four hundred thousand had died "on battlefields, in concentration and labour camps, from hunger," and from murder.[178] On October 29, 1942, Prime Minister Sikorski made an announcement about the mass murder of the Jewish people in Poland, which Arieh Tartakower cited in his reporting. On November 14, 1942, one "rumor of the tragic fate of the Jews in Europe" reached the "Representation of Polish Jews" (Reprezentacja Żydostwa Polskiego) in Palestine. This committee of exiled leaders from Zionist-leaning and Orthodox-leaning parties in interwar Poland was, according to historian Dariusz Stola, alarmed by the report that only one hundred thousand Jews remained in the Warsaw Ghetto. Under the leadership of Anselm Reiss, who had traveled to Palestine soon after war broke out in Poland, the "Reprezentacja requested the Polish Government-in-Exile to check on the news."[179] The response was written on November 16 but cabled only on November 23. In the interim, the London-based Interior Ministry had "begun to decode extensive reports which entirely confirmed the horrible rumors."[180] The ministry did not pass this intelligence onward immediately. In November and December 1942, the underground courier, Jan Karski, spent time in the United States after having crossed the Tatra Mountains. He related his observations from the Warsaw Ghetto and (what he claimed was) the death camp at Bełżec to Tartakower, members of the Polish government-in-exile, and even US president Franklin Delano Roosevelt.

The Polish minister of foreign affairs, Edward Raczyński, had combined Karski's report with other intelligence and produced a pamphlet entitled *The Mass Extermination of Jews in German Occupied Poland,* and he distributed it to the two dozen governments of the United Nations on December 10, 1942. Raczyński chronicled a detailed timeline regarding the Warsaw Ghetto and estimated that upward of one-third of Polish Jewry had already been murdered by the occupying Nazis. In recent months, the pamphlet stated, "new methods of mass slaughter . . . confirm the fact that the German authorities aim with systematic deliberation at the total extermination of the Jewish population of Poland and of the many thousands of Jews whom the German authorities have deported to Poland from Western and Central European countries and the German Reich itself."[181] This report detailed the "Great Deportation" of the Warsaw Ghetto in summer 1942 and the movement of nearly 250,000 Jews from Warsaw and elsewhere toward "extermination camps" in "Treblinka, Bełżec and Sobibór." There, "on arrival in camp, the survivors were stripped naked and killed by various means, including poison gas and electrocution."[182] The report also included news of Adam Czerniaków's suicide and the murder of Janusz Korczak.

Most likely drawing on a draft of the Polish government-in-exile's memorandum, an *NT* headline on December 10, 1942, estimated that 1,000,000 Polish Jews, or one-third of the prewar population, had already been killed by electrocution and gas, including 250,000 Jews from Warsaw.[183] One week after the publication of *The Mass Extermination of Jews in German Occupied Poland,* the Allied governments issued their own "Joint Declaration by Members of the United Nations" broadcasting the latest news of the Jewish tragedy in Europe. The statement was read by Foreign Secretary Anthony Eden on the floor of the British House of Commons and was also published prominently in the *New York Times.* By the end of 1942, David Engel notes, reliable eyewitness accounts alongside substantiated reports from the governments of two Western Allies led to the estimate that two million Polish Jews had already been killed.[184]

Reading numbers in official reports or seeing ghastly statistics in the paper, however, does not necessarily translate to acceptance or understanding. Tartakower recognized this in the wake of Raczyński's pamphlet. "Who knows," he wondered, "if there will be Jews who themselves start to doubt that mass exterminations will take place? Hundreds of thousands would pray to God that these messages turn out to be untrue."[185] According to Riegner in an interview that he gave to the *Washington Post* in the 1980s, "Nobody really believed it. Not even Jews who knew it. For instance, at the height of the extermination policy I counted four million Jews as dead."[186] Riegner sent his reports to the WJC's New York office, but during the same period, they "published the figure of only 1.5 million."[187] Few, it became clear, wanted to accept the "worst" estimates personally even if they wanted the international community to do more.

A few examples will suffice. Consider a meeting of the American Emergency Committee of Zionist Affairs on December 25, 1942. There, surrounded by Zionist-leaning exiles from American and European circles, Tartakower's colleagues Stephen Wise and Nahum Goldmann discussed the prospect of several million Jews who would need food, clothes, and rehabilitation after the war. In January 1943, Anselm Reiss and Ignacy Schwarzbart both evidenced disappointment in what seemed like the Polish government's "lack of concrete action in matters of aid and rescue." Schwarzbart admitted that he had to fight for "every inch" of attention that the Polish government gave to Jewish issues.[188] A few months later, in March 1943, Joseph Tenenbaum and Anselm Reiss spoke optimistically about postwar Poland. Tenenbaum described Polish Jewry as an "unbreakable, immortal nation." Hitler may have murdered millions of Polish Jews, but "you should not think that Polish Jews have ceased to exist." Not "even the Nazis," he declared, "will be able to destroy the forces of the Polish visions." Out of ashes a "new generation of heroes [would] be created," and Polish Jewry would "work and build a new world" after Hitler's defeat.[189] Reiss harbored similar sentiments. Seven years after he assumed the podium at the inaugural meeting of the WJC and spoke about the rootedness of Polish Jews, he walked to another podium to speak to a changed world. Reiss remembered that, "after centuries of captivity, after the previous World War," Polish Jews, as a national minority, had enjoyed Polish freedom and independence. Polish banners proclaiming "for our freedom and yours" were welcomed with "sincere joy and deep insight" by Polish Jews. Now, Polish Jews were fighting to defend the Polish state. The new world, Reiss projected, would know "liberation and freedom" when the "Jewish people fulfill[ed] their eternal hopes by creating a free national residence in Palestine and granting Polish Jewry full equality in the new Poland."[190] That world would also have two million fewer European Jews. A May 1943 article in *NT* publicized that horrific number, which according to Engel was estimated already in December 1942. But was it accepted as an accurate depiction of the Jewish loss?[191] Not necessarily.

And after news of the Warsaw Ghetto Uprising reached New York, soon after the largest armed revolt against Nazi authority in occupied Europe began and news of the ultimate destruction of this place covered the June 1943 edition of *NT,* Tartakower's reaction was sadness coupled with hope. In fact, the mildness of Tartakower's initial response shocked and angered his colleague Zorach Warhaftig, who worked with the sociologist at the Institute of Jewish Affairs and would, as my next chapter reveals, help Tartakower craft relief policies and positions for international audiences. Writing in his memoirs decades later, Warhaftig cast his thoughts back to the spring of 1943, to "the day [he does not mention which day] we heard of the Warsaw Ghetto uprising." On that day, Tartakower invited Warhaftig "to his office and disclosed to [him] plans to shower leaflets over the Warsaw ghetto as a sign of encouragement. 'That is the absolute end' [Warhaftig] burst out hysterically. It was clear that a rebellion against the armed hordes of the Nazi regime was tantamount to suicide. 'You think they need your leaflets!' [he] blurted out. 'They need arms.'" Warhaftig banged his fist on Tartakower's desk. He was "beside" himself. Warhaftig proceeded to "rush out of the room slamming the door. All day long [he] wandered the streets and alleys of New York. [He] dared not and could not go home." The reason was clear. How could he look his "wife in the eye knowing that her parents and extended family had all stayed in Warsaw?"[192]

And yet, a few days later in an editorial, Tartakower's optimism continued. Reflecting on the tragedy of the Warsaw Ghetto uprising, Tartakower proclaimed that "we will build a monument to these heroes" and "build it on the free Polish soil, where new life will blossom, based on solidarity and cooperation of all Polish citizens."[193] Warhaftig was distraught. Szmuel Zygielbojm, on May 12, 1943, had committed suicide in response to reports concerning the nearly complete liquidation of the Warsaw Ghetto and the certain death of his wife and young son. And Schwarzbart confided in his diary six days after his colleague Zygielbojm took his own life that there was "blackness all around," that the "Jewish question in Europe has been eliminated almost completely," and that he "could not see a way out, only extermination."[194] Still, Tartakower held on to some optimism in May and June 1943. Most likely, Warhaftig and Schwarzbart did as well. And perhaps Tartakower's naivete was not unfounded. The numbers crossing his desk were contradictory.

In June 1943, for instance, Tartakower had a long conference with the financial counselor of the Polish Embassy. In the counselor's prognosis, "thousands or perhaps tens of thousands of Jews may be saved by being hidden in Polish homes."[195] Further on in the same report, Tartakower hypothesized that "hundreds of thousands or perhaps even millions of Jews live and will probably continue to live after the war in the territories encompassed by . . . Poland, Hungary, Czechoslovakia and Rumania [*sic*]."[196] Sources from the

Polish government-in-exile partially supported Tartakower's high estimates. On May 4, 1943, Prime Minister Sikorski issued an explicit appeal for the Polish Christian population to aid "threatened Jews."[197] In July 1943, the Polish Ministry for Commerce, Industry and Agriculture prepared "special plans to feed the population in Poland after the war" and assumed that "after the war there will be 1,500,000 Jews in Poland."[198] A hopeful assessment of the situation remained in August 1943, when Tartakower met with representatives of the exiled Polish government and Polish Jewry in New York City. At this meeting, the parties responded to a long report reviewing the current state of the Polish underground press. Those involved, including Jan Karski, held talks about the "mass extermination of the Jews of Łódź" and the "extermination of remnants of the Ghetto in Warsaw" alongside conversations regarding the overall "tragedy of the Polish population which is being systematically robbed, deported and exterminated by the Germans or is being subjected to an artificial process of Germanization."[199] Tartakower's interest in topics aside from Jewish destruction may indicate his continued optimism. Also, in July 1943, following the unexpected death of General Sikorski and reflecting on preparations for the upcoming UNRRA conference in Atlantic City (covered in chapter 3), Tartakower declared that "Polish Jews have the right to demand from their own government the most effective and the most purposeful help" and further that "the Polish government must consider the problem of helping Jewish citizens as one of their most important tasks."[200] His message is clear here: the survivors would have to depend on the Polish government for help, and a large number of Jews would return to Poland.

Around the time that Tartakower penned this article, a list of questions that he had written with Schwarzbart and Reiss on June 26, 1943, traveled to the network of individuals who constituted the Jewish National Committee in Warsaw. The Jewish National Committee worked as a coordinating committee for the hundreds of people attached to the Żydowska Organizacja Bojowa (Jewish Fighting Organization) and thus played a role in orchestrating the 1943 Warsaw Ghetto Uprising. By the time leaders such as Lejzor Lewin, Yitzchak Zuckerman, and Adolf Berman received the twenty-six-part questionnaire, many months later, the questions on the survey did not correspond to the reality at all. The WJC affiliates in exile asked about schools "at a time when almost all Jewish children have been murdered and when those few who still survive are living in hiding, since according to Nazi code, no Jewish child has a right to live."[201] Another query inquired about "religious life and synagogues" in occupied Poland, but in the wake of the liquidation of the Kraków Ghetto, "no new Judenrat has ever been set up."[202] The questions asked by Schwarzbart,

Tartakower, and Reiss in exile indicated to the corresponding members of the Jewish National Committee that the rest of the "outside world" realized very little about the "enormity of the catastrophe which had struck at Polish Jewry" in the wake of the Warsaw Ghetto Uprising.[203]

In their defense, few members of the exilic community could know what members of the Jewish National Committee in occupied Poland knew from the summer and fall of 1943 onward. Their intelligence, filtering throughout the exiled universe from a network of informers of both Jewish and non-Jewish backgrounds across occupied Poland, did not necessarily include what happened to the Polish Jews in the Soviet Union or what became of every trainload of Jews "deported towards the East." And if they had inklings of what was happening, they most likely did not fully believe it. The reality of the Jewish National Committee in occupied Warsaw was not the reality of Schwarzbart, Tartakower, and the exiled community in the summer and fall of 1943. Increasingly, however, the knowledge of the Jewish tragedy was expanding beyond the borders of the Generalgouvernment.

Schwarzbart wrote Tartakower again in October 1943 with a tragic update. This time, his communication contained a horrific estimate and not revelations about Edvard Beneš or his shift away from minority rights. Estimates of the number of surviving Jews on Polish territory ranged from a maximum of 1.2 million people to a minimum of 200,000 people.[204] According to new sources, as of October 4, about 300,000 Jews currently lived in Polish territory, and an unknown number remained abroad in Soviet exile. This broad estimation range suggests the ambiguity in Schwarzbart's data and perhaps an attempt to maintain some hope in the face of the devastating new reports. Just a few months prior in July 1943, the Polish government-in-exile had detailed rehabilitation plans for upward of 1.5 million Jews. Even Tartakower writing in August 1943 had maintained hope that more than a remnant of Polish Jewish civilization would survive. Another report from London traveled across telegram lines toward Tartakower's office at 330 West Forty-Second Street later that same month. The staccato message from Schwarzbart added up to one ominous conclusion: "We have to face complete annihilation even of the small remnants."[205] These reports were, as we have seen, not the first to detail Polish Jewry's destruction, but Schwarzbart's gloomy estimates on the eve of the first meeting of the UNRRA conference in Atlantic City constituted two more beads on a string of warnings that defied rationality. Most of Polish Jewry would not survive. And in fact, the harshest estimates would soon become the numerical reality publicized by the Jewish National Committee. On December 1, 1943, Schwarzbart lamented in his diary that this broader historical moment marked "the end of Polish Jewry. Lord, my spirit is broken. Truly, there is nothing to live for."[206]

CONCLUSION: THE DIPLOMATIC SURPRISES OF 1943

Surprises riddled the Allied universe in 1943. Four surprises in particular create the contours of this book's postwar world. First, as referenced above, reports about the extent of the Jewish tragedy filtered into east central European exilic communities and cast increasingly pessimistic news about the survival of Jewish populations throughout Europe. Second, a Nazi broadcast on April 13, 1943, revealed that their forces had found the mass grave of thousands of Polish officers in the Katyń Forest. When the Polish government-in-exile requested that the International Red Cross lead an international inquiry to discover the circumstances of this slaughter, the Soviet Union promptly broke off relations with Sikorski's government.[207] For more than the next two years, the Allies could not agree on who constituted the "real" Polish government.[208] Caught between the Soviets and the London-based Poles, the Czech government-in-exile increasingly gravitated toward Moscow, thereby imperiling plans for the Polish-Czechoslovak Confederation. As it did so, another ingredient required for Beneš's organization of postwar Europe became more accepted over the course of this important year. This constitutes the third surprise of 1943. By the time Edvard Beneš traveled to the Allied conference in Tehran in November 1943, he had convinced high-ranking representatives from the United Kingdom (Churchill), the United States (Franklin Delano Roosevelt), and the Soviet Union (Maisky) that the Sudeten Germans should be removed from a reconstituted Czechoslovakia after the war. By the end of December 1943, as noted above, Beneš also had Stalin's support.[209] And just as Beneš convinced leaders of the biggest Allied states that population transfers were a necessary tool of statecraft moving forward, so too, surprisingly, did members of the WJC draw closer to his vision of the future.

Between his meetings at the White House, the State Department, and the offices of other powerbrokers, Beneš held private audiences with WJC leaders to discuss the issue of Jewish belonging during his trip to the United States in the spring and summer of 1943. On Friday, May 21, 1943, Wise and Goldmann reached an agreement of sorts with the Czech president, and the animosity between the WJC and Beneš heretofore evidenced through internal WJC correspondence cooled substantially. In a letter written three days later, Kubowitzki explained to Arnošt Frischer (the representative appointed to the

Czechoslovak State Council to speak on Jewish issues) how the meeting had unfolded.[210] The entire discussion focused on correcting misunderstandings and aligning each representative body's platform with the other. Early in the visit, Beneš noted that "in connection with the Jewish postwar demands, he asked to be informed of [the WJC] program as he would regret it if he would have to defend a viewpoint opposed to [the WJC]."[211] In response, Goldmann expressed "how sorry we had been to hear of certain views President Beneš had voiced on minority rights, views which seemed difficult to be reconciled with the great liberal ideals he had always defended."[212] Beneš "replied that he had only expressed serious doubts concerning the vision of demanding simultaneously a Jewish State in Palestine and political minority rights in the countries where Jews live."[213] What the WJC wanted, Goldmann continued, was "only recognition of the fact that there is a Jewish people in the world, that Jewish citizens of the various states have the right to remain members of this Jewish people; that they may continue to instruct their children in the Hebrew language and in Jewish values, to display a deep interest in Palestine and in the Jewish fate everywhere, to cultivate their heritage and cultured ties."[214] Goldman insisted, "This is what we mean when talking of minority rights. We do not for instance, ask for separate Jewish wards in elections." Beneš countered, "Whoever told you that I oppose such legitimate demands misunderstood me."[215] The meeting ended on positive terms, with Beneš promising to meet with other Czechoslovakian Jewish representatives during his extended time in the United States.

Commenting on the meeting between Beneš, Goldmann, and Wise, Frischer offered an exhaustive analysis. His reflections on this meeting center on the continued use of the term *minority rights*.[216] Writing from London on June 21, 1943, Frischer explained how the idea of minority rights had been misunderstood. Minority rights, he maintained, do not give extra privileges; rather, they make minorities (particularly those who tend to live in the same regional spaces) on legal par with the larger majorities. Jews in interwar Czechoslovakia, Frischer noted, did not benefit from minority rights like Sudeten Germans did. Moreover, since the term *minority rights* had been tainted by the likes of Konrad Heinlein and Adolf Hitler, Frischer did not "think that we should make ourselves the champions of 'minority rights' in general in the presentation."[217] Furthermore, he added, "the definition Dr. Goldmann gave about 'what we want' is really a very fine one, but he himself was aware that it is not identical with what the world calls 'minority rights.'"[218] Conceding how important definitions could be "in the diplomatic and political sphere," Frischer proposed that the WJC "should apply a term more modern and more popular, and above all, more suitable for our cause." He suggested the term "'right of man.'"[219]

The language so important to Frischer had ceased to matter as much as it once mattered in the not-so-distant past. Goldmann's exchange with Beneš seems conciliatory and mellows the former rancor of WJC reports regarding Beneš's statements on the postwar world. Beneš was not, he claimed, opposed to Goldmann's specific definition of minority rights. In fact, Beneš himself recognized the existence of the Jewish people in the world, and he wanted to help Jewish people obtain what was owed to them: their own polity. Goldmann did not counter emigration to Palestine, nor did he insist that a discernible Jewish people living in Czechoslovakia enjoy group rights. The parties reached a more palatable middle ground not because Beneš had receded, however. Instead, Goldmann had moved closer to what Beneš now believed.

Beneš did not speak about Palestine at this particular meeting. He did, however, discuss the topic in fall 1943 in a meeting with Chaim Weizmann, the president of the World Zionist Organization. A few weeks before he visited Premier Stalin of the Soviet Union, Beneš stated that "the establishment of a Jewish national home is as certain as the restoration of Czechoslovakia, whose resurrection I do not doubt."[220] A letter that he received from Weizmann one month later asked Beneš to reveal the extent of his support for a Jewish state. On November 12, 1943, Weizmann asked Beneš to ascertain whether Soviet leaders would support WZO claims related to Palestine before the United Nations.[221] Clearly, by the end of 1943, Beneš had become an influential ally for some voices in the Zionist movement. Surprisingly, by the end of 1944, other voices in exile that vigorously supported the reestablishment of the Jewish diaspora in east central Europe, including a unified collective of voices within the World Jewish Congress, would consider Beneš an ally as well.

THREE

NEGATING THIS DIASPORA

The World Jewish Congress and the Prioritization of Postwar Life in Palestine, 1942–1944

JAKOB APENSZLAK WATCHED HIS FRIENDS, his adversaries, and some of his countrymen uproot a significant remnant of the European Jewish diaspora over a handful of emotional days in November 1944. In that month, as "smoke remained in chimneys of the unheated crematoria" thousands of miles away in Poland, the World Jewish Congress's War Emergency Conference convened in Atlantic City. The largest transnational Jewish gathering convened in wartime resembled, in Apenszlak's opinion, a wake more than a typical congress. Hundreds of delegates hailing from all corners of the globe could not avoid the fact that over "five million Jews had been starved, strangled, gassed and murdered in the cruelest way," and acknowledgement of this fact initiated a "powerful reflex of self-preservation."[1] If, Apenszlak wrote, "someone would ask the delegates where they feel happy and safe, where they imagine a safe Jewish future, they would respond in one unified voice: in Palestine."

This was the reality, Apenszlak admitted, despite the fact that "not all of them were Zionists." When a speaker announced with "a thundering voice" that "life in the diaspora, in the *golus* was a sin" and "that everything Jews created outside of Palestine was destined to fail," "storms of applause" greeted this violent statement. In his attempt to understand this turn of events, Apenszlak explained that a "sense of insecurity" dominated the general mood. Aware of the Jewish tragedy and afraid of assimilation that might appear in the wake of it, "the slogan of the Jewish state" shone with the "splendor of one's only hope." It seemed that all the world's Jewish people, including even the wealthier representatives from the Americas, had "lost confidence in all other ways of solving the Jewish problem, except for the Palestinian one." Without Palestine, Apenszlak observed, "everything is uncertain, unstable, unreliably dangerous."[2]

Although he disagreed with them, Apenszlak could understand them. "Psychologically, the negation of Europe after this bloody abyss is natural and understandable." Regardless, Apenszlak firmly held his ground: "The program [of diaspora negation] is unacceptable. The contribution of Jewishness to European civilization is too great to renounce. It would be a renunciation of enormous moral and material good."[3] Roots, Apenszlak reminded his readers, flowed in Europe and throughout the entire area of the diaspora or, in Yiddish, the *goles*. Furthermore, "the future of Israel cannot be built upon *Golus* negation." And yet, despite the fact that the resolutions "regarding the reconstruction and rehabilitation of Europe's Jewry" were adopted without objection, everything had seemingly changed. Drawing near the end of a war and a genocide that had nearly obliterated the Jewish people on the European continent, attendees of the War Emergency Congress had one unified reflex: to turn their faces toward Palestine and ensure that Jews from elsewhere would have the ways and means to get there.

Talk of diasporic negation began on the first day of the meeting. During the opening session of this conference, before 267 representatives from twenty-two countries, Nahum Goldmann approached the podium. Goldmann described the organization's deep commitment to the establishment of a Jewish Commonwealth in Palestine and suggested that the United Nations should financially and logistically support the movement of European Jews there.[4] Also, he contended, Jewish rights must be restored, Jewish property must be restituted, Jewish organizations should help facilitate rehabilitation, and "criminals who have committed crimes against the Jews" should be punished.[5] Even if all these actions were taken, however, the problems facing European Jews would remain unresolved. Only the creation of a Jewish homeland in Palestine could rectify the Jews' position in the world community. "Had there existed a homeland when Hitler came to power, willing and ready to take in all those Jews who could have escaped," Goldmann (problematically) hypothesized, "millions of Jews who are buried in the fields and forests of Poland and Russia would have been alive today."[6] At this unique moment in the history of the Jewish people, Goldmann enthusiastically declared that "no programme of Jewish demands has meaning or historical significance if it does not culminate in a demand for a Jewish commonwealth in Palestine."[7]

Speaking to those members of the World Jewish Congress who were potentially, like Jakob Apenszlak, satisfied with their lives in the diaspora, Goldmann offered a caveat. He was not pleading, in fact, "for [the] enforced evacuation of European Jewry. Those who want to stay have the right to stay and be restored to their former status."[8] There would most likely be, however, "many who will

Fig. 3.1. Nahum Goldmann speaks at the WJC's War Emergency Conference in Atlantic City, 1944. Photo courtesy of CriticalPast.

reject this solution and the minimum one can do for them is to give them the right to start a new life in a country of their own, where, whatever may happen to them, such a catastrophe will not occur again."[9] For these reasons, the proposed demand for a Jewish Commonwealth was "no longer a so-called Zionist demand." It had "superseded the limits of party Zionism." The "tragedy of the past decade" demanded but one reparation: the "establishment of a Jewish homeland in the full sense of the word, a place where every Jew from Europe or elsewhere, who wants to go or is forced to go will be received and find refuge in his own homeland."[10] And therefore, Goldmann crisply shouted at the crowd with the sides of his face slick with perspiration and his fingers poking at those assembled, "this World Jewish Congress session, [despite] not being a Zionist body in its constitution, cannot begin even its deliberations without proclaiming the principle that . . . the real solution of the Jewish problem cannot be brought about unless the Jewish people will be given the right and will be helped by the United Nations to establish Palestine once and for all as its own Jewish homeland."[11]

It seemed that Goldmann could read the crowd. The delegates at the War Emergency Conference overwhelmingly agreed with vigorous applause in the moment and later when they unanimously endorsed a resolution calling for the establishment of Palestine as a Jewish Commonwealth.[12] In an effort to initiate the "definitive and permanent termination of the national homelessness of the Jewish people," the conference urged the British government to abrogate the policy set out in the 1939 White Paper and "to open Palestine to unrestricted Jewish immigration and resettlement." Moreover, the conference "appealed to the United Nations to ensure that the general scheme of postwar reconstruction shall include the establishment of Palestine as a free and democratic Jewish Commonwealth and that appropriate public financial and other resources be provided for that purpose, including the speedy *transfer* [emphasis mine] to Palestine of all Jewish survivors of Nazi persecution who desire or need to have a part in the rebuilding of the Jewish National Home."[13] Going further, the amendment supported by delegates from five continents called for the "the opportunity of free departure from their places of temporary residence and freedom in the choice to be repatriated or returned to their former homes or to be resettled elsewhere."[14] As an "overwhelming majority of such persons will desire to go to Palestine," the Intergovernmental Committee for Refugees and UNRRA should give "large financial assistance to cover the cost of the transportation of the refugees and the process of resettlement."[15] Thus, the establishment of a Jewish political entity in Palestine and the United Nations' support for Jewish refugees to move there became two out of a handful of resolutions emanating from the War Emergency Conference to the assembled press corps and international observers.[16]

The language contained in this amendment includes a number of verbs that indicate repetition. Jews born and raised in Europe were to be "resettled" in Palestine. Survivors from internment camps had the right to partake in the "rebuilding" of their national home far away from their prewar "homes." Jews would not be evacuated to a foreign land; rather, they would be "repatriated" to an entity where political belonging awaited them.[17] The boldness of the language emanating from a meeting of the (formerly?) diaspora-centric World Jewish Congress is striking. Seven months before V-E day, those assembled at the War Emergency Congress did not hesitate to speak for "many" Jews or an "overwhelming majority" that wanted to move away from Europe. By the penultimate month of 1944, this organization publicly stated that the United Nations Relief and Rehabilitation Administration, the Intergovernmental Committee for Refugees, and the international community should fund the transport of uprooted Jewish survivors away from their prewar homes and toward a presumed ethnic home in Palestine. Apenszlak noted this irony soon after the event. And although Goldmann promised that he was not negating the diaspora, the thrust of his argumentation indicated otherwise at this moment and, we will soon see, at others as well.

How did these twinned assumptions—that a Jewish Commonwealth in Palestine should be envisioned as a reparation for the wartime Jewish catastrophe and that Jewish refugees from Europe should have the financial and political support of the United Nations to move toward that perceived homeland—emerge and spread throughout the highest echelons of the World Jewish Congress thereafter, emanating at the 1944 UNRRA meeting in Montreal, the War Emergency Congress in Atlantic City, and beyond? Additionally, how did the organization so threatened by Czechoslovak president Edvard Beneš's calls in the early 1940s for the creation of a Jewish state populated by the "unassimilating" Jews of Europe come to publicly endorse similar plans just a few years later? This chapter attempts to answer these questions using a vigorous analysis of committee minutes, organizational reports, editorials, and personal writings that World Jewish Congress members composed between June 1942 and the War Emergency Congress in November 1944.

And so, the first part of this chapter demonstrates how Nahum Goldmann transferred ideas from the American Emergency Committee for Zionist Affairs (AECZA), a New York–based circle of American-born Jews and Jews exiled by war, to the Office Committee of the WJC by the spring and summer of 1944 and suggests that three key developments influenced this stark change in WJC policy. First, a growing realization of the extent of the Jewish tragedy, the precedence of wartime Jewish displacement, and the stalled reaction of world leaders to both situations encouraged WJC leaders to consider wide-scale emigration plans away from Europe as viable solutions to the so-called Jewish problem in east central Europe in general and in Germany in particular. My evaluation of Nahum Goldmann and his colleagues in the AECZA offers a new vantage point from which to understand the complexity of the "Zionist movement" in the United States and globally in 1942 and 1943. Zionism as a concept fundamentally changed from the late 1930s to the mid-1940s. Goldmann suggested as much in the War Emergency Congress speech quoted above. What emerged by 1944 was an "empirical Zionism" that equated Jews uprooted by the Second World War and the Holocaust with the citizens destined to populate a Jewish political entity in Palestine. This "empirical" form of Zionism arguably made numerical and emotional sense to a wide, sympathetic, and presumed audience of both Jews and non-Jews.

Second, this chapter focuses on how the work of a small organization like the WJC impacted the nascent relief and rehabilitation machinery of the United Nations Relief and Rehabilitation Administration, and thus contributes to a growing body of literature that unearths how the Allied powers and nongovernmental organizations prepared for the postwar world as well as the millions of refugees and displaced persons (DPs) that would populate it. Newspaper coverage and archival documentation about the first two UNRRA conferences (first in Atlantic City in November 1943 and later in Montreal in September 1944) reveal that even as the extent of the Jewish tragedy became increasingly evident, the members of UNRRA had no clear plans to enshrine a distinction for Jewish victims persecuted under racial laws within emerging international legal codes. In 1943 and the first half of 1944, plans to create a category delineating "Jewish DPs" from other displaced people and Axis nationals failed to congeal. WJC officials began to worry that surviving Jews would be forced by UNRRA repatriation plans to return to obliterated communities, or worse, be implicated in postwar vengeance schemes directed toward Nazi Germany and her allies. As they prepared for the (delayed) second meeting of UNRRA in the spring and summer of 1944, the Office Committee of the World Jewish Congress made decisions to exacerbate the displacement of European Jews by prioritizing Palestine as a safe haven in the present and the future, as well as considering plans to negate the European diaspora in response to this failure of the international legal community. The second and fourth sections of this chapter cover both UNRRA meetings, the important seasons between them, and the emotionally driven decisions WJC officials made throughout 1944.

To better grasp the inner dynamics and the policy changes in the WJC, this chapter leans heavily on the frequent meetings of the so-called Office Committee, a small group of between five and ten WJC officials who led organizational departments and represented the WJC publicly at events and in private meetings with officials. Periodically each week for nearly six years, the handful of members who constituted the WJC Office Committee convened to discuss developments both ordinary and exciting. The preserved minutes of this committee from 1944 reveal the endless grind of daily correspondence, the scheduling nightmares that accompanied intermittent meetings with government leaders from across the Allied world, and, in some instances, contentious debates regarding WJC's policies and organizational philosophies. Two particular discussions provide us ideal opportunities to enter the headspace of these actors, isolate when they change their minds, and identify the nuanced conflicts behind the unified public platforms: the first on June 8, which explored whether German Jews should return to Germany after the war, and the second three weeks later on June 30, which debated whether the global role of the WJC should change moving forward. By mid-1944, the WJC could no longer afford to give precedence to the diaspora. The time to emphasize Palestine was ripe.

Finally, this chapter argues that members of the WJC embraced the movement of European Jews away from Europe as one element of an increasingly acceptable postwar plan to replace the protection of minorities with the movement of minorities. The scope of this plan, which partially emerged from the imagination of Edvard Beneš and gained powerful adherents over a short time, would fall under the financial purview of the United Nations. Accordingly, the continued uprooting of the Jewish diaspora in Europe would be financed and sanctioned by the member governments of this new international institution. Just as the idea of population transfers of ethnic Germans gained acceptance throughout the Allied diplomatic world, so too would the idea that Europe's Jews should be transferred into their own ethnicized polity. And so, the organization founded in 1936 to represent Jews living outside of Palestine vigorously advocated for an empirical form of Zionism and thus the further uprooting of the east central European Jewish diaspora in the wake of Hitler's defeat.

NAHUM GOLDMANN AND THE AMERICAN EMERGENCY COMMITTEE FOR ZIONIST AFFAIRS, 1942–1943

Less than one month after a declaration from the 1942 Biltmore Conference called for the opening of emigration to Palestine and the creation of a Jewish commonwealth there, the Jewish members of the AECZA had a unique problem.[18] To increase American support for Jewish migration toward Palestine in the present and the future, the Office Committee of the AECZA deemed it necessary to draft a definition of Zionism that a large variety of Jews, even those of non-Zionist stripe, could support. On June 3 of that year, more than a dozen high-profile characters including David Ben-Gurion (chairman of the Executive Committee of the Jewish Agency), Maurice Wertheim (president of the American Jewish Committee), Meyer Weisgal (assistant to Chaim Weizmann), Stephen Wise, and Nahum Goldmann gathered to "arrive at a common program so that American Jewry could appear as a united group before the Peace Conference to get the best possible settlement for Palestine."[19] The task proved arduous—nearly impossible, in fact. To recall a notable quote about interwar Polish Jewish politics, it seemed that only a Talmudist could understand the Zionist movement in America and the disagreements connecting the personalities within this particular room.

For example, Nahum Goldmann "could not conceive of any formulation on Palestine which would be acceptable to" everyone in attendance. Those speaking for the American Jewish Committee, for instance, could not "agree to any formula about Palestine which included 'commonwealth' or 'national home for the Jewish people.'" President of the American Jewish Congress and founder of the WJC Stephen Wise "warned against being rushed into any formulation," as he "would not delegate the power to formulate Zionism to any individual."[20] And so discussions within this committee, which had been established in the late 1930s to serve as an umbrella group for Zionist organizations and those with Zionist sympathies working in New York City and the United States, came to a standstill. To expedite the debate between non-Zionists (a classification used at the time), Zionists, and the variations therein, Ben-Gurion met with Wertheim privately to reach an agreement on a shared definition of Zionism and enable American Jews as a whole to endorse postwar plans that included the establishment of a Jewish commonwealth in Palestine.[21]

Two days later, the Office Committee of the AECZA reconvened to learn about the conversation between these two leaders. Ben-Gurion imparted good news: Wertheim and the American Jewish Committee would support a program quite similar to the one endorsed in May 1942 at the Biltmore Hotel. His agreement with Ben-Gurion was predicated on two (soon to be deemed impossible) conditions: that the Emergency Committee offer a conclusive formula regarding the "ties which bind Jews together" and that the WJC cease their operations in the United States.[22] Wertheim had good reason to tie his endorsement of a Biltmore-esque platform with these two conditions. He asked the Emergency Committee to clarify exactly which "ties . . . bind Jews together," because without such a clarification, the Biltmore Program's promise to increase "Jewish immigration" to Palestine remained hopelessly ambiguous. Which Jews would become the Jews who settled in Palestine once immigration restrictions eased? Suspicious of WJC political activities within the United States, Wertheim wanted Goldmann and Wise to stop their activities in New York City, Washington, DC, and beyond. Unsurprisingly, Wertheim's conditions sparked animosity among WJC members assembled at the June 5, 1942, AECZA meeting. In an effort to register his anger at such a brash request, Wise noted that "he would consider any decision to alter the status of the WJC" as a "betrayal of the Jewish people."[23]

The animosity detailed in these meeting minutes from June 1942 reveals deep fissures between key Jewish personalities and organizations working in America after the Biltmore Conference, when more than six hundred authorities with Zionist leanings from a variety of political parties assembled in New York and the World Jewish Congress lent support to the broader program agreed on there. Reflecting on the importance of Biltmore, Goldmann approximated the pronunciation of this platform as a watershed in Zionist politics overall. Until this declaration, Goldmann "had been among those who went along with Weizmann in opposing any official demand for a Jewish state." This, Goldmann clarified in his autobiography published two decades later, was a matter of practical politics, not principle. As long as there was "no realistic prospect of attaining a Jewish state in Palestine, if only for the simple reason that we were outnumbered by the Arabs, it would have been harmful to issue such a demand." Although Goldmann considered the demographic reality in the Mandate a "great obstacle," he also considered the time ripe for a declaration of collective Zionist intent.[24] Goldmann pinpointed moments important to the evolution of his thinking in other writings. In the same autobiography, Goldmann affirmed that "the massacre of the Jews made me more certain than ever that after the war we would have to come out with a demand for a Jewish state."[25] However, he did not necessarily have this awareness at Biltmore. In fact, in the spring of 1942 (as the Operation Reinhard camps at Bełżec, Sobibór, and Treblinka began their murderous operations), more than two million Polish Jews remained in the ghettos and towns of occupied Poland. The so-called Great Deportation of the Warsaw Ghetto would begin that summer, in July 1942. And so, to understand Goldmann's deeper feelings about Palestine and about the diaspora, we must go back much further, arguably to his childhood.

Throughout his life, Goldmann simultaneously supported the emergence of a Jewish state and life in the diaspora, and his autobiography emphasizes this repeatedly. Goldmann reflected on his early childhood under his grandparents' roof in Congress Poland, explaining that as a child he was a "Zionist without knowing it."[26] After moving to Germany to commence schooling there, Goldmann delivered his first speech for a Zionist organization at age fourteen.[27] Despite his strong affinity for Zionism in his youth, like other "Zionists" he vehemently rejected the thesis that Jewish movements toward Palestine negated the importance of the diaspora for future generations. Goldmann cast the diaspora as a spiritual necessity for the Jewish people, fulfilling "some deep need of the Jewish spirit or of the collective Jewish soul." Reflecting on the entirety of Jewish history, the man who notoriously possessed eight passports throughout his life observed that since the destruction of the Second Temple, Jews had "shifted back and forth between" two "poles": one marked by the "adventurous spirit of a world people" and another that "yearned for the homeland." This realization pointed Goldmann to a conclusion that the Jewish "situation cannot really be normalized by assembling a small portion of people in Palestine and writing off the rest." In short, the "diaspora must survive along with the Jewish center."[28] Near the end of his life, even after the Jewish state came into existence, Goldmann regarded this tension between "the" Jewish homeland and multiple diasporic homelands as the "central Jewish problem of our time."[29]

In June 1942, Goldmann and others were satisfied with the results of the Biltmore meeting, but other individuals and organizations remained unconvinced. In October 1942, the Zionist Executive in Jerusalem adopted the postulates related to the opening of Palestine to unlimited Jewish migration under the supervision of the Jewish Agency.[30] This idea, however, did not resound among a significant subsection of American Jews such as those in Maurice Wertheim's American Jewish Committee, a non-Zionist-leaning organization.[31] And since a "goodly number of question marks [were] inherent in the Biltmore Program," a new series of discussions was initiated to include the American Jewish Committee within this new thrust of Zionist politics.[32] The questions asked at the two late-spring meetings of the AECZA in 1942 concerning the ties binding the Jewish people or what constituted Zionism, however, elicited neither easy answers nor the desired consensus. Later that summer, Wertheim and the American Jewish Committee withdrew official support for any statement resembling the Biltmore Program. The WJC did not dissolve. And it remained difficult to define the concrete "ties" that bound the Jewish people together.

The dynamic between Wertheim, Ben-Gurion, Wise, and Goldmann preserved in the records of these two meetings reveals the precarious state of "Zionism" in America in mid-1942. While some consensus materialized between so-called Zionists and non-Zionists in the wake of the Biltmore Program, serious questions plagued the leaders involved in these discussions.[33] If Palestine became a "Jewish commonwealth," which Jews would emigrate there? Who belonged to the Jewish people, and what obligation would American Jews have to a Jewish political entity thousands of miles away? How could constituents of the WJC support plans for a Jewish commonwealth while also speaking for Jews in the diaspora? As his remarks at these two meetings in June 1942 indicate, Nahum Goldmann did not yet possess the answers to these questions. After a year and a few more meetings of the AECZA Office Committee, however, Goldmann's plan for the postwar world and the Jews' position within it would coalesce more clearly and, in turn, would shape the official platform of the WJC.

Goldmann's direct trajectory toward viable answers to Jewish wartime and postwar questions continued in late December 1942. Near the end of this month, the AECZA Office Committee met to "clarify fundamental questions of policy and objectives."[34] The most pressing concerns centered on two topics: what type of governmental structure would emerge if the British Mandate system collapsed and how that hypothetical government structure would inhibit or encourage the emigration of the Jewish masses.[35] Crackling discussion ensued on Christmas Day and again three days later. Rarely a shrinking violet, Goldmann suggested that the ideal political structure would be an "international trusteeship for Palestine entrusted to the administration of a neutral country, not tied up with the Arab World and not motivated by power politics."[36] Three others in attendance responded with enthusiastic disagreement, claiming that Goldmann's dream of a neutral power taking over this particular slice of the British Empire was far too unrealistic. Goldmann disagreed. He envisioned the United Nations as a neutral force, able to support the establishment of a Jewish political entity and willing to force Great Britain to revoke their promises to Arab states and encourage migrations toward it. As usual, conversations about Jewish governance in Palestine almost always led to conversations about Jewish immigration.

From the foundation of the modern nationalist movement labeled Zionism in the fin de siècle and the debates I covered in the Polish Jewish political sphere back in chapter 1 to this particular meeting held in late 1942, demographic concerns had been fundamental to all Jewish nationalist projects focused on increased Jewish settlement in Palestine.[37] Those in support of massive, expedited Jewish settlement in the Levant had to contend with one primary practical and logistical concern: how would Jews logistically move from their former "homes" to their new "home" elsewhere? At this juncture, Goldmann envisioned a link between United Nations support for a Jewish political entity and a revision of British-imposed immigration barriers. He did not offer a financial plan to subsidize this movement. Two other participants at this meeting, Chaim Weizmann and Meyer Weisgal, did.

Before Weizmann arrived, his assistant Meyer Weisgal detailed his views on Jewish immigration, which he understood as "quite independent of the provisional form of government which might be set up and the ultimate establishment of a Jewish Commonwealth."[38] Primarily, in Weisgal's opinion, there were two basic problems, "the need of the Jewish people for Palestine and to get a majority in the country." Both of these problems could be solved by "immigration." Since there would be "several million Jews who will have to be fed, clothed and rehabilitated after the war by the United Nations," this mass of humanity had the potential to become the immigrants so desperately sought. Consequently, "by securing the agreement of the United Nations to take these people out of occupied countries immediately after the war and sending them to Palestine," Weisgal believed they would "then be doing something constructive." Within three to five years, the refugee Jews of Europe could constitute "a Jewish majority in Palestine," and "the entire immediate problem will be solved."[39]

Weisgal's call to have Jewish authorities cooperate with the United Nations and facilitate the postwar migration of Jews toward Palestine echoed words that Goldman and others offered in this private apartment on this late December day. But it also represented something new. The direct connection he proposed between Jewish postwar refugees, the United Nation's endorsement and financial underwriting of migration plans, and the metamorphosis of the liberated Jews of Europe to Palestinian settlers had precedent neither in the official proclamations of the Biltmore Conference nor within the confines of this committee. In the wake of the Polish government-in-exile and the Soviet Union establishing relations in the summer of 1941, a general amnesty coupled with state-sponsored evacuations had moved roughly 115,000 Polish citizens deported throughout the Soviet Union to Iran and elsewhere. Thousands of those citizens were taken further onward, to places that included Palestine. But Weisgal was not talking about a movement born out of wartime expediency and an effort to bolster Allied forces in the Middle East. While the activists on the AECZA could not agree on what political entity would emerge in Palestine after the conflict, they spoke in unison regarding Jewish movement toward the Mandate. When he entered the meeting late, Chaim Weizmann joined this pro-emigration chorus with much élan and seconded Weisgal's thoughts.

For Weizmann, postwar Jewish immigration was to ensue with great speed after the war. He "favored a plan of bringing over a large number of people immediately after the guns have ceased firing."[40] Such a plan was "necessary and would to a great extent solve the whole problem." Then Weizmann offered a poignant hypothetical. "Suppose," he posited, "you bring over a quarter of a million or 300,000 Jews, you would then . . . have effectively a majority in Palestine. If these people who will in any case have to be fed and clothed are fed and clothed in Palestine, the country will be rebuilt in the process." Weizmann continued, with attention to presumed public opinion, "If this plan is combined with the development of the country we are more or less in the unassailable position." Arab refusal, he claimed, would not "be tolerated in the post-war world." And such a logical plan could "win the interest and sympathy of the liberal world and is the key to the solution of our problems." In the end, 250,000 to 300,000 Jews could be brought to Palestine as a "10% installment on future Jewish immigration."[41] This, in Weizmann and Weisgal's viewpoint, constituted "the most pressing Zionist goal for the immediate postwar period."

What they wanted, to borrow a term that both Weizmann himself and Edvard Beneš had used to refer to other circumstances a year prior in the January 1942 issue of *Foreign Affairs*, was an internationally funded and sanctioned population transfer across the Mediterranean. As described in chapter 2, Beneš suggested that the transfer of Germans and Hungarians away from Czechoslovakia would preserve the peace in central Europe. Weizmann suggested that Arabs could be transferred away from Jewish-held territory in Mandate Palestine. The intervention here in December 1942, nearly one year after *Foreign Affairs* published those two articles, drew on this language but was also different. Arguably, Weisgal's intervention and Weizmann's specific numbers mark two of the earliest statements envisioning the European Jewish refugees as the precise settlers needed to ensure a Jewish majority in Mandate Palestine. Also arguably, this calculus makes the most sense when situated alongside Beneš's plans to unmix ethnicities and minorities in east central Europe. At subsequent meetings of the AECZA and the Office Committee of the World Jewish Congress, Goldmann returned to this formula equalizing Jewish refugees from Europe as Palestinian immigrants. Eventually, half a year later, Goldmann adopted the ideas espoused by Weisgal and Weizmann at this particular meeting as his own and subsequently transferred them to circles within the WJC. To understand how Goldmann became an empirical Zionist, however, it is necessary to understand what happened during the six months between the Christmastime gatherings of the AECZA and a subsequent AECZA meeting on June 1, 1943.

Decision, or Lack Thereof: The Bermuda Conference, April–May 1943

To put it bluntly, the stakes of the discussions at hand drastically changed in response to two events that commenced at nearly the same time. In April 1943, the much-anticipated Bermuda Conference convened on the same day that Jews remaining in the Warsaw Ghetto initiated their uprising. Known officially as the "Anglo-American Conference on Refugees," planning for it began when the British Foreign Office proposed a joint meeting between British and American officials to discuss the continuing problem of refugees in Europe.[42] Held over eleven days in April, official discussions were closed to private organizations and observers.[43] A close review of diplomatic correspondence before, during, and after the meeting reveals that the assembled parties worked to secure transport for the small-scale resettlement of Jewish refugees in some places (Palestine and Mexico) but not others (North Africa and Madagascar), crafted a joint statement, attempted to clarify which organizational bodies would care for refugees in the coming months, and, overall, made few conclusive decisions. The problems encountered and left unsolved at Bermuda eventually became key issues for both UNRRA and the World Jewish Congress over the next two and a half years.

The British and the Americans made small but demonstrable promises leading up to the Bermuda Conference, and these commitments continued once diplomats convened in Bermuda. For example, British authorities expressed their willingness to admit Jewish children and some adults into Palestine with varying numbers of caveats. An agreement to admit Jewish children in January 1943 included specifics stating that the immigration would be capped at seventy-five thousand to accord with the "limits imposed by the 1939 White Paper" and excluded adult males because of the "acute security problem" there.[44] One month later in February 1943, plans for the British to admit "many thousands of Jews from Southeastern Europe" hinged on the ability to secure "the necessary transport for them" and a promise given by Sikorski of the Polish government-in-exile that "after the war all Polish Jews would be welcomed back to Poland." The United States established a $2,500,000 fund right before the Bermuda Conference convened on April 15, 1943, to help refugees move from Spain.[45] Transport questions were inevitably linked to refugee questions. Those assembled considered the twenty-one refugees in Spain, the three thousand Czechs and Poles of military age within that group, and the four to five thousand Jewish men, women, and children who were either enemy nationals or stateless. "If all or part of these" refugees, William H. Beck, the consul general at Hamilton, wrote to Secretary of State Hull, "could be removed to a temporary home, the Conference would have led to some definite practical result."[46] While certificates of admission for Palestine could be accrued for fifteen hundred families or twenty-five thousand persons, transport posed a severe difficulty. At the time, "transport arrangements [did] not permit of them proceeding beyond Portuguese Southwest Africa."[47]

Alongside questions of transport, the role that Madagascar or Palestine could play in sheltering refugees also became a topic of Allied conversations throughout 1943. In February of that year, by way of example, a US official working in the UK drew on his prewar recollections and asked if Madagascar could become a "home for oppressed Jews" under the current circumstances.[48] Discussions on April 20 in Bermuda turned to the issue of Polish refugees remaining in Iran after a large-scale evacuation of their fellow citizens. In the wake of the recent breaking of diplomatic relations between the Soviet Union and Poland over the Katyń affair, some Polish refugees remained unevacuated.[49] The Intergovernmental Committee would assume authority over these uprooted Polish citizens and potentially direct them to Madagascar. De Gaulle had "so far agreed to accept 200 Polish families," but the availability of Madagascar depended on the question of France's representation on the Intergovernmental Committee.[50] Finally, the British government considered "asylum in Palestine to Jews (mainly children, with a proportion of women) from Rumania [*sic*] and Bulgaria." Because these two governments refused to allow Jews to leave, diplomatic considerations took precedence over humanitarian considerations once again.[51]

What decisions, then, were finalized at Bermuda? In short, only a handful and none of great consequence.[52] Notably, the Polish Jewish evacuees in the Soviet Union remained outside the scope of the conference.[53] And after the conference dissolved, a decision both positive and negative emanated from the White House. On May 14, 1943, American president Franklin Delano Roosevelt sent a memorandum to Secretary of State Cordell Hull agreeing that North Africa could be used as a depot for refugees but not transition into a permanent residence without the approval of relevant authorities. Roosevelt admitted that there was "plenty of room in North Africa," but he thought the idea of sending "large numbers of Jews there" was "extremely unwise."[54] Those assembled in Bermuda did manage to produce a so-called Joint Declaration, which was proposed on April 26, 1943, and stated that the assembled Allied parties would, "at the termination of this war, admit to their territories all of their nationals who may have been displaced by the war into other countries." Pursuant to this, they promised to "ensure such conditions . . . as will enable all such persons, of whatever nationality, to return to their homes after the war."[55] The ideas of prewar homes and postwar homes were made one.[56] This statement was subject to further scrutiny after it was approved by both the Americans and, six months later, the Soviets. After many months of questions and answers, the Soviet government approved the statement written in Bermuda only in late November 1943.

Bermuda did not alleviate the plight of European Jews. And the timing of this failure deserves notes. While most Polish Jews (in both the Generalgouvernment and eastern areas of interwar Poland that had been taken over by the Nazis in the wake of Operation Barbarossa) had been murdered by March 1943, millions of Jews remained alive in Europe.[57] Even as the Warsaw Ghetto went up in flames in May 1943, hope remained for Europe's Jews, especially those living outside of occupied Poland. In a special pamphlet published by the British Section of the World Jewish Congress in July 1943, they urged the United Nations to fulfill immediate measures because they still believed that "more might be done, and can be done now, to save European Jewry from extermination."[58] Larger interventions, however, did not ensue. Furthermore, after the Bermuda Conference, it remained unclear which organization would have authority over refugees.[59] As Allied diplomats left the British Overseas Territory, another called the Conference on Food and Agriculture assembled from May 18 to June 3, 1943, under the auspices of the United Nations. At this conference, an "Interim Commission" was established that "immediately set about the task of preparing the framework for a permanent and genuinely international organization in its allotted field."[60] And out of this initiative, the United Nations Relief and Rehabilitation Administration coalesced.

Back to New York: The American Emergency Committee for Zionist Affairs, June 1943

Chaim Weizmann had many thoughts on June 1, 1943, but none of them directly related to the imminent conclusion of the Conference on Food and Agriculture. His depression was palpable, and he bared his deepest regrets to the AECZA assembled in New York on that day. The disappointing results that had issued from the Bermuda Conference dovetailed with the dismal news of death coming out of occupied Poland. The Warsaw Ghetto was no more.[61] The largest center of Polish Jewish culture and life had become ground zero of a battle between Polish Jews and the occupying Nazis. And when Chaim Weizmann spoke, he responded to this crisis of epic proportions with anger and disbelief.

Due to leave America after a yearlong stay, Weizmann availed himself of the opportunity to offer "a few summary remarks." And so, he began to speak frankly about the state of the Zionist movement and the fate of European Jews. Both were imperiled. Weizmann viewed the situation in the Zionist movement with the utmost gravity. The fact, he declared, that "European Jewry [was] being decimated imposes quite different problems. Where will the millions of Jewish come from who are to go to Palestine?[62] . . . There may be, perhaps a million or a million and half Jews left to emigrate but the wisdom of talking in very large figures seems questionable."[63] Aware of the suppression of the Warsaw Ghetto Uprising and other reports filtering slowly out of Europe, Weizmann lamented that most of his prospective Palestinian émigrés had been killed. Weizmann was "sure of one thing: the old methods and slogans and clichés have gone never to return because the position is changing and Zionist organizations all over the world must make up their minds that new methods must be sought." He had little hope that American Jews would make aliyah or that the British would relax immigration restrictions. Since the destruction of the Second Temple in 70 CE, the Jews had never "faced so tragic a period." Dr. Weizmann, due to depart the United States imminently, would leave with "with a heavy heart."[64]

The jubilation that had wreathed Weizmann with the passing of the May 1942 Biltmore Resolution had evaporated. That accomplishment should be understood as a "symbol" and a "flag" but not necessarily practical. As European Jewry could not provide enough immigrants to populate Palestine, "Zionists must continue to build, infiltrate and expand industrially and economically without expecting millions of Jews to come." Rather than dwell in naive dreams that a Jewish commonwealth could immediately come into being after the end of hostilities, he deemed it necessary to characterize the Biltmore Resolution as "impractical." Moreover, "the fact that the Jews have been allowed to disappear and there was no reaction to it or to the Bermuda Conference is depressing." In summation, as far as the Jews were concerned, "Hitler has won the war," and Hitler's "poison has spread deep."[65]

Weizmann's frank comments elicited a variety of responses, including a notable one from Nahum Goldmann. He emphatically disagreed with Weizmann's characterization of the Biltmore Program and still "believed there was a good chance of even the eldest among the Zionist leaders seeing its implementation." In Goldmann's eyes, the Biltmore plan remained a "practical program for this generation and at this particular juncture of Jewish history." The main uncertainty from the Biltmore Program remained the question of which step should be taken first—namely, should the establishment of a commonwealth or the initiation of emigration constitute the greatest priority? When asked by a member of the State Department which platitude of the Biltmore Program he would immediately choose, Goldmann replied "that he would ask for the immigration of half a million Jews in the two years immediately after the war."[66] He strongly believed that the US State Department and Great Britain "would accede to the demand for the immediate immigration of half a million Jews" before they would endorse the creation of a Jewish commonwealth.[67]

Concerning debates regarding which Jews should move toward Palestine, Goldmann provided a concrete resolution. In general, he considered "the dispute about the number of Jews to immigrate to Palestine ridiculous." Quite simply, "the formula should be that all those Jews who have been uprooted from their countries and have to be cared for immediately after the Armistice, should be assisted by the UN." The "uprooted" Jews "should be forced neither to return to their countries of origin, nor to be dispersed." Succinctly, if individual states or the community of the United Nations inquired what the "Zionist demands will be step by step," Goldmann recommended that the AECZA pronounce demands "coached in his formulation for immigration." Directly recapturing Weisgal and Weizmann's words from the end of December 1942, Goldmann reminded his colleagues that there would be a "tremendous job of housing, feeding and transportation which, if successful will lay the basis for the demands for a self-governing Commonwealth."[68] In Goldmann's assessment, the immediate emigration of Jewish refugees should be the primary demand for all Zionists. And most importantly for our analysis, the relief bodies of the United Nations—which had not even been fully formed yet— should, in part, finance this emigration.

Goldmann's "empirical Zionism" found acceptance among the assembled participants. The specific demand linking UN support for postwar Jewish refugees with transit toward Palestine that Goldmann delineated at the AECZA meeting in June 1943 would soon resonate among the members of another office committee, that of the World Jewish Congress. In this way, Goldmann served as a link between discussions among prominent Zionist-leaning leaders and WJC members, some of whom harbored conflicting views regarding their organization's support for mass Jewish migration to Palestine. The sharing of formulas would not be immediate, however. At the first meeting of the United Nations Relief and Rehabilitation Administration, the WJC would endorse calls for a Jewish state in Palestine and unfettered migration there, but in more abstract terms.

Just a few weeks after the conclusion of the Conference on Food and Agriculture and the June 1 AECZA meeting when Nahum Goldmann adopted Weizmann's formula as his own, conversations about the administration of refugees continued among the top diplomats in American circles. On June 25, 1943, US Secretary of State Cordell Hull wrote to John Gilbert Winant, the US ambassador in the United Kingdom, with news about how this new UN-sponsored relief organization UNRRA would administer relief and rehabilitation to the refugees after the conflict. Preliminarily, UNRRA agreed to maintain refugees "until the end of the war" after they arrived "at place of refuge." At the end of the war, refugees could "return to their homes" or "be transferred to places of permanent residence."[69] In this way the concept of home began to broaden. It was still unclear how UNRRA would deal with all refugee situations and when the Intergovernmental Committee for Refugees would assume control over the fate of individual refugees who could not (for a variety of reasons) return "home," and it would remain so at UNRRA's inaugural meeting in Atlantic City and until late 1946, as chapter 5 details.[70] While the head of the Intergovernmental Committee for Refugees, Myron Taylor, did not travel to southern New Jersey, hundreds of other diplomats, observers, and nongovernmental organization members made the journey and walked the famous boardwalk. At least one of them had jurisdictional boundaries between refugee agencies at the forefront of his mind: Arieh Tartakower.

ARIEH TARTAKOWER AND HIS WORK FOR THE WORLD JEWISH CONGRESS: NOVEMBER 1943–MARCH 1944

Arieh Tartakower got things done. He did so as a widely published sociologist in the 1930s. He did so as an editor and editorialist at *NT* in New York City in the first half of the 1940s. And in his leadership role in the World Jewish Congress, he did so across continents between the fall of 1943 and the spring of 1944 and, as we will see, beyond that. In fact, when Tartakower traveled away from New York, as he did in the winter and spring of 1944, many decisions of the Office Committee were stalled until he returned. In November 1943, soon after receiving new intelligence from Ignacy Schwarzbart in London, which indicated that he and the WJC should prepare for the complete annihilation of Polish Jewry, he traveled from New York City to Atlantic City to get things done in a new setting: the first meeting of the United Nations Relief and Rehabilitation Administration.

At the First Meeting of UNRRA in Atlantic City

Armed with pamphlets, lists of visiting dignitaries, and the desire to speak with as many relevant parties as possible within a busy three-week period, Tartakower arrived in southern New Jersey twice in November 1943 eager to disseminate WJC plans for a postwar Jewish program. But the wheel of history could not turn, to hark back to an editorial he wrote in 1941, more quickly than his circumstances allowed. The forces bringing UNRRA into existence as a functioning, transnational relief organization moved slowly—frustratingly slowly. Even a few months after this first meeting, the WJC and Tartakower himself had few guarantees that their demands and basic Jewish "postwar" needs would be met by UNRRA.

Unlike Foreign Minister Jan Masaryk of the Czechoslovak government-in-exile and Vice Premier Jan Kwapiński of the Polish government-in-exile, Tartakower did not attend the exclusive meeting at the White House on November 9, 1943, when representatives from forty-four nations signed the covenant committing them to participation in UNRRA. He could attend the inaugural meeting in Atlantic City as an observer and representative of the WJC.[71] In the days leading up to his departure southward, the Office Committee of the WJC had adopted guidelines that would inspire both UNRRA representatives in their work toward "a democratic world order."[72] Besides supporting the establishment of a "new international structure based on the Four Freedoms and the Atlantic Charter" and an International Bill of Rights, the WJC had specific guidance for the new body regarding the rights of refugees.[73] "All refugees, deportees and other victims of Axis persecution" should be allowed to "return to their places of de facto residence and to the opportunities of which they were deprived . . . if they desire to do so." These victims had a right to indemnification, and, finally, "appropriate measures should be taken in preparation for the restoration of normal conditions to expedite the reintegration of all sections of the population into the economic life" of liberated countries.[74] Jews were thus encouraged to return to Poland, Czechoslovakia, Hungary, Germany, and other European destinations. Finally, the first part of the WJC proposal ended with an important condition. The Office Committee recommended that UNRRA delegates devote special attention "to the distinctive Jewish problems created by the policy of extermination of the Jewish people, ruthlessly carried out by the Axis authorities and their accomplices" during the war.[75] To solve the special problems facing postwar Jewry, their unique status as Hitler's preeminent victims was to be established within UNRRA policies.

Tartakower's effort to secure a special status for Jews and publicize the Jewish tragedy at UNRRA's first official meeting stemmed from his belief that the uniqueness of Jewish suffering had to be recognized by this international body. In a July 1943 letter to Jan Stańczyk, minister of labor in the Polish government-in-exile, Tartakower outlined his general plans for the yet-to-be-announced "International Conference concerning relief after the war which will probably take place during September of this year."[76] Tartakower expressed his desire to have one representative of Polish Jewry included in the Polish delegation. He explained that "this has nothing to do with any tendency on the part of the Polish Jews to segregate themselves."[77] Instead, the WJC understood "that the Jewish populations suffered much more during the present war than all other nations and that, therefore, relief activities for it must necessarily have a special character." A few months later in October 1943, Tartakower conferred with prime minister of the Polish government-in-exile Stanisław Mikołajczyk and Vice Premier Jan Kwapiński via telegram.[78] Again, Tartakower wanted to ensure that the Polish delegation to Atlantic City included an official Jewish representative or, in the least desirable case, paid heed to the special situation of Polish Jews specifically and Jews overall.

Tartakower was not alone in his lobbying. In an aide-mémoire published on November 1943 with the support of the WJC and distributed at the UNRRA meeting in Atlantic City, two members of the Czechoslovak Jewish Representative Committee (an affiliate committee of the World Jewish Congress) elaborated on the distinctiveness of the Jewish problem. The writers, Frederick Fried and Hugo Perutz, noted that it was incorrect to assume "that a social and economic order based on democratic principles would automatically provide the benefits of relief and economic reconstruction to Jews and non-Jews alike." In fact, those "who so regard Jewish postwar problems are not being realistic enough to evaluate the basic cultural and economic differences affecting the Jews, which require that these people be given special attention to the occupied and war-stricken countries."[79] The years-long Nazi program and pogroms meant that "a clear recognition of the partly basic and partly gradual differences [between Jews and non-Jews] is imperative." At a most basic level, "Jews are receiving far less foods than the other elements of the population." For these reasons, Fried and Perutz recommended that "an expert should be delegated" to the UNRRA conference, and it would be "the task of that expert to plan and to prepare," in collaboration with the newly established administration of the organization, a "program in the interest of our unfortunate brethren who are yearning for their deliverance from plight and suffering that was inflicted on them by Nazi oppressors, the common enemy of mankind."[80] The proposals that Fried and Perutz offered in the aide-mémoire dovetailed nicely with the aforementioned plan that the leadership of the World Jewish Congress proposed. Published around the same time as Perutz and Fried's report, the WJC's plan demanded that "a representative entitled to speak for the whole of the Jewish people and recognized as such" should be "constituted."[81]

Alongside the demand for a (vague) Jewish body interfacing with national and international actors, the WJC Executive Committee Platform advocated for the creation of another sovereign entity that was distinctly Jewish in nature: a Jewish commonwealth in Palestine opened by the British for immigration.[82] Moreover, echoing the platform of the Biltmore Conference, the "Jewish Agency should be vested with control of immigration in Palestine and with the necessary authority for upbuilding the country." In sum, "Palestine [should] be established as a Jewish commonwealth" and "integrated in the structure of the new democratic world." Furthermore, "an indispensable element in the implementation of this policy is the recognition of the right of every Jew who desires to settle in Palestine to emigrate and to take his possessions with him."[83] Three days into UNRRA's first official convention in Atlantic City, Tartakower submitted an official memorandum to the leaders of the organization that mirrored the document Fried and Perutz had written and included this general language on Palestine. Jewish representatives from seventeen different countries endorsed this official document.[84] The document did not, however, clarify who would pay for the movement of Jews toward Palestine or how those Jews would negotiate the complex journey from Europe across the Mediterranean. In short, Goldmann's formula equalizing the uprooted Jews of Europe with the new emigrants to the Jewish portions of Mandate Palestine had not yet pierced the WJC's more general platform.

The fortnight-long inaugural session of UNRRA marked an important milestone in Allied cooperation and provided hundreds of delegates the opportunity to meet each other and recently appointed members of the organization's hierarchy. For Arieh Tartakower, it represented four days of frenzy spread over two short visits that added up to disappointment. A report he submitted detailing work he did during his second two-day stint, for example, bursts with activity and meetings with important figures such as Jan Masaryk, representatives from the Polish delegation, and a member of the British team.[85] Despite a full schedule, Tartakower tended to evaluate his work in negative terms. He had failed to meet face-to-face with the Soviet ambassador. He had failed to broaden the definition of the war's victims. And he had failed to ensure that UNRRA's mandate and work would reflect the special nature of the Jewish tragedy.[86]

Two particular failures seem most problematic for our narrative. First, UNRRA representatives refused to create a special status for Jewish war victims in their foundational documents. Upon receiving memoranda from the WJC and the Jewish Labor Committee, UNRRA counsel general Herbert Lehman passed both documents on to the Subcommittee on Social Welfare Policies, "because its jurisdiction also includes UNRRA relations with voluntary relief agencies."[87] There in committee, chairman Jan Kwapiński and secretary Harry Greenstein—a native of Baltimore who worked for the Associated Jewish Charities—debated how to respond to these two requests. The majority of the committee decided that "appropriate plans for dealing with special Jewish problems can be worked out within each afflicted nation—and that for UNRRA to undertake to give them extraordinary treatment might, in the long run, react to the Jews' own disadvantage." In other committees, the exceptional discrimination faced by Europe's Jews was recognized, notably by the Norwegian minister of reconstruction Anders Frihagen.[88] Of course, open-ended phrasing emerging from committee meetings did not preclude the possibility of distinctive treatment, but the debate over granting Jews "unique and special" status did not seem to point in Tartakower's favor.

Second, in the wake of the Atlantic City assemblage, UNRRA's scope of activity was not confirmed vis-à-vis the scope of the Intergovernmental Committee on Refugees (IGCR). It remained unclear how people unable or unwilling to be repatriated to their former "countries of residence" would be supported. As the conference drew to a close, Sir George Rendel, a member of the British delegation, noted that while UNRRA "will cooperate with the Intergovernmental Committee on Refugees in seeking the repatriation of exiled Jews . . . UNRRA could not force governments to take back aliens."[89] The committee report stated that the Intergovernmental Committee on Refugees "has long dealt with those persons who have been obliged to leave their homes for reasons of race, religion or political belief." After the war, "UNRRA will assist in the care and repatriation of such of these persons as can, and are willing to return to their countries of origin or of former residence." Another body, the IGCR, would be responsible for finding "places of settlement" for those who "cannot or do not desire to be so repatriated.[90]

There might be a gap in the timing of these two distinctive initiatives. Regarding "the care of... those refugees as cannot be repatriated," it would be the "responsibility of the relief organs of UNRRA to assist, for a reasonable period," those who did not wish to return home. UNRRA would support these refugees who could not be repatriated "until the Inter-Governmental Committee [was] prepared to remove them to new places of settlement." Thanks to the efforts of Director-General Lehman, the "UNRRA's willingness to undertake a large share of the responsibility in repatriating refugees" was clearly stated in the official communiqué.[91] This differed remarkably from the original draft Sir George Rendel wrote. The first manifestation of this document "gave almost the whole responsibility to the Intergovernmental Committee on Refugees," whose leader, Myron Taylor, did not even receive an invitation to Atlantic City.

Writing about the first UNRRA meeting a few weeks later in December 1943, Aryeh Leon Kubowitzki alerted his colleagues in the Office Committee to the jurisdictional space separating UNRRA and the IGCR.[92] In response to this jurisdictional gap, Kubowitzki asked, "What if the IGCR states that it does not have to find new places of settlement for people who have been deported?" Would these people be "returned to their countries of origin or of former residence?" Kubowitzki suggested that the attention of the State Department be called to this "discrepancy." In short, the WJC should suggest that the "mandate of the IGCR be defined by the terms adopted at Atlantic City and should read as follows: 'and transport those persons who have been obligated to leave their homes for reasons of race, religion and political beliefs.'"[93] A booklet the WJC produced called "The Importance of UNRRA," written in 1943 but published in 1944, zeroed in on the same problem that Kubowitzki noticed. Repatriation, it noted, "is one of the most complicated and delicate questions of relief work."[94] And yet, UNRRA and IGCR representatives struggled to outline how repatriation for the Jews and other refugees or "displaced people" across the globe would unfold and be subsidized, especially for those who could not or would not return "home," at this inaugural meeting and afterward.[95]

Reflecting on the much-anticipated eleven-day meeting in the November 1943 issue of *NT*, Tartakower pled for global understanding of the Jewish plight amid the war's terrible destruction.[96] The Wehrmacht's advance and occupation combined with the German extermination policy had unleashed "millions and tens of millions who will have to be brought back to their homes, brought back to health, given roofs over their heads as well as a rational basis for their future." It would take a dozen years, Tartakower predicted, to complete this work. But this daunting European reality paled in comparison to the Jewish reality. "Our institutions, our schools, municipalities and synagogues have all been destroyed completely," and "we became strangers" not just as "individuals but as a nation." The "great Jewish misfortune" demanded "appropriate cooperation." Better times could then ensue, Tartakower suggested. He did not, notably, suggest that better times could ensue in Palestine. Despite being disappointed by the results of the WJC's lobbying in Atlantic City that November, Tartakower did not dismiss a collective Jewish future in Europe. He obviously and sadly did not know that by November 1943, with the exception of Jews in hiding and a relatively small number used for forced labor, the so-called Generalgouvernment was basically *judenrein*. Jakob Apenszlak did not know this either.

The first UNRRA conference in Atlantic City propelled Apenszlak back to a familiar idea: creating a congress of Polish Jews to speak on behalf of the entire Polish Jewish community. Apenszlak predicted that the "greatest Jewish concentration" would "remain in the Polish lands" and that Jews would need help from the "victorious democracies."[97] Funding could help "increase the population potential of Jews in Poland" by subsidizing "the repatriation movement of refugees who managed to survive the war in the countries of asylum." Apenszlak could not assume "automatic rehabilitation of the European system after the war." There was a "danger that when planning the future world, Polish problems may be overlooked in Jewish and non-Jewish communities." To call attention to these issues, Apenszlak proposed the convocation of a "congress of Polish Jews in America, including both American Jews of Polish descent and those of Polish nationals who are in this country."

Representatives of the Bund, however, derailed Apenszlak's plans quite quickly. They thought that Apenszlak's attempt to assemble Polish Jews in America had Zionist undertones, and, once again, they were will not willing to reconcile the creation of a commonwealth in Palestine with the "full reconstruction of our life and the new rooting of Jews in Poland."[98] Apenszlak considered this claim to be "unfounded," and he admitted to not liking the Bund representation. The "essence of the Zionist ideology," Apenszlak clarified, "is the simultaneous development of Jewish foundations of national culture in the *golus* and the development of the Jewish national headquarters in Palestine." Apenszlak invited the Bund to agree to the convocation of the Congress of Polish Jewry in America to facilitate the rebuilding of Polish Jewry and securing rights in the new Poland without "reinforcing the divisions constructed of false, anti-Zionist arguments." It was yet unclear whether the Congress of Polish Jews in America would resemble Baruch Zuckerman's effort in the late 1930s. According to an announcement in

January 1945, the Program of the World Conference of Polish Jewry was set to convene on April 28, 1945, more than a year after Apenszlak first discussed the idea in *NT*.[99] Apenszlak's plan can be read alongside Tartakower's assessment of the first UNRRA conference. Whether both men embraced full-scale emigration plans toward Palestine or not, they both kept working to reroot European Jewish diasporas. And for the first few weeks of 1944, that precise work would take Arieh Tartakower away from the editorial offices of *NT* for a multiweek business trip to London. He would not contribute to the paper that he coedited for more than three months.

Amid Colleagues, Allies, and the Governments-in-Exile in London, England

After spending some time recuperating from an undisclosed medical condition, Tartakower traveled to London. He met with Jewish and non-Jewish leaders alike.[100] Regularly, he interfaced with WJC employees such as Noah Barou, A. L. Easterman, Sean Rubenstein, and Lady Reading. He met with Chaim Weizmann, who carried the WJC memorandum to the UNRRA conference in his hand during their discussion about confidential information relayed from Goldmann and Weizmann's recent conference with Churchill. Weizmann asked Tartakower about the WJC's work concerning the "rescue of European Jewry" and listened closely as Tartakower detailed information concerning rescue plans for Hungary and Romania. Also, Tartakower met with his colleagues Arnošt Frischer, the Czechoslovakian delegate to the WJC, and Ignacy Schwarzbart, the Polish Jewish delegate to the WJC. Recall that both Frischer and Schwarzbart sat on the councils of their respective governments-in-exile. And finally, he endured a four-day meeting with the leadership of the WJC in London in mid-January. There, he leveraged his role as a research fellow in the Institute of Jewish Affairs and the troves of information percolating through transnational telegraph lines as the group attempted to grasp the extent of the Jewish loss in Europe.[101]

Not surprisingly, UNRRA-related issues filled his schedule as well. Besides his work with Jewish leaders, Tartakower branched out to meet Gustav Kullman from the Intergovernmental Committee on Refugees and various UNRRA leaders, such as Fred K. Hoehler, John Henry Gorvin, and Sir Herbert Emerson. With Kullman, Tartakower discussed the situation of refugees in various countries, the rescue of Jewish children in France, planned relief activities, and relations between UNRRA and the IGCR. Tartakower's last talking point harked back to discussions regarding the management of refugees held in Atlantic City just a few weeks prior.[102] A few weeks after the Atlantic City conference, the scope of both organizational bodies still remained undefined. So, in London, Tartakower sought to delineate which organization would control the various aspects of refugee policy.[103]

This proved increasingly difficult once Tartakower and his colleagues realized that the words promulgated in Atlantic City were not necessarily decisive and the machinery of UNRRA remained unassembled well after its inaugural meeting. Still, Tartakower maintained that "Jewish advisors" could be appointed in a "semi-official standing to serve as a liaison officials between UNRRA and the organized Jewish people."[104] Director-General Emerson, however, had "some doubts whether it is worthwhile to have a special position granted to private organizations" and lobbied instead for direct communication channels between UNRRA and national governments. Emerson did seem open to Tartakower's input at other junctures. He asked Tartakower "to transmit to him the final text of the respective resolutions adopted in Atlantic City." Upon reviewing the WJC's documentations, Emerson revealed that "he may be inclined to reconsider the entire problem" of Jewish refugees during and after the current war.[105] Tartakower's interactions with Emerson and others from UNRRA and the IGCR in the early months of 1944 indicated how ad hoc refugee and relief policies remained. The Atlantic City conference represented a watershed moment of sorts, but the discussions held there did not cement policies regarding the power of nonstate actors and the position of Jewish advisors. As Tartakower noted in his final report, "in the field of UNRRA much more must still be done."

In addition to meeting officials in UNRRA and IGCR hierarchies, Tartakower convened with individual governments-in-exile concerning the relief and rehabilitation work that would potentially commence on their sovereign territories upon the war's conclusion. Tartakower wanted governments to back certain WJC plans, such as the one to send "Jewish candidates to train relief workers" on the ground and another to disseminate Jewish aid workers into "liberated territories in cooperation with the machinery of UNRRA."[106] He spoke with Norwegian, Danish, Dutch, and Czechoslovakian bureaucrats during his ten weeks in England. More than any other government, however, Tartakower met with seemingly all the high-ranking members of the Polish government-in-exile. Tartakower spoke with these officials regarding Polish Jewry and the mass of European Jews who had been deported toward Polish territory. From Prime Minister Mikołajczyk, to Minister of the Interior Banaczyk and Minister of Foreign Affairs Romer, to Minister for Social Welfare Stańczyk, Minister of Information Kot and Minister of Reconstruction and

Peace Problems Seyda, Tartakower met with them all during his stay in England. Indeed, he felt that a "tremendous burden of work [had been] imposed upon" him.[107] But his labor paid off a bit, at least in the short term, in the form of fruitful conversations about reversing discriminating interwar laws, outlining parameters for postwar reconstruction, and helping establish a Polish-government-in-exile-backed organization to rescue Jews (called Żegota) along with his colleague Anselm Reiss.[108]

It is notable that in January 1944, the rescue of Jews remained a primary concern for Tartakower and many of the exiled government officials he encountered. Despite ghastly reports of Jewish exterminations, the majority of leaders in London held out hope that Jews from all countries could be saved. In fact, in Tartakower's assessment, public opinion in England now tended to favor doing more for the Jews in need of rescue on the continent.[109] Since hundreds of thousands of Europeans deemed Jewish by the Nuremberg Laws had been transported to former Polish territory, rescue efforts engineered by Tartakower and the WJC needed the support of the relevant member governments (such as the Belgian, French, and Czechoslovak) as well as the Poles. With personal connections and fluent Polish, Tartakower proved to be an ideal interlocutor to broker any proposed rescue efforts. For example, across a handful of meetings with Minister Stańczyk, with whom Tartakower had corresponded since the beginning of his term at the WJC, he "discussed problems of refugees in different countries" and problems of relief in Poland itself.[110] During his meetings with Polish representatives, however, Tartakower encountered a distinction that had the potential to inhibit relief efforts for Jews. Just as in Atlantic City, Tartakower had trouble convincing his contemporaries that Jews as a whole deserved special categorization.

According to Tartakower, in all of his conferences, he "spoke about all Jews of the respective countries independent of their actual citizenship," and "representatives of at least two governments, namely the Dutch and Norwegian, expressly accepted this principle."[111] Two governments proved hesitant, however, in envisioning all Jews as a distinctive collective: the Poles and the Czechs. When Tartakower discussed rescue efforts with his Polish colleagues, he "stressed the principle that help on the part of the Polish Underground is to be granted not only to Polish Jews but also to Jews deported to Poland." Accordingly, "the Polish government accepted this principle with the understanding that they will be reimbursed for expenses incurred in this work as far as non-Polish Jews are concerned."[112] Discussions with Stańczyk regarding the rescue of children mirrored this stance. If the Polish underground networks in France helped move Jewish children to safety in Spain, the "Polish government [would] be reimbursed for expenses incurred in helping children of non-Polish nationality whereas the entire expense for Polish Jewish children up to the moment of arrival in Spain will be covered by the Polish government."[113] Of course, Stańczyk wanted to imagine Jews divided into their European nationalities—paying for only Polish Jewish rescue missions directly would reduce his government's cost.

Tartakower's interaction with Ján Bečko, the Czechoslovak minister of social welfare, also revealed how problematic it could be to imagine Jews as part of a transnational collective. Talking about Jewish representation in UNRRA, Bečko asked Tartakower to "please explain to me what are the particular interests of the Jewish population in the machinery of UNRRA. Why should I make any difference between my people? There is no difference between Czechoslovak Jews and Czech Gentiles . . . why should I appoint special representative of the Jewish population?" What was obvious to Tartakower was hidden to Bečko. So Tartakower responded, "Yes, I agree with you perfectly, there is no distinction, there is no discrimination by the Czechoslovak government, but, unfortunately, Hitler does not share your views and he makes a great distinction between Czechoslovak Jews and other parts of the population of your country." Citing the memo he had submitted to the Atlantic City meeting, Tartakower noted that "because of this discrimination there will be the necessity of doing certain relief activities specially for the Jews." Bečko eventually agreed that "something must be done in order to have Jewish representation secured within the Czechoslovak sector of UNRRA," but this short interaction as well as Tartakower's interaction about Jewish children in France reveals the gulf between his thinking and that of his government-in-exile peers.[114]

During his two and half months in London, Tartakower realized that UNRRA's machinery continued to be unbuilt, that the jurisdictional divide between UNRRA and the IGCR continued to be fuzzy, and that diplomats throughout the Allied universe continued to imagine Jews in "national" terms and were not, overall, imagining Jews as a collective body deserving of specific relief or classification. On top of this, Tartakower noted in *NT* that relations between Polish Christians and Polish Jews in London were perhaps "worse than in the country before [the] war."[115] His work with Schwarzbart and Reiss did achieve some "serious results" in meetings with different governmental ministers, and there were some "signs of improvement" overall. But there remained "difficulties and complications."[116] Despite the issues he traced in his departing report that March and at a symposium held in honor of his return at the Hotel Newton in New York City on April 29, 1944, Tartakower felt that his trip had been productive. He remarked a few weeks before arriving back in

New York that "there is a feeling that something happened here in connection with our visit."[117] Something was happening back in New York as well. And soon, new language and new ideas incubating within the WJC would come to dominate policies and platforms showcased at two delayed meetings in 1944 and, arguably, challenge the modus operandi of the entire organization while altering the texture of the diaspora.

PALESTINE FIRST, DIASPORA SECOND? THE CHANGING MINDS OF THE WJC OFFICE COMMITTEE, MAY–SEPTEMBER 1944

Timing is everything. And 1944 was no exception. The WJC planned to convene their much-anticipated War Emergency Conference in May. The leadership of UNRRA anticipated that the second meeting of their organization would commence in June. Both meetings were delayed by a number of months.[118] In this interim, across the spring and summer of 1944, key tenets of the philosophy of the WJC's Office Committee and the words used to enunciate it changed. When UNRRA reassembled in September and the War Emergency Conference opened in November, men such as Nahum Goldmann, A. L. Kubowitzki, Arieh Tartakower, Zorach Warhaftig, and Maurice Perlzweig spoke less about the rootedness of the diaspora and more about the diaspora's desire to take root elsewhere. And by the late summer and fall of 1944, that elsewhere increasingly equaled but one place: Palestine. The WJC Office Committee came to vigorously support a formula equating the uprooted Jews of post–World War II Europe to the UNRRA-subsidized "repatriates" to a Jewish polity in Palestine and thus imperiled their organization's commitment to preserving the right of every Jew to live in the diaspora.

And so, members of the WJC Office Committee seized an unprecedented political opportunity to fundamentally change the demographic distribution of the Jewish people and the landscape of modern Jewish civilization. This unique political opportunity emerged out of three contexts: the increasing obviousness of the horrific Jewish tragedy in Europe, a broader revision of international norms related to both minority rights and population transfers, and, finally, the inability of Allied diplomats and statesmen to protect certain categories of persecuted Jews in evolving United Nations legislation. Cocooned within these three contexts, leaders of the WJC amended their policies regarding the reconstitution of Jewish life in east central Europe by the fall of 1944. Even without confirmed numbers of the Jewish dead and without full awareness of what surviving Jews would want in their postwar futures, this group of European

Fig. 3.2. Leaders of the World Jewish Congress, including Arieh Kubowitzki, Maurice Perlzweig, Nahum Goldmann, Stephen Wise, Arieh Tartakower, and Zorach Warhaftig, at the War Emergency Conference in Atlantic City, 1944. Photo courtesy of CriticalPast.

exiles spoke their new vocabulary with certainty at times and with doubt at others. This doubt diminished over time and was almost entirely extinguished when the situation demanded a clear commitment to the Palestinian project.

The next section of this chapter focuses on some key decisions made by members of the WJC Office Committee over the span of a few months in 1944 to substantiate the reality and sharpness of this change. First, Tartakower and others began speaking about the "many European Jews who could not return to their European homes" and eventually inserted this language in booklets and publicity destined for the second meeting of UNRRA. Second, WJC Office Committee members prioritized Palestine at key turns: in discussions about the rescue of children in May 1944, in discussions about what type of resettlement the War Refugee Board would subsidize, and in discussions about the convocation of the War Emergency Conference in April 1944. And third, they moved toward a policy steeped in the impossibility of a numerically significant, post-war Jewish diaspora in places such as Germany and beyond. A close look at two important committee-wide discussions shows this third point while exhibiting the complications inherent in this decision. Furthermore, the documents used over the next few pages bring us intimately closer to the actors in our narrative and reveal some of the emotions influencing their intellectual trajectories.

Decision: "Many" Who Would Not Return Home

After three and a half years writing for *NT* and two decades of articulating dense sociological studies in Polish, Yiddish, and Hebrew, Arieh Tartakower had something new to say on the cusp of the second scheduled (and soon to be postponed) UNRRA meeting. "Not everyone," he wrote in May 1944, "will return to Poland after the war. There are many who would like to move to another country . . . many of whom will be eager to move to our national headquarters in Palestine."[119] And so, because of this reality, UNRRA had to take decisive steps at their next meeting in Montreal that they did not take during the Atlantic City meeting in 1943. Tartakower did not want Polish Jews "to be treated like other repatriates." Instead, "they should be helped by UNRRA as well as the others. They should be protected until their departures, the costs of their journey should be covered and they should be helped to rebuild their lives." And so, the "current provisions of the UNRRA constitution must be changed so that they should take into account this fundamental and decisive point of view." Beyond the situation of Polish Jews, Tartakower demanded that the next UNRRA session must clarify whether Jews of German, Austrian, Bulgarian, and Romanian citizenship would be treated as victims or as "an enemy population." Since the first UNRRA meeting in Atlantic City, these points had not been clarified. Despite dozens of meetings in London, Washington, DC, and New York City, Tartakower and his colleagues in the WJC did not have answers to these very specific questions. This article constituted a plea for more precise legislation as well as an alert to the reading public that a problematic gulf remained in the UNRRA legal code.

This article also represents something much more consequential than perhaps meets the eye. Arieh Tartakower had not been to Poland since 1939. Almost all of the Polish Jews with whom he interacted had also spent most if not all of the war away from Polish soil. He had had little to no contact with the hundreds of thousands (the full number was not clear yet) of Polish Jews who had been deported to the Soviet Union. Since the spring of 1943, however, he had been reunited with his wife, Malvina, who had left Poland moving eastward in 1939, spent time in the Urals, and then, after the general amnesty in 1941, evacuated to Persia and Palestine. She arrived in the United States at some point before an interview with her appeared on the pages of *NT* on April 12, 1943.[120] He had, of course, interactions with other citizens of Poland and east central Europe during his ten weeks in London early in 1944. He had access to research conducted by the WJC's in-house Institute of Jewish Affairs. He had letters from occupied Poland, transcripts of meetings with secret couriers such as Jan Karski, and access to the Polish government-in-exile and information that they would share with him. And yet, what he had and what he did not have begat this profound statement in May 1944: "Not everyone will want to return to Poland after the war ... *many* would like to move to another country ... *many* ... will be eager to move ... to Palestine" (emphasis mine).[121]

Of course, echoes of this idea predated Tartakower's article. For instance, speaking at the War Emergency Session of the American Jewish Congress on May 18, 1942, director of the Institute for Jewish Affairs Dr. Jacob Robinson harbingered Tartakower's more drastic prediction in a speech entitled "Problems of Jewish Reconstruction after the War." He was more careful in attributing opinions to others and open to multiple destinations. "It is, of course," Robinson conceded, "extremely difficult to predict how the people of Europe will feel toward the Jews when the war is over. As a matter of fact, we know little enough regarding their present attitudes; the reports that reach us are conflicting."[122] Regardless of this lack of knowledge, Robinson continued, "whatever the efforts that will be made to reintegrate the greatest possible number of Jews into the economic and social life of their respective countries, it is safe to assume that there will still be great masses of Jews who, because of age, the condition of their health, or for social or psychological reasons, may not fit into the new picture," and so "provision must be made for them." Specifically, "those who may be forced to emigrate, or desire to do so will need the assistance of intergovernmental and private Jewish and non-Jewish bodies." Where would they go? Robinson cited many destinations: Latin America, Palestine, and other "underdeveloped territories for Jewish colonization for the eventual purpose of forming Jewish settlements outside of Palestine." In May 1944, Tartakower was much more certain about what the "many" wanted and where they wanted to go. He was also certain that UNRRA, the IGCR, or an amalgam of both would pay for those who needed to be repatriated elsewhere, even though a May 1944 meeting with an UNRRA official revealed that neither organization had the necessary funds to subsidize this.[123]

Regardless of exactly how Arieh Tartakower arrived at this precise conclusion more than one year before V-E Day, his words echoed throughout the WJC in 1944 and into the future. In fact, this idea theorizing that Polish Jews and other east central European Jews, especially those of German or Austrian or other Axis citizenship, would prefer to move to Palestine instead of returning to their prewar homes or interwar citizenships became one keystone of a broader argument casting European Jews away from Europe. It echoed sentiments expressed by Weisgal and Weizmann at the December 1942 meetings of the American Emergency Committee for Zionist Affairs and nicely complemented the formula that Goldmann had made his own by June 1943. In fact, it made the equation of the uprooted European Jews with the Jewish settlers in Palestine even more convincing. This movement was something the uprooted themselves personally desired. And moving forward in 1944, 1945, and 1946, Tartakower's precise language appeared in official WJC literature distributed at the UNRRA meeting in Montreal (which we consider in the next section of this chapter), in meeting minutes of the WJC Office Committee between 1944 and 1946, and in *NT* articles alike.

Iterations of Tartakower's May 1944 words also continued and appeared in more high-profile contexts. On November 13, 1944, Tartakower wrote to Major General G. H. Hilldring, the director of the Civil Affairs Division in the US War Department. As he estimated that one or two million Jews remained in Europe, Tartakower welcomed a recent statement declaring that "Jewish displaced persons, regardless of their former nationality, are considered as friendly elements by the military authorities and are treated accordingly."[124] He stressed to General Hilldring the "fundamental difference" between the Jewish DPs and the DPs of other nations: the Jews were "scared to return" to their former homes. Tartakower made a similar argument before Earl Harrison on March 20, 1945, soon after US president Roosevelt had appointed Harrison as representative on the Intergovernmental Commission on Refugees. After the war, Tartakower explained, nearly 350,000 Jews of interwar German, Austrian, Hungarian, Romanian, and Polish citizenships would fall into the category of displaced persons "who cannot or do not desire to be repatriated" to their country of prewar citizenship. An "overwhelming majority of these people will certainly wish to go to Palestine," Tartakower continued, and "it is the duty of the Intergovernmental Committee to enable them to do so with the close cooperation of the Jewish agency for Palestine."[125]

A few months after Tartakower met with Harrison and soon after the latter submitted his famous report on displaced persons to President Harry S. Truman, Tartakower again raised the issue of "persons who on account of political reasons do not intend to return to their home-countries" at the third meeting of UNRRA in London. Within this group, "the first and foremost victims would be Jewish displaced persons, whose reluctance to be repatriated has nothing to do with the political reasons, but is in the majority of cases dictated by their will to go to Palestine."[126] And finally, at the first session of the General Assembly of the United Nations in November 1946, a WJC memo said the following about 250,000 displaced Jews in Germany, Austria, and Italy: "It is universally recognized," the memo argues, "that Jewish displaced persons and refugees do not wish to return to their countries of origin and, indeed, that repatriation would inflict unbearable psychological hardship on them."[127]

What was universally recognized by the end of 1946 was pinpointed by Tartakower in a Polish-language newspaper article in May 1944. As far as I can tell, he is one of the first high-ranking members of the World War II–era exile community to publicly circulate this particular idea, which became a central component describing the postwar desires of surviving Jews to a popular readership.[128] Simultaneously, however, Tartakower continued his gesturing to the rerooting of the diaspora in Poland. A June 27, 1944, issue of *NT* contains an article in which Tartakower prophesied that "we will need to build a Jewish life on the Polish lands, strong and dignified, based on the principles of equality and cooperation of all peoples with no difference to faith and nationality" regardless of "how many Polish Jews will see" the war end.[129] It was not a dichotomous switch. But, increasingly, Tartakower and his colleagues prioritized the center over the diaspora, essentially prioritizing the "many" Jews that could not return home over those that potentially could.

Decision: Palestine for the Uprooted Children in Portugal and the War Refugee Board

May 1944 marked an important threshold for one particular group of surviving Jews, those unattached children who had managed to make it to Portugal.[130] The WJC connection to this group began near the end of 1943, when the French Resistance informed WJC officials about a secret operation to hide Jewish children in private homes and Catholic institutions in the areas of France under German control.[131] After learning about this plan, the WJC followed the movements and subsidized the care of thousands of Jewish children. Frequently, these children had Polish citizenship. Emissaries of the World Jewish Congress found these children throughout 1944.[132] The WJC Office in Geneva helped secure passage for them to neutral countries such as Sweden, Switzerland, and Portugal. In Portugal, government authorities agreed to let three hundred of these children in the country at a given time. Thus, Portugal's outlet to the sea meant that if visas could be secured from other states, these children could get even further from the Nazi menace, and others could be brought in after the first set departed.[133] The safety of these children, however, became politicized in the same month that Tartakower published his "many" article in *NT*.[134] One destination would be privileged above all others regardless of the time it demanded: Palestine.

On May 13, 1944, Kubowitzki disseminated a letter and an attached memo to his colleagues on the Office Committee from Isaac Weissmann, the WJC representative in Portugal.[135] Weissmann had sent this letter to Arieh Tartakower in London on January 25, 1944, and now the letter had been received in New York. It demanded an answer. Weissmann's inquiry was both simple and complicated: would the WJC contact UNRRA and secure their support for the transportation of upward of thirty-five thousand Jews from Portugal to Palestine? Earlier that January, Weissmann had overseen the successful departure of a ship from Lisbon to Palestine carrying 750 uprooted Jews.[136] In the wake of this event, "interest for Palestine immigration" increased "everywhere." Drawing on this enthusiasm, Weissmann saw a unique opportunity to attribute the thirty-five thousand open emigration spots available for Palestine to Jews that had managed to arrive in Portugal. He needed funding, however, and lots of it.

"Private charity funding," he admitted, "cannot cover the enormous expenses involved."[137] And since this movement of people displaced by war technically fell under the purview of UNRRA, this organization was responsible for "guaranteeing the means [of] large-scale emigration." Moreover, if UNRRA started transporting these refugees now, an important precedent would be set. "If we do not start now to pave the way," Weissman offered, "the end of hostilities will find us unprepared." Even though the "details of this task naturally belong to the work of the Jewish Agency," Weissmann felt that the "World Jewish Congress is the body that can best do the preparatory work in respect to building the basis on which to organise a great *Aliyah*." In the memorandum draft attached to his letter, Weissmann stated his philosophy succinctly: "It must be the task of the World Jewish Congress to find the ways and means for a close cooperation with UNRRA for tackling this immense task of repatriating the Jews that survive the disaster."[138] Weissmann was careful to acknowledge the problematic overlaps between the Jewish Joint Distribution Committee (which he classified as non-Zionist), the Jewish Agency, and what he was asking the WJC to do.[139] For Weissmann, the WJC could be a proactive force for subsidized migration toward Palestine.[140]

One day after Weissmann's letter and his draft memorandum fluttered through the WJC offices, the Office Committee assembled to consider his request, which predated their meeting by more than three months.[141] They did not take long to issue their opinion. First, the WJC planned to transfer $10,000 to Weissmann in a few days. Second, Weissmann was to be informed "that even if this means a delay of a few weeks, our preference is Palestine for the children rescued in Portugal . . . this is also our attitude towards the War Refugee Board."[142] And so the WJC emphasized their "clear preference" to direct the movement of Jews away from Europe toward Palestine above all other destinations.[143] This new line of policy regarding the movement of refugees resurfaced two months later with regard to refugees in Switzerland. On July 6, 1944, the Office Committee suggested that Riegner in Geneva be "informed by cable of our line of policy which is opposed to any action which may divert the refugees from concentrating their efforts on going to Palestine."[144] When they could not choose Palestine, the Office Committee chose separation. For instance, a majority of the committee endorsed a special school specifically for Polish Jewish children uprooted to Kenya and Tanganyika where they could have a "Jewish education" separate from other Polish-speaking citizens.[145] Soon, they were interfacing with governmental officials to further these decisions in more official ways.

Three weeks after the Office Committee decided to prioritize movement toward Palestine for those Jews in Lisbon and almost one year after the meeting of the American Emergency Committee for Zionist Affairs where he reiterated the formula linking uprooted Jews to Palestinian Jews, Goldmann sat down with other leading members of the WJC to discuss domestic developments in refugee policies—namely, the January 1944 creation of the War Refugee Board. Recently, Goldmann had visited John W. Pehle, a former US Treasury lawyer who had become the executive director of the War Refugee Board soon after its creation.[146] Kubowitzki also shared meeting rooms with Pehle in the War Refugee Board's short existence. During this particular meeting, Pehle showed Goldmann "a draft of a statement which read that America will be ready to take refugees."[147] Such a change in US policy toward European refugees should arguably have been greeted with enthusiasm. Goldmann quickly registered his disagreement with the War Refugee Board's proposed proclamation. He told Pehle that the part of the draft stating that "after the war these refugees will be returned to their countries of origin" was problematic. Furthermore, Goldmann stood "opposed to the formulation of the draft since a possibility must be secured for refugees to go to Palestine after the war." Relaxed US immigration quotas might preclude Europe's Jews from choosing new postwar homes in Palestine. Therefore, Goldmann suggested that a draft "be prepared in a new form securing a possibility for the refugees to go to other countries wherever they wish."[148] This demand dovetailed nicely with the decision about the destination of those Jews marooned in Portugal. Palestine increasingly gravitated toward the center of the WJC's thoughts, even when they spoke about the convocation of their upcoming War Emergency Congress.

Decision: Palestinian Jewry and the War Emergency Congress

On Saturday, April 22, roughly one month before the much-anticipated WJC-sponsored War Emergency Conference would convene, Goldmann wondered if the WJC should postpone the meeting. At times simply calling it "the Conference," the leadership of the WJC had thought about convening an international event bringing together all constituent countries of the World Jewish Congress throughout most of 1944. Once it became clear that the Allied cause was gaining unquestionable ground and that an organization-wide gathering would help clarify the WJC's postwar visions, members such as Baruch Zuckerman and Maurice Perlzweig started suggesting venues and making deposits. The meeting was designed to assemble as many country delegations as possible and represent the second official international gathering of the organization after its inaugural meeting in Geneva in 1936, and it had already been delayed twice. Now Goldmann wondered if it should be delayed again on account of the Palestinian delegation. Goldmann was "of the opinion that it was impossible for the Palestinian Delegation to come in time."[149]

Zuckerman asked if air priorities could be secured for the delegation. Goldmann said they could not. Perlzweig weighed in as "as strongly in favor of postponement . . . in view of the fact that the most important and most active part of World Jewry—the Palestinian Jewry—would not be represented at the Conference, but has asked for its postponement." Tartakower agreed with Perlzweig and offered another reason as well: "It is his impression that [they] are not ready with our preparations." Argentina also asked for postponement. Zuckerman, always the contrarian, was strongly against postponement. If it was postponed, Zuckerman feared, the WJC "shall have no Conference at all or only after the war." If the WJC could be sure "of the Conference for October, it would be otherwise, but we cannot be sure of it because of the greatest military operation in history." Dr. Robinson disagreed. "A conference without Palestinian Jewry," he said, "is of no importance and unrealistic. This would mean that the best remnants of the destroyed Jewish communities—if not in numbers then in quality—could not come over from Palestine too." Kate Knopfmacher, an important administrator in the WJC's New York Office who sometimes voiced her opinions as she took notes, agreed with Zuckerman that the conference should move forward. The WJC "would lose prestige by postponing the Conference for a third time." Dr. Robinson's reasons, she admitted, were impressive but should have been raised six months ago. Robinson retorted that he was "never consulted."

Robinson had a way of interjecting a snippy comment when emotions warmed up. The meeting minutes impart the tension. Next, Perlzweig assumed the floor again. A rump conference would cause the WJC to lose prestige. "Palestine," he declared, "is more important for us than England." The WJC should issue a statement affirming conference preparations but publicizing that both Palestine and Argentina had "asked for postponement." Goldmann insisted that they call Wise and discuss postponement with him over the phone. It was done, and the matter was settled. The conference was delayed until the end of August 1944. It would be delayed again and opened in November. When it did open, as Apenszlak's editorial from the first pages of this chapter revealed, Palestine and policy toward it remained the most important topic of conversation among those assembled, which included a delegation of Palestinian Jews.

Discussions concerning the uprooted European Jews in Lisbon, the plans of the War Refugee Board, and which delegation's attendance should define the War Emergency Conference demonstrate the growing importance of Palestine in the collective thinking of the World Jewish Congress' Office Committee. The decisions that I focus on in this particular subsection should not, however, lead us to believe that the east central European diaspora instantly became inconsequential or that dual commitments to Palestine and life elsewhere instantaneously evaporated. Ten days after the WJC selected Palestine as the preferred destination for uprooted Jews in Lisbon, for instance, Arieh Tartakower challenged his peers on another decision concerning halutz-inspired education. "Doesn't this topic," he questioned, "belong under the purview of the Jewish Agency and not the WJC?"[150] In June, Perlzweig promised, despite his vigorous pro-Palestine sentiments, that the diaspora still mattered even if minority rights did not.[151] Office Committee members continued to interface with east central European leaders in exile such as Jan Masaryk and Jan Stańczyk to ensure that official representatives to UNRRA would invoke Jewish themes as they spoke more generally. One particular meeting with Prime Minister Stanisław Mikołajczyk of the Polish government-in-exile captures the complexity of WJC demands.

Tartakower, Goldmann, and Wise united to meet with Mikołajczyk in mid-June 1944.[152] First, the trio spoke on behalf of the Delegation of Polish Jews about a potential law mandating that the "property of Jewish individuals" and institutions "with no legal heir" remaining after the war should be turned "over to a special fund for Polish Jewry." In his report from this discussion,

Tartakower indicated that this fund should be used "for the reconstruction of Jewish life in Poland and for assisting such Jewish persons who may wish to emigrate from Poland." A "special committee of experts on behalf of the representatives of Polish Jewry" submitted a draft of this law to Mikołajczyk and asked that it be "taken up immediately by the Polish authorities."[153] Here, the contradictory ideas percolating through the minds of WJC officials resurfaced in an official conversation. Tartakower, Goldmann, and Wise would not condemn the rebuilding of Jewish life in Poland before a Polish official. However, they also would not forsake those Polish Jews who favored emigration elsewhere leaving their hiding places or returning to Polish soil.

In this way, a fund established for the Jews of Poland potentially helped some to stay and others to leave. Tartakower does not register Mikołajczyk's reaction to this proposition. Nor do we know how the plans for this fund evaporated over the next few months. What remains is clear evidence of an organization with a mission that was in flux. But the flux bent increasingly toward one particular outcome: harnessing all intellectual, logistical, and diplomatic energies to facilitate the movement of uprooted European Jews, especially those from east central Europe, toward Palestine. The documentation showcased thus far in this section and emerging out of the Office Committee suggests this shift. A close analysis of two more intimate office meetings from June 1944 provides more evidence of it. And then, in the last part of this chapter, the official words presented by the WJC at the second UNRRA meeting in Montreal and at the War Emergency Conference in Atlantic City in the late summer and fall of 1944 confirm it.

Decision, or Lack Thereof: Should German Jews Return to Germany? (June 8, 1944)

The time had come, finally, for "honest, personal opinions."[154] Men such as Perlzweig, Goldmann, Tartakower, Kubowitzki, and Zuckerman saw each other quite frequently, often every few days unless transoceanic travels called them away. Their professional work was entwined with their personal lives, especially as these men were often away from their families for months or years at a time (personal conversation between the author and Michael Kubovy, son of Kubowitzki, July 1, 2022). And yet, their personal opinions rarely entered organizational discussions, at least openly. But at 4:00 p.m. on June 8, 1944, the masks came off. Perlzweig began the meeting, which was called to discuss the draft of the statement of policy of the German Jewish Representative Committee, by offering his "honest, personal opinion," which he expressed because he had "to protect" his "children and their children."[155] It is exhilarating, I must admit, to read what these men "honestly" thought about a complicated topic: whether or not the World Jewish Congress should support the return of German Jews to Germany after Hitler's defeat.

This special meeting, originally scheduled for April 26, 1944, convened after a "regular" meeting of the Office Committee at 1:00 p.m.[156] Information shared at that meeting included updates on Weissmann's work in Lisbon (it had been stopped, and some members of the Office Committee thought that Kubowitzki should travel to Lisbon in order to facilitate work there), the War Refugee Board (did it have information that was not being communicated?), UNRRA (it was, finally, developing "rapidly," especially the Displaced Persons Committee), and how to approach the American Jewish Congress, which owed the WJC thousands of dollars. At this meeting, Tartakower relayed new intelligence from the Polish government-in-exile: the Jewish National Committee in Warsaw had received $20,000 sent by the WJC, a transport of seven thousand Jews from Terezín had arrived at the "famous extermination camp in Oświęcim," and, most horrifically, "the first transports of Hungarian Jews, deported to Poland, already arrived there and were sent immediately to extermination camps."

This depressing information sat alongside a more general optimism regarding the June 6, 1944, D-Day invasion two days earlier. To mark this event, Zuckerman stated that it was "decided" that that the French Committee should produce a statement promising that the French population and the Jews of France "shall be assured that the leaders of French Jewry in the United States will do their utmost to establish Jewish life in France."[157] When the members of the Office Committee met with representatives of the German Jewish Representative Committee on the afternoon of June 8, 1944, this news had most recently percolated through their discussions. And while those assembled could envision a statement promising the renewal of Jewish life in France, the verdict on the same circumstances in the German context proved much more vexing. While no clear consensus emerged from this discussion, a majority of the voices felt ambivalent about the viability of renewed Jewish life in Germany, and a few found themselves advocating a much different position than before.

Near the beginning of the meeting, Maurice Perlzweig stated succinctly, "He who goes back to Germany goes at his own risk."[158] This Polish-born resident of London served the WJC as the head of the Division for International Questions and chairman of the British Section. He drew on his rabbinical education as well as extensive diplomatic experience to substantiate why the WJC should discourage Jews from returning to the postwar, defeated German state. Notably, Perlzweig harbored fears that Jews returning to Germany would become entangled with overall retribution and incur punishment targeted for the non-Jewish German population. While "it is a human right to go back," he "who does it must meet the German fate and we cannot defend him."[159] The German case was different from, say, the Belgian, Czechoslovak, or French case. Germans would become targets after the war. Jews in Germany could become targets as well.

Following Perlzweig's example, Dr. Goldmann also decided, for the first time, to speak his "personal opinion." Reflecting on the draft of the statement of policy before him, Goldmann, the man who had accompanied Perlzweig when he first arrived in the United States in 1940, respectfully disagreed with his position. He also disagreed with those who advocated an "evacuation" from the German context. If, Goldmann argued, they were "against a return only to Germany, this would be a triumph for Hitler, Germany would become *judenrein* and this would happen with the approval of the WJC." Moreover, if the WJC dismissed return to Germany as a viable option based on German aggression and acquiescence to Jewish extermination, what about other countries where Jews were also killed? Other countries such as Romania and Hungary had murdered Jews as well, and if the WJC banned "Jews from all these countries," the organization would "destroy Jewish life in the diaspora."[160]

On the contrary, Goldmann believed that "the greatest triumph of Jewry would be if Jewish rights in Germany would be internationally guaranteed." In response to Perlzweig's fears regarding retribution and punishment misdirected toward Jews, Goldmann figured that "the Jewish community will return to Germany later" and thus "will not be in Germany when the punishment of the Nazis will take place." Worried about Jewish rights in the diaspora in general, Goldmann felt that a ban on Germany could have severe consequences for the rights of Jews wanting to remain in other European countries. "We have a right," Goldmann stated, "in a democratic world to live wherever we want." How could these statements coexist with Goldmann's equation of Jewish survivors with potential Palestinian émigrés? Understanding Goldmann's support for a postwar German Jewish community hinges on our ability to differentiate between those Jews who wanted to return to their prewar homes and those who decided to relocate elsewhere. It seems that Goldmann sought in this particular discussion to protect individual choice, regardless of where that individual chose to abide. Perhaps for this reason, Goldmann remained against a mass evacuation despite being able to "understand its logic." Each Jew possessed the prerogative to live in Tel Aviv, Warsaw, or even Berlin.

Whereas Goldmann refused to take away options, Baruch Zuckerman saw only one. This longtime member of the WJC, who had traveled to Poland in a failed attempt to organize Polish Jewry at the end of the 1930s, agreed with

Goldmann that "the problem of whether Jews should return to Germany or not should be considered as part of the whole problem of the return of Jews to Europe." In contradiction to Goldmann's views, however, he believed that a WJC or a Jewish Joint Distribution Committee statement of policy "must have historic significance." Those assembled should act as if "the representatives of the Free Nations will pay great attention" to what they said. From his standpoint, the Jews of Europe were entitled to three distinct rights: "to decide whether he wants to return to the country from which he was displaced," "the right of ethnic groups to maintain their identity and develop their own religious and cultural life," and, most importantly, "the demand for the equalization of the Jewish status as a people with all the other peoples of the world." For Zuckerman, who had made aliyah to Palestine in 1932, there was "only one way to achieve such a goal: the recognition on the part of the world of Palestine as a Jewish state or commonwealth." Accordingly, only after offering a declaration concerning Palestine could "the principles contained in the first two spheres of rights" be addressed. Thus, to analyze the problem of "whether Jews should return to Europe or not," the WJC had to clarify its position on Palestine.[161]

Already, Zuckerman possessed a clear position on Palestine and who should constitute the citizenry of a hypothetical Jewish commonwealth. "With the exception of those individual Jews who will insist on returning to their former countries," he declared, "Jewish representative bodies must demand from the world the concentration of all the remaining displaced Jews in one country: in Palestine." And so the WJC should not release an isolated document merely dealing with Jewish return to Germany, because "nobody in the world will understand the mentality of the Jews who after having passed through the greatest catastrophe in their history are merely repeating the demands which they put forward after the first World War."[162] Rather than "leave to humanity a heritage of a renewed German Jewish problem, a Polish Jewish problem, a Romanian Jewish problem, a Hungarian Jewish problem," Zuckerman asked the "world" to "facilitate '*yeSiath Europa*' [the exodus from Europe] for the Jews." Only after a formulation regarding the migration of European Jews toward Palestine should the WJC consider "supplementary political formulations" concerning the right for Jews as individuals to return to their old countries, if they so chose, and the right of Jewish groups to "maintain their group identity if such groups remained in Europe."[163] The most pressing priority centered on securing a Jewish political entity in the Levant and populating it with survivors of the catastrophe. The man who had learned so much about Polish Jewish life during his extended stay in the country during the 1930s did not entertain a commitment to rooting that complex life once again.

A few minutes after Zuckerman finished his statement, the leader of Belgian Jewry, Aryeh Leon Kubowitzki, assumed the floor. At the previous meeting with this group, Kubowitzki had "defended" the idea of a policy statement encouraging the return of Jews to Germany. Now, however, "we are driven by the terrible force or events to proclaim a ban on Germany." Why, Kubowitzki asked aloud, did he "change [his] mind?" Kubowitzki, a founding member of the WJC, still considered himself a supporter of Jewish life in the galuth. He stood "opposed to the idea of collective responsibility," realized that "many Germans have helped Jews at the risk of their own lives," and recognized that "there are other peoples [besides Germans] who have not behaved very well." More practically, he envisioned "all the difficulties we would have to face if a ban was proclaimed, because of the mere fact that Germany is in the heart of Europe."

Just one year prior, Kubowitzki "believed that the masses of the German people did not know the details of the horrible massacres of helpless old people and children in which their kinsfolk participated." But "now no doubt is possible anymore." Ordinary Germans "must have been informed through innumerable channels," and "yet not one outstanding German tried to come out from Germany in order to disassociate himself and his people from these crimes." Moreover, "a year ago we did not know the appalling dimensions of the exterminations. We knew that hundreds of thousands had been killed. We did not know that we had lost the two thirds of the Polish Jews . . . we had finally hoped that we would save Hungarian Jewry . . . but they [the Nazis] do not give us any respite. They are bent upon killing all of us."[164] Recall that he had just heard reports about the Hungarian transports headed toward Auschwitz earlier that day.

Kubowitzki, who in Goldmann's assessment was a "dynamic man with a thoroughgoing knowledge of European Jewish Affairs," changed his position partially because of this chilling realization and partially because of something even bigger than that annihilation.[165] "History," Kubowitzki declared, "imposes upon us the obligation of giving an answer to what happened in our existence in these historical times. The answer must be commensurate with the magnitude of the tragedy."[166] Compelled by the "moral safety" of Jewish people and the need to tell his own son "how the Jewish people reacted," Kubowitzki viewed the present situation as markedly different from "normal wars" or "average pogroms." Like Perlzweig, he had his descendants on his mind. This "apocalyptic occurrence" demanded that he and his colleagues "give an answer to the world, not only to the Germans." He had to "bring back to his Belgian neighbors a Jewish answer which should be adequate, striking, majestic." This answer should be "dramatic enough to shake the world and to give our people the moral support and respect of the nations of the world."

And while the WJC Administrative Committee was not prepared to "proclaim a ban" on return to Germany, they could "start negotiations with other Jewish organizations and with our religious authorities so as to be ready when our War Emergency Conference will convene" in the future. Moved by his obligation to his four-year-old son Michael, to the "victims who are dead, cremated helpless dust," and to history, Kubowitzki could not foresee a future involving a substantial Jewish community in Germany.[167] The dramatic frippery of Kubowitzki's remarks does not diminish the force of his argument. Rarely do the WJC archives produce a speech more compelling or vivid. After reading through years of documents in search of his deepest beliefs, I found that an abrupt alteration in his thinking produced this visceral and impactful language. His mind had changed. Had the collective thinking of his peers changed as well?

After Kubowitzki's rousing comments, a patient Arieh Tartakower assumed the floor to "emphasize the practical aspects of the matter." Today, Tartakower reminded his colleagues, "we are discussing only the question of German Jews and not the question of principle whether European Jews are to be left in Europe or enabled, all of them, to go to Palestine." All should bear in mind that "since there would be scarcely any noteworthy numbers of Jews in Germany after the war," the WJC did not need to issue an official document. Tartakower could not foresee significant numbers of German Jews from Palestine, the United States, or Great Britain returning to Germany "unless we encourage them to do so." Even if "there would be Jews willing to go back there, they would not be able to live together with the Germans," as the German people had been "systematically educated during the long years to consider Jews as their worst enemies." In fact, for "the time being after all that happened," he did not "see the slightest possibility of Jew and German living together." Widening his gaze beyond the German Jewish issues, Tartakower admitted that global public opinion would "not understand how Jews are still thinking of Jewish life in Germany." Other countries, such as Poland, were different because the population there remained, "despite it all, not anti-semitic, whereas in Germany, Jewish hatred must be considered as a rule."[168] This was not the first time the behavior of local populations or neighbors breached the conversation of the Office Committee. In fact, this topic would become an important theme linked to the conversation on why Jews would not want to return to their homes. At this meeting, however, Tartakower seemed the most concerned about relations between Jews and non-Jews after the war. And surprisingly, the next speaker had recently changed his mind like Kubowitzki. His mind had changed, however, in the opposite direction.

After conceding that the opinion of the United Nations regarding the post-war Jewish life in Germany could not be known, Dr. Martin Rosenbluth, a member of the Executive Board of the German Jewish Representative Committee, lent his voice to the discussion. For a long time, Rosenbluth had been "against the policy of the WJC because" he believed that they "should concentration on Palestine. But in view of the tragedy [they] now witness[ed], [he] came to the opinion that it was necessary to do something for the Jews in Europe."[169] Jews in the labor and concentration camps "might prefer to return to the places of their previous abode," and "both protection and guarantee" was needed for them. In contrast to Kubowitzki, who felt compelled to forsake Germany because of the European Jewish tragedy, Rosenbluth used the example of Hitler's war against the Jews to justify continued support of Jewish life in Europe

This discussion tugged at the heartstrings of all involved, caused Kubowitzki and Rosenbluth to reverse their previous opinions, and reveals how complicated the crafting of organization-wide policies could be, especially when emotions ran high. Almost of all the participants who spoke during this meeting had close yet contentious ties with Europe. Stepping back and reflecting on the conversation, the anonymous notetaker concluded that the proposed "statement of policy [was] not merely a practical question and as such it [was] not confined to Germany alone. It [was] part of a general policy which [had] to be defined and which appear[ed] in every item of post war planning as for instance in the question of retributions."[170] Perhaps a "final policy of the WJC" for the future of Jews in Europe could be "drawn up along the line of what Dr. Goldmann term[ed] a policy of concentration in the Diaspora" whereby the WJC "should not make efforts to rebuild lost Jewish positions at any price but rather fortify those positions which [held] out some hope for the immediate future."[171] And so the document and the conversation ended, at least for that day.

In a broader sense, this particular discussion demonstrates how members of the WJC Office Committee's relationship to the diaspora and the Zionist project had changed over a few short years. Language calling for the movement of uprooted Jews toward Palestine with little attention to individual choice was not ostracized. Even Zuckerman's calls for mass evacuation found space in this discussion. In sum, a range of opinions existed, and no committee-wide consensus emerged easily. The document reveals, however, that minds had changed in a variety of directions. Goldmann ended the discussion with a reminder that a "final decision" regarding the return of Jews to Germany "will remain with the Emergency Conference in the fall."[172]

Decision, or Lack Thereof: The Postwar Role of the WJC

At the end of June 1944, WJC Office Committee members converged once again on Goldmann's apartment to revisit the contradiction inherent in a policy encouraging both support for Palestine and the diaspora. Jacob Robinson, WJC founding member and head of the Institute for Jewish Affairs, was a brilliant legal mind who served in the Lithuanian Parliament and possessed intimate familiarity with the Minority Treaties.[173] Upon emigrating to the United States in 1940, he plunged into New York's exilic milieu and gained a sound reputation for his research work benefiting both the WJC and the American Jewish Congress. On this summer day in 1944, Robinson called a special "all-out" meeting to "reconsider the basis of all [WJC] activities and to discuss them fundamentally, as conditions have changed since the WJC met in August 1936."[174] The core members of the WJC Office Committee, many of whom could date their membership in the WJC from the 1930s, congregated on the western edge of Manhattan's Central Park to reimagine the Congress's role in a Jewish world very much altered.

Robinson hoped that an honest debate with his colleagues would allow the WJC as a whole to chart a new course after the current conflict. However, one of his colleagues, Maurice Perlzweig, suspected that Robinson's proposal to reconceive the WJC stemmed from other, more Zionist motives. Threatened by the call for a reevaluation of the WJC, Perlzweig assumed that Robinson wanted the WJC to simply merge with the Jewish Agency in Palestine and cease promoting Jewish life elsewhere. Specifically, Perlzweig took issue with Robinson's presumed negation of the WJC's influence, as the "Jewish people [still] consist of two fragments: in Palestine and those for whom Palestine is the solution and to the others who are not there." The interwar system of minority rights had collapsed, Perlzweig continued, "but not the diaspora," as there would be Jews in the Soviet Union, South America, the British Commonwealth, and the fringe in western Europe. Zuckerman joined Perlzweig's attack on Robinson's idea of WJC negation. As long as the World Zionist Organization refused to represent diaspora Jews, Zuckerman said, "we must continue with the WJC."[175]

In Tartakower's assessment, a misunderstanding plagued the conversation among his colleagues and stifled their collective ability to reach a viable mission statement for the postwar WJC. "We cannot," he opined, "speak now of the

Jewish people as one entity." Instead, four components should be distinguished from each other: American Jewry, Palestinian Jewry, Jewish communities scattered all over the world, and European Jewry. This last segment of world Jewry should be, in his words, "written off." Ironically, Tartakower continued, the WJC had gone "from one extreme to the other. Before the war we considered European Jewry as the only decisive factor." In contrast, now "we say that there is nothing to be reconstructed." This reality, he conceded, was "terrible." In sum, Soviet Jewry and the European Jews scattered "all over the world" numbered at least "four million." Hundreds of thousands of Jews would remain on the European continent after the war. What, Tartakower asked, would be the "fate of European Jews" after this war?[176]

Various possibilities existed. If, he declared, they had "the possibility of bringing them to Palestine in the next few years," then they could discuss Robinson's point of view. But he reminded his contemporaries that the WJC had already worked "to organize emigration of European Jewry in the years before the war." No consensus had been reached to this point, and no viable plans to transport Jews toward Palestine existed yet. Despite the grim prognoses emanating from the death camps of Europe, WJC officials still needed to "think in terms of an organized people."[177] There needed to be an "organized Jewish body," and the WJC could fill that demand. Tartakower foresaw a role for the WJC in the postwar world. He could not, however, imagine how Jews would get to Palestine or elsewhere specifically. It was premature, he thought, to declare European Jewry extinct, but the situation had irrevocably changed.

After Tartakower offered his thoughts, Kubowitzki raised his voice to condemn, once again, Robinson's suggestion that the WJC should be dissolved. As long as the "diaspora exist[ed]," the WJC would remain. The WJC should, in Kubowitzki's assessment, alter their program. The basic template from 1936 Geneva should remain. The WJC would "always" be there and promised to consider the "Jewish problem from a universal Jewish aspect." Kubowitzki assumed that the congress would be "terribly attacked from two camps: from the assimilation camps and from the tendencies of the Jewish Agency." He added that the "conception of a Jewish state to which citizens of Europe belong" remained, in his assessment, "very dangerous." Kubowitzki's keen reflection on citizenship deserves pause.[178] He appears to speak against the transfer of Europe's Jews away from the continent, understanding the Jews as belonging to the states that gave them political rights. But these remarks starkly contrasted with the views he had enunciated less than a month before in similar company. Across these two discussions, Kubowitzki refused to support the renewal of Jewish communities in Germany but later exuded unease in response to plans enabling Europe's Jewish citizens to populate a state in the Levant.

Near the end of this late June meeting, Goldmann offered his comments. He noted that the "small Jewish communities will need us more than before and therefore the WJC has to exist."[179] Committed to the idea of Jewish migration toward Palestine and willing to voice his support for this movement in Zionist, non-Zionist, and diplomatic circles, Goldmann pledged the WJC's continued support for diaspora life. This promise to Jews remaining in Europe became part of the postwar WJC platform unanimously approved at the War Emergency Conference five months later. The twinned ideas espoused by Weisgal and Weizmann in the spring of 1943, one equating Jewish survivors with potential Palestinian citizens and another tasking the UN with repatriating these migrating Jews toward the Mandate, were included in the WJC's public statement as well. As an organization founded to speak for the Jews of the diaspora, the WJC could not quickly negate the diaspora outright. And yet, by beginning to advocate for the transfer of European Jewish populations, especially those in east central Europe, toward Palestine, they came quite close to liquidating the entity that justified their own existence. The "grand, sweeping," and "majestic" solution proposed by Kubowitzki within the Office Committee would soon have grand, sweeping, majestic, and tragic consequences not only for the German Jewish community but for Jews throughout all of Europe when internal discussions became external recommendations.

ZORACH WARHAFTIG, "RESETTLEMENT AS REPATRIATION," AND THE SECOND UNRRA MEETING, SEPTEMBER 1944

Hundreds of diplomats from across the world convened in Montreal late in September 1944 for the second meeting of the United Nations Relief and Rehabilitation Agency.[180] Tucked within the white reams of memos, schedules, and directories bestowed on each participant was a freshly bound two-hundred-page book produced by the Institute of Jewish Affairs, the research arm of the WJC, and written by Dr. Zorach Warhaftig.[181] While offering specific amendments to existing UNRRA code and requests for further definitions of nebulous language, Warhaftig also argued for UNRRA language recognizing Jewish exceptionalism, for UNRRA policies to take precedence over state and local laws, for the special circumstances surrounding the resettlement and "homes" of Polish Jews who lived in areas that would be ceded to the Soviet Union, and, finally, for the inclusion of Palestine as an approved destination for postwar resettlement. Distributed to all invitees of this UNRRA session, Warhaftig's *Relief and Rehabilitation* marked perhaps the precise moment when the WJC first publicly called for a population-transfer-esque plan targeting Europe's Jews.

Warhaftig's journey from his 1930s home at 13 ulica Świętojerska in Warsaw to the second official meeting of UNRRA in Montreal was circuitous to say the least. Born six years after the turn of the century in Volkovysk (a town of five thousand Jews and five thousand Christians), Warhaftig began life as a Russian subject until the creation of the Second Polish Republic in 1918, when he became a citizen of Poland. Trained in his youth as a rabbi, Warhaftig moved to the Polish capital as a young adult to study at the University of Warsaw, where he earned a doctorate in law in the 1930s. There he opened a private law practice while simultaneously serving the Central Bureau of He-Halutz ha-Mizrachi and as a vice president of Mizrachi and acting as a leading executive member of the Tora va-Avodah movement. He also, as noted in chapter 1, attended a meeting held to support the WJC's effort to assemble a Congress of Polish Jewry in 1938. Soon after that meeting, Warhaftig married Naomi, who came from a "warm house" at Nowolipie 39. There, in "Jewish Warsaw, the pride of Jewish communities throughout Europe, with its masses of Jews, scholars and writers, the vibrant seat of trade and industry of crafts and arts, of *cheders*, schools and *yeshivot*, of academic institutions and centers of Torah learning, of theaters," there in the "blooming" capital city of Poland, Zorach and Naomi built their first shared home.[182]

The Warhaftigs scrambled back to their Warsaw in late August 1939 from the World Zionist Organization meeting in Geneva as threats of war became increasingly real. Reflecting on this moment in his eighties, Maurice Perlzweig remembered begging his WZO colleagues not to return eastward. As Perlzweig recalled, he spent "the rest of the Congress trying to persuade people not to go back to Poland but did not succeed. Practically everyone went back to Poland."[183] Warhaftig, his wife, and the others arrived in Warsaw after nearly a week of travel.[184] The group arrived home to find the city mobilizing. Warhaftig hurried to the Muranów railroad station to help build antitank trenches in those early September days. Like many Polish Jews that tense autumn, Warhaftig fled east toward the city of Vilnius, which the Soviet Union had ceded to Lithuania.[185] After a few months there helping other Jews escape from Lithuania toward Palestine and other destinations, Warhaftig traveled to Vladivostok by train and then on to Japan by boat, where he and a few thousand Polish Jews sought refuge in 1940 and 1941. When he was encouraged to cancel his departure to Palestine planned for December 19, 1940, due to the difficulties inherent in such a long journey, members of Mizrachi and the World Jewish Congress intervened to secure Zorach Warhaftig a visa to the United States instead. He traveled to New York on his visa, alone.[186]

In New York, Warhaftig waited for his family to join him and worked as a researcher for the Institute of Jewish Affairs. His colleague Arieh Tartakower suggested on April 18, 1944, that Warhaftig attend the next UNRRA meeting. Goldmann disagreed at the time, asserting that "Warhaftig was not good for official contacts."[187] Goldmann was overruled one month later when the Office Committee decided that Warhaftig would accompany Tartakower and Perlzweig as an advisor to the second UNRRA meeting in Montreal and produce a book that would be distributed at that event. Like Tartakower and others on the WJC, Warhaftig remained concerned that UNRRA's Subcommittee for Social-Welfare Policies "decided against making any recommendations for special treatment of Jewish war victims" at their first meeting in Atlantic City. Instead, the subcommittee had endorsed the idea that each nation would deal with the "Jewish problem" individually. Warhaftig wanted to accentuate Jewish difference and pave the way for a transnational category that would apply to all Jews regardless of prewar nationality.

Worried that stateless Jews or Jews possessing German or Austrian citizenship would be categorized as enemies, he recommended amendments that clarified how UNRRA relief activities would extend to enemy territories, to those with residence in Axis countries, and to those who experienced discrimination from 1933 onward.[188] Notably, Warhaftig wanted to include language to ensure that UNRRA would assist displaced people in repatriating to both their "country of origin" and "their places of settled residence." Those eligible for repatriation should include those who had been "obliged to leave their homes for reasons of race, religion or political belief since 1933—regardless of the nationality of these persons."[189] Of course, Warhaftig had Jews in mind. He also wanted to clarify a key concept within this passage.

What qualified as "settled residence"? In fact, "certain interpretations of it might fail to include all types of factual residence."[190] What about, for example, Polish Jews living in 1930s France, German Jews forced to flee to Italy, or stateless Jews living throughout Europe?[191] In general, resettlement as a concept profoundly interested Warhaftig. Since "great numbers of people deported or expelled to foreign countries and also many of those displaced within their own country" were unable or unwilling to be repatriated to their former homes, "a solution other than repatriation and return" had to be found. Policies and infrastructures designed to channel displaced people back to their preconflict homesteads seemingly ignored complex realities on the ground. International borders, such as interwar eastern borders of Poland and Czechoslovakia, had shifted because of invasion and occupation, and more changes to boundaries in this carved-up region could be expected. For most in this "unrepatriable" group, "there is only one other possibility, namely, resettlement in other countries as immigrants."[192]

Besides the problem of shifting borders, Warhaftig evinced doubts about the postconflict return of Polish Jews in general. He referred to a report supposedly emanating from the Polish Underground that claimed "that the return of the Jews to the cities and to their homes and concerns would be regarded as an invasion and might invoke opposition by force." Quoting the report despite the Polish government-in-exile's claims that the report did not originate from "any responsible Polish underground quarters," Warhaftig alerted UNRRA members that "the non-Jewish population has occupied the place of Jews in the town and cities and over a large part of Poland." And so the Polish "population would regard the mass return of the Jews not in the light of a restoration of a prewar status but as an invasion against which they will defend themselves even by force." In sum, it stood to reason that a majority of Polish Jews would prefer to be resettled elsewhere.

Warhaftig opined that UNRRA should "facilitate this urgent movement and do so quickly because" there was "no logical difference between repatriation to former places of residence and resettlement."[193] In fact, "resettlement of uprooted people, especially in the case of the Jews, is only another form of repatriation." And so, Warhaftig submitted, if UNRRA officials considered the resettlement of the Polish Jews from Soviet-occupied Poland to new homes in another part of Poland as a legitimate form of resettlement, then perhaps these same officials could support the movement of these displaced Polish Jews to other "homelands" as well. With regard to the resettlement of the Jews in Palestine, Jews would go there "with the aim of reconstituting their ancient home, their *patria*."[194] Thus, Warhaftig recommended that representatives convening in Montreal alter language, specifically in paragraph 5d, to read that UNRRA "should also assist those nationals of the United Nations and those stateless persons who have been driven as a result of the war, from their places of settled residence in countries of which they are not nationals, to return to those places, *or to be settled in other countries* [emphasis in original]."[195]

Why should European Jews and these Polish Jews specifically be moved away from the continent of their birth? First, "normal humanitarian considerations," Warhaftig observed, "impose the obligation to take into consideration the preference of refugees themselves." Second, UNRRA had already recognized "the desirability" of family reunion as an "important principle." Third, the Soviet Union had already permitted "23 Jewish refugee families" to relocate to both Australia and Palestine. The accumulation of humanitarian concerns, UNRRA preferences, and global precedents led Warhaftig to argue that "the settlement of Jewish refugees in Palestine, in fulfillment of the principles of the Palestine Mandate, should be regarded as *repatriation* in its highest sense" [emphasis in the original].[196]

Warhaftig's submission to the delegates of the second UNRRA meeting marked the first time that a WJC official publicly drew the connection between the repatriation of displaced persons to their "homeland" and the sponsored movement of European Jews far away from their prewar "homes" to Palestine. At the first UNRRA meeting in Atlantic City, the question of displaced Jews who chose not to return to the place of their last domicile was entertained but not clarified. Afterward, in meetings with Secretary General Lehman and his colleagues on the Intergovernmental Committee for Refugees, WJC officials discussed how the process of resettlement and repatriation would be complicated and contested for those Jews who wanted to move elsewhere. When Warhaftig declared that "the settlement of Jewish refugees in Palestine . . . should be regarded as repatriation in its highest sense," he drew on a multitude of private and internal discussions from the WJC circles, some of which were covered in this chapter.[197]

Exactly one month after its release on August 25, 1944, WJC officials delivered Warhaftig's book to every delegate attending the Montreal UNRRA conference along with a "short memo" and a summary of the main arguments contained within.[198] According to Sofia Grinberg, who attended the conference in Montreal, Warhaftig's book was "read by all delegates of governments and was considered by them as a very helpful document."[199] In his memoir written nearly four decades after the conference, Warhaftig recalled that "the guidelines suggested in [his] research played a partial role in framing UNRRA and in directing its activities." A leading Polish Jewish journalist, Chaim Shoshkes, later told Warhaftig that he saw *Relief and Rehabilitation* on the desk of the Canadian prime minister Lester B. Pearson. When asked about Warhaftig's treatise, Pearson told Shoshkes that he used the book as "a manual in mastering the problems of UNRRA and in the implementation of its program."[200] Some of Warhaftig's ideas arguably morphed into UNRRA policy.

The UNRRA General Assembly at Montreal endorsed two of the three fundamental demands enunciated in Warhaftig's book: the first concerning "full equality in the treatment of displaced persons regardless of their nationality" and the second regarding "relief to be administered in enemy or ex enemy territory to victims of persecution." A proposal submitted by US delegate Dean

Acheson at a closed meeting of the policy committee requesting that "the UNRRA constitution be amended to authorize relief to all 'displaced' Jewish victims of Nazi persecution found in German and other enemy" territories gained noticeable support. Acheson's addition "was made as an amendment to a British resolution giving power to UNRRA with the consent of the occupying military authorities, to take care of Allied nationals found in enemy or ex-enemy territories." Specifically, the words "or other persons who have been obliged to leave their country or place of origin or former residence or who have been deported there by action of the enemy because of race, religion or activities" came under consideration. Acheson's proposed insertion was "discussed at length and put over for further action."[201] Two days later, on September 24, 1944, the resolution unanimously passed the Policy Committee, which included one member from each of the forty-four assembled nations.

Canadian prime minister Pearson argued that the "extension of UNRRA activities to cover persecuted racial and religious minorities and extension of the agency activities to aid political anti-Nazis of technical enemy nationality would look after many who were hitherto unprovided for in the scope of UNRRA activities including the inhabitants of Nazi concentration camps and German Jews deported to Poland."[202] Less than seventy-two hours later, the language approved by the Policy Committee was endorsed by the entire council. And so two-thirds of the fundamental demands elaborated by Warhaftig in his well-distributed book and reinforced by Tartakower in Montreal passed into the UNRRA legal code. On September 29, Tartakower joined Miss Jane Evans of the American Jewish Committee at 138 West Forty-Third Street to publicly celebrate their joint accomplishments at Montreal. The codification of this particular language took center stage at their joint press conference.[203]

The third demand articulated by Warhaftig in his book and reinforced in person by Tartakower at the Montreal meeting elicited interest but not legislation. Those assembled in Montreal did not offer a solution to the question of DPs "who cannot or do not wish to be repatriated."[204] Poignantly, UNRRA policies emanating from Montreal contained no mention of Palestine as a viable destination. According to Tartakower's final report of the conference, "the demand concerning participation of UNRRA in the resettlement of persons who cannot or do not wish to be repatriated had no chances whatever of being adopted at that session."[205] Perhaps the silence with regard to this issue came as a surprise. Just a few days into the hurricane-delayed conference, the American delegation "indicated it was giving urgent consideration to appeals from the World Jewish Conference and the American Jewish Conference . . . asking it to support amendments to the UNRRA constitution, one of which would provide for resettlement in Palestine of millions of Jewish refugees who do not want to return to Germany and other countries in which they formerly lived."[206] Since "resolutions [had] been introduced to authorize UNRRA operations to resettle elsewhere in the western hemisphere those Jewish refugees who had obtained a temporary haven in the new world and wish to remain on this side of the ocean," discussions concerning movement toward Palestine could not be considered completely unprecedented.[207] Resettlement elsewhere, however, proved a very contentious topic, and official debates about it did not materialize.

Reflecting on the proposed amendment in the Policy Committee authorizing relief for all "displaced" victims of Nazi persecution regardless of prewar citizenship, Acheson explained that the amendment did not cover the problem of repatriation, which was a "matter for the individual governments to handle." Specifically, "the question of resettlement of Jewish refugees in Palestine had not been discussed," thus "clarifying a misunderstanding which had given rise to the impression that the US delegation had interested itself in this project."[208] Clearly, resettlement in Palestine was not tantamount to repatriation in general for Warhaftig's audience. As hundreds of diplomats departed Canada to return to forty-four member governments, Warhaftig's equation of resettlement and repatriation remained a hypothetical formula.

Despite the measurable legislative successes in Montreal, the triad of WJC delegates who attended the event expressed profound discontent upon their return. In a long report submitted on September 29, 1944, Tartakower revealed his frustrations and diverged from the opinion of Pearson cited above. "The atmosphere of deep understanding for the sufferings in Europe, the willingness to help and sympathy for the idea of a broad cooperation of all nations in the field which we faced in Atlantic City," he lamented, "did not exist in Montreal."[209] In sum, his report persuaded the WJC to extend help to "persons unable or unwilling to be returned to their former homes in the same measures as help is accorded to repatriated persons with the Intergovernmental Committee on Refugees" and have that organization approach UNRRA in the future.[210] After Tartakower added these unofficial remarks, his colleagues Sofia Grinberg and Zorach Warhaftig shared their thoughts as well.

Both Grinberg and Warhaftig offered conflicting comments on the unresolved demand of resettlement. In a conversation she had with Patrick Malin of the IGCR, Grinberg discussed the group of unrepatriable Jews that seemed to increasingly garner attention. Malin noted that the IGCR, not UNRRA, planned to care for these refugees. While the IGCR had no "funds of its own," it planned to accumulate finances from specific governments upon submitting definite projects to them for consideration. Malin was confident that

Fig. 3.3. Delegates from other countries attend the WJC's War Emergency Conference in Atlantic City, 1943. Photo courtesy of CriticalPast.

the organization "will be in a position to fulfill its task concerning these persons."[211] Warhaftig could not disagree more. He argued that "resettlement [presumably to Palestine] should now be [the WJC's] main concern."[212] The Montreal Conference, in his assessment, "did not deal with the subject" of resettlement because "in his opinion they were afraid of the word resettlement in connection with Palestine."[213] Rather than wait for the IGCR to draft indefinite plans, Warhaftig suggested working with the JDC on questions of resettlement. Technically, they already were. Both the JDC and the WJC subsidized Isaac Weissmann's work in Lisbon beginning in early 1944. Warhaftig wanted something more official. A little more than two months later, the convocation of the War Emergency Conference provided an occasion to make the implicit explicit.

CONCLUSION: NOVEMBER 1944

The decisions considered, made, postponed, and outlined in this chapter found a second life at the WJC's November 1944 War Emergency Conference (WEC). The largest Jewish gathering during the war included debate across four official languages (Spanish, English, Hebrew, and Yiddish) and resulted in a number of resolutions. Under the "Resolutions for Relief and Rehabilitation," the WEC decided to make recommendations for Jewish orphans, those living in Christian houses, surviving in monasteries, or wandering at large. This group could not be rehabilitated in "places and countries filled for them with memories of blood and horror in the areas where they were hunted day and night by their inhuman persecutors." For those assembled in Atlantic City, it followed that "only the speedy removal of these unfortunate children from the territories where they experienced the most nerve-shattering experiences, and their upbringing in new areas, in a healthy atmosphere, among children of their own faith and background can restore them to the requisites of sound and healthy life." One place, one ideal place, could provide these children with this future: "The place where these unhappy Jewish children will find full retribution is Palestine, where thousands of Jewish child victims of Nazism have already found shelter and happiness since long before the actual outbreak of the war and during the present day."[214] And so the WEC suggested that the "joint efforts and exertions of Jewish as well as of international organizations should be mobilized in order to collect with all possible speed all parentless Jewish children in the liberated areas, and in enemy territories as soon as they come under Allied domination, and to bring such children to Palestine to be brought up and rehabilitated there under the auspices and care of the Jewish people."[215] The germ of an idea related to the orphaned children marooned in Lisbon had evolved into a much larger policy and a request that the rehabilitation of these children include their subsidized movement toward Palestine.

These orphaned children would not be the only displaced Jews destined for Palestine. In the WEC's "resolution on Palestine," the WJC associated itself with the program of the Jewish Agency for Palestine and its claims that "there must be a definitive and permanent termination of the national homelessness of the Jewish people by the establishment of Palestine as a Jewish commonwealth." As part of a "general scheme of postwar reconstruction" of the United Nations, the "appropriate public financial and other resources [should] be provided for that purpose, including the speedy *transfer* [emphasis mine] to Palestine of all Jewish survivors of Nazi persecution who desire, or need to have part in the rebuilding of the Jewish National Home."[216] The "Resolutions on Relief and Rehabilitation" expanded on this idea and harked back to a word Tartakower enunciated in his May 1944 editorial: *many*. It would be, the resolution continued, "impossible for many hundreds of thousands of Jewish displaced persons to return to their pre-war places of residence." This group of "many" should have the "choice to be repatriated or returned to their former homes or to be resettled elsewhere." Without citing the opinions of surviving Jews in Europe, the resolution concluded that "it will be certain that the overwhelming majority of such persons will desire to go to Palestine, where they will find not only a refuge but a home."[217] And finally, with regard to the future mission of the WJC, the WEC hoped that an "International Jewish Reconstruction Commission" would be created to organize work on the ground after liberation, work with individual governments, and "participate in the deliberations of the United Nations." The WJC would be part of this initiative.[218]

The idea of Jewish homelessness in Europe stands in sharp contrast to the ideas expressed by, for example, Anselm Reiss and the united statement given by the Polish Jewish delegates to the first WJC gathering in Geneva in 1936. The same Anselm Reiss arrived in New York with Ignacy Schwarzbart in mid-November 1944, before the convocation of the WEC and before a special poetry night dedicated to the Warsaw Ghetto on November 18, 1944. The Polish Jewish community in New York remained active, imbibing Polish-language poetry by Czesław Miłosz and Julian Tuwim in a special poetry issue of *NT* to complement the Warsaw Ghetto remembrance event and convening in a special session on the first of November at the Hotel Diplomat in New York. There, the seats filled to hear speeches given by Reiss and Schwarzbart. Words those attendees heard sounded more like the program of the WEC than the 1936 unified declaration of the rooted Polish Jews. There, Ignacy Schwarzbart, the Jewish representative to the Polish government-in-exile and active member of the WJC, declared that "the Jewish state in Palestine is the only solution for the Jewish nation for the future."[219]

Schwarzbart's words recorded in the December issue of *NT* mirrored a similar quotation that Tartakower offered in an English-language edition of the same paper published while the WEC delegates traveled to the St. Charles Hotel in Atlantic City for the beginning of the conference on November 26. He was a changed man when he wrote these words, and not only because of his intellectual evolution across the spring and summer of 1944. He had been appointed as professor of sociology at the Hebrew University in Jerusalem and looked forward to relocating to Jerusalem as early as 1945, in just a few months. The good professional news Tartakower shared with his colleagues on September 29 would soon be overshadowed by tragedy. Around the same time that Tartakower informed the WJC Office Committee about his new professional appointment, Tartakower's nineteen-year-old son Jochanan died on the battlefields of western Europe. A small announcement in *NT* recognized Jochanan's death but did not include any words from the father of the fallen.[220] A book that Tartakower published that fall with his colleague Kurt Grossman, *The Jewish Refugee*, memorialized Jochanan in its dedication. And perhaps the memory of his son's commitment to his leadership role in the Zionist youth movement Habonim was entwined with a November 1944 editorial he offered in *NT*. In Tartakower's assessment, "the fate of European Jewry in the last five years" would "serve for eternity as a warning of what the curse of homelessness and of a permanent minority status must mean in the world as it is now constituted." The Jews still alive in Europe had to be saved so "that they might build up a new Jewish life of security and dignity in the postwar world and to proclaim again the idea of the Jewish commonwealth in Palestine as the only real solution to the Jewish problem."[221]

In August 1936 the refrain was rootedness. In November 1944 the refrain was *haTikvah*.[222] Nahum Goldmann promised that he was not calling for an evacuation from Europe, but in his next breath he declared that the only solution to the Jewish question was Palestine. In his remarks to the WEC assembly, Noah Barou of the British Section of the WJC stated that "'no Jewish evacuation of Europe' is one of the most important things for the WJC to say clearly and pointedly. This must be an unequivocal statement, so that there will be no confusion about it."[223] And then, in his next breath, he spoke about Palestine being the only center toward which "all the Jews who want to leave Europe" could come. Ignacy Schwarzbart noted that "we haven't the right to order that European youth should go to Palestine. We must ask them what they want." And then, in his next breath, he dictated what their "want" should be: "It is our hope that if they can enjoy the sunshine and beauty of their rightful home, if they can walk hand in hand with [their] own parents through the streets of a city which belongs to them, conscious of a national pride, then we will have achieved our purpose."[224] Those refusing to call for the evacuation of the diaspora, and specifically the east central European diaspora, seemingly did just that. The nuance and disagreement evident in the meetings of the WJC Office Committee and, specifically, captured in the special meeting of the Office Committee and the German Jewish Representative Committee had dissolved into a more simplified and unified program: Palestine first, the diaspora second. After seeing the resolutions of the WEC, it should come as no surprise that the German Jewish Representative Committee issued a ban on collective German Jewish life in postwar Germany at the beginning of December 1944.

FOUR

UNCERTAIN CITIZENSHIP

Anxious Postwar Returns to East Central Europe, 1945–1946

"AFTER EVERY WAR," WISŁAWA SZYMBORSKA reminds us, "someone has to clean up. Things won't straighten themselves up after all."[1] Szymborska's exquisite poem "The End and the Beginning" showcases a variety of postwar work. Rubble is pushed, corpse-filled wagons pass, doors are hung, bridges and railway stations are rebuilt, and memories of the conflict are kept alive by the aging survivors until awareness passes into oblivion. After this particular war, however, other things had to be straightened up as well. Ethnic communities—or, to be more specific, "perceived" ethnic communities—were separated, minority rights were erased, and belonging to the state became equalized with belonging to the "nation."[2] And so, the contents of conversations about the rerooting of the Jewish diaspora in east central Europe, agreements hatched between Edvard Beneš and the Allied powers regarding the probability of population transfers, and reconstruction plans offered by new international organizations intersected as the calendar flipped toward 1945.

The "end" of one type of Jewish belonging in Europe and the "beginning" of another type of Jewish belonging elsewhere coalesced in the minds, words, and activities of a group of east central Europeans living in exile during the Second World War and the Holocaust. As that war ended, this new type of belonging cemented in the form of policies, procedures, and precedents for some Czechoslovak and Polish citizens identified as Jews by wartime persecution. Across roughly a score of months leading up to the end of 1946, when my narrative in this book crests to a halt, the citizenship and thus the future belonging of "Jews" from Subcarpathian Rus', "Jews" who listed German as their nationality in the 1930 Czechoslovak census, and more than a hundred thousand Polish "Jews" who survived the war in the Soviet Union remained uncertain in some ways but increasingly certain in others. More and more Jewish and non-Jewish activists in the Allied universe agreed that these Jews belonged elsewhere, ideally in Palestine.

This consensus prioritizing Palestine did not, as we have already seen and will see again, necessarily dovetail with the desires of individual Jews returning to their postwar homes, who often wanted to remain, at least in the immediate future, in the states where they had citizenship or join remaining family members in various locations, most notably in the United States, the United Kingdom, and Australia.[3] Of course, the consolidation of the intellectual foundations and the diplomatic preconditions that theoretically supported the ethnic unmixing of this region and the further displacement of Jews within broader plans did not foretell the history that followed. As we know by now, nationalism, especially the hyperethnic variety of it, required hard work. The narrative capturing how east central European Jews returned to changed postwar circumstances, found their political belonging compromised, and then moved safely and efficiently elsewhere (but mainly toward displaced camps in occupied Germany and Austria) proceeds from this point onward. The broader story extending over this chapter and the final one, moreover, demands an awareness of four postwar realities that can help explicate the "chaos" that ensued as occupation came to an end and new political forces consolidated power.

Across 1945 and 1946, a series of unanticipated events, decisions, and indecisions ensured that a majority of Jewish survivors from east central Europe would remain uprooted. First, the emergence of a particular type of postwar antisemitism specifically in Poland made postwar lives in the region for some Jews impossible.[4] This reality perplexed WJC officials and others, including those still committed to diaspora life. Even Jakob Apenszlak conceded by the second half of 1946 that continued, violent manifestations of this particular antisemitism nearly precluded the ability of Polish Jews to reroot themselves. And when Ignacy Schwarzbart and Zorach Warhaftig encountered this new iteration of antisemitism in occupied Germany a few months after Hitler's defeat, contact with it helped consolidate their commitment to removing Jews from the region. Postwar anti-Jewish violence and the antisemitism imbued in it "was not just a consequence of rigid ethnic categorization but an agent actively reinforcing hostility along ethnic lines after the war."[5] Portions of this chapter and the final chapter explore this changed antisemitism and the consequences it generated.

Along with this new antisemitism, the circumstances coalescing on the territory of the former Third Reich stumped WJC officials while also providing Jews in the region with an in-between, temporary option during a turbulent time. The swarming and languishing of displaced Jews on occupied German and

Austrian soil constituted the second reality that pointed plans for the postwar world in a specific direction. When the International Union of Anti-fascist Immigrants and Refugees proposed, in December 1944, that a Jewish state called "Israel" should emerge in a northwestern portion of defeated Germany, the Foreign Affairs Ministry in the exiled Czechoslovak government did not take the proposal seriously. Neither did officials in the US State Department. Remember that at the War Emergency Conference, the WJC in conjunction with the German Jewish Reconstruction Committee had vehemently discouraged the collective return of Jews to Germany. And yet, just half a year later, tens of thousands of displaced Jews and others had pooled into camps on formerly Axis territory. This space had become, in essence, a no-man's-land of sorts protected by civilian and military entities that encouraged in-between and sometimes unclear statuses for those who assembled there. In 1945 and 1946, as many as two hundred thousand Jews remaining in east central Europe spent time in these camps and by doing so prolonged their postwar displacement on the continent.[6] From these camps, the surviving east central European Jewish diaspora dispersed all over the world, to the Americas, Australia, and western European states as well as, sometimes, to Palestine and (after 1948) Israel.

Lagging machineries, clunky logistics, and conflicting policies in UNRRA and in national and local government circles propelled Jews to these displaced persons camps and kept them there indefinitely. More than all other postwar circumstances, this reality prolonged Jewish uprootedness in east central Europe in seemingly indefinite ways. This is the third and, I argue, the most important context to consider as we attempt to unravel the process by which the preconditions for the continuance of a thriving Jewish diaspora in east central Europe evaporated in 1945 and 1946. Citizenship became uncertain and later untenable as international bodies, domestic actors, government ministries, and powerbrokers on the border offered conflicting decisions about where certain people, especially those persecuted as Jews during the war, belonged. This chapter's exploration of the convoluted policies concerning Czechoslovak Jews from Subcarpathian Rus' and German-speaking Jews with interwar Czechoslovak citizenship, for example, shows how a lack of direction from the centralized state resulted in uncomfortable confusion for both Jews on the ground and their advocates at home and abroad. The uncomfortable confusion evident in the Czech legal code existed in international law as well and is contextualized at the end of this chapter and in chapter 5's excavation of the "unsuccessful repatriation" of Polish Jews from the Soviet Union in the first half of 1946.

Emotions matter as well in these last two chapters, even if diplomatic language exchanged between powerbrokers does not reveal them explicitly.

Fig. 4.1. A group of Polish Jewish children and their caretakers on Staroměstské náměstí in Prague. Photo archives of the United States Holocaust Memorial Museum.

For Czechoslovaks such as Jan Masaryk and his Jewish colleague from the Czechoslovak government-in-exile, Arnošt Frischer, emotions mattered. For WJC members such as Tartakower, Schwarzbart, and Warhaftig, emotions mattered. For international observers such as Bartley Crum, James McDonald of the Anglo-American Committee, and Jose Guttierez-Sanchez, the Cuban representative to the United Nations Special Committee for Economic and Social Affairs, emotions mattered, too. Emotions mattered for journalists such as Joel Cang and Jakob Apenszlak as well as for decision makers such as Marian Spychalski and Yitzchak Zuckerman. We will encounter all of these emotional and psychological beings in the final two chapters of this narrative.

Yes, the emotional shock of encountering the human remnants of the Jewish Gehenna (a biblical Hebrew word meaning "hell" that Tartakower used to name what had come to pass) and the unbearable absence of the Polish Jewish masses amplified nearly everyone's commitment to find a "final solution" for the postwar European Jewish question. Across the following pages, we will encounter strong words gleaned from committee minutes, editorials, and letters. But emotions alone cannot explain how the diaspora of east central European Jews became even "more" uprooted. Neither can an argument driven primarily by antisemitism, violence, or "chaos" explain how the ideas formed by men such as Beneš, Goldmann, and Kubowitzki became realities and were endorsed by others in the postwar world with much more influence. The first three chapters of this book showed how supporters of the diaspora in the WJC came to agree, by mid-1944, with Edvard Beneš that the ethnic revolution in east central Europe demanded the simultaneous embrace of a Jewish polity in the Middle East and the UN-subsidized transfer of European Jews who "could not return home" to that destination. In 1945 and 1946, decisions, indecisions, and legal uncertainties lent causal force to this particular trajectory. These decisions, detailed in this chapter and the next, began in earnest as the war's end enabled new beginnings.

JAN MASARYK AND HIS ANSWER TO THE GERMAN, JEWISH, AND STATELESSNESS QUESTIONS, 1942–1945

Stories about the end of the Second World War and return after the conflict rarely begin with a document about luggage. Most people had very little to carry. Edvard Beneš was, as usual, an exception. On February 3, 1945, all of his diplomatic luggage was packed. Two suitcases, five parcels, a bag, and a box weighing more than 100 kilograms in total would accompany the Czechoslovak president and his wife, Hana, as they traveled from Paris to Cairo, Tehran, and then Moscow, where Beneš would continue his circuitous journey home.[7] Many officials in the new Czechoslovak government known as the National Front, including communist party delegates such as Klement Gottwald and Vladimir Clementis, would accompany Beneš back to Prague.[8]

And so, on the morning of May 16, 1945, Beneš boarded a special train in Blansko. Red, white, and blue banners of the republic adorned houses along the one-hundred-mile route from Moravia to Bohemia.[9] At two o'clock in the afternoon, the bands of the Czechoslovakian and Red Armies played the fanfare from Bedřich Smetana's opera *Libuše* as Beneš's train crested into Prague's central train station, Wilsonovo Nádraží. Minutes later, when Beneš emerged from his carriage, the bands received him with renditions of the Czechoslovakian state anthem and the "Internationale." A fantastic, winding car trip through the golden city ensued. Beginning in the New Town, a caravan of thirty-four automobiles followed Národní třída (National Boulevard) to the National Theater and the banks of the Vltava River toward the Old Town Square, where Beneš addressed the cheering crowds. Afterward, he proceeded across the Charles Bridge, through Malá Strana, and up the hill to Prague's castle complex.[10] His second exile was finally over.[11]

Jan Masaryk's exile would continue for a few more weeks. As Beneš traveled eastward in early 1945, the Czechoslovak foreign minister and son of Tomáš Garrigue Masaryk prepared to travel westward toward California. There, Masaryk took part in the inaugural session of the United Nations at the elegant War Memorial Opera house in San Francisco.[12] He met the delegation from the WJC as well as many heads of state during the weeks-long affair. He did not, however, meet his Polish contemporary. The Big Three Allies, who had recently convened for the Yalta Conference in February 1945, did not yet agree on which group of bureaucrats and statesmen constituted the official government of Poland.[13] Thus, a severe sovereignty dispute resulted at the convening of the first meeting of the UN without Polish representation: neither of the "Polish governments" was present in San Francisco. In a way, Masaryk represented more than his state; he represented an entire region.

The first part of this chapter begins in the first half of the 1940s and considers notes scribbled on postwar planning pamphlets, confidential government letters, and private conversations to chart the development of Masaryk's views on German-speaking Czechoslovak citizens, the place of Jews in postwar Czechoslovakia, the viability of Palestine as a Jewish state, and the issue of statelessness. Unlike his colleague, President Edvard Beneš, who publicly expressed strong views concerning the future of Palestine as a homeland for nationally minded Jews in the early 1940s and deviated little from those ideas publicly for the duration of the war, Masaryk visibly labored over Jewish questions, sometimes even contradicting himself during the same meeting. Masaryk's picaresque journey toward endorsing a Zionist-compatible solution to the "Jewish question" and Jewish migration toward Palestine cannot be unwoven from his less-convoluted intellectual trajectory concerning German exclusion from Czechoslovakia.

Wartime Ruminations on the German and Jewish Questions

Like his colleague Edvard Beneš, Masaryk decided early on during the war that postwar Czechoslovakia should no longer contain an ethnic German minority theoretically. In a way that Beneš seemingly did not, however, Masaryk publicly struggled to clarify what that meant. Over the radio waves on the evening of Wednesday, October 23, 1942, for example, Masaryk addressed the Nazi-appointed state secretary of the Protectorate Karl Hermann Frank on BBC Czechoslovak-London radio.[14] Masaryk used vivid vocabulary to describe the despicable "Germans who are very quick at putting the noose around peoples' necks throughout Europe." Masaryk declared with certainty that after this current conflict, Germany would be defeated, and the "disgusting spider of the swastika will be swept away." Punishment would ensue, and "evil doers" would face "terrible severity." Masaryk's opinion of German elements within his occupied state rang loudly: they must face their crimes and the consequences.

Masaryk and Beneš agreed that culpable Germans should be punished and excised from Czechoslovak society. But how to weed out the "good Germans" from the "bad Germans"? Furthermore, how to differentiate those persecuted as Jews under Nazi racial laws from others listed as German nationals on the 1930 Czechoslovak census? While Beneš and Masaryk agreed on the exclusion of Germans in postwar Czechoslovakia, they issued sometimes contradictory opinions about Jewish belonging in Czechoslovakia and elsewhere. Masaryk seemed notably less certain than Beneš regarding his stance on Zionism and Jewish settlement in Palestine in the early war years. As an example, in a speech given at the Royal Albert Hall in London on October 29, 1942 (a few days after the radio broadcast), Masaryk mentioned Palestine but guaranteed that Jews could return to postwar Czechoslovakia as well. Addressing an assembly of British Jews, Masaryk reminisced about the equality Jews enjoyed in his interwar state: when "Czechoslovakia again takes its rightful place in the heart of Europe, our Jewish brethren will be welcome and I count on their cooperation in building up what Hitler has destroyed." He noted that, although the audience's "longing eye often rests on the country of your past glory, Palestine," deliverance would come only if those Jews in the audience fulfilled their "duty one hundred percent as citizens of Great Britain."[15]

Like his colleagues in the WJC, Masaryk spoke more openly about Jewish migration from Europe as the war progressed. However, unlike WJC leaders who debated to what extent they should negate the diaspora in Europe or reinforce Jewish culture within a region that had cradled a unique and demographically numerous Jewish collective, Masaryk had a more overriding concern. He endorsed plans to build up a Jewish polity in Mandate Palestine partially as an attempt to solve Czechoslovakia's "German question." For if non-Jewish Germans belonged elsewhere—namely, in an ethnic German state—then German-speaking Jews belonged elsewhere as well. Because he could not justify the expulsion of German Jews who were suffering under Nazi racial laws, the establishment of a Jewish state allowed Masaryk to solve a very real conundrum: how to completely eliminate German speakers from the Czechoslovak body politic.

Even when Masaryk was invited by Jews to speak about Jews, his thoughts repeatedly turned to Germans instead. While delivering the Lucien Wolf Memorial Lecture at the Jewish Historical Society of England on September 14, 1943, Masaryk reflected on national minorities in interwar Czechoslovakia. Although he mentioned the Jewish "religious minority" in his former state, his emphasis fell on the German "racial minority" and the disastrous consequences of their existence. Offering some historical context, Masaryk explained how, soon after the conclusion of the First World War, Czechoslovaks as a whole realized they would have to "share [their] citizenship with Germans, Magyars, Little Russians [Ruthenians from Subcarpathian Rus'] and others."[16] Once the government "found the solution for the German minority" within Czechoslovakia's borders, it could "easily find the solution to other minority problems."[17] Beginning in 1918, the "German question" and Czechoslovakia's response to it served as twin foundations for the entire minority rights system. By the 1930s, moreover, rabid German nationalism had corroded the cement binding ethnic German nationals to their Czechoslovak citizenship.[18]

Unlike the Jews in the Weimar Republic, who "blended love of country, the true patriotism, with [their] European citizenship," many Germans living in interwar Czechoslovakia "believed in a hierarchy of races," thus destabilizing the political life of the First Republic and making the Munich Agreement seemingly inevitable. For this reason, he could not envision a postwar reality in Czechoslovakia that included a replication of the interwar minorities system and asked that "the minority problem be settled drastically and with finality."[19] As the problem of the German minorities transcended Czechoslovak borders, the nation as a whole "must take steps to ensure that minorities shall never again act as a lever for power with aggressive designs."[20] Overall, the Czechs and Slovaks had to consummate their national life in their own homeland. In Masaryk's view, "members of minorities in all countries have before them a compelling, momentous and irrevocable choice—to work faithfully for the welfare of the countries in which they are living or to get out!"[21] Masaryk did not employ the word *expulsion*, nor did he explain how population transfers of ethnic minorities would proceed. The message underlying his vision of the postwar world, however, comes across in unnuanced, ethnic terms.

Intellectual Percolations throughout Masaryk's Foreign Office

Just a few weeks after his lecture at the Jewish Historical Society in London, Masaryk traveled to Atlantic City, New Jersey, to attend the first conference of UNRRA. Tartakower met with him during this event, and, as described in the previous chapter, Masaryk had agreed to make a statement about Jewish issues if and when he was summoned to the podium to speak about displaced people. Like other representatives to the event, Masaryk received a mailing from the British arm of the WJC soon after his return from New Jersey. Entitled "The Atlantic City Conference of UNRRA" and printed in January 1944, it garnered the attention of at least two Czech Foreign Ministry employees working in London exile under Masaryk's charge: Zdeněk Procházka and Hubert Ripka. Both men left evidence of their readership on the worn flyer in the form of thin, wobbly underlining, thick red highlights, and their signatures.[22] Ideas concerning the repatriation of DPs to their countries of residence and to other countries willing to accept them attracted their black and red pens more than other issues.

One of the two men underlined that "displaced populations" constituted the "most acute rehabilitation problem." The UNRRA council and the subcommittee dedicated to "Displaced Persons" did not specify protocols for Jews, instead advocating that the "sole rule of procedure in the case of deportees should be 'repatriation' and that 'repatriation' should mean solely the return of United Nations citizens to their countries of origin."[23] The British Section of the WJC noted a fatal flaw in this logic. Both readers drew attention to the next section and declared that many Jewish refugees after the war "will not find it possible or will not prefer to return to the countries of homes from which they were removed and who should by every rule of justice be aided to resettle elsewhere."[24] As a corrective, the WJC British Section proposed that the "repatriation of deportees can take the form not only of returning citizens to their countries of origin but also of returning displaced residents who were not citizens of their country in question to the countries of their 'settled residence.'" The British WJC wanted UNRRA to make their proposed solution to the larger DP problem more lenient. In this way, personal choices gained leverage, whereby citizenship would not be the deciding factor animating repatriation schemes. These ideas disturbed Procházka and Ripka, not necessarily because they wanted to impede the resettlement of European Jews but because they wanted to ensure that German nationals would be excluded from postwar Czechoslovakia.

Another official in Czechoslovak exile circles found UNRRA discussions regarding displaced persons insufficient as well. In a report dating from the end of November 1943 and disseminated to all government departments in December of that year, a Czech delegate to UNRRA named Josef Hanc detailed the dissonance that plagued discussions of these topics.[25] During subcommittee meetings, "many opinions" were voiced. The Czechs agreed with the Yugoslavs that governments must agree on evacuations, but the committee as a whole did not issue an opinion on this statement. The "general resolution given in the end" was that the "delicate and complicated question be solved humanitarily."[26] Hanc, the former Czech consul general in the United States, did not comment on this vague formulation in the larger UNRRA report. Procházka and Ripka, however, saw a link between the WJC literature received in January 1944 and Hanc's report. They exchanged a handful of letters in early 1944 in an attempt to flesh out what was clear and what remained complicated.

In reading over the subcommittee minutes dealing with DPs that Hanc had referenced, Ripka noticed that a slight change in wording could inhibit Czechoslovakia's ability to control the ethnic makeup of its postwar population. In an early meeting of the Subcommittee for Displaced Persons, those assembled—including two Czechoslovaks, Jiří Stolz and Evzen Loebl—confirmed that nationals of UN states or stateless people should "be repatriated to their countries of residence, provided these countries are willing to receive them."[27] Ripka agreed with this formulation, whereby the individual state ultimately decided on the process of repatriation. However, in a subsequent subcommittee meeting, the language did not necessarily guarantee the same level of state autonomy. In fact, the will of individual states was completely erased from the repatriation equation. Instead, UNRRA would work "in consultation with member governments to assist in the return of nationals of UN states and stateless people who had been displaced as a result of the war to their countries of settled residence."[28] Ripka saw this slight change as intensely problematic. If an individual state such as Czechoslovakia could not control the displaced Germans filtering back to their pre-1939 Bohemian and Moravian homes, then Czechoslovak plans to expunge the body politic of the German national element would be threatened. If Stolz and Loebl had protested this revision in the subcommittee, Ripka would have had precedence to offer disagreement. He asked Procházka for clarification and direction.

Procházka responded quickly to Ripka's letter, labeled the situation "serious," and promised to ask Masaryk for guidance moving forward upon the foreign minister's return. Nearly five weeks later, Procházka wrote back to Ripka with Masaryk's response to this repatriation quandary. Procházka had spoken to Masaryk about Ripka's concerns, and Masaryk had offered clear directives. First, even though Czechoslovakia had agreed to welcome stateless individuals and refugees from Germany and Austria across her borders, future meetings of UNRRA might allow for further discussions and different solutions regarding this matter. More importantly, Masaryk directly addressed Ripka's fundamental concern regarding the ability of individual states to control the ethnic composition of their body politic. According to Procházka, Masaryk offered assurances that "the expulsion of Germans will be our own affair," despite the "formal adoption" of UNRRA proposals indicating the contrary.[29]

Inconsistent Solutions and Anti-German Prejudice

The report submitted by the British Section of the WJC in early 1944 belonged to a conversation in Czech government circles that did not necessarily relate to Jewish postwar life in Czechoslovakia. The more meaningful questions for these exiles revolved around the German issue. Problematically, Masaryk endorsed UNRRA proposals demanding universal policies toward stateless DPs while simultaneously crafting backroom plans to push German nationals beyond Czechoslovakia's borders. Notably, there was no differentiation in these UNRRA-inspired discussions between non-Jewish Germans, Jewish Germans, German-speaking enemies, and German-speaking dissidents working against the Third Reich. As Masaryk and his colleagues privately worked through UNRRA proposals, they cast the world in monolithic ethnic terms. Publicly, however, Masaryk vacillated between more nuanced understandings of ethnicized belonging and spoke of the Jews as a discernible entity deserving of their own state.

For example, when Masaryk spoke with the press after attending the inaugural 1943 UNRRA conference in Atlantic City, he offered an evaluation of the event infused with Jewish exceptionalism. The so-called Jewish problem, Masaryk opined, demanded "a specific treatment," and it was "laughable" to think otherwise.[30] The nations of the world could not "build a permanent peace" without treating Jewish concerns as such in the rehabilitation program. For two thousand years, Masaryk said, "we Christians have been discriminating against Jews. Let us this once have the courage to discriminate in order to help them finally solve their problem." Masaryk implicitly declared that a permanent peace depended on this particular kind of "positive" discrimination.

A few months later, however, Masaryk promised to oppose discrimination in all its manifestations. At a dinner arranged in his honor by the Czechoslovak Committee of the United Jewish Appeal on May 24, 1944, he reiterated that the UN had a "duty" to deal with the Jewish problem "thoroughly and for all time." It did not follow, however, that there would be "any differentiation on religious grounds among the citizens of the future free and democratic Czechoslovakia." Instead, Masaryk declared that neither he nor Beneš "would be a part of any such indecency." When people returned to Czechoslovakia, "we are not going to ask: are you a Jew or a Catholic or a Protestant?" Rather, the "people at home will ask 'have you done your duty during the terrible crisis that all of us together have been facing the last half a dozen years?'" Thus, actions, not perceived religion or ethnic belonging, would provide the foundation for postwar Czechoslovak citizenship.

Perhaps Masaryk revised his call against Jewish discrimination because he stood at a lectern in the midst of fundraising for the United Jewish Appeal. After all, calling for continued, albeit positive, discrimination vis-à-vis the Jewish people might have ruffled the feathers of American Jews advocating for continued support of Jews in the diaspora and equality overall. But the juxtaposition of these two public statements focuses attention toward the precarious position Masaryk held as a public figure intent on securing the most favorable postwar conditions for his state. Publicly referred to and privately regarded as a loyal friend to the Jewish people by the WJC and others, Masaryk's words carried weight in public opinion and diplomatic circles. His commitment to the Jews functioned in two, sometimes contradictory, ways. First, he advocated for the reentry of Czechoslovak Jews into postwar Czechoslovakia. Second, he insisted that the "nations of the world, among them the Jews," gather at peace conference tables to deal with the Jewish problem "intelligently and humanely."[31] Sometimes, these two commitments opposed each other. The small number of Czechoslovak Jews who claimed German nationality on the 1930 census complicated Masaryk's first commitment while also solidifying his allegiance to his second commitment. Masaryk did not expect the Czechoslovak people to ask whether one was a Jew or a Catholic or a Protestant in the wake of liberation. He did, however, assume that his countrymen would ask, "Are you German?"

The dissonance evident in Masaryk's sometimes conflicting visions for Jews in the postwar world appeared once again in a meeting between the Czechoslovak foreign minister and two representatives of the WJC. Maurice Perlzweig and Frederick Fried met Masaryk in Washington, DC, on May 16, 1944, to discuss Beneš's comments concerning the repatriation of Jews in general and Czechoslovak Jews in particular after the war. In this intimate meeting, Perlzweig explained that disquiet had emerged in Jewish circles from Beneš's declaration "that the return of Czechoslovak Jews must depend on the adoption of some international machinery for the repatriation of Jews."[32] In response, Masaryk "wished to explain the background of the statement" and "indicated at the same time that he did not see eye to eye with Beneš on this question." Briefly, in Perlzweig's shorthand, "the background was the Sudeten question." During a visit to Churchill before Masaryk left London, "Winston had expressed the hope that the Czechs would get rid of the Germans."[33] When Masaryk exhibited "hesitation," "Winston reassured him that he meant no harshness, but said that it might be done gently, by giving them 48 hours notice to go for example." Offering no comment on whether such a short time frame would be harsh or not, Perlzweig continued with his description of the meeting: "Having told this story [about Churchill], Masaryk turned on me and with great conviction said 'there will be no more minorities, Brother Perlzweig.' The rest of the conversation left it crystal clear that the Czechs felt that their loyal support of special minority rights under the old system had been very ill rewarded and that they did not propose to repeat it."

In response, Perlzweig pointed out that the Sudeten German problem "was not the issue and that it was important to reassure public opinion that the citizenship rights of Jews in regard to repatriation would be observed." Masaryk prevaricated and proposed "to make a strong statement about it at a forthcoming meeting of the United Jewish Appeal" and, subsequently, "offered to write out a statement immediately." Perlzweig attached the statement in full. Dated May 16, 1944, and signed by Jan Masaryk, it read, "I wish to go on record once again in stating that decent citizens of Czechoslovakia regardless of race or faith will be treated in the same fair manner as was the case before this terrible war started. The treatment of Jews in my country is a matter of personal pride to me and there will be no change whatsoever in this respect. This little statement can be considered as the concerted opinion of the Czechoslovak Government-in-Exile." Commenting on this statement in his memo, Perlzweig observed that "there is no explicit reference to repatriation, but apparently it is implied in the reiterated promise of equal rights." During the meeting, Perlzweig and Fried had directed Masaryk to this admission. In response, Masaryk "repeated one of his stock sayings: 'I will not go back without my Jews.'"[34]

Thus, a gathering initiated to offer clarification actually resulted in thicker confusion. In response to a serious question about the status of Jewish repatriates overall, Masaryk offered, to use Perlzweig's wording, "a stock saying" and an incomplete glimpse of a broader context that he did not fully describe. This meeting reveals that even in May 1944, after Beneš had received private guarantees from Roosevelt (June 1943) and Stalin (December 1943) concerning the homogenization of the Czechoslovak body politic and further reassurances on population transfers more generally from the Big Three at Tehran, the Sudeten Germans haunted conversations about postwar Jewish life in Masaryk's state. The inability of Masaryk to tease out Jewish concerns from the broader "German problem" arguably abetted citizenship confusion on the ground in the wake of Hitler's defeat.

Just how deep did Masaryk's suspicions concerning German-speaking Czechoslovak Jews strike? A radio address Masaryk delivered on Rosh Hashanah on September 29, 1943, provides an informative glimpse: Masaryk reminded his Czech-speaking listeners in the United Kingdom or perhaps those intercepting the signal illegally on the continent that on this day Jews in "America, England, Russia, and Palestine" prayed for the "poorest of the poor, who had their synagogues torn down by the German barbarians and were massacred by the millions."[35] Reflecting on Jews in the diaspora worldwide, Masaryk admitted that "it is true that every nation is known by how it treats the Jews, and we behave admirably."[36] However, Masaryk continued, in a different and provocative tone, "It is also true that some Jews did not behave well. They walked repeatedly through Prague cafés and acted like Germans [*němčili*] even after 1933."[37] After the war, however, Masaryk predicted, "it will be difficult to find a Czechoslovakian who will make these mistakes again."[38] Regardless, Masaryk had also known "many, very many decent, proper, faithful Jews," who "belonged among us as our own." As he closed his radio remarks, Masaryk assumed a self-congratulatory posture, saying that after the war "our children and the whole world can say that we helped the Jews and we remained descent people amidst German horrors."[39]

Fundamentally, Masaryk's decision to recognize the Jewish New Year is exceptional. Masaryk had offered condolences for the wartime Jewish loss, maintained a note of hopefulness moving forward, and exhibited a sensitivity to a religious calendar that was not his own. On the other hand, this address, which was meant to mark the passage of Jewish time, contains references to "Germanizing" tendencies among Czechoslovak Jews. Poised before a microphone and intent on reaching out to Jews across occupied Europe and in liberated areas as well, Masaryk cast accusations concerning regretful interwar behavior and a prediction that Germanizing Jews would not operate in the same haughty manner after Hitler's defeat. Why include such negative reminiscences in an address containing Rosh Hashanah greetings at a very somber moment? Masaryk's words are best understood against a backdrop of paranoia. So worried was Masaryk about the ethnic German element in Czechoslovakia that a New Year's speech for a decimated people became an opportunity for pointing fingers and offering a guarantee that Jews in postwar Czechoslovakia would never "Germanize" in the same way again. For Masaryk, only "Czech Jews" belonged in postwar Czechoslovakia.

Statelessness: Current Problems and Possible Solutions

Germanizing Jews could not easily rejoin, Masaryk predicted, the Czechoslovak body politic.[40] Neither would they be stateless. Discussions of statelessness were omnipresent in international circles during the Second World War. Statelessness and citizenship are mutually exclusive. Therefore, to eradicate statelessness, a political entity must bestow citizenship or an international organization must create a new category for political belonging that transcends state borders. As the Second World War drew to a close, few serious discussions at international levels entertained the reintroduction of Nansen passports or the creation of a new status that would simply prolong statelessness. Instead, it became "generally accepted doctrine that statelessness is undesirable."[41]

Thus, nationality law had to be reformed in such a way that "every individual may have a nationality and statelessness may be eliminated." In the words of a booklet produced by the British Section of the WJC, which arrived at Czechoslovakia's Foreign Ministry in March 1945, the "abolition of statelessness can only be a humanely satisfactory remedy if nationality warrants the enjoyment of fundamental human rights by all nationals."[42] In other words, for statelessness to vanish, the category of citizenship needed to guarantee basic rights for all people regardless of nationality.

The author of the article, legal scholar Paul Weis, explained that "there is no basis in present international law for a right to a nationality; neither has the individual a right to acquire a nationality at birth, nor does international law prohibit loss of nationality after birth by deprivation or otherwise."[43] This situation placed the individual at the mercy of the "nationality-granting" state. Due to an "exaggerated conception of the state," "the unlimited exercise of its sovereign omnipotence," and the "lack of effective international machinery for the enactment and enforcement of universal rules," the individual floated alone on the high seas, cast off from political lifelines. As long as "nationality is the link between the individual and the benefits of the Law of Nations, legal policy regarding nationality must see its task in providing this link." Nationality should be conceived of as a "means" toward a specific aim: the "enjoyment of the benefits of the Law of Nationals and—ultimately—of the Rights of Man by all of those rights which are common to all men."[44]

To foreground his argument, Weis referred to a series of denaturalization laws passed in the 1930s that stripped groups of citizenship rights. These laws had had a sizable impact on his own life. Born in Vienna in 1907, Weis had been a law student when he lost his citizenship and faced internment in Dachau in 1938 and 1939.[45] While describing the revisions of German and later Austrian law, Weis emphasized the Jewish predicament that emerged in a variety of occupied countries as Nazi German law was instituted by the occupiers. Stateless people were by default "unprotected."[46] The status of statelessness was hereditary, and only stateless people codified as refugees could claim international protections. Statelessness evaporated only after repatriation, naturalization in another state, marriage, or death. Notably, migrations directed toward Palestine and America did not lead to statelessness, as these immigrants were in a position to "acquire the nationality of the country of immigration."[47]

Seeking a solution to the problem of statelessness, Weis argued that simply "allotting stateless persons a nationality" would not ameliorate the situation. Rather, the "question has to be decided whether the nationality to be allotted is the nationality of the State with which the person is in fact most closely connected."[48] So the "will of the people" had to be ascertained before nationality could be fixed. As the individual and the group were entitled to state belonging as a basic human right, the power and authority of individual states were necessarily constrained. The state could no longer indiscriminately deprive someone of nationality and could not arbitrarily cast out citizens until those people had acquired political belonging elsewhere.[49] To cite Weis directly, "Under existing customary International Law, no State may refuse to receive back into its territory any of its nationals or former nations unless the latter has acquired another nationality. It is desirable that this rule should be laid down unconditionally and unambiguously by contractual legislation."[50]

Therefore, Weis recommended that in countries such as Czechoslovakia, where Jews might want to live again, returning prewar citizens should obtain their former political status ipso jure, as legislation initiated by occupying powers was to be rescinded. Those Jews who possessed wartime citizenship in Axis countries, however, could decide not to reacquire their prewar nationality. Compulsory repatriation may have been out the question, but decisions regarding citizenship were to be made by individuals and not necessarily by state powers. For example, a reinstatement of interwar citizenship laws across Nazi-occupied Europe would allow Jews to return to their former countries of residence. For those Jews refusing to return to their prewar homes in Germany, Austria, Italy, Bulgaria, Romania, and France, the eradication of statelessness would have opened up an aperture for the creation of new citizenships elsewhere, as in Palestine or the western hemisphere. Weis himself would have fallen into this category had he not acquired British citizenship in 1947. After being released from Dachau in 1939, he had managed to emigrate to England, where he continued his law studies and began his work for the British Section of the WJC. On the question of whether Jewish DPs should have the right to emigrate directly to Palestine, as the final resolution of the WJC's War Emergency Congress had demanded four months before his article was published, Weis was silent. He did not address this specifically in his paper as "it requires special and most careful examination in connection with the entire Palestinian problem."[51]

In the end, Weis articulated a handful of distinct demands. First, he asked that "nobody should be deprived of his nationality for reasons of discrimination (political, racial, religious or other)" in the future.[52] Second, he suggested that old nationalities should be restored "from the date on which they were deprived of it."[53] Both of these fundamental demands were translated into Czech and sent from Procházka's desk in the Ministry of Foreign Affairs to the Ministry of the Interior soon after the pamphlet arrived at the ministry's

London office in March 1944. Why did these two demands provoke concern in Czechoslovak government circles? The memorandum attached to the translation does not offer an explanation. Perhaps, however, we can deduce from the evidence presented in this chapter why Weis's revision of "statelessness" as a viable political category would threaten postwar plans for a reconstituted Czechoslovak body politic.

As illustrated by numerous examples, Masaryk and many of his subordinates in the Czechoslovak government-in-exile desperately wanted Germans out of postwar Czechoslovakia. Accordingly, they approached the issue of statelessness with this paramount concern woven throughout their thoughts. So, if German-speaking Jews from Czechoslovakia could automatically regain their prewar citizenship with the backing of international law, a small but noticeable number (arguably between fifteen hundred and two thousand people) would potentially have legal rights to stay in Czechoslovakia, thereby complicating the expulsion of Germans. Both Paul Weis and the WJC wanted to guarantee that Jews could not arbitrarily be deprived of political belonging in the future, and both wanted previously annulled citizenships to be reinstated. In general, Masaryk hoped that citizenship would be reinstated for Jews as well. He did not, however, want German-speaking Jews to remain in his Czechoslovakia, despite their prewar citizenship status as Czechoslovaks. Herein lies the contradiction: Masaryk, the perceived, steadfast friend of the WJC in Allied diplomatic circles, wanted German-speaking Jews to gain citizenship elsewhere, perhaps in an ethnically Jewish state, so that Czechoslovakia's plans for the expulsion of "Germans" could be more completely realized. The emergence of Palestine as a state for "ethnic" Jews offered Masaryk a solution to the perennial "Jewish question," the problem of statelessness, and the problem of the German minority and minorities in Czechoslovakia overall.

Infinite Returns

A litany of wartime communications between the Czechoslovak foreign minister and the WJC came to an end in July 1945, when Maurice Perlzweig wrote Masaryk to wish him luck on his return, thank him, and remind the foreign minister what the WJC wanted for the Jews of Czechoslovakia. A note of caution rang through the short letter and the memo. "There is scarcely an active Zionist anywhere," Perlzweig claimed, "who is not now convinced that President Beneš has made up his mind that the price of Czechoslovak citizenship henceforth must be the loss of any real Jewish identity."[54] Perlzweig asked Masaryk to correct him explicitly if his assumption, which in fact was raised in the May 1944 meeting quoted above, was indeed correct. Already the idea that Czechoslovak Jews would "be presented with the alternative either of emigrating to Palestine or of becoming totally identified spiritually and culturally, as well as politically" with one of the other nationalities that made up the Czechoslovak population at that time had caused "considerable disquiet" throughout the Jewish world and beyond.[55] Specifically, Perlzweig asked Masaryk to reexamine internal government policies toward Jews while also sharpening their treatment of another group: Jews with German citizenship in Czechoslovakia.

According to Perlzweig, a "thousand German Jews" did not "desire to return to Germany" for "reasons which need no elaboration." The WJC asked "the Czechoslovak Government not to compel these victims of Nazi oppression to return to places where they have now become strangers. The same, in greater or less degree, may well apply to some Jews of other nationalities." These Jews should have permission to stay in Czechoslovakia for a few months. On the one hand, Perlzweig was adamant that Czechoslovak Jews have the ability to stay in Masaryk's state as a discernible entity. On the other, Perlzweig wanted to ensure that Jews, of German citizenship and others, could leave for Palestine or elsewhere and be supported by the Czechoslovak government in the meantime. These grand requests indicate an unusual intimacy between Perlzweig, the rest of the WJC, and the Czechoslovak foreign minister. Perlzweig hinted at this closeness in the letter attached to this memo. As he wished Masaryk luck on his homeward journey, Perlzweig wrote that he need not tell Masaryk "how deeply indebted" the WJC felt to him for his "truly magnificent support of [their] cause during a most tragic period and for all the marks of [his] friendship, especially during these recent years."[56] Perlzweig had relied on Masaryk in the past and anticipated that he could do so in the future. His prediction would soon be tested. By the end of 1946, Masaryk's proximity to the WJC and his belief in Palestine as a destination where Jews belonged would pay dividends for those convinced that Europe's Jews belonged elsewhere. In the meantime, however, Masaryk had more traveling to do.

So, in fact, did millions of others. After the western Allies reached German territory in early 1945, military oversight of refugees had "proceeded smoothly." Uprooted civilians in France, Belgium, and Italy found military-organized transports home relatively quickly. In the months after D-Day, the "blueprint" issued on June 4, 1944, by the Refugee Displaced Person and Welfare branch of the Supreme Headquarters Allied Expeditionary Force (SHAEF) prepared for the needs of the 11,332,700 uprooted in western European countries. According to that plan, "all the uprooted persons would return to their countries in about six months," with the soldiers ensuring an orderly passage and the provision of relief supplies.[57] It proved difficult to anticipate for such large numbers.

From the beginning of 1945 toward the days when Masaryk and his colleagues traveled to San Francisco, nearly seven million civilians, millions of uprooted "ethnic" Germans, and countless prisoners of war demanded SHAEF's support. Michael Marrus notes that a massive military-orchestrated repatriation effort utilizing "passenger trains, open boxcars, barges and army trucks" managed to move 5.25 million people "home" over just two months. That's a rate of 80,000 people, Marrus reminds us, each day. Remarkably, "of seven million displaced persons under the control of the western Allies, fewer than two million remained by the end of September."[58] Many of those two million spread into displaced persons camps across the newly created military command zones in western Germany and Austria. And while they were not a static group (some were repatriated "home," some came back, and others arrived, some multiple times), they were stubborn. Of course, long-term sojourns in DP camps were especially precarious, as they could be closed at any time. They almost were in February 1946, until US president Harry S. Truman intervened. Fatefully for some, they remained open and would remain so well into the 1950s. And for those future displaced persons moving within and from the east, access to these camps in the American zone of occupied Germany, of course, went directly through western Czechoslovakia and under Masaryk's nose.

ENCOUNTERING POSTWAR REALITIES: TARTAKOWER, WARHAFTIG, AND SCHWARZBART

This next section examines how three WJC officials encountered postwar realities in exile and back in east central Europe in 1945 and early 1946.[59] These encounters combined with more overarching reports from 1945 drove home the vicious results of Hitler's failed war against east central Europe and his successful war against Europe's Jews. Across the first months of 1945, the enormity of both of these wars spread across the pages of *Nasza Trybuna* as the Red Army swept over what had been Nazi-occupied Poland. Four days before the liberation of Auschwitz-Birkenau on January 27, 1945, the paper included the report of a speech by Polish Jewish leader Emil Sommerstein, who had attended the first WJC meeting in 1936, survived the war in the Soviet Union, and was poised to assume the position of chairperson of the Central Committee of Polish Jews (the central Jewish organization for postwar reconstruction and repatriation in liberated Poland under the purview of the Polish government assembled in Lublin). The speech quoted in *NT* mentioned that 6.1 million Jews were killed throughout the war, including 3 million deported toward Polish territory from other countries. The February 1945 issue included a byline stating that the "Jewish population [had been] reduced to 1% in Nazi-ridden cities," and a report from April 30, 1945, noted that the Central Committee of Jews counted 30,000 Polish Jews on liberated Polish territory and only 500 children. The majority of those remaining were between twenty-five and forty years old.

Besides confirming the extent of the annihilation, these pages also conveyed the extreme uprootedness of Polish Jews and other Jews as Axis forces retreated. An English-language edition of the serial noted that twenty thousand Polish Jews were in Belgium as of January 1945. An evocative editorial that Tartakower wrote in advance of the first meeting of the United Nations on March 28, 1945, mentioned that "five-sixths or perhaps even more" of this "community of remnants" remained outside their former country.[60] And finally, in a long article published the month the Nazis met complete defeat, Tartakower paid heed to the tragedy and extent of Polish Jewish displacement. "For the few hundreds of thousand Polish Jews left after the inferno of the last few years no more than a fraction resides on the territory of Poland," he observed. "The great majority, a quarter of a million, are scattered as refugees in the vast interior provinces of the Soviet Union, tens of thousands are in Germany, in France, Belgium and in countries outside of Europe."[61] Jewish displaced persons in general, Tartakower noted, were still ruthlessly uprooted. Two-thirds of all surviving Jews were refugees, deportees, stateless, or displaced from their original homes in some way. "There can be no justice and no peace in the world," Tartakower posited, "unless and until this tragic problem will find its solution." Repatriation was necessary. The majority of these refugees, Tartakower suggested, wanted to go to Palestine and should be supported. It remained unclear, however, whether Tartakower's suggestion would morph into practical policies.

Encounter with Earl Harrison, March 1945

A policy began to coalesce at a meeting in Philadelphia on March 20, 1945, when Tartakower met with Earl Harrison. Roughly three months before he traveled to postwar Europe on the orders of President Truman and less than one week after his appointment as the American vice-chairman of the Intergovernmental Committee for Refugees, Harrison hosted Tartakower and his colleague from the American Jewish Congress, Chaim Fineman, to discuss a short but significant list of wartime and postwar issues. After devoting time to the problems of aliens in western Europe, refugees "deprived" of liberty, and "relief" for Jews in territories under Red Army control, the dialogue turned to an unenviable issue: "the resettlement of Jewish persons who cannot or do not desire to be repatriated."[62] Specifically, Tartakower focused on east central European Jews who would not want to return to communities devastated by genocide and instead desired settlement and citizenship elsewhere.

What would happen to these uprooted Jews, in some instances deprived of their citizenship from the mid-1930s onward, living outside their countries of citizenship during war's outbreak and in other circumstances forced to return to once-populated communities as sole survivors? As we have observed, Tartakower and his colleagues at the WJC became increasingly captivated by this particular problem in their preparations for the two UNRRA meetings in 1943 and 1944. They had not yet received a satisfactory solution to this problem and did not necessarily anticipate that the next UNRRA meeting in August 1945 would prove any different. But on this day, Tartakower sat beside a newly powerful man in Pennsylvania, thousands of miles and a handful of exiled years away from the country of his citizenship, with well-matured advice. After years of writing and conversing with Allied leaders as well as his own colleagues in the WJC, Tartakower knew with certainty how this particular "problem" should be solved.

After the war, Tartakower explained, nearly 350,000 Jews of German, Austrian, Hungarian, Romanian, and Polish citizenships would fall into the category of displaced persons "who cannot or do not desire to be repatriated" to their country of prewar citizenship. This urgent problem, one of the "most important within the program of the Intergovernmental Committee," could be solved swiftly. Tartakower and his colleague Fineman told Harrison that the "overwhelming majority of these people will certainly wish to go to Palestine and that it is the duty of the Intergovernmental Committee to enable them to do so with the close cooperation of the Jewish Agency for Palestine." In response to the presented numbers and this provocative suggestion, Harrison was "very impressed," and, in Tartakower's memory, the vice-chairman "agreed that the solution we suggest may be the best."

When encouraged by Harrison to "confidentially" transmit "their opinion of the work which was done thus far by the Intergovernmental Committee," Fineman and Tartakower vocalized their dissatisfaction with the situation, the "poor achievements" of the committee, and the unfairness of a "policy which frequently is directed against the vital interest of the Jewish refugees as it happened especially in the case of Palestine." Commenting to Harrison on the work of his organization, they "stressed how inhumane it is not to allow a person on account of certain political motives to go to the only country in which they may find a permanent home and how much more inhumane it is to send such persons to camps for refugees instead of enabling them to proceed to Palestine where they may start a new and dignified life." Tartakower reported that Harrison was "grateful" for this explanation and receptive to learning more. He asked Tartakower to forward the "facts and figures quoted during the conference" to him in the form of a short document before he left for his upcoming trip to London.[63]

Two months after his meeting with Tartakower, Earl Harrison traveled throughout the displaced persons camps in the American zone of occupied Germany, and he eventually submitted the fateful report that historically bears his name to President Truman calling for separate facilities for Jewish displaced persons and the immediate granting of one hundred thousand entry certificates to Palestine.[64] To quote from the August 1945 report directly, Harrison argued that "for some of the European Jews there is no acceptable decent solution other than Palestine.[65] This is said on a purely humanitarian basis with no reference to ideological or political consideration so far as Palestine is concerned." In his conclusion, Harrison declared "that the main solution" and "in many ways the only real solution to the problem lies in the quick evacuation of all nonrepatriable Jews in Germany and Austria who wish it to Palestine." In fact, he added, "the evacuation of the Jews of Germany and Austria to Palestine will solve the problem" for the military authorities.[66]

Truman apparently agreed. Writing to US commander general Dwight D. Eisenhower at the end of August 1945, Truman noted that he was "communicating directly with the British Government in an effort to have the doors of Palestine opened" for the displaced persons who "wish to go there."[67] Reviewing the publication of the Harrison Report a few months later during the initial meetings of the Anglo-American Committee of Inquiry in 1946, the *New York Times* proclaimed that the report constituted "the first official proposal for the immediate settlement of 100,000 Jews in Palestine."[68] Thus, it became an important node of precedence for others who eventually supported this plan. In 1946, for example, the WJC quoted these lines directly for their memo delivered to the Fifth Plenary Session of the Intergovernmental Committee on Refugees. While the ideas were attributed to Earl Harrison in this memo, their provenance should have extended back to Arieh Tartakower, who presented this formula to Harrison during their visit in March 1945.

Encounter with the Shocking Postwar Reality and UNRRA's Inefficiency

During the five months between Tartakower's visit with Harrison and the publication of his famous report in August 1945, the war against the Nazis had ended, but other conflicts had begun. As Stefan-Ludwig Hoffmann reminds us, the "greatest number of deaths in the war occurred between 1944–1945," and the greatest waves of displacement crested in the wake of Hitler's suicide.[69] Concerned with the psychology of war survival and trauma's repercussions on the postwar era, Marcin Zaremba notes that "everywhere the ending of military activities brought chaos and a sense of uncertainty."[70] Anxiety, violence, and aggression were "present in all spheres, civil war, inter-ethnic conflicts, state violence against the opposition" and combined to cause a "lengthening of inter-ethnic distance" throughout the region between Berlin and Moscow. Those who expected "rapid stabilization" were quickly disappointed. The "post-war 'migration of peoples,' looting, personal score settling, the exacting of sometimes brutal vengeances against collaborators and Germans" further damaged war-torn societies. In the wake of liberation, this lack of stabilization and the pooling of uprooted Jews in what had become occupied Germany (and to a lesser extent Austria) came to shock Tartakower and his colleagues at the WJC. At the War Emergency Congress in November 1944, those assembled had supported the decisions of the German Jewish Reconstruction Committee to proclaim a ban against Jews returning to Germany en masse. Now, as the summer of 1945 progressed and Tartakower planned to visit the United Kingdom for three conferences (the third meeting of UNRRA, the WJC-organized meeting of European Jews, and a meeting of the World Zionist Organization), he received reports about Jewish DPs in the heart of the former Third Reich and reacted with his journalistic pen.

Things were simply not moving fast enough to satisfy Tartakower after "Victory in Europe" had been declared. At the end of May 1945, he insisted that "Jewish DPs must be authorized to stay where they are at the present, until means and ways will be found for their repatriation or emigration to other countries." Repatriation should transpire "as soon as possible," and persons "who cannot or do not desire to be repatriated" should be taken care of as well. "The majority of them," he argued, "are anxious to go to Palestine and they are to be enabled to do so," and "for all others, new countries of settlement will have to be found." He was discouraged by the results thus far. "Much more must be done," he wrote, "if the problem is to be solved."[71] One month later in June 1945, he struck a more somber tone over the work of UNRRA in particular. There was, he observed, "a strong feeling of disappointment with the activities of UNRRA. Compared not only with the magnitude of the disaster and the tremendous needs in the countries devastated by war and overrun by Nazis... the achievements of UNRRA are so far not very encouraging and in many cases may even dwindle into insignificance."[72] In fact, the "tasks ahead of us were just as overwhelming today as they were a year or two ago." Tartakower demanded UNRRA's attention toward the "internment camps in Germany" and "the people within those camps." "Where has UNRRA been," Tartakower asked, in the "two months since liberation?" What had UNRRA done, he continued, for those in the camps, who "had every reason to expect that their unspeakable martyrology would now come to an end and that a helping hand would be given to them by the Allied nations?"[73]

His questions continued. "How should former German or Austrian Jews who have nothing except hatred and contempt left in their hearts for their so-called fatherlands be repatriated? And what should become of the tens of thousands of Polish, Hungarian or Rumanian [*sic*] Jews who are now in the camps in Germany and are most reluctant to return to their home countries . . . ?" To Tartakower, it was clear that most of them "dream about going to Palestine," and "some may wish to go to other countries." But a string of queries remained: "Who is responsible for this work of resettlement? Whose concern is it? Who makes the necessary preparings? Again I am afraid that the final answer to these questions must await the coming of the Messiah." Nobody seemed willing to take responsibility for the displaced persons milling around Europe. Tartakower observed that the "people of UNRRA may be tempted to say that this is the concern of the Intergovernmental Committee of Refugees and they unfortunately may be right from their point of view." Yet again he used the first-person pronoun as he offered a response to his own series of questions. "I say 'unfortunately,'" he scoffed, "because after the experience of the last few years, I have very little if any confidence in the efficiency of this body."[74]

In July 1945, UNRRA claimed to be in full operation, with 2,656 workers in 332 teams spread across the newly created western zones of Germany. But significant gaps in UNRRA's work would remain until UNRRA disbanded in 1947 and especially until the end of 1946, when millions still clogged Europe's highways, byways, and camps. In September 1945, for instance, the WJC Office Committee learned about some significant problems in UNRRA's work. Neither the Jewish population in Czechoslovakia nor that in Austria had yet obtained UNRRA assistance. Despite the fact that Sweden welcomed refugees, UNRRA delegates in occupied Germany prevented their departure. In principle, the WJC leaders decided "to bring refugees from Germany to Sweden from where they can also proceed to Palestine." Tartakower communicated these views in Washington within the week. On Goldmann's suggestion, Tartakower also inquired about the possibility of sending WJC representatives to Europe in UNRRA uniforms. Despite UNRRA teams on the ground, the situation among DPs in the American zone remained, in Tartakower's assessment, "terrible."[75]

It seemed that Tartakower's prediction about UNRRA's inability to act in the wake of organizational meetings rang true. The third UNRRA meeting, which convened from August 7 to 14, 1945, offered no conclusive solutions to the "problem" of Jewish DPs waiting in occupied Germany or the "problem" of DPs who did not wish to be repatriated to the countries of their former citizenship. Neither did, it should be mentioned, the inaugural meeting of the United Nations, which convened in San Francisco that May.[76] The "question of non-repatriable displaced Jews," like the "stateless" Jews, Jews from Germany and Austria, and the "majority" of the Polish, Romanian, and Hungarian Jews, remained at the end of August 1945 "one of the most complicated and gravest problems facing" the readers of *NT*.[77] The WJC "asked that special steps be taken" by UNRRA and the IGCR "to facilitate the entrance of the Jews to Palestine." Nothing seemed to happen in response. And still, significant obstacles to immigration remained for east central European refugees in both the American and British (vis-à-vis Palestine) contexts.[78]

Encounter with a Small Group of the Polish Jewish Remnant: London 1945

"The delegation from Poland had arrived."[79] The announcement stopped the conversation in the meeting room full of delegates to the World Zionist Organization's first postwar conference in London.[80] Arieh Tartakower became silent. "Divided from each other for six years," it seemed "unbelievable" that they would reunite in a sterile meeting room. Yitzchak Zuckerman would be there soon, as well as Chaja Grosmann. Adolf Berman would speak at the assembly, but it remained unclear if he would join the others for this more private salutation. And then, finally, the leader, Emil Sommerstein, entered the room. Tartakower could not describe "the welcome scene." No one knew whom to hug, what first words to say. "We did not know," he admitted, "what to share among ourselves." Neither Sommerstein nor Tartakower could, in fact, "take control of emotion." The recognized leader of Polish Jewry had "changed so much that he was unrecognizable, as if he himself were the entire tragedy of Polish Jews." His "enormous, gray beard" and his walking staff masked, temporarily, the "majestic rest that never leaves him." When the words finally poured out, they were words full of information. They spoke of "underground work, about armed struggle with the Germans, about ghettos and death camps, about what is happening in Poland now, about the hunger and dreams for Palestine, about the . . . *chalutz* movement, about those who are coming back to Poland from Russia and those who emigrated or want to emigrate."[81] In his official speech before the entire World Zionist Congress, Sommerstein reiterated many of these facts. He also discussed the new Polish government and its policies toward equal rights and toward emigration.

Reflecting on this emotional, seemingly indescribable encounter, Tartakower was hesitant to offer much commentary: "This is not a place for details." But he wanted to convey one point. "It is evident," he wrote, "that the best and most convenient solution to the question of Polish Jews would soon be to transfer them, possibly all, to Palestine."[82] In the meantime, he wanted to defend Jewish rights and Jewish society, but those aims were temporary. His meeting in London, his first with a number of Polish Jewish survivors of Hitler's Gehenna and Soviet deportation, pushed him to negate this particular diaspora with even more vigor. He had a similar reaction when he traveled to South America in September 1944 and across the continent encountered reminders of the Polish Jewish civilization that had been his own. I have written in this book about seizing political opportunities, weighing diplomatic options, and strategizing as a small organization in a broader ocean of Allied voices. The emotions hatched in the June 8, 1944, Office Committee meeting concerning the return of Jews to Germany marked one moment on a more personal, humanizing trajectory. This meeting between Tartakower and Sommerstein's group indicates another. Next, Warhaftig and Schwarzbart supply us with more.

Encounter: Zorach Warhaftig Proposes a "Final Solution" in Germany, Fall 1945

On his first trip to occupied Germany, Zorach Warhaftig failed in his mission to rescue five hundred children and shepherd them away from postwar internment camps to France.[83] The Central Committee of the Liberated Jews in the US zone refused to let them go. Warhaftig had traveled to Europe as an envoy of the Union of Orthodox Rabbis.[84] Besides his hands-on relief work, Warhaftig spent part of his time in Europe during the fall of 1945 researching and drafting a report commissioned by his colleagues in the WJC after they learned of his travel plans. And in this report, Warhaftig described what happened to hundreds of Jewish children destined at first for French homes "prepared there by the *Mizrachi* and *Aguda* organizations for a temporary stay of six months."[85] In the final stages of this plan, as Warhaftig and others were selecting which children would leave for France, "the Central Committee informed us of its opposition to our undertaking." At a joint meeting with the Central Committee, UNRRA, and the JDC, Warhaftig and his colleagues were "presented with a final and determined refusal to let the children go." The Central Committee instead "wanted the children to go to Palestine."

While the Office Committee of the WJC had prioritized Palestine for Jewish children in Lisbon more than one year earlier, this insistence on Palestine over every other temporary destination was unique in this particular postwar context. Warhaftig explained to his WJC colleagues how from October 1945 to November 1945 the prioritization of Palestine came to eclipse other options. In the final month of summer, Yitzhak Grünbaum, whom we first met as an increasingly radicalized Zionist leader returning to Poland in the 1930s from his home in Mandate Palestine, had made a declaration on behalf of the Jewish Agency. It was "most important and urgent," Warhaftig recalled Grünbaum saying, to "get the Jews out of Germany to any neighboring countries" even if that movement was technically illegal.[86] The visit of David Ben-Gurion helped change this position in October and November.[87] According to Ben-Gurion, with whom Warhaftig had audience, "taking a Jew out of camps in Germany, to any country outside of Palestine is, in the present conditions, as big a crime as taking a Jew out of Palestine itself."[88]

Warhaftig's unpublished report is replete with numbers, information, and individual snapshots of the daily DP existence in an uncertain time. Like generations of historians who would come after him, Warhaftig relied on estimations when writing about DPs. It was difficult to be more accurate. Eighty thousand Jews were spread around camps in both occupied Germany and Austria.[89] Already by November 1945, ten thousand Jews from the camps had departed to Belgium and France; some claimed prewar residence in those places and joined a massive "repatriation movement," while others traveled westward because they had assurances of a certificate enabling them entry to Palestine or a visa to another country.[90] The lack of consulates in Germany and Austria meant that DPs often traveled westward in the hope of obtaining a visa. In general, Warhaftig described a situation best characterized as "that of people 'on their way.'" Especially among Jewish populations in Poland and Hungary, there was a "continuous movement of evacuation."[91]

Midway through his report, Warhaftig focused on one evacuation stream in particular: the so-called *bricha*. Like the first phase of the *odsun* (expulsion) or the semiorganized movement of those deemed German away from Czechoslovakia, which began chaotically in the summer and fall of 1945 and then continued in a more organized fashion in the first half of 1946, the movement of Jews away from east central Europe began in an unorganized fashion, and it was, in Warhaftig's assessment, "wild."[92] Across the first three months of the postwar era, eight hundred thousand "Germans" left Czechoslovakia under a variety of different circumstances. That event, the *divoký odsun* (wild expulsion), was not necessarily coordinated by the central state, which was in fact just coalescing on Czechoslovak territory.[93] Around the same time this massive movement of humanity began, "people from Poland particularly smuggled themselves out to Czechoslovakia and there via Plzeň and Prague."[94] From western Bohemia, fleeing populations crossed frontiers into the American zone.

Some semblance of order had appeared by November 1945, despite the fact that the *bricha* remained, according to Warhaftig, mostly unorganized. Only recently had particular halutz organizations "set up a kind of liaison officer in the border cities to help" give advice and directions and indicate transportation facilities. The so-called "organized *bricha*" provided documents and organized care facilities for newcomers to Germany and Austria and is covered in the next chapter. With regard to governmental responses to the movement he witnessed, Warhaftig had the following to report. The legal authorities in Poland and Hungary felt positive about this *bricha*.[95] The British were hostile; the Americans were friendly. Czechoslovak authorities had been particularly helpful, because, Warhaftig suggested, "they wanted to get rid of these undesirable transients." Perhaps they were motivated as well by their desire to move as many "Germans" away from the Sudetenland as quickly as possible. Warhaftig asks that readers of his report understand the entire European Jewish context, but he does not necessarily demand an understanding of the broader European situation from himself. Occurring at the same time and in the same spaces, the wild *bricha* cannot, of course, be completely separated from the wild *odsun*. Even the adjectives used to describe both indicate a striking similarity. Both events were fueled by racism, albeit in different forms.

Warhaftig's visit to occupied Germany near the end of 1945 convinced him even further that Palestine provided the ultimate answer to almost all postwar Jewish questions: "What the displaced Jews are more interested in are not the problems of relief but those of their final solution." There was, Warhaftig lamented, "terrible disappointment," "bitterness, nervousness," and "depression because of the unclear prospects for their future. The overwhelming majority of the survivors, particularly the youth have one wish only, to go to Palestine." And while "an important fraction of Jews . . . would prefer emigration to the United States," for Warhaftig the "final solution" equaled Palestine.[96]

Like Warhaftig before him, Tartakower used the fraught phrase *final solution* in April 1945. In a memo to Jacob Robinson on "Jewish stateless aliens," Tartakower wrote that "the final solution of [this] problem will be secured only by encouraging such persons to find new homes in other countries and especially in Palestine."[97] Encounters with survivors and others reaffirmed what both Polish Jews already knew in the fall of 1944. Six months, nine months, and one year later they spoke the same words with more confidence. Nearly twelve months after the War Emergency Congress, the Executive Committee of the WJC adopted a resolution in response to words offered by Ernest Bevin, the British foreign secretary. On November 13, 1945, Bevin drew a distinction between Zionist organizations and "Jewry as a whole." Wise, Kubowitzki, Goldmann, and Frischer responded with speed and clarity. "The WJC and Jews everywhere," they stated, "will continue to give to the Jewish Agency for Palestine which is authorized under the Mandate to speak for the Jewish people as a whole in matters affecting Palestine and which expresses the views of the Zionist organization and very large numbers of non-Zionists."[98] As documents from 1944 demonstrated and these documents from 1945 reinforce, the idea of continued Jewish life in the diaspora was problematic for a wide array of "Zionists" and those without established Zionist leanings as well.

Encounter: Schwarzbart and the Polish Jews in the US Zone of Germany, January 1946

As he traveled across southeast Germany encountering convents full of orphans, dining rooms full of survivors, conference rooms reserved for the inaugural "Conference of Jewish Refugees in Munich," and unexpected Yiddish speakers in darkened, chugging train cars, Ignacy Schwarzbart struggled to envision Jews as a unified group. In a report he filed two weeks after his visit to the US zone in Germany in the second half of January 1946, he stated that he was "against 'Polish Jewish' grouping" but, in the next half sentence, admitted that "there exists a special aspect of the problem of the Polish Jews."[99] Evidence of this special aspect dominated his forty-three-page report and thirteen pages of conclusions and suggestions that followed it. Wherever he went, names, faces, and places from prewar Poland followed him.

Polish Jewry remained real for Schwarzbart. At the Munich-based headquarters of the Central Jewish Committee and the JDC, a man named Bochner from his hometown (Chrzanów) "greeted Schwarzbart 'with joy'" in a random hallway. En route to a building at a DP camp, Schwarzbart's "brothers from Galicia asked [him] many questions, all inquired about relatives." At a banquet, while singing Palestinian songs, Schwarzbart saw "the natives of Kraków. [His] eyes could not leave them and they looked at [him] through tears. Their last Jewish representative in the Polish parliament!" While visiting Polish Jewish children in a convent, he discovered that relations between these children and other Polish Christian orphans had been "full of hatred" just a few months prior. He gave them copies of *NT*, which they gobbled up; then they begged for more Polish books. At this meeting, "pain beat in [their] hearts as if it would tear them apart." And in addition to the endless talks he had with Chaim Weizmann, General Myers, and representatives of the Jewish Central Committee, Schwarzbart convened his own gatherings open only to Polish Jewish survivors.

Besides taking part in the first occupation-zone-wide meeting of Jewish DPs during his trip, Schwarzbart used his time in Bavaria to have as many meetings as possible and gain a better understanding of the current situation impacting Jewish DPs in general and the Polish Jews in particular. His report recounts an interesting exchange among Jewish DPs concerning, once again, emigration outlets for Jewish children. At this particular meeting, the statement dating from October 14, 1945, which prohibited the evacuation of children to the "countries of the diaspora," was overruled by some Jewish DPs anxious to capitalize on a Swiss-generated proposal to take children from occupied Germany southward to Switzerland. Elsewhere, Schwarzbart learned that the DPs lacked clothing and underwear but not food. He suggested that the WJC organize a clothing and underwear drive as well as oversee the creation of a "Ministry of Internal Affairs" to streamline relief on the ground. In Zeilsheim DP camp and in the packed hall where he spoke for a half hour, Schwarzbart encountered many conationals who had known him in the past. Hundreds of people assembled to hear him answer questions, five of which he could recall for his report.[100] Even in a broader audience, the special Polish Jewish context warranted Schwarzbart's attention. His reports about UNRRA machinery and the violence embedded in postwar antisemitism mirrored those that Warhaftig and Tartakower expressed. Schwarzbart did express, however, more complex ideas about the (continuous but unsteady) Polish Jewish flight into German space and the causal force behind antisemitism in Poland.

In his long report, Schwarzbart articulated a denser explanation of the antisemitism that sprouted up in Poland after liberation than encounters with Tartakower and Warhaftig reveal. He agreed with his WJC colleagues that antisemitism in 1945 and 1946 was "worse than before the war." Despite the fact that only "scores of thousands of Jews remain . . . everywhere in Poland the Jew is a main topic of conversation." Underground newspapers were both antisemitic and antigovernment. These two trends dovetailed as Jews occupied an inordinately larger number of high-profile government offices. Schwarzbart noted that Jews were drawn to government service for protection, but this push to associate themselves with the government backfired insofar as it generated more antisemitic language linking the government to Jews. This prevalence of antisemitic rhetoric "bears all the characteristics of an organized drive." The drive was not necessarily government led; in fact, the government had offered declarations and official prohibitions against antisemitic language. But conversely, some members of the government were "content to be rid of Jews" in order to facilitate "national homogeneity." In sum, Schwarzbart envisioned the antisemitic campaign as intentionally designed (it was unclear by whom) to "discourage Jews in the USSR from coming back" to Poland. Schwarzbart filed his report as the mass repatriation of Polish Jews and Polish Christians settled deep inside the Soviet Union began, in February 1946. Thus, his chronological position allowed him a vantage point that Tartakower and Warhaftig could not have accessed.[101]

Schwarzbart wrote months later, but he still agreed with Warhaftig and Tartakower. All three men thought, throughout 1945 and early 1946, that UNRRA could do more ("UNRRA support is considerable but not sufficient," Schwarzbart wrote) and that those Jewish DPs who did not want to be repatriated and were increasingly assembled in the American zone of occupied Germany should move toward Palestine. The fact, Schwarzbart wrote, was "beyond doubt that the overwhelming majority want to go to Palestine." Interestingly, "this desire [was] not always motivated by Zionist ideals."[102] If all the Jewish DPs could not be admitted to Palestine, Schwarzbart suggested a partial solution as an alternative plan. "The transfer of Jews up to the age of 40 to Palestine" could alleviate the dire DP situation. The final solution to the postwar Jewish question, all three Polish Jews on the WJC agreed, demanded subsidized transfers of Jews from east central Europe away from their former homes.

In essence, new problems, new information, and new voices that Schwarzbart, Warhaftig, and Tartakower encountered throughout 1945 and early 1946 reified their dedication to a plan that had come to maturity in 1944. Their deep and emotional encounters with the surviving Polish Jewish remnant seemed to confirm what they had already believed for roughly a year: the east central European diaspora was in peril and was on the verge of being negated voluntarily. As another contemporary scholar of Jewish DPs, Koppel Pinson, wrote in April 1947, those in camps throughout occupied spaces "conceive[d] of this epoch as the liquidation of European Jewry as a whole." Those who had not been Zionists before the war now believed in a "complete rejection of the diaspora" and a "clear and unmistakable Palestine-centrism."[103] Of course, Pinson, Schwarzbart, Tartakower, and Warhaftig encountered the individuals who had left Poland and other countries, so their conclusion was made less nuanced by this self-selection or imposed travel restrictions. They also tended to discuss the problems of transfer, displaced persons, and failed returns in distinctly Jewish terms. When we zoom outward from these encounters in this particular year, we can begin to see how Jewish issues were at times exceptional, at times not exceptional, and almost always linked to the broader movement of east central European peoples at a time dominated by hyperethnic motives, population transfers, expulsions, and repatriations.

UNCERTAIN CITIZENSHIP: GERMAN-SPEAKING CZECHOSLOVAK JEWS, CZECHOSLOVAK JEWS FROM SUBCARPATHIAN RUS', AND THEIR COMPLICATED BELONGING IN THEIR POSTWAR STATE, 1945–1946

"Every Jew returns to Czechoslovakia as a repatriate," Imrich Rosenberg, former WJC official and Prague bureaucrat, observed in July 1945.[104] In the two months before this meeting, according to historian Tara Zahra, "five and a quarter million Europeans were repatriated by Allied authorities in May and June of 1945 alone."[105] It was a season of movement. Rosenberg said this telling statement during the so-called "wild expulsion" of German-speaking Czechoslovaks and a wave of undocumented individual returns that crisscrossed the unblocked roads of Bohemia and Moravia. Military authorities, UNRRA officials, dispersed repatriation teams under the guidance of the reconstituted Ministry of the Interior, and individual train stewards helped nearly forty thousand Czechoslovak Jews return to that state's slightly truncated territory in the summer of 1945.

Arriving back on Czechoslovak soil, however, did not necessarily restore their Czechoslovak citizenship. For a small but notable percentage of two distinct groups of these returnees—those who lived in prewar Subcarpathian Rus' and those who were listed as German nationals on the 1930 census—plans for their return and the return itself sparked new uncertainties. Before both groups even set foot on government-sponsored forms of transport, they were compelled to sit in repatriation offices in Cairo, Jerusalem, or Katowice, where they had to demonstrate their "Czechness" to inconsistent officials. After the first group returned to their old towns in the "wild" and "sad" hills of Subcarpathian Rus', the easternmost part of the prewar state, they had to decide if they would become Soviet citizens or head off toward evacuated, Sudetenland homes that had belonged to Germans before the wild expulsion.[106] Once resettled, they had to convince power-seeking and gun-carrying local officials on national committees that they were loyal to Masaryk's state despite their census data indicating otherwise. And even after the citizenship of both groups of Jews was restored, it could be taken away. Between 1945 and 1946, the eight thousand Czechoslovak Jews from the first group who hailed from Subcarpathian Rus' and, to a lesser extent, a few thousand German-speaking Czechoslovak Jews who came from larger cities and the interwar Sudetenland became combatants in a citizenship war.

Over this period, panicked members of the WJC interfaced with Jan Masaryk and other officials such as Arnošt Frischer, who by 1945 had been elected chairman of the Council of the Jewish Communities in Bohemia and Moravia-Silesia, to protect the rights of small groups of both to return and live in Czechoslovakia.[107] A combined analysis of both situations plunges us into the messy and often contradictory world of repatriation committees, national committees, government policies, and international organizations. What emerges is a chaotic picture of a society in the midst of a massive ethnic cleansing enterprise against German-speaking Czechoslovaks as well as that of a fragile state negotiating carefully with the Soviet Union about its new eastern border and broader geopolitics. By the time the Ministry of the Interior included a designation of Jewishness in their own policy books in September 1946 (thereby resolving most of the questions about uncertain citizenship for these two populations), networks, pathways, and precedents supporting movement away from Czechoslovakia were already established. And others could use them. Indeed, the uncertainness of citizenship statuses for some Czechoslovak Jews in the first year and a half after V-E day initiated real repercussions for Jewish belonging across the entire region. We come back to the regional context in chapter 5. For now, let us begin with returns to Czechoslovak spaces, be they unofficial or official, successful or unsuccessful.

Unraveling the Process of Postwar Repatriation

As President Beneš arrived back in Prague amid pageant and celebrations, as Foreign Minister Masaryk departed San Francisco, and as Arieh Tartakower composed his contributions to *NT* in New York City, Isaak Martin Weiss (known by his nickname Marty) spent his days in a hospital bed near the Mauthausen Concentration Camp. There, this sixteen-year-old gathered up strength to begin his own journey back to Polyana, a small village folded between the hills and valleys of Subcarpathian Rus'. During the interwar period, roughly one hundred thousand Jews or just under a quarter of the entire Jewish population in Czechoslovakia were rooted here alongside a small number of Czechoslovak officials who moved here in the wake of the establishment of the new state and a majority population of Ruthenians. A majority of the Jews in this historically underdeveloped region felt nationally Jewish, and a large number of them were Hasidic.[108] Marty's home was "traditional" in his telling, not Hasidic. He spent his prewar school years commuting between his cheder, where the rabbi taught him the Hebrew of the Torah, and a state school, where pictures of the President-Liberator Tomaš Garrigue Masaryk decorated the walls. The youngest son in a large family, Marty watched one older sister migrate to America, another sister study at the state gymnasium in nearby Mukačevo, his older brother join the Czechoslovak army, his father discourage another brother from emigrating to Palestine, his two younger sisters celebrate Christmas Eve with their Orthodox Christian neighbors, and, finally, the Hungarian army invade his town in the wake of the 1938 Munich Agreement.[109]

Seven years later, after five years of occupation, after their deportation to Auschwitz-Birkenau in 1944, and after his mother and sisters were killed on arrival there and his father died a few months later in a death march, Marty left occupied Austria with his cousin and traveled, without tickets, on a number of trains to his native hamlet in June 1945. Only by returning to Polyana could Weiss ascertain who else in his immediate and extended family had survived and who had perished. Unlike President Beneš, no one met Marty with jubilation when he arrived in Polyana just a few weeks later. He stayed there for only one day. As far as he can recall, he did not register with a repatriation commission at any point on his journey. His only memorable interaction with an "official" was in the drawing room of his uncle's former house, the biggest one in town. There, a Soviet official gave him "papers" after Marty declared his name and citizenship in front of him. From Polyana he moved to Svalyava, a larger city nearby, where he learned about the survival of two of his siblings.[110]

Like the *odsun* and like the *bricha*, repatriation happened wildly immediately after the war and, frankly, wildly at times over the next few months. Teens like Marty broke free of hospital beds and marauded through the countryside looking for places to sleep and food to steal and eat.[111] Individuals, temporary families, and large groups liberated together repatriated themselves. Officially, however, repatriation unfolded in commission offices spread across Europe, the Soviet Union, Asia, and the Middle East. And repatriation was a story shared by many. As Ori Yehudai estimates in his work on emigration from Palestine to Europe in the immediate postwar years, UNRRA and its successor the International Refugee Organization (IRO) repatriated twenty-five hundred Greek, Polish, Austrian, and Czechoslovak citizens from Palestine between 1945 and 1947.[112] Some numbers suggest that half of all Polish citizens due to be repatriated from Palestine were of Jewish descent! As an "event," repatriation should be understood as a contingent process that engulfed an overwhelming number of individuals, families, caretakers to help them, and officials that organized the larger operations.

Take, for example, Director Artur Opsal of the Czechoslovak Repatriation Mission in Katowice, Poland. Opsal admitted in a detailed report filed in October 1945 that his day-to-day operations required "very hard work."[113] Working under the purview of the Ministry of Employment and Social Care, Opsal helped a variety of people from across east central Europe, some of whom had been displaced since 1933. Sometimes, Opsal admitted, it was difficult to know the "state affiliation" of the person that wanted to leave Poland. He was upset by his colleagues in the Polish repatriation offices who sometimes let Jews leave Poland without following proper procedures. Overall, he had a negative view of the Polish offices that were equivalent to his own. According to Opsal, Polish officials did not respect the repatriation agreement signed with Prague officials. They sometimes let people stay on Czech territory without a Czech visa.

In the late summer and early fall of 1945, nearly 180 people a day or 5,000 people a month passed through Katowice on their way to Czechoslovakia and in the process greatly increased Opsal's already difficult work.[114] Each transport, for instance, had to be carefully compared with the transport document. The train cars had to be searched thoroughly to ensure that "no person had been added."[115] Opsal was also concerned about the amount of time that transports to occupied Germany and Austria spent on Czechoslovak territory. And so, he wrote that "a sufficient number of convoys should be arranged" so that the transport could be adequately guarded. He worried about illegal migrants as well as germs. Typhus was a perennial problem. So were false passports. He noted that women and children often took advantage of repatriation officials to divert their attention from the fact that they did not carry the correct travel documents.

Opsal devoted his last paragraphs to the situation of Germans and German Jews. His repatriation office was not designed to handle ethnic Germans. This reality resulted in German Jews waiting for the same trains as ethnic Germans in offices elsewhere. The Czechoslovak ambassador in Warsaw had told Opsal that he could not admit German Jews to Czechoslovakia, as it went against the policies of American troops. Only the US Embassy could legally intervene. Opsal did predict that it was "very likely that the Jews who previously had German citizenship will be allowed to return to Germany." In this case, Opsal recommended, "it will be necessary to organize closed transports through the shortest route through Czechoslovakia." Earlier that month, Opsal recalled, some Jews of Polish citizenship had joined a transport of Germans and Austrians. Delegates of the Austrian Red Cross, along with other governmental members, allowed the transport to continue even after realizing this mistake. In light of this situation, Opsal demanded that the whole territory of Czechoslovakia and the Polish-Slovak border in particular be carefully guarded to reduce illegal crossings.

In my final chapter, I return to the topic of repatriation, the Polish-Czech border, and Opsal's October 1945 missive when I discuss another mass repatriation, that of nearly 150,000 Polish Jews who had spent most if not all of the Second World War in the Soviet Union. For now, this short introduction to Repatriation Officer Opsal and Marty's unrecorded repatriation helps bring into focus the main stories of this chapter's third section, those of the contests over belonging for two sets of Jewish populations returning to Czechoslovakia in 1945 and 1946. Whether they arrived quickly and under the repatriation radar like Marty Weiss or waited for organized UNRRA, military, or state transportation to return them to their prewar states, millions of east central Europeans experienced repatriation after the Second World War. Repatriation had different consequences depending on one's registered nationality or place of domicile. Jewish survivors who had registered as "Jewish nationals" on the 1930 Czechoslovak census as well as their descendants found themselves embedded in a fresh set of political structures as their state reemerged on the map and as local and state officials consolidated power in an uncertain era. Those with power, mainly returning state officials and local politicians (who usually had weapons, strong anti-Nazi reputations, and a presumed history of loyalty to all things Czech and Slovak), possessed strong ideas about the ethnic composition of the postwar body politic.

Locating Power in Postwar Czechoslovakia: National Committees, the National Front, and the President

At least three entities controlled political power on Czechoslovak territory in the immediate wake of Hitler's defeat: the office of the president, a handful of cabinet members leading government ministries who assembled nearly every day beginning in April 1945 to discuss the status quo and offer recommendations to the president, and the so-called national committees (*národní výbory* [plural], *národní výbor* [singular]), at both the regional and local levels. President Beneš issued a series of decrees to consolidate power over his state well before the first postwar elections in the spring of 1946—he did so while in exile in London, in Moscow where he formed a government with Czechoslovak communists before his return to his state, in May 1945 upon his arrival on Czechoslovak territory, and during his initial days back in Prague. These decrees clarified the law of the land and created the space for the expulsion of Sudeten Germans, the attribution of Czechoslovakian citizenship, and the nationalization of large swaths of private property. In the postwar power vacuum left by fleeing Protectorate administrators and occupying forces, a handful of advisors assembled around Beneš. Some of them had spent the war years in exile with Beneš, others with communist leanings had found asylum in the Soviet Union, and a handful had survived the war on Czechoslovak territory. Together, they constituted the "first government of the liberated republic" (*první vláda osvobozené republiky*) that coalesced in May 1945.[116] A coalition of politicians from six parties (the so-called Národní Fronta [National Front]) served as a sounding board for Beneš as he conceived of his presidential decrees.[117] These political bodies should be understood, furthermore, as operating in a power hierarchy that included military forces, from the Soviet, American, and Czechoslovak armies to the Secret Police and the National Security Corps (Sbor národní bezpečnosti), which technically fell under the purview of the Czechoslovak Ministry of the Interior.[118]

From their initial meeting on April 5, 1945, the first government of the liberated Czechoslovak republic assembled many times before Beneš promulgated decree number 33/45, arguably the most infamous declaration made by the president of the Second Czechoslovak Republic.[119] These men spoke about the German question frequently. They almost never discussed Jewish issues. Chad Bryant describes how the first presidential decree "defining German nationality on 19 May 1945 stated that whoever had belonged to a German national group, association, or political party after 1929 or had marked German on any census since then was to be considered 'German.'" Those who had "opposed the Nazi regime" would constitute an exceptional case.[120] On May 25, 1945, in their twenty-second meeting, these leaders discussed the expulsion (*odsun*) of Germans from their republic for the first time on the record. Over a series of a few meetings that transpired over the next two months, Václav Nosek, Jaroslav Stránský, Zdeněnk Nejědlý, Jan Procházka, Klement Gottwald, Zdeněk Fierlinger, and their colleagues explored how they would deprive Germans and Hungarians of citizenship, how they would delineate between good and bad elements of both populations, and how the Czechoslovak economy would survive the massive outflow of human capital as millions departed important industrialized lands.

The issue of expelling Germans and Hungarians, Minister of the Interior Nosek noted in a meeting convened on July 10, 1945, must be linked to a revision of Czechoslovakian citizenship rights overall.[121] Discussions on that day considered how the potential presidential decree should define a "German" (according to racial calculus, the interwar census, or Protectorate-era records?); whether or not the Interior Ministry should have final authority over who stayed in the republic (should the process be completely centralized? Nosek argued on behalf of his ministry possessing final authority); and when forced movements away from the Sudetenland should begin (after the harvest?). As those in this assemblage and subsequent meetings contemplated the draft of the final expulsion decree, it became apparent that the proclamation should contain some mechanism for contestation. And so, the final draft of presidential decree number 33/45 written on August 2, 1945, and filed in the wake of discussions held at the Potsdam Conference did just that and more.[122] It deprived citizens registered as German and Magyar nationals on the 1930 census of Czechoslovak citizenship and property rights in the reconstituted republic.[123] Putting into motion ideas spun in his 1942 *Foreign Affairs* article, Beneš initiated a proclamation that would dictate the future of upward of three and a half million Germans and half a million Hungarians.

Officially, presidential decree number 33/45 included an important caveat: German and Magyar nationals could contest revocation of citizenship before the national committee within their geographical jurisdiction.[124] These local national committees defined political life, citizenship, and the contours of nationality in post–World War II Czechoslovakia just as they had after the Great War.[125] The Beneš decrees and communiqués from the ministerial level publicized laws, but individual "national communities enjoyed considerable latitude to interpret and implement these decrees."[126] Allegedly, these popular-elected national communities worked from guidance given by the centralized Interior Ministry, but orders were "often vague or contradictory." Over the course of nearly fourteen months beginning in the summer of 1945, however, it became evident that the rules distributed from Prague were incomplete, especially with regard to Jews from Subcarpathian Rus' and those Jews classified as German on the last Czechoslovak census.

To Be a Czechoslovak Jew Is Not an Easy Thing

In 1937 a short black-and-white tourism film called *Píseň o Podkarpatské Rusi* introduced moviegoers throughout the interwar Czechoslovak state to the smallest and most remote portion of their country. Rolling mountains cradle fog, wildflowers sway under levitating clouds, and the "mountain people" sprinkled throughout the lenses till the soil, tame the rivers, sing on horseback, and walk on landscapes that have impossible angles. This short film by Jiří Weiss was also known as the "Song of the Sad Land," a direct quote from the words delivered in conjunction with the pictures. While Marty's chunk of Czechoslovakia was indeed quite hilly and rural, this region had a thriving urban population, Czechoslovak high schools and administrators, and a regional population that was more than 10 percent Jewish. Although Czechoslovak and Soviet officials frequently discussed it after reestablishing diplomatic relations in 1941, by the close of 1944, it was obvious to the Czechoslovak official František Němec that this portion of the state would belong to the Soviet Socialist Republic of Ukraine after the war.

The series of agreements finalizing this reality included one treaty signed by Molotov, Fierlinger, and Clementis on June 29, 1945. Now that Subcarpathian Rus' (or Podkarpatská Rus, the PKR) would be officially attached to the Ukrainian Soviet State, all remaining citizens with Czechoslovakian nationality would be allowed to move into Czechoslovak territory until January 1, 1946.[127] Furthermore, those people who qualified as Czechoslovak citizens could apply to a local repatriation commission and have their move subsidized by the Czechoslovak government. At a time when many Jewish residents of the region were still making their way home (Marty, if you recall, had just left the hospital at this point), this news traveled through local communities via town mayors and Soviet officials. A dicey issue emerged from this proclamation. How exactly would Czechoslovak citizens demonstrate their citizenship in the absence of official papers and local records? Moreover, would the categories established by the 1930 census be amended with regard to Jews who now identified themselves as Jewish nationals?

A fifteen-page communiqué issued by the Czechoslovak Ministry of the Interior a few weeks later in August 1945 attempted to resolve these specific issues regarding PKR Jews and unresolved nationality issues in general. Entitled "How to Confirm Citizenship," the statement directed the actions of regional representatives scattered throughout the republic on national committees (*národní výbory*) whom the Interior Ministry charged with determining citizenship.[128] The rules clearly singled out German and Hungarian nationals from the 1930 census and any person guilty of collaborating with the occupiers as undeserving of Czechoslovak citizenship. Those ensured citizenship included those who had been imprisoned during the war for "religious or racial reasons" and those who had fought on behalf of Czechoslovakia as soldiers. The long guidelines concluded with a reminder for those serving as Interior Ministry representatives. They should send "requests to the Ministry of the Interior when doubts occur" over which citizenship an applicant possessed.[129] Notably, individual representatives could bestow citizenship as they individually saw fit, albeit with some consultation from the ministry. Given this constellation of power, the representative of the local national committee (such as the one who sat in the drawing room that had belonged to Marty's uncle) occupied quite an influential position.

Notably, this directive from the Ministry of the Interior in Prague dates from August 1945 and only arrived to the national committees throughout the state near the end of summer, a full three months after liberation.[130] Already, citizens filtering through transit nodes and across Czechoslovakia's busy rail and road grid (made busier by destroyed railways elsewhere in east central Europe) had plodded toward the buildings housing the offices of their respective national committees. And also notably, the August 1945 communiqué from the Ministry of the Interior elicited legal confusion soon after its dissemination. Just as UNRRA policies in 1944 and 1945 did not account for those displaced people who would not or could not return to their place of former residence, the Czechoslovak Interior Ministry had not accounted for a particular subset of survivor. How, for instance, should a Jew listed as a German speaker in the 1930 census be classified? Did the experience of internment in a concentration camp for racial reasons trump the linguistic identification of such an example? As usual, the devil lurked in the details, and the lack of details impacted a small but visible Jewish population.

Striving for clarity on this issue, an attorney named George Weiss wrote Arnošt Frischer an inquiry on November 28, 1945.[131] Weiss, who had worked with Frischer during the war at a research institute that Frischer created to study legal issues related to postwar restitution, now represented a handful of German-speaking Jews in the fall of 1945 who wanted to secure Czechoslovakian citizenship, lest they be forced to leave their ancestral Bohemian home.[132] Frischer was by this point a private citizen with a relevant background. He had served as the Jewish representative in the Czech government-in-exile during the war and in that capacity had frequent if not daily correspondence with the WJC. He has entered our narrative previously at many junctures. It seems to me, however, that now is the ideal time for this personality to come into sharper relief.

Weiss had many questions, and he assumed that Frischer could offer the most coherent answers. "Are we right," Weiss queried, "to advise people who reported in 1930 as Jewish but were educated in German schools and spoke German at home to apply for confirmation [of Czechoslovak citizenship]?"[133] From this point, more questions logically followed: "What if they reported in 1930 as Jewish, spoke at home Czech but went in their youth to German schools?" Moreover, what if the citizen in question had parents who spoke different mother tongues? Weiss developed an example. "If they reported themselves

Czech," he posited, "but if one of the parents was a German speaking Jew, if therefore some German was spoken at home," and if the citizen in question had a German-looking last name, "is it thought in Prague that such a man would apply even if he went to the Czech schools only?"[134] No doubt the parameters Weiss sketched out applied to one of his retained clients. The lack of clarity in the ministry's directives was indeed baffling.

Going further, Weiss demanded, "How is a German speaking Jew expected to answer the question on his nationality? Jewish?"[135] Furthermore, Weiss asked, "Is nationality further unchangeable and meant to be the same as reported in 1930? Is it possible to declare oneself to be of Jewish nationality?"[136] Weiss negatively concluded that "to all these questions no advice is forthcoming and people here are quite helpless."[137] The questions George Weiss raised in 1945 illustrate the intrinsic dilemma Jews faced in a new Czechoslovakia. At that moment, the laws aimed for the convergence of citizenship and nationality. Accordingly, the possibility of a multinational citizenry disappeared in the wake of plans for large-scale population transfers ensuring that political states aligned with ethnographic maps. A category of Jewishness existed in at least two forms (racial persecution during the war and according to the interwar census) but not in the principles enshrined in Czechoslovak law.

One month after Weiss's inquiries, Arnošt Frischer detailed some answers to these valid and troubling questions in a report entitled "The Jewish Position in Czechoslovakia."[138] In a statement addressed directly to President Beneš, Frischer detailed the reality of the approximately forty-three thousand Jews remaining in the Czechoslovak state. Quick to remind Beneš that almost thirteen thousand within that number maintained no religious affiliation and were Jewish according to Nuremberg criteria only, Frischer detailed how these citizens "encountered great difficulties" and were "excluded from privileges and rights which belong to Czech, Slovaks and members of other Slav ethnic groups."[139] To amend this injustice, Frischer began, on September 25, 1945, to "advise citizens who registered previously as of Jewish nationality, to register in the future as being of Czech or Slovak nationality respectively." Frischer did this, he argues, "presuming that the Government would consider this act as a contribution made by the Czechoslovak Jews to the political homogeneity of the Republic, provided that their former declaration of Jewish nationality would not be detrimental to them and that they would be treated in all cases equally as Czechs and Slovaks." Frischer had sent a letter to the Ministry of the Interior detailing his change of policy a few weeks prior. He still awaited an official reply.

Finally, Frischer turned his attention to the Jews from Subcarpathian Rus'. In Frischer's assessment, "these Jews have always been supporters of the idea of the Czech state. They sent their children to Czech schools and they professed in the vast majority of cases, Jewish nationality."[140] In the wake of the annexation of this region to Soviet Ukraine, these Jews "did not get the right of option for the Czechoslovak Republic and their situation remains very precarious, whether they are in Subcarpathian Rus' or whether they have [already] moved to Czechoslovakia."[141] Frischer alerted Beneš to rumors circulating "that they are to be expelled from the western provinces [of Bohemia and Moravia] within the next few days if not hours."[142] Frischer lobbied Beneš to treat these people "sympathetically" even if it was not possible to create a supplementary agreement with the USSR concerning the "right of option for Czechoslovakia."[143]

Frischer's colleagues in the WJC followed the situations he detailed in his memorandum to Beneš carefully. They too were concerned that prolonged uncertain citizenships would be detrimental to Jews in this particular state and perhaps others bordering it. Near the end of 1945, for example, WJC official Paul Reiner argued in a memo that presidential decree number "33/45 must be amended and a specific solution in the instance of the small remaining Jewish population is required."[144] Echoing sentiments espoused by the WJC at UNRRA meetings in 1943 and 1944, Reiner argued that Jews should be entitled to a special political distinction under state law. Specifically, he maintained that "Jews should be distinguished from Germans and Hungarians and upon proof of Jewish origin or denomination, should be automatically exempted from the burden of proving their loyalty to Czechoslovakia."[145] Reiner invoked a Nuremberg-esque definition of Jewishness, lumping those of religious conviction with those of Jewish heritage.[146] Both positions espoused by Reiner and Frischer called for positive discrimination toward all those Czechoslovakian residents considered Jewish by the Nuremberg laws, regardless of what nationality they possessed in 1930. German-speaking Jews seemed to be the most vulnerable, but Jewish nationals from Subcarpathian Rus' also remained in a political no-man's-land of sorts, even six months after V-E day. These circumstances worsened further across the first months of 1946. A nadir was reached when some Czechoslovak Jews possessing "certain" citizenships faced very real threats of expulsion to the Soviet Union.

Citizenship Given and Citizenship Taken Away in 1946

In February 1946, Marty Weiss plunged himself into a training program in Liberec, the unofficial capital of the German national minority in interwar Czechoslovakia.[147] The teenager who had never lived in an electrified house would learn to become an electrician. Marty was like many Jews from Subcarpathian Rus' and hundreds of thousands of Czechoslovaks from elsewhere in the state inhabiting schools, jobs, apartments, and addresses that had just recently belonged to "ethnic" Germans. In the economic free-for-all of the *odsun*, people deemed Czechoslovak by state authorities shuffled into the region via trains, cars, and blistered feet. Czech speakers from Poland were returning with the help of repatriation commissions, Czech "nationals" who had spent the majority of their lives in Volhynia traveled to a homeland they had never seen, and people declaring their "Czechoslovak" citizenship arrived in emptying cities where rooms were available to them—and only then thanks to another presidential decree of the republic on July 20, 1945. According to the proclamation issued by the office of President Beneš, "Czechs and other Slav nationalities" could apply for an "allotment of land" according to the regulations issued by the Ministry of Labor and Social Welfare and according to procedures followed by, of course, the national committees.[148] Economic enticements dovetailed with ethnic and national belonging even during the chaotic phase of the "wild" *odsun*.[149] The so-called Settlement Offices scattered throughout the areas of the former Sudetenland (a word that was banned in the wake of Hitler's defeat) coordinated the influx of Czechs, Slovaks, and Jews and the outflow of Germans in an attempt to prevent labor shortages. After the July 1945 Potsdam Conference, economic, demographic, and ethnic changes would continue with the explicit approval of the Allies. By the time Marty arrived in Liberec, the second stage of the *odsun* was underway, and more than two million Germans would be expelled from Czechoslovakia over the next dozen months, in an "orderly and humane" manner.[150] In reality, daunting logistical challenges ensued in the wake of this drastic uprooting.[151]

Within this milieu of people coming, going, hiding, and staying, Jews from Subcarpathian Rus' like Marty attracted the attention of a local community official in Liberec. The official, identified as Dr. Macháček, filed a report to the Interior Ministry on February 4, 1946, about "ten thousand persons of Jewish origin and often of Jewish nationality, formerly Czechoslovakian citizens who ha[d] residence or right of residence in the territory of Subcarpathian Rus [*sic*]" and who had in the past few months "crowded into the border regions."[152] According to Macháček's report, these Jews had become "unproductive elements" with few exceptions. They "lived mainly by black market activities" and engaged in profiteering by "looting German flats."[153] Perhaps most tellingly, the greatest part of them did "not know either the Czech or Slovak language," and they were not of "Czech or any other nationality." Macháček elaborated, stating that "persons of Jewish origin and religion in Subcarpathian Rus' formed a quite independent nationality" and for this region never "integrated," never becoming Slovak or even Czech.

Macháček had already learned via correspondence with the Interior Ministry that according to agreements signed between Czechoslovakia and the Soviet Union, these Jews labeled as "Jewish nationals" were "not permitted to opt for [the Czechoslovak] Republic." Furthermore, the Ministry of the Interior had deemed certificates issued to these Jews as "invalid" and would deny "without any exceptions" applications of these persons to stay in Czechoslovakia.[154] Consequently, these Jews could be forcibly repatriated to the Soviet Union immediately. Such a policy indicated an abrupt change from the ministry's initiative to allow those of Jewish nationality to demonstrate to national committees their "Czechness" or "Czechoslovakness" by way of language use, school certificates, or proof of their war experiences. This did not matter to Macháček, who proceeded to outline some recommendations to the National Committee of Liberec in early 1946. As soon as possible, "all offices of the town of Liberec must be informed that every person coming from the former eastern part of the Republic should not be regarded as a Slav unless he is able to prove the contrary."[155] Only by "submitting confirmation from the census of 1930" could a person prove the contrary. Even those people "who submit provisional certificates of Czechoslovak citizenship" would be required to demonstrate how the census categorized them sixteen years prior.[156] Imagine if sixteen-year-old Marty had had to comply with these new steps. Many wartime survivors of "Jewish origin" had been children, infants, or unborn at the time of the last interwar census.

A few weeks after Dr. Macháček filed his report concerning those Jews of "Jewish origin or nationality" in Liberec, an internal document circulated through the Interior Ministry regarding the establishment of national belonging in postwar Czechoslovakia. In an attempt to delineate who enjoyed the right of settlement in the Sudetenland, an anonymous author reminded his readers that the law of June 29, 1945, granted those with Czechoslovakian nationality, those with permanent residency in Czechoslovakia, and military people of Ukrainian or Russian nationality who had fought in the Czech army or were "members of army families" as those entitled to citizenship.[157] Those who had declared Jewish nationality on the 1930 census, however, fell outside these categories despite the fact that "Jews have always been an element of state building, attendees of Czech schools," and supportive of "Czech institutions." To rectify this imbalance, the Interior Ministry submitted that "nationality can be proved with other documents such as the general certificate of public Czech schools or [evidence of] attendance at Czech schools." This anonymous

March 1946 directive corresponded mainly "to those who during the war left their homes and shortly after liberation returned from concentration camps or as members of the army and settled chiefly in the borderlands [*pohraniční území*]." In conclusion, and in stark contrast to Macháček's reasoning just a few weeks prior, "economic losses for the modest labor force" would ensue if these Jews were not permitted to stay in the republic.[158] For this Interior Ministry official, those of Jewish nationality from Subcarpathian Rus' served an intrinsic purpose for the Sudetenland's economy. This back-and-forth paper trail had real implications for the citizenship status of Czechoslovakian Jews.

It should come as no surprise that WJC officials were paying attention. In mid-March, around the same time this Interior Ministry report was written, Arnošt Frischer met with Foreign Affairs Minister Jan Masaryk to discuss the worsening situation in northern Bohemia. In a report sent to the WJC a week later, Frischer explained how he related "the whole situation according to formal laws and to reality."[159] Noticing departmental cleavages in Czechoslovak governmental policies, Frischer asked Masaryk to merge his opinion with that of the minister of the interior and "recommended a benevolent attitude" with relation "to Jews who had reported an option for Czechoslovakian citizenship" so that they would no longer "be harassed."[160] Moreover, Frischer implored Masaryk to talk with the Russian repatriation commission and urge them to "give up claims to the Jews."[161] Masaryk expressed his agreement with Frischer and promised to intervene because he "could not tolerate anti-Jewish policies in Czechoslovakia."[162] And yet, a few days after the meeting, Frischer still could not "state the results of the meeting."[163]

Soon, another high-profile governmental official added his voice to the conversation surrounding the uncertain citizenship of Czechoslovaks that had declared Jewish nationality. Ambassador Laurence Steinhardt, the highest-ranking American diplomat in Czechoslovakia, appeared in communication written by Arieh Tartakower. According to Tartakower, Ambassador Steinhardt had stated that "officials of the Jewish communities in Bohemia and Moravia have no evidence of Soviet pressure on the Czechoslovak government for the return of any Subcarpathian Jews to Ruthenia (or Rus'-SC)."[164] While the distinction drawn in Czechoslovak law between citizenship and nationality complicates the situation, the status of these Jews did not appear to be under "imminent threat" as of March 1946.[165]

A few days later, Francis T. Williamson, the acting assistant for the Chief Division of Central European Affairs, related another intervention with Ambassador Steinhardt. On this occasion, Steinhardt reported that "not more than 20 persons were handed over by the Czechoslovak police to Soviet repatriation offices" and that the "Ministry of the Interior [acted] sympathetically to the Jewish refugees" from this region. Notice how Jews like Marty were mischaracterized. They were not "refugees"; instead, they were Czechoslovak citizens displaced, like millions of others, into evacuated territories within the Czechoslovak state. Despite the small number of Jews involved in this forced repatriation to the USSR, Steinhardt told Williamson that the Jewish Community of Prague harbored concerns that the increased public pressure on the Ministry of the Interior would result in a Jewish exodus from Subcarpathian Rus' toward occupied Germany.[166]

In the Office of the Czechoslovak Foreign Minister, in the American Embassy on Vlašská Street, and even at the conference table within the Jewish Town Hall across the shallow alley from the Old New Synagogue, conversations regarding the uncertain citizenship status of Jews like Marty continued, albeit with new twists. On March 24, 1946, Frischer sat down alongside officials of the Prague Jewish Community and the Jewish Communities of Bohemia and Moravia for their regular bimonthly meeting. Frischer detailed the facts of the problem and referenced his meeting with Masaryk (and the minister's promise of help) a few days earlier as evidence of his response to the impending citizenship crisis.[167] According to Frischer, the Ministry of the Interior had agreed to protect those Jews with certificates confirming their right of option to settle in Czechoslovakia and not be subject to deportation to the Soviet Union.[168] Frischer considered the situation regarding approximately fifteen hundred of these with presumed Jewish nationality to be quite serious, as the position of the Interior Ministry toward this group was not "favorable."[169] Three weeks later, the same group reconvened in the same conference hall and opened the right-of-option controversy for discussion once again. From Frischer's standpoint on April 10, 1946, the situation of the Jews from Subcarpathian Rus' was "worsening and critical."[170] Those assembled listened as Frischer detailed instances of property confiscation, citizenship revocations, and other problems that he had discussed of late with an Interior Ministry representative.[171] After some debate, those in attendance decided that in the following days a multipronged intervention with heads of political parties and governmental leaders was necessary.

The concern that Frischer and his colleagues expressed during meetings across the spring of 1946 found voice throughout the WJC as well. In a memo dating from March 26, 1946, Alexander Easterman, Maurice Perlzweig, and Aryeh Leon Kubowitzki critiqued an official government announcement from Prague regarding the Subcarpathian Rus' situation. Specifically, "persons producing certificates of option for Czech citizenship" should not be forced to register for repatriation to the Soviet Union. These persons would be considered Czechoslovak citizens until their application obtained a "final decision."[172] In their assessment, this constituted "a satisfactory improvement and [would] likely stabilize temporarily [the] situation."[173] These WJC officials advised that citizenship should depend on nationality status in 1930 or attendance at Czech schools. A second memo from Easterman alone just a few days later, however, relayed a worsening situation. On April 2, 1946, he wrote to Wise and Perlzweig observing that the status quo for Jews from Subcarpathian Rus' had "gravely deteriorated."[174]

Obviously, Jewish leaders in Czechoslovakia and Jewish observers from international perches took note of the drama surrounding this small remnant of prewar Czechoslovakian Jewry who originated from Subcarpathian Rus', an area now ceded to the Ukrainian Soviet Socialist Republic. Throughout the spring of 1946, conflicting accounts concerning the gravity of the situation and how Jews on the ground responded to back-and-forth pronouncements from a variety of government officials produced anxiety and confusion. By May 1946, records from the WJC point to a resolution of this drama. On May 13, Frischer met again with President Beneš and discussed the matter of the Jews from Subcarpathian Rus'.[175] Moreover, "Mr. Easterman of the British Section of the WJC visited Prague recently [regarding] the same matter. He reported that all Jews who had opted for Czechoslovakia are permitted to remain there."[176] Roughly a year after V-E Day, as the communists "scored a stunning victory in the Czech provinces," securing more than 40 percent of the vote, obtaining the premiership, and retaining power over the important Ministry of the Interior, these Czechoslovaks of Jewish nationality from Subcarpathian Rus' had seemingly secured Czechoslovak citizenship.[177] The position of these Jews as well as those Czechoslovak Jews with German ties, however, was definitively outlined only a few months later.

At the end of September 1946, as the *odsun* of "ethnic" Germans and the wave of Polish Jews sweeping across the border (which is covered in chapter 5) began to show signs of waning, the Interior Ministry issued its most direct postwar ruling concerning Jewish inhabitants in Czechoslovakia.[178] In a memorandum distributed throughout the country to national committees in towns of all sizes, the ministry offered guidance concerning "person(s) who by the occupants were considered as 'persons of Jewish origin.'"[179] Beginning with historical background, the memo noted how the "barbarism of the Nazis, supported by the racial theories and by the deep hatred of everything that was not proved to be Nazi raged at first and increased in measure against persons of so-called 'Jewish origin'; and against so-called 'Jewish half-castes,'" or those declared

Jewish according to Nazi racial ideology. In response to the despicable Nazi behavior during the Protectorate time, "the Czech and Slovak nation refused the call of discrimination of these unfortunate victims of the Nazi persecution from the other citizens who survived the terrors of the concentration camps." Glossing over the fact that the Czech and Slovak lands were divided during the entire period of the Second World War and that, in fact, the Slovaks were allied to the Nazi state, the memo promised that Czechs and Slovaks would repudiate "every discrimination regarding religion and native language and the difference in treatment accordingly," with the exception of German and Hungarian nationals who had committed crimes against the republic during the war. As of the date of this decree, "persons of Jewish origin would be categorized as Jews and Jewish half-castes by the Czechoslovak authorities" to differentiate Jews from German and Hungarian nationals.[180] Succinctly, a Jew in the eyes of Nazi law remained a Jew according to this Czechoslovak law. The ministry also "made it clear that it was henceforth explicitly forbidden to include Jews ('Jews or the people of Jewish origin') in the deportation trains leaving for Germany."[181]

This document ends with special instructions for *národní výbory* members asserting that "it is necessary that the respective National District Committees should investigate thoroughly every case according to specific directives."[182] Overall, this decree attempted to solve at least two problems. First, Czechoslovak authorities promised to recognize Jewish origin as a viable category in the state's legal code because such a distinction persisted from the Protectorate era. To account for those Jews who had registered as German or Hungarian in the 1930 census, the ministry agreed to make a distinction between Jews, Jewish half-castes, and the rest of the population. Second, this ruling attempted to integrate the actions of the national committees on the ground with those of the ministry above. In the end, the ministry itself could offer decisions in individual instances, thereby overriding the authority of the local body. Sixteen months after liberation and a full year after the August 1945 communiqué detailed above, the Ministry of the Interior codified "Jewishness" into state law. In a sense, the Czechoslovak Interior Ministry did what the WJC had consistently lobbied UNRRA to do at that organization's 1943, 1944, and 1945 meetings: to make a legal distinction of "Jewishness" in order to offer positive discrimination to those classified during the war as Jews. This also meant that categories introduced by Nazi legislation had meaningful postwar afterlives. And soon, a similar category would appear in transnational legislation impacting Jewish survivors with interwar German and Austrian citizenship spread across shattered Europe.

ANOTHER CATEGORY OF JEWISHNESS: WRITING THE CONSTITUTION OF THE IRO

Two and a half years after he dramatically changed his mind at the June 1944 meeting convened to discuss whether the WJC should endorse the return of the Jewish community to postwar Germany, A. L. Kubowitzki's opinion remained consistent. He still did not want Jews to live in postwar Germany. He was, however, effectively powerless in the circumstances encircling his precise historical moment. Tens and hundreds of thousands of Jews had migrated or returned to (occupied) Germany in the war's wake, and now these displaced people seemed destined to remain in camps and temporary housing until a larger solution could be found. Months and a year after the war ended, plans to resolve their displacement remained elusive. By the end of 1946, 640,000 "unrepatriable displaced persons," including roughly 250,000 Jews (mainly from Poland but from elsewhere as well), waited indefinitely in the American zone of occupied Germany.[183]

Of course, Kubowitzki could not have predicted this eventuality at the meeting with the German Jewish Representative Committee in June 1944 or even a year later in June 1945. Indeed, few narratives in the modern European experience of migration seem stranger. Notably, in the first months after the war, the number of non-Jewish displaced people decreased overall, save for those categorized as "Poles." It soon became evident to members of UNRRA, the WJC, and government officials that Poles of both Jewish and Christian backgrounds constituted the most stubborn portion of DP camp populations. And then, as the repatriation of Polish citizens from the Soviet Union commenced in February 1946 and the less-than-stable situation reigning throughout the fragile Polish state continued to destabilize, the influx into the occupied areas of Germany and to a lesser extent Austria and Italy gained more steam. The next chapter explores this migration in detail. For now, note that throughout 1946, Jews, and especially Polish Jews that had recently been repatriated from wartime experiences in the Soviet Union, flocked toward Hitler's former state, finding there an in-between and collective status as "unrepatriable displaced people." Kubowitzki and his colleagues had correctly anticipated that such a group would emerge in the abstract. They had not anticipated their pooling in occupied Germany and Austria.

While the practice of granting preliminary political asylum had become quite normalized by the early 1950s, protections prohibiting the forcible repatriation of refugees to the country of their previous citizenship were not necessarily in place in the mid-1940s. Thus, the travel, admittance, and continued residential attachment of these refugees to occupied German spaces cannot be assumed as conventional. States had refused and consequently would "refuse to admit the principle" of granting political asylum.[184] The circumstance of unrepatriables in occupied areas, however, was unique and thus offers scholars of international law a provocative precedent. Refugees in general and the Jewish refugees in particular who fled toward occupied spaces in Germany and Austria were, for the most part, accepted to those spaces indefinitely. There they met Warhaftig and Schwarzbart in 1945 and 1946. There they enjoyed a higher caloric allowance than the "ethnic Germans" arriving in droves from Polish and Czechoslovak territory. There they waited for a solution, a "final solution" that would make their belonging certain. An important node on the trajectory toward that complicated solution came to pass in December 1946, when the draft constitution of the International Refugee Organization was sent to United Nation member states for their approval at the second meeting of the UN General Assembly. On the eve of this event, Kubowitzki had last-minute directives that he wanted to share with the secretary-general and others.

On November 12, 1946, Kubowitzki sent a memo "concerning Jewish refugees and displaced persons" to the UN secretary-general in advance of that body's second official meeting.[185] The ideas contained across these three succinct pages echo thoughts showcased in memos that Tartakower or Warhaftig wrote, which were destined for earlier international meetings such as those of UNRRA in 1943 and 1944. But unlike previous instructions issued by the WJC, Kubowitzki's memo from the end of 1946 is remarkable for what it does not demand—more precisely, for what it does not *have* to demand. Across 1945 and 1946, as Czechoslovak authorities and legal observers debated how German-speaking Jews and Jews from Subcarpathian Rus' could demonstrate their "Czechoslovakness," delegates to the UN and specifically to that body's Economic and Social Council also worked through knotty questions concerning where Jewish displaced persons and others who could not be repatriated belonged. And while the draft constitution of the International Refugee Organization mentioned the word *Jewish* only once, as a whole it was keenly attentive to Jewish-related issues raised by members of the WJC throughout the 1940s.

Kubowitzki's memo both reacted and contributed to language coalescing in an entity called the United Nations Special Committee on Refugees and Displaced Persons (UNSCRDP) across a few months in 1946. The Special Committee, one of many special committees convened by the nascent UN, was convened at the direction of the aforementioned UN Economic and Social Council and tasked with creating a draft of the constitution for the soon-to-be-established International Refugee Organization. The documented created by this committee was adopted by the UN at the end of 1946, helped dictate an interim agreement in July 1947, and came into force in September 1948. In sum, this constitution did three things. First, it protected the rights of displaced people to refuse repatriation to their former countries. Second, it allowed the IRO to investigate, promote, or execute (i.e., fund) "projects of group resettlement or large-scale resettlement."[186] And third, besides the establishment of these new precedents in international law, the IRO constitution included language protecting certain refugees defined as "Jewish" by Nazi persecution. Just like the September 1946 directive from the Czechoslovak Ministry of the Interior, the IRO Constitution included a reference to a postwar category of Jewishness stemming from wartime discrimination. Also like the Czechoslovak Interior Ministry memo, what became official IRO language and policy took months to coalesce and in essence came into finalized written form only as the stream of Jewish displaced people arriving in occupied Germany from Poland slowed to a trickle. International law tends to grow slowly.[187]

Since the summer of 1944, WJC officials such as Aryeh Leon Kubowitzki, Arieh Tartakower, and Zorach Warhaftig had argued that Jewish displaced persons were nonrepatriable. In the late winter and spring of 1946, international committees working on refugee-related issues, such as the Anglo-American Committee of Inquiry on Palestine and the UNRRA Special Subcommittee on DPs, were ready to agree with them.[188] The theme of "unrepatriability" was also apparent when the UN Social and Economic Committee organized a special committee to consider how the impending end of temporary UNRRA operations impacted broader refugee and DP issues in February 1946. In the second month of 1946, as loaded repatriation cars of Polish Jews and other Polish citizens crossed the Soviet Union and Jews from Subcarpathian Rus' laid down shallow roots in the Sudetenland, a plan to convene a new UN-sponsored committee to investigate the current state of DP and refugee issues took shape.

Three principle ideas would guide the proposed conversation that would begin at the United Nations Special Committee on Refugees and Displaced People in April. First, the displaced person and refugee problem proved to be international in scope. Second, the committee should study policies enabling return to countries of origin, as they were preferable to the alternatives. And third, no refugee or DP who expressed valid objections to returning to his country of origin "should be compelled to return against his will."[189] Besides offering these guidelines, the Social and Economic Committee also produced draft definitions of DPs and refugees in advance of the Special Committee's first meeting. Writing in May 1946, Warhaftig tended to agree with the guidelines laid down by the UN Social and Economic Committee and seemed optimistic that the UNSCRDP would enable progress. He also wanted to push their debates and conclusions a bit further. "The problem of the Jewish refugee," he suggested, "is indissolubly tied to the future of Palestine."[190]

The document created by the UN Social and Economic Committee, and then debated by the UNSCRDP a few months later, included Jewish-specific language that fulfilled, in part, two crucial demands presented by the WJC in 1943, 1944, and 1945: namely, the recognition of the wartime Jewish experience in UNRRA policy or UN law and positive discrimination for Jews in postwar legal structures.[191] As we saw in chapter 3, such a distinction of Jewish suffering and such a promise for positive discrimination did not easily enter UNRRA's policies at meetings in Atlantic City or Montreal. Like the Czechoslovak Ministry of the Interior, the United Nations officially did not want to perpetuate racial categories enshrined in Nazi law. In February 1946, however, the UN Social and Economic Committee included Jewish-specific language in their draft of resolutions for the UNSCRDP to consider. It read as follows: "The term refugee also applies to a person of Jewish origin who was a victim of Nazi persecution in Germany or Austria and who was detained in or who was obliged to flee from and was subsequently returned to one of those countries as a result of enemy action or of any war circumstances and who has not yet been firmly resettled there."[192]

In part, this statement was meant to protect those German and Austrian Jews who had never been deported outside of the Reich and now, postwar, wanted assistance in leaving former Axis territories.[193] Thus, it pertained to a very small group of potential refugees. The number did not necessarily matter. In May 1946 when the United Nations Special Committee on Refugees and Displaced Persons convened, the solitary insertion of the word *Jewish* elicited much more discussion than the three insertions of the word *Spanish* to refer to those displaced by the Spanish Civil War because of what such an insertion implied.[194] For some, the usage of *Jewish* demanded clarification about Palestine. The colonial power in Palestine, the United Kingdom, led the charge against the inclusion of the word *Jewish* in the draft of the IRO constitution.

The UK delegation outlined its disagreement with the word *Jewish* and its hesitancy to support the movement of displaced people away from Europe in a minority report filed to the UNSCRDP on May 17, 1946. Unlike the Nazis, the minority report argued, the UN should not make a "distinction" between "the various racial, religious or other minorities existing in any country."[195] Moreover, since the "main business" of the IRO "will be to repatriate to their countries of nationality or former habitual residence those DPs who are outside their countries and can return there or alternatively to resettle in new homes those who cannot be repatriated," this addition to the IRO constitution could imply that "the concern of the new organization insofar as Germany and Austrian Jews are concerned will be to remove them from Germany or Austria and resettle them elsewhere." This should not come to pass. In fact, "His majesty's government cannot subscribe to the policy so strongly advocated by the Nazi regime that there is no place for Jews in central Europe or as citizens of the state which will eventually be established there." While the UK delegation admitted that "in certain cases it may be difficult for Jews to return to places where they have suffered so atrociously or where the Nazi tradition of anti-semitism has not yet been completely eradicated," "fear" propelled these diplomats to speak out against it—namely, "fear that the new provision might well involve the new IRO in schemes for Jewish immigration into Palestine, a matter which is being separately dealt with by bodies specially concerned with that problem."[196] The linkage of Jewish issues with Palestinian issues propelled the UK delegation at the UNSCRDP to call for the neutralization of this language related to German and Austrian Jews. The UK delegation wanted to separate what members of the World Jewish Congress and some other members of the UNSCRDP considered indissoluble: Jewish displacement in Europe and Jewish settlement in Palestine.

Such a connection, however, would not necessarily be made explicit when the final draft of the IRO constitution was submitted in the late fall of 1946 for approval by member nations. The United Nations General Assembly officially created the IRO in December 1946.[197] The document included Jewish-specific language alongside a mention of statelessness. And so, the word *refugee* also pertained to "persons who, having resided in Germany or Austria, and being of Jewish origin or foreigners or stateless persons, were victims of Nazi persecution and were detained in, or were obliged to flee from, and were subsequently returned to, one of those countries as a result of enemy action, or of war circumstances, and have not yet been firmly re-settled therein." The IRO constitution contained no mention of Palestine, however. It did retain language from February and May 1946 allowing the IRO to pursue "the investigation, promotion or execution of projects of group re-settlement or large-scale re-settlement" and created within the provisional budget a sum of $5,000,000 for "large-scale resettlement."[198] After years of lobbying and memo-pushing, an international body had finally given the WJC some of what it most desperately wanted: language distinguishing Jews as uniquely persecuted, the financial and theoretical support for massive resettlement, and designation as a consultative organization. By the end of 1946, the tens of thousands of Jews in displaced persons camps could look forward to the establishment of a new organization that, according to its bylaws, could legally move them far away from east central Europe. A majority of these displaced Jews had Polish citizenship and had survived World War II and the Holocaust because they had spent most of the first half of the 1940s in the Soviet Union. Their postwar story of prolonged uprooting begins next.

FIVE

UPROOTED

The "Miraculous" Remnant of Polish Jews Who Survived in the Soviet Union and Their Postwar Migrations

SOMETIMES YITZHAK ZUCKERMAN TOOK SANDWICHES and a small bottle and sat in the ruins of the Warsaw Ghetto. There, he did some "soul searching."[1] When I visualize Zuckerman eating his lunch in 1945 or 1946, he is surrounded by heaps of stone and dust. But Zuckerman's vivid memory could transform the rubble left in the wake of two devastating uprisings into city avenues and busy addresses that had pulsed with people, his people, just a few years before. Forty years later, he could still summon that space, and he did so in his memoirs "in case someone knows the area."[2]

Regrettably, few people did "know" the area when he dictated his memoirs decades after his participation in the 1943 Warsaw Ghetto Uprising and the 1944 Warsaw Uprising. Few people, in fact, knew the area even in 1945 and 1946 when Zuckerman worked in a variety of capacities for the postwar Central Committee of Polish Jews and ate his lunch gazing at ruins.[3] So many Polish Jews never came back to their Warsaw. Zuckerman came to terms with this realization in January 1945, as the Red Army crossed Polish territory and the "war" came to an end there.[4] It was at that moment, Zuckerman admitted, that he "saw the vacuum left after the murder of [his] people" for the first time. In the wake of this awful awareness, he "broke down."[5] Zuckerman regained his composure, however, because some of his "people" remained alive.

His realization that "180,000" Jews would return to Poland from the Soviet Union was "decisive—and who would greet them? How would they be organized?" Zuckerman could not, he remembered many decades later, "leave them alone."[6] And so, although he questioned "Jewish life in the diaspora, in Poland," although he continued to believe that "'catastrophic' Zionism was correct," although his future wife, Zivia Lubetkin, made aliyah herself in 1945, and although he believed that "this was no longer Poland, but one big cemetery, with no room for Jewish life," he simply could not "abandon the Jews."[7] Of course, Zuckerman was not the only Polish Jew to find hope in the news that a noticeable number of Jews had survived the war in the Soviet Union. WJC Office Committee minutes and *NT* contain repeated, hopeful references to this population throughout the early 1940s. It was unclear how many had survived, it was unclear how many would return, and it was unclear how their postwar futures would unfold. But they were alive. So Zuckerman, along with Tartakower, Schwarzbart, Apenszlak, and Kubowitzki, waited for them to come "back."

Building on the narrative of the previous chapter, this final chapter focuses on the failed "return" of more than one hundred thousand Polish Jews who survived the war in the Soviet Union spread across scores of localities.[8] Over a few months in the first half of 1946, these survivors boarded repatriation trains, which over days and weeks brought them westward.[9] In many cases, these Polish citizens returned to their prewar state but not necessarily their location of prewar domicile. Entire towns had been obliterated. The interiors of many major cities had been destroyed.[10] And significantly, the eastern and western borders of the Second Polish Republic had moved roughly 120 miles westward. East Prussia and other historically German lands adjacent to the new western border (known as the "Recovered Territories") had been annexed to Poland, and the overall size of the prewar state had been reduced by Soviet annexations of eastern lands. Many repatriated Polish citizens from the greater Soviet Union (including formerly Polish lands now under Soviet control) were directed toward the so-called Recovered Territories and into spaces left by evacuating "ethnic Germans." For a majority of these Polish Jews, uprootedness did not end with repatriation. Some Polish Jews who repatriated from the Soviet Union continued moving and joined in the so-called *bricha*.

Bricha means "flight" in Hebrew, and already in the 1940s this term was used to describe the semiorganized and semilegal movement of east central European Jews away from their prewar homes as well as the clandestine network that (to varying degrees) supported this uprooted diaspora along their uncertain way. Numerous transit routes emerged within this network over time and depended on local, regional, and state officials who allowed passage across borders and offered sustenance in an organized way.[11] Those east central European Jews who left behind their interwar citizenships surprisingly found themselves living for indeterminate amounts of time along their migration route, in places such as government-subsidized housing in Czechoslovakia or in so-called displaced persons camps in occupied Germany and Austria. Finally, *bricha* trajectories culminated (if they "culminated" at all) in many places, such as France, Belgium, the United Kingdom, the Americas, Australia, and Palestine. The particular *bricha* path under consideration here commenced in the Recovered Territories in early 1946, cut across the border with Czechoslovakia, and pushed "the uprooted" toward DP camps in the American zones of occupied Germany and to a lesser extent Austria.[12] As this movement of Polish Jews gained momentum in the year after V-E Day, actors spread across local, communal, governmental, humanitarian, and international entities enabled it by actualizing some precedents and ignoring others. Notably, both before and after the infamous Kielce pogrom on July 4, 1946, UNRRA, WJC, American, Czechoslovak, and Polish authorities helped Polish Jews definitively uproot themselves from Poland by crossing into Bohemia and crossing "over" to Bavaria.

Beyond reconstructing events within Poland and Czechoslovak government circles, along the Polish-Czechoslovak border, and across the complex Allied universe of observers, relief workers, and powerbrokers, this chapter also problematizes the triumphant causality inherent in *bricha* historiography. Like all narratives that become important foundation stories, the telling of the movement of east central European Jews away from east central Europe often assumes a sophisticated degree of planning and coordination that appears both in contemporary documents written to support a specific end goal and for testimony-givers, memoir-writers, and observers of the past in retrospect. Historians must find neutral language to explore the *bricha* as a highly contingent event that depended on a vast array of actors beyond the Jewish emissaries (*shlihim*) who were "sent" (often from Palestine) to instruct Polish and other Jews how to "leave."[13] Polish Jews hurrying toward the Czechoslovak border collided with border guards, enforcers of government policies, UNRRA representatives, and Jewish community officials who collectively dealt with the multiple population transfers unfolding in the region as millions were expelled and resettled. In what follows, I chart how the day-to-week-to-season work of Polish and Czechoslovak state officials who worked to consolidate postwar boundaries and reorganize populations within their states intersected with and diverged from the recommendations of officials in the World Jewish Congress, leaders in UNRRA, and the military/government/local authorities who assumed control of spaces emerging from wartime occupation. Decisions taken by surviving Polish Jews who returned from Soviet spaces as both individuals and members of young, expanding families must be understood within the realm of options available to them. Power dynamics, we will see, fluctuate through this chronological telling.

In addition to the actions of individuals, states, and international organizations, multiple realities coalesced to further uproot this particular diaspora. The larger story about the "miraculous" remnant of Polish Jews returning from the Soviet Union, their largely unsuccessful repatriations, and their prolonged displacement as DPs elsewhere pays special attention to four of them. First, a chaotic climate in "liberated" Poland marked by civil war, Red Army military occupation, a homegrown socialist revolution, the presence of militia groups (including Ukrainian and other Polish irredentists), and overall political unrest made the idea of postwar life in Poland range from difficult to unbearable, especially for vulnerable populations such as minorities and children.[14] Second, changing international norms accepting population transfers as a viable statecraft tool morphed into a transregional commitment to the reorganization of populations in east central Europe along perceived ethnic lines and concrete postwar policies prioritizing the unmixing of populations in a region notable for its heterogeneity. Within this context, the inclusion of Jews as "only" Jews (not Polish Jews, Czech Jews, German Jews, etc.) bound for a Jewish polity had to gain traction in the minds of those with power to act in decisive ways at opportune junctures. Third, a new form of violent antisemitism (fueled in part by the concept of *Żydokomuna*, a Polish word that loosely translates as "Judeo-Communism") emerged during and after Nazi occupation. This influenced how Jewish individuals and families calculated risk and the extent to which "others" within this story were willing to offer humanitarian help. And, finally, continued access to opened borders on either side of Czechoslovakia enabled the pooling of Jews in, specifically, the American zone of occupied Germany. This particular precedent, over time, combined with an uncertain legal category (rendered as "displaced persons unsuccessfully repatriated") and the reluctance of Great Britain to open up Jewish emigration toward Mandate Palestine to result in a precarious, stagnant reality by the end of 1946.[15]

As that year, the last year of this book's chronology, drew to a close, almost two-thirds of all Polish Jews who had survived the Second World War (and tens of thousands of non-Jewish Polish citizens and others of both Jewish background and non-Jewish background) waited in DP camps throughout Allied-occupied Europe or had already immigrated to other destinations, mostly to France and Belgium, alongside a great human mass of others. For all the uncertainty hovering over these uprooted east central Europeans by the end of 1946, one truth seemed clear. Like almost all the members of the WJC Office Committee born in Poland and east central Europe more broadly, these Polish Jews would have postwar and post-Holocaust citizenships elsewhere.

THE "MIRACULOUS" REMNANT: PERCEPTIONS, REALITIES, AND PLANS FOR THE POLISH JEWS SAVED IN THE SOVIET UNION

By the late summer and fall of 1945, Tartakower, Schwarzbart, Zuckerman, Apenszlak, and their contemporaries began to accept a devastating fact: more Polish Jews had survived the Holocaust and the Second World War in the Soviet Union than outside of it.[16] Most of these Polish Jews—residents of the eastern territories of the Second Polish Republic ceded to the Soviet Union under the terms of the 1939 Molotov-Ribbentrop Pact as well as refugees from elsewhere in Poland—were deported by the Soviets in 1940 and 1941 alongside hundreds of thousands of other Polish citizens.[17] Then, after Nazi forces invaded Stalin's state and Soviet officials issued an amnesty for Polish citizens as part of the larger realignment within the Allied universe in the summer of 1941, a majority of this group pooled in central Asia and lived there for half a decade.[18] In places such as Kazakhstan, Uzbekistan, and Kyrgyzstan, they spent nearly half a decade working, moving, living, and dreaming of returns that must have seemed improbable at times. Studies dedicated to this uprooted group count and sort this "majority" remnant as individuals. And yet, more often than not, those within this collective experienced wartime flights from prewar Polish territory; the dynamic years of displacement that ensued in gulags, *kolhozy*, and Soviet cities; and decisions made between 1939 and 1946 as growing families anxious for news from home.

Before exploring their journey away from Poland, which captivated diplomats, statesmen, and border patrols alike in 1945 and 1946, this first section draws on existing literature and fresh primary evidence to briefly introduce these Polish Jews: family, belonging, and futures. To begin, I focus on families. Testimonies collected from oral history projects, the archival record, and one particular registry that memorializes data from one repatriated group of Polish Jews in Szczecin during 1946 contain three generalizable revelations: that returning Polish Jews from Soviet central Asia included exceedingly young couples (including a majority who had welcomed their first child during the war), that these pairs had reproduced at an above-average rate, and, apparently, that these mothers and fathers had found cities such as Tashkent and Osz to be particularly hospitable places to start a family.[19] Roughly a quarter of the Polish Jews who returned to Poland in 1946 from the USSR were under the age of seven, and one-eighth were under the age of two.[20] The presence of so many young people, toddlers, and babies exerted demands on their caregivers and should make us reconsider how we tell their wartime and postwar stories. Their lives in Soviet exile across seven wartime and postwar years were dominated by the realities of "family creation," including fertility, family planning, childbearing, and childrearing, and populated with caregivers who helped these families grow.[21] The decisions these mothers and fathers made, then, to return to Poland in 1946 or to leave Poland after their repatriations to a state riven by violence, civil war, and the trauma of Nazi occupation and the genocide that accompanied it should, it follows, also be cast in familial terms.[22]

How did Polish Jewish mothers and fathers living in Soviet exile raise their children in both linguistic and cultural terms, and, concomitantly, how did all of those within this collective define their own linguistic and cultural belonging? Such questions beget, of course, a diverse range of answers across a geographically dispersed group of so many people. Briefly at this juncture, however, I would like to suggest that for the Polish Jews (and all Polish citizens) spread out across the Soviet Union, local participation in transregional activities sponsored by the Union of Polish Patriots (Związek Patriotów Polskich or ZPP) encouraged a unique sense of belonging.[23] As a political and cultural organization led by Polish communists but meant to encompass all Polish "patriots" living in the Soviet Union during the Second World War, the ZPP created a community and sustained spaces infused with Polishness, (sometimes) Jewishness, and, to harness a concept coined by Jakob Apenszlak in 1946, "Jewish Polishness."[24]

Of course, discernible levels of "Jewishness" depended on the numbers of Jews in a given locality. Thanks to detailed ZPP records, we can estimate how many Jews lived in a certain area and how their percentage within broader communities changed over space.[25] From their home base in Moscow, the ZPP established an extensive system of orphanages, schools, clubs, and day homes that offered Polish language instruction, jobs for Polish citizens, and support for overstretched parents. The ZPP also supported adult education initiatives, Polish-language working groups, and a wide array of cultural programs to entertain Polish citizens far from their prewar home. One iteration of these cultural programs had a particularly extensive reach in the spring of 1945. Commemorations of the second-year anniversary of the Warsaw Ghetto Uprising can be interpreted as reinforcing both a continued iteration of "Jewish Polishness" and a strong belief in a Jewish future on postwar Polish territory.

On the banks of the Ural River in Czekalow (Orenburg) at 3:00 p.m. on May 19, 1945, hundreds of Polish citizens came with Polish flags and red candles to commemorate the uprising of Jews in the Warsaw Ghetto. After opening hymns, two Jews, one Pole, one Ukrainian, and one Czech acted as masters of ceremony for this public remembrance celebration, which included lectures and recountings of ghetto life and partisan activities in both Polish and Yiddish.[26] Eighteen hundred miles away, another group commemorated the Ghetto Uprising with a public declaration. In Czymkient (Shymkent), a city in southern Kazakhstan, those assembled on April 22, 1945, began with ten minutes of silence, listened to papers in Polish and Yiddish on the uprising, and heard a lecture on the cooperation between the Jews and Poles in the "war for liberation." The declaration included statements of alarm about Zionism, glorified the very "idea of Polish Jews," and ended with a promise: the combination of Polish and Jewish blood that "flowed in the Ghetto" harbingered a "new springtime in Polish-Jewish brotherhood that will wash away anti-semitism and Judeophobia forever."[27] And finally, a few days later in Tashkent, the local ZPP organized a memorial evening for the "Heroic Uprising in the Warsaw Ghetto" in the clothing maker's club. The event commemorated the diverse political life in prewar Warsaw, which included Agudah, the Zionists, the Poale-Zionists, the Bundists, and the Communists.[28] Each of these events cast the uprising in terms that served unique political ends. It should not surprise us that the meaning of the Warsaw Ghetto Uprising depends on the circumstances of its telling and the ideological voice of the teller.[29] Clearly, this cluster of commemorations reveals expressions of Polishness, Jewishness, and Jewish Polishness existing in tandem. All three concepts could belong in postwar Poland.[30]

The specifics of that future in Poland for these evacuees, refugees, and survivors were not certain for most of the early 1940s. Polish citizens in the Soviet Union, of course, did not have a repatriation guarantee, which is why some Polish citizens returned on their own volition well before the organized repatriation in 1946. While it difficult to know how many Polish citizens "stayed" behind in the Soviet Union, estimates indicate that a majority of Polish Jews who spent the war in the "east" returned to Poland at some point after mid-1945. Oral testimonies from this remnant suggest that returning was perhaps the only way to know the unknown—namely, who still survived and what had happened to those who did not.[31] And while some testimonials admit that return to Poland in 1946 would simply lead to more migration options to Palestine, the United States, or other destinations where often family lived, the collective continuance of displacement and migration after repatriation should not necessarily be assumed.

In 1945, Arieh Tartakower assumed these things regardless. In the first "postwar" issue of *NT*, Tartakower came to terms with the numerical reality of the Polish Jewish Gehenna and the geographical reality of those who remained alive. "The great majority" of Polish Jews, he admitted, "a quarter of a million, are scattered in the vast interior provinces of the Soviet Union." Like the rest of Polish Jews deported far away from the places of their permanent residence, these Jews "must be taken care of" according to their own wishes. Their "maintenance should be secured," discrimination against them should be "abolished," their desire for repatriation should be "effectuated as soon as possible," and, finally, those "who cannot or do not desire to be repatriated" should be helped to emigrate. Despite having little to no systematic contact with the Polish Jews in the Soviet Union, Tartakower was certain about them as he was about all surviving Polish Jews. He declared that "the majority among them are anxious to go to Palestine and they are to be enabled to do so."[32]

By the end of the war, Tartakower had lumped Polish Jews in the Soviet Union together with the others that had survived the tragic war and occupation. He envisioned their futures in Palestine. In April 1946, the Anglo-American Committee of Inquiry did so as well. Writing about the Polish Jews remaining in the Soviet Union, the committee's report suggested that "it appears to be the general view that the majority of Jews returning will not wish to remain in Poland."[33] The report did not explicitly indicate that Polish Jews in the Soviet Union preferred Palestine over Poland in this section, but the paragraph preceding this declaration noted that a "homeless" Jew wishing to leave Poland "will in all likelihood be advised to express his preference for Palestine." The futures envisioned by the largest segment of the surviving Polish Jewish remnant, however, proved far more complicated than Tartakower imagined or the Anglo-American Committee presented. It turns out that it is difficult to speak about the collective wishes of an oversimplified majority either as a contemporary observer or as a historian.[34]

As the year 1945 waned, as office workers in the Moscow offices of the ZPP boxed up their vast archive, as men, women, and thousands of children readied themselves for multiweek journeys on often-unheated trains, the Central Committee prepared for the "great task" that awaited them. Before even one repatriate had returned, the funding earmarked to welcome repatriates and help them settle into homes recently evacuated by ethnic Germans and jobs that the devastated Polish state desperately needed filled already seemed insufficient. And so, the Central Committee issued a public statement in an attempt to obtain more financial support for those returning from the Soviet Union. As many millions of Jews died "under German systematic terror," in gas chambers and crematoria, those who escaped from the German catastrophe and found refuge mainly in the Soviet Union were "miraculous" thing and a source of "consolation and hope."[35] More than 150,000 of them would return to Poland. They would bring with them vast employment experiences from the previous six years in the Soviet Union. They would surely "raise the cultural level of Jewish life in Poland."[36] The optimism shrouding their return could not eclipse, however, the fact that it would be difficult to find them housing and work. While

Fig. 5.1. Polish Jews near the emergency reception center set up in Náchod, Czechoslovakia with hills in the background, summer 1946. Photo by Al Taylor, courtesy Photo Archive of the Jewish Joint Distribution Committee.

the government of National Unity had shown "great understanding," more than two hundred million złoty would be needed to set up transit posts and arrange for special shelters, financial help, medical care, children's centers, laundry facilities, restaurants, baths, adequate lodging, kindergartens, and training.[37] And so, in this undated plea, the Central Committee asked the Polish government and Jews living abroad to help them prepare for this massive return. Ready or not, the repatriation of this miraculous remnant was nearly underway. For a majority of this surviving remnant, their repatriation morphed into the beginning of a trajectory that would take them away from postwar Poland.

THE ROAD OUT OF POLAND CROSSES CZECHOSLOVAKIA, 1945–1946

Tucked into the emerald hills of northeastern Bohemia, the town of Náchod lies about three miles west of the Polish border. In good weather, it would take less than an hour to walk from Náchod's town hall to the small rocks that represented the boundary between these two states. With no mountains, hills, or roaring rivers separating them, these borderlands were knitted together by economies, accessible footpaths, and roads. Even in 1945 and 1946, when instability plagued the other borders encircling Poland, the stretch of the so-called "green border" slicing this territory remained relatively stable and well traversed.[38] Tens of thousands of Polish Jews crossed the border near Náchod between September 1945 and December 1946.[39] Most scholars who study how Náchod became a key exit point from Poland focus on the summer and early fall of 1946, when Polish Jews traveled toward the town in relentless droves under summer skies. At the peak of this wave, upward of one thousand people journeyed in and around the town daily. Older residents in Náchod had encountered refugees before. The movement after the Second World War was larger, however, than previous crises and required the work of international, national, and local actors.

What happened in and near Náchod in 1945 and 1946 offers a multilayered case study about aid distribution, fluctuating migration laws, recognized and unrecognized powerbrokers, and emergency improvisations. Perhaps most significantly, the events unfolding here compelled a new category of displaced people to crystallize in the policies of the United Nation's Relief and Refugee Administration: those referred to as "displaced persons unsuccessfully repatriated."[40] The creation of such a category to protect and subsidize Polish Jews moving away from Poland resulted from the accumulation of some precedents and fateful decisions hatched in Polish and Czechoslovak government buildings, in meeting rooms populated with UNRRA officials, and within US military circles in Bavaria and on the border itself. The story of how Náchod became the "most important spot in Europe" for world Zionists in the late summer of 1946 begins before that season when hundreds of Polish Jews swarmed the town's streets daily, before the Kielce pogrom on July 4, 1946, which initiated waves of panicked movement away from Poland, and, in fact, before Zuckerman met the first official trainload of repatriates returning from the Soviet Union. Náchod is epiphenomenal of a much larger shift in thinking about where the Jewish diaspora belonged in an ethnically homogenous postwar east central Europe.

Fall 1945

A full year before the infamous Kielce pogrom, Polish Jewish refugees were streaming across the "green border" into Czechoslovakia. Some, including thirteen to twenty thousand soldiers and officers in the Berling Army, had

Fig. 5.2. Polish Jews, their children, and a Czechoslovak authority in Náchod, summer 1946. Photo by Al Taylor, courtesy Photo Archive of the Jewish Joint Distribution Committee.

arrived back from the Soviet Union. Others, including tens of thousands of children, had survived the brutal Nazi occupation without crossing Poland's borders. Those who wanted to leave Poland could do so by accessing repatriation offices, such as the busy one in Katowice, and used funds allocated by local philanthropic organizations such as "Charita."[41] In the summer of 1945, Charita focused on cases that "national delegations and official legations" had ignored. According to a report circulated to a variety of nonprofit and governmental bodies by Lt. František Schönborn (liaison between the Czechoslovak General Staff and Charita), a particularly Polish Jewish stream began because they were "anxious to go to Palestine" and knew that if they moved toward "the camps of Landsberg and Feldafing" in the American zone of occupied Germany, they could get closer to that destination.[42] For about five weeks beginning in July 1945, eleven thousand Polish Jews traversed the "green border" easily, joining a movement that Zorach Warhaftig would call the "wild" *bricha* in the wake of his visit to DP camps in occupied Germany just a few months later. From

Schönborn's repatriation department in Katowice, most of these uprooted Polish Jews crossed Bohemia in a west-southwest direction toward Bavaria.

En route, they traveled in parallel with millions of others. Upward of five million "ethnic" Germans panicked and left the so-called Recovered Territories in the last weeks of the war.[43] Hundreds of thousands of "ethnic" Germans evacuated Czechoslovakia during the "wild" *odsun* in the summer of 1945. In June 1945, the Polish Army took control of resettling more than two hundred thousand Germans from the German-Polish borderlands.[44] Between May 1945 and August 1945, more than seven hundred thousand Czechoslovaks had been "repatriated from elsewhere.[45] Prague's train tracks and sleeping quarters bulged with refugees, expellees, and repatriates because it was the most important east central European transport node north of the Alps in the weeks, months, and years following Hitler's defeat. In mid-August 1945, however, this wild *bricha* hit a stubborn human roadblock just as the wild *odsun* was dissipating. According to Schönborn's report, the Twenty-Second US Army Corps, "situated in Czechoslovakia, stopped accepting individuals or transports of such [Polish Jewish] people, giving [as] a reason that Great Britain had closed entry into Palestine."[46] Now, six thousand Polish Jews were stalled on Czechoslovak territory. And the stream of the displaced flowing out of Poland continued.

Schönborn insisted that the refugee crisis unfolding before his eyes was severe and demanded an immediate solution. In September 1945, he sent his ideas to Walter Menzel, the delegate of the International Red Cross in Prague, while also forwarding them to the Czechoslovak General Staff, the Czechoslovak Ministries of Labor and Social Welfare and of Foreign Affairs, and the Jewish Joint Distribution Committee (JDC) offices in the Czechoslovak capital. In Schönborn's telling, the wave of terrorism in some parts of Poland against the Jews and a lack of protection from the Polish government had induced an unspecified number of young concentration camp survivors of both sexes to leave. The refugees even went so far as to carry forged repatriation cards "stating that they [were] German Jews born in Germany." It would not be easy to forcibly eject them from Czechoslovakia back into Poland. He noted that "150 US soldiers with bayonets" were needed to "force 640 Polish Jews to return to inner Bohemia" after they gained entry to an area controlled by the Twenty-Second US Corps. Thus, because the US Army authorities would not accept them, because the Jewish organizations in Czechoslovakia were "hopelessly inadequate to handle this problem," because some in the Bohemian lands considered this population a threat, and because winter was coming, Schönborn had formulated an impressive, transnational plan.[47]

For this "international problem with delicate aspects," Schönborn's approach involved funding and organizational support from international Jewish organizations, the immediate establishment of camps for thirty to forty thousand Polish Jews, protection from the Polish government, and, finally, support for temporary stays from the Czechoslovak government. Czechoslovak authorities, in fact, would play a key role in administering the camps, choosing camp personnel, and controlling access to and from the places of temporary internment. The refugees would stay in Czechoslovakia only until they could leave for the American zone in Germany or elsewhere. Schönborn drew on the principles of President T. G. Masaryk to cement his requests to the two government bodies included on his mailing list. Furthermore, Schönborn had definite ideas about the long-term future of these uprooted Polish Jews. "Palestine," he wrote, "must be the ultimate goal." For the one hundred thousand Polish Jews in question, "their admittance into Palestine would practically solve the Jewish problem in Eastern Europe."[48]

Already in the summer of 1945, during the wild *bricha* and immediately afterward, thousands of Polish Jews used the repatriation infrastructure and Poland's border with Czechoslovakia to exit their country. Their desire to leave Poland pressured officials in different ways. On the first of July 1945, Foreign Minister Jan Masaryk met with high-ranking representatives of the WJC to discuss the postwar situation of Jews in central Europe. Masaryk promised "to use his influence for the opening up of emigration for those who want to emigrate, especially those with close family ties abroad."[49] Orphans within this group of Polish Jews garnered special attention. American and Polish officials worked to ensure that UNRRA would subsidize the departure of "Jewish orphans from the concentration camps in Germany to England and Switzerland."[50] Plans for the "resettlement of Jewish children and adults" were based on the "assumption that very few of the Jews would be returning to their countries of origin" and "on the choice expressed by the Jewish people themselves for resettlement in Palestine or in some other country." Children between the ages of ten and thirteen were deemed "capable of expressing their future wishes," and no child would be "forced to go anywhere."[51] As more refugees pooled, however, these promises proved hard to keep. Faced with an influx of almost three hundred thousand Polish citizens in the US military zone in Germany, American officials made plans to return ten to twelve thousand Polish citizens to Poland every day, even though Polish officials estimated that their state could absorb only half that many.[52]

These Polish citizens returned to a chaotic situation in "liberated Poland" that was deadly for everyone, including Jews. At least 351 Polish Jews were killed from the surrender of Nazi Germany to the end of 1945. Jewish deaths peaked in March, June, and August. By October, November, and December 1945, the "murders and attacks" had undermined the "confidence of the Jewish population severely," and a "tendency towards panic and emigration" became clearly noticeable to the writers of a report issued by the Polish Ministry of Public Administration.[53] An estimated thirty-three thousand Polish Jews left Poland by the end of that year. By the beginning of 1946, this movement of Polish Jews away from Poland and toward Allied-controlled territories began to capture the attention of WJC leaders, UNRRA officials, and members of a new body, the Anglo-American Committee of Inquiry.

Winter 1946

James McDonald, the former high commissioner for refugees in the mid-1930s who we first met in chapter 1, prepared to return to Europe at the beginning of 1946.[54] Now part of the newly constituted Anglo-American Committee of Inquiry, McDonald and a handful of international colleagues had plans to conduct research and interviews on the postwar Jewish question in both Mandate Palestine and east central Europe. Like others attentive to the humanitarian disaster taking shape in occupied Germany, he could not avoid the public relations crisis that unfolded in the highest echelons of UNRRA during January 1946. On the third day of the new year, Reuters quoted Lt. Gen. Frederick Morgan, the chief of UNRRA in Germany, as "stating that he had seen 'an exodus of Jews from Poland on Russian trains on a regular route from Łódź to Berlin. All of them were well-dressed, well-fed, healthy and had pockets bulging with money.'"[55] Moreover, he "asserted that a secret Jewish force is seeking to organize a mass-exodus from Poland to Palestine."[56] This language provoked a response from the WJC.

A. L. Easterman of the British Section of the WJC accused Morgan of attempting to "influence the findings of the Anglo-American Inquiry Committee" with this antisemitic description of these uprooted Polish Jews. Other officials in UNRRA found Morgan's language offensive as well. He was dismissed from his post on January 6 after he refused to resign. Two weeks later, Morgan flew to the United States to appeal his dismissal, and by the end of January, Executive Director Herbert Lehman had reinstated Morgan after a public expression of his "sympathy for displaced Jews." Genuine or not, this sympathy was challenged as more Polish Jews left the Soviet Union, trickled back to Poland, and decided to leave the country of their prewar citizenship. The "problem" that Morgan had identified continued to grow, not only for those relief workers in occupied Germany and for members of

Fig. 5.3. Polish Jews at a border crossing with a Czechoslovak border guard, winter 1946–1947. Photo by Arthur Zeigart, courtesy Photo Archive of the Jewish Joint Distribution Committee.

the Anglo-American Committee of Inquiry but for officials at all levels of Czechoslovak governance.

By late January and February 1946, a new crisis had formed on the Czechoslovak-Polish border, just as the first Polish Jews returning from the Soviet Union reached Polish soil and the "organized" phase of the *odsun* was about to begin. Less than half a year after the "green border" became a point of transit for roughly sixteen thousand Polish Jews, the small stones that represented the international border between Czechoslovakia and Poland beckoned a new group of travelers, those Polish Jews repatriated under the terms of the July 1945 agreement between the Soviet Union and the Polish government.[57] On January 7, 1946, for example, a large group of Polish Jews arrived at the border along with others hoping to cross into Czechoslovakia. At first, the Czechoslovaks refused their crossing, protesting that they did not have the papers. But on January 12, 1946, their entry was approved as long as they promised not to "settle in Czechoslovakia" permanently.[58] This same report, written by a Polish border guard identified as "Grajscomorska," also referenced the illegal border crossing of 160 other Polish Jews around the same time. How should Polish Jews arriving at Grajscomorska's station, Border Point Number 11 near Náchod, or elsewhere along this boundary be handled?

Compelled to partially answer this question, a varied team assembled for a meeting regarding the increased flow of Polish Jews across the Bohemian border on February 1, 1946. Representatives from the Czechoslovak Ministry of Foreign Affairs, the Czechoslovak Ministry of the Interior, the Czechoslovak Ministry of Health, UNRRA, and the Jewish Joint Distribution Committee and Dr. Karel Stein of Prague's Jewish Community gathered to discuss the Jewish refugees who "cannot stay in Poland" and "need help."[59] This international coterie decided together that these Polish Jews could "stay [in] Czechoslovakia for a while during their passing." Moreover, because of reported "anti-semitism in Poland they can have asylum in Czechoslovakia." Legally, these so-called transmigrants fell between categories. They had already been repatriated once to Poland, but now they were displaced again. At this meeting they were categorized as "displaced persons unsuccessfully repatriated."[60] According to all assembled, their entry into Czechoslovakia would be legal, transit visas would be given for their subsequent movement into occupied Germany or Austria, and the government of Czechoslovakia would provide "two camps for those leaving Poland."[61] Finally, an agreement between UNRRA and the Czechoslovak Ministry of Foreign Affairs clarified that UNRRA, not Poland, would be financially and legally responsible for these Polish Jews.[62]

Up until this point, official UNRRA guidelines did not necessarily offer support to "doubly" displaced individuals like these. The agreement made between the Czechoslovak Ministry of Foreign Affairs and UNRRA in early February 1946 challenged this precedent and extended UNRRA's jurisdiction in a novel way well before the United Nations' Social and Economic Council's Special Committee on Displaced People and Refugees clarified their own language in April 1946 (as we learned in chapter 4).[63] Warhaftig, Tartakower, and their colleagues at the WJC, as we learned in chapter 3, worked to include such language about doubly displaced people at UNRRA meetings in 1943, 1944, and 1945. They were largely unsuccessful. The reality coalescing on the border near Náchod in early 1946, however, urgently demanded a more specialized articulation of displacement.

It did not take long for the consolidation of this "new" category to dramatically alter daily life along this part of the Czechoslovak border more generally and in Náchod particularly. Less than three weeks later, on February 21, 1946, the state border police in Náchod "detained a group of Polish Jews for crossing the border and left them in detention" at the International Red Cross facility in town. The border police report indicated that "members of this group should have been punished for crossing the border," but instead "they were transmitted by the Repatriation Department in Náchod and without punishment removed to Bratislava." This surprising turn of events fell under the command of Consul Václav Novák from the Ministry of the Interior; the joint representative in Náchod, Rudolf Beck; and Elfan Rees, an UNRRA functionary. Furthermore, the police report confirmed that these Polish Jews "planned to travel to the American zone in occupied Austria from Bratislava."[64] Beck and Rees communicated instructions from the Minister of the Interior to Czechoslovak border police, a body that technically fell under Novák's direct command. On a practical level, these Polish Jewish migrants, who should have been punished for their illegal transgression, were given clearance to proceed onward. Other streams of migration continued as well.[65] Like in the summer of 1945, the border near Náchod had become an important exit point from Poland. But the passage of Polish Jews through the border near Náchod depended on the opening of further outlets—mainly those belonging to the occupation zones run by American officials.

As the "displaced persons unsuccessfully repatriated" arrived in the American occupation zones in Austria and Germany across the winter of 1946, authorities struggled to deal with the influx of people as well as rumors that came in their wake. Military authorities in occupied Germany tried to open a special camp in Wewelsburg at the end of January for Poles that had recently arrived from Poland so that this new group would not "mix with other DPs" or tell "exaggerated stories of conditions in Poland and thus influence DPs on the question of repatriation."[66] The plan to separate "old" Polish DPs from "new" ones quickly encountered resistance. In the end, military authorities in the American zone of occupied Germany decided that "it may not be advisable in all cases to remove DPs who have returned [to the camps] from Poland." Such forced removals might cause "unrest or the wrong impression."[67] Soon, under the glare of a particular media spotlight, the movements of some "displaced Jews" came to matter even more.

Some of the Polish Jews who passed through Náchod in early 1946 had arrived in the American zone in occupied Germany by mid-February.[68] There, they and other Polish Jews met face-to-face with Bartley Crum of the Anglo-American Committee of Inquiry over three days to discuss, in part, how the DP problem should be solved. In a visit to the DP camp Funk Kaserne, for example, Crum, James McDonald, and others in the committee interviewed some "young Jews who recently fled Poland," and "they denied that there was an organized underground railway out of Poland." Instead, "local committees in the cities through which they passed" had helped them get to Germany "because they had heard that that was the best way of getting to Palestine."[69] Besides these young Jews, Crum and his fellow committee members spoke with more high-profile voices such as UNRRA camp director Harry Lerner and Israel Guttman, the chairman of one thousand displaced Polish Jews living together in Stuttgart and survivor of the Warsaw Ghetto Uprising.

At one point during his seventy-two-hour visit, Crum asked Guttman directly if he believed that there was "no future for the Jews in Europe" and "that Hitler has won the war against the Jews." Guttman replied "yes" and accused the "democratic world" of facilitating Hitler's victory over the Jews. Besides Guttman, Crum interacted with thousands of Jewish survivors in DP camps. Near Munich, Crum visited other camps in Leipheim, Freiman-Siedlung, and Fahrenwald. At the last camp, he was greeted by hundreds of people in a silent procession carrying a banner that read, "Open the Gates of Palestine." Finally, he saw the results of an UNRRA-organized vote, "which showed that of 19,311 refugees, 18,702 wanted to go to Palestine, 393 to the United States, 13 to Germany and the remainder elsewhere." All this led Crum to recommend that hard-core Jewish "unrepatriables" should be immediately evacuated from DP camps to permanent homes.[70]

Bartley Crum was not alone. Soon, two prominent American women echoed his thoughts and joined a growing chorus initiated in the early 1940s: Palestine equaled the immediate solution for the so-called hard-core unrepatriables languishing in DP camps. After her visit to a DP camp, Eleanor Roosevelt conceded that "it is true that [the displaced Jews] want to go back to Palestine," and she encouraged the United Nations and "existing international organizations" to solve the entire problem.[71] Mrs. Herbert H. Lehman, the wife of the UNRRA director general, agreed with the former First Lady. Edith Altschul Lehman pinpointed one particular international organization directly: the American Jewish Joint Distribution Committee. In a statement presented on behalf of her husband, she "stressed that the UNRRA cannot handle many important aspects of the relief problem in Europe and that the work of the JDC was indispensable." She promised that UNRRA would "do everything possible . . . to assist Jewish refugees, and, if the political situation allows, facilitate the transfers to Palestine of those who desire to go there."[72] Permissive language related to Jewish displaced persons had decidedly changed from the first two meetings of UNRRA.

Recall that in Montreal at the second general meeting in 1944, UNRRA delegates were reluctant to openly discuss Palestine. At that time, Warhaftig and Tartakower suggested that the other Allies did not want to alienate British leaders, who tried keep the DP problem separate from the Palestinian problem.

No such fear of alienation remained as 1946 moved forward. As the deliberations of the United Nations Special Committee on Refugees and Displaced Persons in the previous chapter already revealed, British voices against debating Palestinian issues were increasingly in the minority. As Tartakower prepared for the fourth general meeting of UNRRA in March 1946, the language he used to articulate WJC demands did not seem much different from earlier statements. In a joint memorandum on behalf of the WJC, the American Jewish Conference and the Board of Deputies of British Jews stated that the "vast majority" of the five hundred thousand Jewish displaced persons in Europe preferred to go to Palestine.[73] The words that Tartakower presented had echoes from the past, but now these words fell on more accepting ears.

Spring 1946, from the Global to the Local

UNRRA was meant to be a temporary relief body that would emerge quickly, work diligently on the ground, and then transform into more permanent United Nations–sponsored institutions such as the International Refugee Organization discussed in chapter 4. As 1946 progressed, UNRRA increasingly ceded power to entities, such as the Subcommittee on Displaced Persons created by the UN Economic and Social Committee, that would eventually replace it. Despite this shifting of responsibility, three more general meetings took place during the last full year of UNRRA's short existence: in Atlantic City that March, in Geneva that August, and in Washington, DC, that December. The springtime meeting in New Jersey brought together a collection of important figures to discuss ongoing global efforts of relief and rehabilitation. Many attendees returned to the city where the inaugural UNRRA conference had taken place in 1943.

For two of those returnees, Director General Lehmann and WJC representative Tartakower, the council meeting in March 1946 would be their last. Lehmann stepped down from his position as leader of UNRRA on March 31, 1946, for medical reasons and was succeeded by Fiorello H. La Guardia, who stayed in this position until the end of 1946.[74] As he had for the three previous UNRRA meetings, Arieh Tartakower represented the WJC at this event. In just a few months, however, Tartakower would assume a new position as professor of sociology at Hebrew University in Jerusalem, and thus he would not travel to Geneva for the fifth council meeting in August. Perhaps with this in mind, Dr. Kalman Stein, a Polish Jewish member of the WJC who would eventually replace Tartakower after his (second) aliyah, traveled to Atlantic City as well. Together, on March 21, 1946, these two men met with Jan Stańczyk, who had served first in the Polish government-in-exile based in London and then returned to the continent as the Polish minister for labor and social welfare. While Stańczyk had changed colleagues and positions, he continued to supply the WJC with up-to-date information. He remained, in Tartakower's assessment, "as always, very helpful."[75]

Stańczyk wanted to ensure that UNRRA assistance would extend to all Polish Jews in occupied Germany and Austria regardless of when they arrived there.[76] According to Tartakower's report on his conversation with Stańczyk, Ludwik Rajchman (the other Pole on the committee and a "converted Jew") "took the view that the infiltrees cannot be considered as displaced persons and cannot therefore be assisted by UNRRA."[77] Tartakower noted that "up to the moment of [his] leaving Atlantic City, Rajchman was not successful in having this question brought before the Council which may perhaps be also a result of Stańczyk's intervention." Going further, Stańczyk proposed that the "Jewish population [be] mentioned specifically in the resolution authorizing the UNRRA administration to extend further assistance to DPs." Overall, Stańczyk's stance vis-à-vis the dispensing of UNRRA aid to Polish Jews arriving in the occupied zones dovetailed with the overall view of emigration expressed by the Polish government. And because "very strong tendencies of emigration among some Polish Jewry will grow considerably as a result of the process of repatriation" from the Soviet Union, Stańczyk imagined that the movement into occupied zones would most likely continue unabated as long as propaganda steeped in the new antisemitism encouraged violence against Jews.[78] Because "much more" antisemitism existed in 1946 than before the war, Stańczyk expected the number of infiltrees to increase.

The influx of Polish Jews continued and troubled some UNRRA representatives, who drafted and issued Resolution Number 92 at the Fourth General Counsel Session. This resolution required the "administration to do all within its power in consultation with and by representatives to the occupying authorities, military authorities and the governments concerned to bring about the removal of conditions which may interfere with the repatriation of the DPs."[79] The number of Poles who repatriated back to Poland did, in fact, increase for a time. From March 1 to March 28, 1946, thirty-five thousand Poles repatriated, and in the thirty days that followed, fifty-seven thousand Poles returned to Poland. This increase was marginal, however, when the complete picture of movement is considered. The stalling of repatriation back to Poland coupled with the influx of Polish Jews leaving their country caused American military authorities to warn that they were "rapidly approaching a point where the number of Poles willing to be repatriated will be at a minimum."[80]

The severity of the problem was quickly becoming evident to other relevant parties. In the same month that Tartakower met with Stańczyk, a special report circulated within the Czechoslovak Interior Ministry. The two-page document alerted officials to the "serious" problem of the Jewish refugees from Poland at Czechoslovakia's northeastern border.[81] In addition to "International Jewish Organizations" that were "helping [Polish Jews] to move further west," institutions such as the Czechoslovak Ministries of the Interior, Social Welfare, and Foreign Affairs had "tried to sign an agreement with UNRRA" to offer further help. The agreements, however, had not been signed yet because the UNRRA branch in Czechoslovakia had "not received agreement from their headquarters."[82] In lieu of this cooperation, the Interior Ministry had worked with (unidentified) Jewish organizations to "register the refugees of this kind as long as they live at the present time on the land of Czechoslovakia." Without knowledge of UNRRA's more general opinion on this matter, however, "further infiltrations of these people on the land of Czechoslovakia is impossible."[83] The report encouraged "caution in this matter," as various opinions existed within government circles regarding these Jewish refugees. Humanitarian concerns soon mandated a softening of differences between these opinions.

Neither the Central Jewish Committee based in Warsaw nor individual Jewish communities throughout Poland were financially or logistically prepared for the quick and relentless influx of Polish Jewish repatriates from the Soviet Union.[84] The first of 66 transports to reach Tarnów, Poland, for example, did so on February 1, 1946. Over the next six months, 76,873 Polish Jewish repatriates and, within this group, 12,641 children would pass through this station on their way to destinations further north and west. The percentage of Jews in each transport ranged from 2 to 80 percent.[85] Later reports from Katowice counted trains from 51 origins, 140,393 repatriates in total, 99,672 Jews within that total, 22,870 children, and 6,252 people over sixty years old.[86] The average trip lasted from three to four weeks. In all, the Repatriation Department counted 199 transports returning to Poland between February 8 and June 26, 1946. In total, 207,047 Polish citizens and, within this number, 136,579 Jews streamed back to Poland on official trains originating from more than a hundred origin points in the Soviet Union.[87] Undocumented returnees increased these numbers as well. By March, when UNRRA convened in Atlantic City, individual communities receiving these Jews felt the strain of this sudden action.

In the first week of March, for example, the Jewish Community of Chełm was completely overwhelmed. The town was located just a few dozen miles west of the new border with Ukraine, and trains filled with repatriates passing through had drained the once-substantial community of all its resources.

"Completely out of the money," the telegram sent to the Central Jewish Community declared on April 30, 1946.[88] Immediately, the committee promised to send one hundred thousand zloty to help. In Lower Silesia, money was tight as well. A few weeks later, the regional Jewish committee and the repatriation commission based in Kraków gathered to discuss the situation of the forty thousand repatriates who had already settled in the region and those en route. The committee agreed that it was necessary to "convince Jewish society about the important moment before" them. Moreover, a "sense of brotherhood towards fellow Jews" could, one participant suggested, help local Jewish communities overcome "financial difficulties."[89] Another participant suggested something more concrete: pooling state vouchers for goods into a "money fund for the purpose of repatriation" that would be controlled by the Jewish community. No such plan built on communal kindness, however, worked five hundred kilometers to the north in Bydgoszcz. By the end of March 1946, the number of Jewish repatriates there had exceeded the population of the reestablished Jewish community. This Jewish community's position vacillated between "critical" and "catastrophic."[90] Repatriates themselves were sometimes required to pay for some of their own care. Taken together, examples from Chełm, Kraków, and Bydgoszcz reveal that just a few weeks after the official repatriation from the Soviet Union began, local Jewish communities and the Central Committee of Jews in Poland could not support all the repatriates upon their return to Polish soil.

Spring 1946, Szczecin

A "disastrous situation" had materialized in the "recovered territories" as eighty-five thousand repatriates, including fifteen thousand children, arrived in Lower Silesia.[91] Humanitarian needs exploded as thirty thousand Polish Jewish repatriates descended on Szczecin over one month beginning on May 2.[92] Broader estimates suggest that sixty-three thousand repatriates from the Soviet Union were bound for Szczecin over just a few weeks.[93] Before Polish Jews decided to leave Poland, they exited repatriation trains, encountered officials who waited for them, and "officially" returned to the country of their citizenship. Tens of thousands arrived in Szczecin, a city that had been devitalized from both its recent and distant pasts.

Known for centuries as Stettin when it had been part of a German polity, by 1946 the ethnic Germans were leaving. Between February and June 1946, seven hundred thousand Germans were forced out of Polish territory, two hundred thousand in the month of June alone.[94] As Polish Jews arrived back from the

Soviet Union, Polish citizens from the ceded eastern territories, the bombed-out cities, and the evaporating villages of central, southern, and eastern Poland moved into spaces that had belonged to Stettin's German population. The numbers in general are staggering. Around 1.5 million Polish citizens were "repatriated" from territories that had belonged to the Third Reich between 1945 and 1948.[95] Roughly 1.4 million Polish citizens were "repatriated" from the newly ceded eastern territories that now belonged to the Ukrainian and Belarusian Socialist States. The Polish Jewish repatriates from the Soviet Union seem like a small number in comparison. Part of this larger "ethnic revolution," they arrived in Szczecin beginning in March.[96]

At first, like in Bydgoszcz, the flow was somewhat manageable. By April 1946, 629 had registered with the relevant repatriation authorities and waited to hear where they would work and where they would live. Over a few weeks in May and June, however, the population of repatriates swelled.[97] By June 25, 1946, 25,321 had arrived in Szczecin from places such as Osz, Buchara, Nowosybirsk, and Czakalow, where perhaps some of the repatriates had experienced that community's commemoration of the Warsaw Ghetto Uprising just one year prior.[98] In a short burst of time, Szczecin became one of the largest Jewish communities in Poland, and in the late spring and early summer of 1946, the face of that community was changing nearly every day as more trains arrived at the Niebuszewo station.[99]

There is, as far as I can tell, no systematic answer to the question of how quickly, on average, those returnees decided to leave or keep moving when they arrived back in Poland on repatriation trains and met a variety of interlocutors on railway station platforms.[100] A portion of Polish Jews left immediately, a more significant portion settled for what would become only in retrospect brief stays, and a smaller minority settled for what would become only in retrospect longer periods. If the calculus propelling a Polish Jew to attend a pro-Palestine demonstration in postwar Łódź seems quite complex when placed under a microscope, imagine then how complex a more fateful and impactful decision to leave Poland must have been.[101] Zionist sympathies factored into this calculus, of course, but they did not necessarily determine it. Those carrying babies, clasping the hands of toddlers, and looking for relatives had more pressing, practical concerns.[102]

Repatriation Clerk Jakub Schwalbendorf observed this in Szczecin. As hundreds simultaneously exited trains and reached the conclusion of journeys stretching thousands of miles, Schwalbendorf was "buried with questions."[103] In a guest column he wrote for the first issue of *Tygodnik Informacyjny* (a monthly newspaper produced by the Community of Polish Jews in

Szczecin in 1946 and 1947), Schwalbendorf described the sound of an arriving transport:"'Where are you from? . . . Who elected the Jewish Committee? . . . Why did the Repatriation Administration give us black coffee on the way here? . . . Do the Jews in America know whether anti-semitism or individual train workers made our trip so long? . . . Can we get a free ticket to look around Poland? . . . Does the Central Committee know what the Union of Polish Patriots was doing in Russia?'" Schwalbendorf tried to give "real answers to this hail of questions." Someone asked for help finding the address of an uncle in America. Another wanted to shake his hand. Another voice asked about the kibbutzim and which ones were the best. Schwalbendorf had a question of his own: "Where is the manager of this transport?" Insults against the manager of the transport followed. "We were told," the repatriates said, "that everyone will receive a flat" and clothing and "full board for every month." And at every train station, there would be "a representative of the Jewish community and everyone will receive 'help' without any difference." And yet, Schwalbendorf was the first representative of the Jewish Committee that any of them had seen. Amid all this, another person found him. A second transport had arrived. And, Schwalbendorf noted, "everything starts from the beginning."[104]

Despite the provision of plans that attempted to match the repatriates with professional opportunities in specific places, in June 1946 around 20 percent of the repatriates were unemployed.[105] Take, for example, the work of Jan Kaniewski, a member of the resettlement department in Szczecin who wrote to the Ministry of the Recovered Territories in May 1946. Kaniewski "took charge of arrangements for the Jewish transports" and let a few guidelines dictate his designs.[106] The needs of the district took precedence as well as his desire to avoid "anti-semitic reflexes." He wanted to avoid creating Jewish communities that were "too large," spread the repatriates out across "all the small towns," and, finally, use the Jewish repatriates to "revive industry and trade" left obliterated in the wake of the German removal from the region. In fact, he anticipated that workers, unskilled workers, and Jewish youth could join state campaigns and help with jobs related to the upcoming fall harvest.

Solutions, however, proved scarce. Just one month later, eight thousand Jews were waiting for work. Some factories in the region refused to employ Jews, and the Committee of Polish Jews in Szczecin did not know what to do. Along with the Kierownik Wydziału Produktywizacji (head of the Productivization Department), the committee wrote to the Wojewódzki Wydział dla Spraw Żydowskich (head of the Voivodeship Department for Jewish Affairs) to ask for guidance. While sixteen thousand had found work, thousands still waited and thus needed "immediate help." Perhaps regional authorities could intervene

Fig. 5.4. A Czechoslovak guard lifts Polish Jewish children from a truck, winter 1946–1947. Photo by Arthur Zeigart, courtesy Photo Archive of the Jewish Joint Distribution Committee.

and alleviate the unemployment? Another problem coalesced in June 1946. Despite the work of the "lively and chaotic" Jewish Committee to settle Jews throughout the region, a concentration of twenty-six thousand Jews pooled in the city, and only five hundred Polish Jews spread out in the districts.[107] This demographic distribution exacerbated unemployment, especially because some managers refused to hire Jews.

William Bein, the director of JDC operations in Poland, visited Szczecin in July 1946 because he had heard about the difficult situation there.[108] The JDC wanted to encourage "constructive help," but the conditions in Szczecin would not allow such collaboration. Assistance would arrive instead in the form of cash, clothing, and products. Bein regretted that a "certain percentage of Jews in Poland . . . believe that they should be constantly supported by their American co-religists." He loathed the queues he saw throughout Poland. "A citizen in Poland," he was quoted as saying, "has to be a useful member of society."[109] Bein's criticism borders on the unfair. Officials in the Jewish community and at both the regional and state levels seemed overwhelmed by the sheer number of repatriates. Attempts to direct returning transports to less full destinations did not seem to succeed.[110]

Spring 1946, the One Hundred Thousand Hard-Core Unrepatriables

The border with Czechoslovakia continued to hemorrhage Polish Jews. On April 18, 1946, the Czechoslovak Ministry of the Interior sent out an official communiqué to various state and regional bodies pertaining to the "*odsun* of people of Jewish descent, who were also Polish state citizens." The Interior Ministry confirmed that "some of its departments had cracked down on these people" and that some entities within the Ministry had even "evacuate[d]" these Polish Jews "back to Poland." This report deemed this behavior "inappropriate" and "unsuitable." A new policy was necessary. Moving forward, this memo indicated that "security forces" would "take care of persons of Jewish origin and Polish nationality." Explicit instructions directed border guards and other state officials to "not evacuate [*odsunovani*] them like uncomfortable foreigners to Poland." Because these Jews desired to reunite with relatives in "America, in Palestine, in Canada, in Subcarpathian Ruthenia," and in other states and because "international Jewish organizations like the Jewish Joint and others" would support this "evacuation" away from Poland, those working at the Czechoslovak Interior Ministry had even more incentive to help them exit Poland for good.[111]

This report does not fixate on antisemitism as a cause for this movement away from Poland. Nor does the report explicitly prioritize movement toward Palestine. And even though the communiqué mentioned that an organization like the JDC would subsidize the exit of Polish Jews from Poland, such an eventuality was not guaranteed. As in early February, this mid-April precedent kept the Czechoslovak border with Poland and the Czechoslovak border with the US zone in occupied Germany open. And so, with the continued support of Czechoslovak authorities, Polish Jews could cross the border to Czechoslovakia and arrive in (already full) displaced person camps in the US zone. As more Polish Jews settled in these temporary camps, discussions about their future travel trajectories continued.

Once again, plans to relocate one hundred thousand displaced Jews, many of them Polish Jews, from German spaces to Palestine found high-profile spokespeople in spring 1946. In April, the same month that the Czechoslovak Interior Ministry confirmed their commitment to enabling the Polish Jewish *odsun*, Judge Simon H. Rifkind offered remarks as he left his position as special adviser on Jewish affairs to the US general Dwight Eisenhower. Rifkind circled back to the number Earl Harrison had used in his August 1945 report within the recommendations included in his final memorandum and suggested that one hundred thousand of the remaining Jews in Europe should be moved to Palestine in a scheme of "rapid mass resettlement."[112] The problem of the uprooted Jews in Europe, Rifkind noted, was "actually insoluble without Palestine." He pleaded that "all" of the Jews had "but one earnest wish, to be quit of Europe, and most of them have one other compelling desire, to emigrate to Palestine." Like Rifkind, Herbert Lehman offered his own set of personal thoughts in May 1946, a little more than one month after he stepped down from his position as UNRRA director general. Reflecting on the increasingly untenable situation forming in occupied Germany as Polish Jews kept streaming into the US zone thanks to the "humane" border policies of the Czechoslovak Interior Ministry, Lehman urged that one hundred thousand Jewish displaced people "should be able to proceed to Palestine forthwith" in order to diffuse tensions among displaced people.[113]

Neither Rifkind nor Lehman offered a precise timeline for this transfer of one hundred thousand Jews from Europe to Palestine, but another official, one still employed by UNRRA, did. On April 10, 1946, the Jewish Telegraphic Agency reported some spectacular news. Lt. Gen. Sir Frederick E. Morgan, UNRRA director in Germany, who had come under fire for antisemitic language directed toward Polish Jews earlier in the year, told the Anglo-American Committee of Inquiry "that all the 100,000 displaced Jews in Europe could be transported to Palestine within one month."[114] This satisfied the Americans on the committee such as James G. McDonald, who wanted to see all displaced Jews "admitted to Palestine by the end of the year, while the British want to spread out the 100,000 over a period of years."[115]

The Anglo-American Committee unanimously decided that the number one hundred thousand would be a central component of their April 1946 report.[116] The final version of their recommendations mentioned the number one hundred thousand in relation to Palestinian immigration no less than five times and urged that the transfer between US military zones and receiving ports in the Mandate transpire either "as soon as possible" or "immediately." Speaking about the report at the New York chapter of the American Jewish Committee a few weeks after it was published, McDonald insisted that there was no "justifiable reason for delay" of the prompt relocation of one hundred thousand

European Jewish refugees in Palestine. The British government, he argued, could not hold these Jewish young people as "hostages," President Truman could not fail to press for this movement, and, finally, Palestine had the capacity to absorb "many times 100,000 Jewish immigrants."[117] Like McDonald, Crum spoke to engaged Jewish audiences in the weeks following the release of the committee's report. To the Associated Jewish Organizations in May 1946, Crum urged the audience to advocate not "for a Jewish commonwealth now, but to unite in demanding the immediate transfer of the 100,000 Jews" by the American military.[118] Writing about the committee's report in *NT*, Tartakower declared that the Anglo-American Committee of Inquiry report proved that a "Jewish commonwealth is both possible and necessary and the demand for it is certainly very realistic."[119]

Repeatedly in 1945 and 1946, reports and statements about the "problem" of displaced persons requested that one hundred thousand Jews from occupied east central Europe be moved to Palestine quickly. Tartakower, Harrison, Schönborn, Rifkind, Lehman, McNarney, and the Anglo-American Committee of Inquiry utilized this neat, round number (which purported to represent a substantial segment of the hard-core unrepatriable Jews waiting indefinitely in DP camps) to make an implicit argument as well: the Jews of east central Europe belonged somewhere else and should be transferred away from Europe as a result. Logistics and reality complicated this simplified plan. In a memorandum sent to President Truman, the Jewish Agency predicted that the resettlement of one hundred thousand would cost upward of $45 million.[120] Beyond the question of financing, British officials heavily controlled movement into the Palestinian Mandate throughout 1946. For instance, April 1946 saw an increase in the quota of Palestinian immigration certificates to (only!) fifteen hundred, one thousand of which were designated for children, most of them orphans.[121] These numbers, of course, pale in comparison to one hundred thousand. There would be no immediate transfer, despite calls for and supporters of this increasingly popular empirical Zionism.[122] Despite the lack of viable emigration options and financing, US authorities in occupied Germany made conscious decisions to keep the border between Bavaria and Bohemia open. In the last week of spring 1946, the US Army announced that it planned to leave their controlled borders open to Jewish refugees from the east and even planned to construct five new entry stations and three reception centers.[123]

Calls for grand plans to speedily transfer suspiciously round numbers of European Jews away from Europe should not obscure another reality. At the end of June 1946, Polish Jews could exit Poland, enter Czechoslovakia with little resistance, exit Bohemia into Bavaria, and find housing and support in

US Army and UNRRA-funded institutions in occupied Germany and Austria.[124] Of course, as Tartakower suggested at the beginning of the repatriation scheme from the Soviet Union, "Zionism" was a "serious factor in the emigration of Polish Jews."[125] But allegiance to ideological ideals alone did not open state borders, distribute hot meals and medicine, or adapt temporary housing structures for hundreds to thousands in a short time span. Regardless of the extent to which Jewish operatives within and outside Poland were centrally organized, a transnational route helping Polish Jews leave Poland had coalesced a little more than one year after V-E Day. Actors along the Polish border, in Czechoslovak border towns, within US zones of occupation, and associated with international organizations supported the viability of this route and those along it on a daily basis.

"The Deep Diaspora": Jakob Apenszlak and NT in the First Half of 1946

Much to Jakob Apenszlak's delight, a small but significant part of the remaining Polish Jewish diaspora choose to remain in Poland throughout the first half of 1946. At the end of January, even as Polish Jews began to elicit the attention of Czechoslovak border guards, Apenszlak contributed an article to *NT* entitled, simply, "They Will Be in Poland." Numerically, he predicted, Polish Jews would be small, but they would remain "morally part of our nation."[126] The theory of evacuationism, which gained adherents throughout 1945, had begun to fall out of fashion. This did not surprise Apenszlak. "It is not a coincidence," he noted, "that Jews have been in Poland for thousands of years, staying or leaving the country is not a matter of theoretical arguments." And so, "the remaining parts of Jews in Poland" possessed the same considerations as their ancestors: "attachment to family tradition," ties to "centers of religious life," and even connections "to the Polish people themselves, with whom blood was intermingled." Later in his article, Apenszlak paused to reflect on Einstein, Mendolsohn, and Bialek, whose collective works demonstrated the cultural ties binding Jews to east central Europe more broadly. "The idea of Palestine," he argued, "does not require getting rid of the achievements of the diaspora." Finally, just like those who called for the mass exodus of Jews from Poland in the 1930s, those advocating for a mass exodus from Poland in 1946 would find it difficult to connect realistic plans to words. It was quite easy, Apenszlak admitted, "to utter 'exodus from Poland' without any regrets without even the slightest hope that this goal can be achieved."[127]

Six months later, at the end of June 1946, Jakob Apenszlak continued to feel vindicated: Polish Jews would certainly remain in Poland. "Even those who believed until now," he wrote, "that the complete evacuation of Jews from Poland is the only solution now agree that there will be a Jewish center in the Polish Republic."[128] Despite the movement of "thousands" crossing the Polish border "determined to reach the shores of Palestine" and "thousands" more that would follow, Apenszlak predicted that a "large part of the 200,000 [survivors] no matter how deep their craving to build a new life on a new soil will be forced to remain in Poland." The forty thousand Polish Jews "gradually establishing themselves in Lower Silesia" demonstrated this reality. More than a year before, Apenszlak recalled, the pages of *NT* had expressed this view "when the slogan 'complete evacuation' was on everybody's lips." Twelve months later, "reality confirms that our appraisal of the situation [in 1945] was fully justified."[129]

Of course, postwar opinion pieces in *NT* contained multiple views about the future of Jews in Poland. In an article designed to rally support for the repatriates described in Adolf Berman's April 1946 communiqué to the WJC, Tartakower spoke about the desire of the 160,000 Polish Jewish refugees to "return home," the obligation of "state organs of social welfare to organize non-stop aid campaigns," and the contradictory fact that "maybe the most will not be in Poland," as their "dream is to go further in the majority of cases to Palestine."[130] Contributor Samuel Margoshes noticed a similar trend during his trip to Poland in March 1946. One-third of all Jews in Poland, he wrote, "use assumed names or false passports to pass as Aryan Poles."[131] Among the Jews who did remain in Poland, Margoshes estimated that 95 percent wanted to go to either Palestine or the US. "These Jews were not," Margoshes admitted, "all Zionists." One "doesn't have to be a Zionist in Poland today," he noted, "to want to go to Palestine." Thanks to hostility manufactured by the "majority" of Polish Christians, the "Jews in Poland," he declared, "are living not only in a cemetery but on a cemetery that is on top of a volcano."[132] Even Apenszlak had written in July 1945, at the height of evacuationist talk, that it was "absolutely clear that no other solution can be found for the so-called problem of displaced persons in Europe insofar as it concerns the Jews other than the admission of the majority of Jewish survivors to Palestine."[133] Apenszlak did not think that this fact preordained "a Jewish exodus from Europe," but it did imperil the demographic power of postwar Polish Jewry. In June 1946, Apenszlak tried to convince readers that *NT* had portrayed a unified view of the possibility of Jewish life in postwar Poland. A close reading of all contributors and even articles produced by Apenszlak himself demonstrates a variety of views regarding the future.

Despite this example, Apenszlak consistently proved much more optimistic than his *NT* colleagues about a collective Jewish future in Poland. Arguably his optimism reached its climax in the last few days of June and the beginning of July 1946. Demographically, he envisioned more than a hundred thousand Polish Jews rerooting themselves in Poland. Some would lay down roots in evacuated German spaces in Poland's new "west." Some would return to the great Polish Jewish cities of Łódź, Kraków, and, once it was rebuilt, Warsaw. The shtetlach were gone, and so were the smaller settlements scattered throughout the republic. But a civilization would return and build on a cultural force that had sustained Apenszlak and the readers of *NT* during the Second World War: a form of Polishness that was decidedly Jewish.

Apenszlak named this cultural force on July 2, 1946, in a letter that he wrote to his friend Stanisław Matula in Jerusalem. The postal path of this letter is telling. One Polish Jew sat in New York City and the other in Jerusalem. More than just a language and friendship connected them. Both belonged to the same particular past, the same generation. After seven years in the United States, Apenszlak insisted that he would continue his work with an "irrational institution like the Polish Jewish press in America." While *NT* was only a "weak reflection" of Apenszlak's prewar newspaper *Nasz Przegląd,* he could not "break the connection with the Polish way." Neither could others. The global list of subscribers and the "letters of gratitude received from former prisoners of concentration camps and those staying in occupation zones" demonstrated something to Apenszlak. He was impressed by "how deeply one part of our intelligentsia has grown into Polishness, or into this specifically Jewish Polishness [*żydowska polskość*; underlining in the original]."[134] And from his perch in New York City at the beginning of July 1946, Apenszlak had no reason to question whether this deep attachment to "Jewish Polishness" would find new roots on postwar Polish soil. By the first week of July 1946, around two hundred thousand Jews were counted on Polish soil. Lower Silesia contained roughly ninety thousand of them.[135] Before Matula even received Apenszlak's letter, however, the reality and the possibilities it contained had substantially shifted because of the Kielce pogrom.

Summer 1946: The Kielce Pogrom and Its Aftermath

Yitzchak Zuckerman had a remarkably visual memory. Just as he could summon the streets of the Warsaw Ghetto when only heaping stones remained, so too could he recall specific details about the room where he first learned of the Kielce pogrom. As the (contested) results of the June 30, 1946 Referendum become increasingly known, Zuckerman went with Adolf Berman and Paweł Zalecki to visit Prime Minister Edward Osóbka-Morawski.[136] Their goal on

July 4, 1946, was to brief the prime minister on current events in Palestine and ask him to provide a statement on the Polish government's position.[137] They all convened in a "big hall, with a few telephones along the wall."[138] "Suddenly," Zuckerman recalled, "at the other end of the room, the telephone rang."[139] Osóbka-Morawski went to the phone, listened to the line, muttered words, and then returned to his three guests. He said, "Gentlemen, a great catastrophe, a pogrom in Kielce. A pogrom against the Jews." He knew nothing further save that the "army had been sent there." The official meeting ended abruptly in Zuckerman's memory.

As the group left behind the prime minister, Zuckerman had made up his mind. He was "determined to go to Kielce."[140] After convening with the Central Jewish Committee, collecting a "gun and two or three grenades" from his apartment, and waiting for "two truckloads of medicine, clothing and whatever was necessary in such a case," he got in a car. Driven by a "Jewish driver with Polish documents and with him, his girlfriend who also looked Gentile," Zuckerman arrived in Kielce at dawn a day or two after the deadly and violent pogrom. They arrived in a "ghost town."[141] After passing by army troops, Zuckerman met with the Urząd Bezpieczeństwa (Department of Security) commander Major Sobczyński, who did not know much. What he did know was damning. Dozens of Jews and members of the training kibbutz of the Zionist youth in the city had been killed in Kielce. Even more horrifying, "the pogrom struck Jews in a radius of dozens of kilometers around Kielce—on the same day and at the same time, Jews were taken off trains and murdered."[142] It was, in Zuckerman's assessment, a "great catastrophe."[143]

Like Zuckerman, Joel Cang arrived in Kielce from Warsaw very soon after that "great catastrophe."[144] On July 5, 1946, "pools of blood" remained in the "place where the Jews were killed" by a mob of attackers, which had included women.[145] After nearly six years away from Poland during the war and occupation, Cang had returned to Poland in 1946 as a regular foreign correspondent for the *Manchester Guardian*. He filed a series of postwar reports for that paper, and some of them focused on violence against Jews. Like similar investigative work in the 1930s, Cang researched how the Kielce pogrom had begun and progressed. Despite his experience covering anti-Jewish violence in the 1930s, nothing had prepared him for what he discovered in Kielce. Cang encountered the power of rumors, numerous dead bodies, stories of horror, and an event that had involved, according to the vice governor of the district, nearly five thousand perpetrators throughout the entire region.[146]

Dead bodies seemed to be everywhere. So were the murderers. After seeing the coffins of nineteen Red Army soldiers killed by Polish terrorists in a fight near Radom on July 3, Cang encountered more dead bodies upon his arrival in Kielce on July 5. After seeing the "mutilated bodies of 36 Jews" and the broken bodies of forty-six wounded others, Cang continued his investigation. First, he talked to the Christian boy, Henryk Błaszczyk, who had spread the rumor that he "had been kidnapped by Jews and kept in a cellar where he saw 15 murdered children." Cang asked the boy why he had told this story, and the boy "replied that he was told by older people to tell this lie." The boy's father had believed him. So had some neighbors. The subsequent arrest of a Jew by local police proved to the "agitators," according to Cang, that Jews were guilty of "ritual murder."[147] As the story floated through the town, "crowds armed with pistols and sticks attacked the Jewish community centre and a fight ensued." After the Jewish Community president and other members of the community were killed, the bad situation became even worse. "Workers from a nearby factory" joined the crowd that was "breaking into Jewish homes, demolishing furniture and attacking Jews."

The violence continued in Kielce and beyond. Crowds also attacked Jews "who were traveling on trains in the region." Smaller pogroms transpired around Kielce on that same day and involved people "dragging Jews out of trains, killing them on the spot with stones, sticks, iron bars and, it was stated, even axes." In response to the outbreak of violence, the vice governor ordered the militia to the Jewish community building, the fire brigade unsuccessfully tried to disperse the crowd with water, eventually soldiers came and fired in the air, and by force the army managed to halt the pogrom in town. During the event, the governor of Kielce also tried to intervene with Catholic authorities to "to urge the crowd to stop."[148] The local priest had refused, saying such a matter demanded the bishop's attention, and the bishop was out of town. Polish Christians saved some Jews, and at least two Polish Christians were among the dead. According to Cang, the police chief was unhappy with the united response to the event. The Polish army eventually stopped the five-hour-long pogrom.

Expressions of governmental control did follow and culminated in the organized movement of Jews away from Kielce. Just one day after the event, fifty people had been arrested. The vice minister of security arrived to supervise the investigation and oversee the arrest of policemen. And while the situation was "calmer," Cang wrote that "Jews living in districts around town [were] being evacuated under strong police protection."[149] In fact, Zuckerman helped with one of these evacuations: he escorted the wounded and other surviving Jews away from Kielce under military escort to a sealed train replete with Red Cross nurses from Kraków and a Russian officer who had been appointed by the Polish council. The decision to evacuate most of the surviving Jews happened because, as Zuckerman lamented, he naturally "couldn't persuade all the Jews to leave."[150] About sixteen hours after Zuckerman had arrived in Kielce, "Adolf Berman, officials, army people from Warsaw and a group from the training *kibbutz* of the Zionist youth arrived by airplane."[151] Berman, the head of the Kielce district, the town mayor, and Zuckerman "held a meeting to discuss the idea of removing all the Jews from Kielce to Łódź." The next night, the train that Zuckerman had requested arrived. The other officials returned to Warsaw, and Zuckerman stayed to organize the evacuation.

At a certain point in the process, when someone spoke Yiddish to him and he was afraid that the doctors, medics, and nurses would attempt to sabotage the operation on account of Zuckerman's Jewishness, his steely "nerves gave out," and he "pulled out a gun and ordered all the [Jewish] patients removed in fifteen minutes."[152] Those around him responded by working more quickly. Threats of violence and weapons were endemic in postwar Poland. Both helped Zuckerman facilitate the necessary evacuation of the wounded and the survivors. Traveling with soldiers who guarded the train at each intervening station, the locomotive arrived in Łódź the next morning and was met by ambulances as well as members of the local Jewish community. "Smaller Jewish communities in the areas near Kielce" emptied, Cang observed, "almost overnight."[153] Local defense commissions overseen by the Central Committee of Polish Jews sprouted up, and between July 1946 and May 1947, they intervened "with the authorities in excess of 2,000 instances related to anti-Jewish activities between July 1946 and May 1947."[154]

As Zuckerman recalled many decades later, "Kielce was just an omen."[155] Rumors continued to spread, and they suggested that "nationalist underground forces in many other cities were preparing to fight the government by murdering Jews."[156] A message from the Central Committee of Polish Jews that appeared in the August 20 issue of the Szczecin-based *Tygodnik Informacyjny* pinpointed these "exaggerated rumors" as important causal factors as well.[157] "Some unpredictable elements," the statement claimed, had used calls for the "emigration of the Jewish population to spread panic, fear and doubt." These rumors sowed "chaos and bedlam" while also propelling people to abandon their "jobs, their business and their workshops."[158] These rumors and the reality they painted depressed Zuckerman immensely. At the collective funeral for the deceased in Kielce, Zuckerman was certain that "those who participated in the pogrom also bore banners." Both the Polish Army and the Soviet Army remained in the city to maintain order. Zuckerman interpreted this double presence as an "indication of how shocked the authorities were. They understood clearly that the pogrom wasn't only an assault on the Jews, but also an attempt to bring down the institutions of the new regime."[159] Zuckerman's depression transformed into anger in the hours after the funeral as he traveled home.

As he sat looking out the window on his flight from Kielce to Warsaw, an officer from the security forces "expressed amazement at [his] glum mood." Zuckerman raged in response. He conceded that the government had "goodwill" toward Jewish survivors, but he knew that the government could not "guarantee the lives of the Jews in Poland; what happened is evidence of that." The remaining Jews were caught between a "hammer and the anvil"; they couldn't leave Poland, and their lives were not protected. "They are," he continued, "killed on trains and everywhere else, and then there's a pogrom in Kielce! And there will surely be other places too! Open the door for the Jews to leave!"[160] The security officer did not respond to Zuckerman immediately. Two days later, Zuckerman received a phone call from a senior member of the Urząd Bezpieczeństwa (UB). Two days after this, he met this unnamed man and others at a Warsaw café, where they all decided that Zuckerman, who agreed to be the responsible "Jewish" party, would meet with Deputy Minister of Defense Marian Spychalski about securing government support for the mass movement of Polish Jews across Poland's western border.

When Zuckerman agreed to consult with Spychalski, he agreed to consult with an old "friend from the Underground when, even if [they] weren't seeing one another, each one knew what the other was doing." And so, Zuckerman anticipated that Spychalski would be sympathetic to Zuckerman's request not because of Spychalski's own Jewish background but because of their shared history. Before his visit, Zuckerman told Adolf Berman about his plans to ask the deputy minister of defense for help opening the border for Jews who wanted to leave Poland. Despite not talking about the *bricha* with Berman for more than two years, Zuckerman spoke honestly with his colleague, whom he also knew from their wartime Underground work. Spychalski was, Zuckerman remembered relating to Berman, "the only one who might be able to consider these things globally and calculate Poland's relations with England." He was known from the Underground and was "reliable and imaginative." Berman agreed with Zuckerman "immediately," and the two contacted Spychalski and were accepted for a meeting "without delay."[161]

The process by which Polish Jewish migration away from Poland gained explicit government support happened quickly and easily, according to the next part of Zuckerman's memoirs. The meeting with Spychalski, who was also "shocked by the pogrom in Kielce," was "warm." Immediately after Zuckerman and Berman asked him to open the borders to Polish Jews who wanted to leave, Spychalski called the "general in charge of the borders, a Soviet military man whose name was [Gwidon] Czerwinski." In the presence of Zuckerman and Berman, Spychalski told Czerwinski "one thing": "Do not under any circumstances use the northern borders, that is, towards Berlin; use the southern route, across the Czech border."[162] When Czerwinski offered Spychalski a positive response to this request, Zuckerman arranged a meeting between "his guy" Stefan Grajek and Czerwinski to "fix the border crossings." According to Zuckerman, Grajek gave Czerwinski the preferred border crossings, Czerwinski passed the responsibility to two colonels on the border, and Zvi Netzer, Zuckerman's associate, "agreed to be liaison with them." At a second meeting, Zuckerman proposed that his "people who crossed the border" would receive "a stamp on their transit document." At the border, "the Jew would show a document with [this] stamp, confirming that the person was one of [his] Jews."[163] Notably, Michał Rudawski remembers this process differently. A senior officer in the Wojska Ochrony Pogranicza (Military Border Guard), Rudawski claimed that he, in fact, was the one responsible for the operation.[164]

What about the rest of the Polish government? Did the Soviets support the opening of the borders that facilitated the quickening of the *bricha*? Zuckerman hedged this question. He could only, he claimed, "reconstruct the course of things."[165] In Zuckerman's telling, it took Spychalski only a few moments with Zuckerman and Berman to make a decision about opening the border. Zuckerman was sure that Spychalski "did not pick up the telephone to call the Ministry of Foreign Affairs or any other element in the government." It was therefore conceivable "that Spychalski did it on his own, perhaps out of naivete, perhaps because of his attitude towards Jews, perhaps because of the proximity of the Kielce incident, or because of the clash between his communist theory and the Polish reality." Perhaps it was "these things and God knows what else might have caused that." Much to the chagrin of future historians, nothing was "written and no agreement, no document was signed; it was all an oral conversation."[166] Both the Polish government and Moscow could have intervened soon after Spychalski's actions, but Zuckerman noted that they did not.[167] In the end, Zuckerman pinpointed "*an historical, fateful decision, here, made by Spychalski* [emphasis in the original]" as the reason why Jews were able to cross "the borders as they did."[168]

Of course, Polish Jews had been leaving Poland across the Czechoslovak border for more than a year. But the pace of leaving exploded throughout July, August, and September 1946. Writing for the *Manchester Guardian* on July 17, Cang noted that "foreign consulates in Warsaw [were] almost besieged by crowds of Jews vainly seeking visas to go abroad."[169] The two hundred thousand

Fig. 5.5. A Czech truck passes over the border carrying Polish Jews, winter 1946–1947. Photo by Arthur Zeigart, courtesy Photo Archive of the Jewish Joint Distribution Committee.

Jews in postwar Poland, as estimated by Cang, had been "thrown into a panic." Now, they could "legally" leave without a destination visa.[170] To invoke Zuckerman's memoirs, "the great departure began."[171] To be more precise, a significant number of Polish Jews, many of whom had returned from wartime exile in the Soviet Union, flooded existing exit routes and migration networks in the summer of 1946 to depart Poland toward uncertain destinations.

Summer 1946: Czechoslovakia and Its Borders

As rumors about more organized violence against Jews spread and Spychalski orchestrated the official opening of Poland's border with Czechoslovakia for Polish Jews, local, state, and UNRRA authorities continued to deal with existing refugee problems while anticipating new ones. One week after news of the Kielce pogrom reached Zuckerman in Warsaw, the new director general of UNRRA, Fiorello La Guardia, sat for an interview on July 11, 1946. A reporter asked him, "How many displaced Jews from Europe should go to Palestine?" He replied cheekily, "If you're trying to get me to say 100,000, I say that 100,000 of them should go to Palestine forthwith. I say that as an American." He also announced his plans for the United States to "pool all unused immigration quotas from all countries and use them for any DPs who wished to enter the United States, regardless of their country of origin."[172] Furthermore, La Guardia hoped that American leadership on immigration would propel British foreign minister Ernest Bevin to reconsider his rejection of the suggestions made by the Anglo-American Committee of Inquiry.

The Jewish Telegraphic Agency covered La Guardia's interview as some of the officials under his command traveled to Prague for a series of meetings with high-ranking ministers as well as national and international Jewish leaders over twelve days from mid to late July. The influx of Polish Jews across Czechoslovak borders, or the so-called exodus, *bricha*, or *odsun* of Polish Jews, had demonstrably increased, and Czechoslovak officials seemed willing to support this movement. The drama of some Prague-based high-level meetings that occurred during this pivotal month remains preserved in a report filed by Israel Jacobson, a Jewish American who was serving as director of operations for the JDC in Czechoslovakia after the war.[173] In the second half of July and August 1946, fewer than a dozen men and women working in Prague, in Náchod, and throughout the US zone in Germany, as well as spaces in between, ensured that thousands of Polish Jewish citizens would leave Poland and have lodging and support indefinitely.[174]

Soon after the Kielce pogrom, Jacobson attended a meeting on the dire financial state of the operation straddling the Czechoslovak-Polish border. As the flow of Polish Jews increased, the cost of upkeep and further transportation from Náchod climbed astronomically.[175] The "makeshift arrangements" involving the ministers of social welfare and labor, foreign affairs, and the interior and the JDC proved insufficient when confronted with an increased exodus. To exacerbate matters, the Czechoslovak government had spent upward of twenty-one million crowns on food over the past six months "without any clear-cut decision as to who was ultimately responsible" for distributing it. Acting on the verbal assurance of Elfan Rees, a repatriation officer of the UNRRA mission to Czechoslovakia whom we encountered at the meeting where the category "displaced persons unsuccessfully repatriated" was created, Prague government officials assumed that UNRRA officials would offer a special allocation for these people classified as unsuccessful repatriates. In the second week of July 1946, the UNRRA deputy director general for Europe, Mary Louise Gibbons, came to Czechoslovakia to clarify her organization's obligation with officials from various government ministries and the JDC. She brought debilitating news.[176]

In meetings with minor government authorities during her time in Bohemia, Gibbons informed her colleagues that "they had either misunderstood or been misinformed" by Rees about UNRRA's "responsibility in supplying these additional funds and food products necessary to feed and to transport the unexpectedly large number of refugees." Upon the reversal of Rees's promise, shockwaves spread throughout bureaucratic and diplomatic circles. In Jacobson's assessment, "great anxiety and confusion amongst the lower echelons of Governmental employees who had been carrying out the program of aid to Polish travelers without authorization from their chiefs" (i.e., the heads of various ministries) followed in the wake of Gibbons's declaration. Jacobson scheduled a meeting with Foreign Minister Jan Masaryk and his vice minister, Václav Clementis, concerning the dire situation at hand.[177]

At the meeting, Masaryk assured Jacobson that "everything would be done to keep the Czechoslovakian border open." Moreover, he declared that "Czechoslovakia must remain a haven of refuge for these Jews fleeing from terror." Emphatically, Masaryk promised that if Czechoslovakia closed its borders, he "would resign" in protest. Masaryk's vice minister Clementis, who had spent the war years in the Soviet Union with other Czechoslovak communists, "also agreed that everything would be done to keep the border open" once he was assured that the Polish Jews would stay in Czechoslovakia only for the duration of their "transport out of the country."[178] Jacobson and the JDC now had a clear mandate from the Ministry of Foreign Affairs that the movement of Polish Jews would continue.

Fresh off his meeting with Czechoslovak leaders, Jacobson welcomed another UNRRA leader for a conference lasting more than two hours a few days later. Unhappy with the remarks of Gibbons, Jacobson sat down with her associates, Piotr Alexejev (the current chief of the UNRRA mission in Prague) and Gertrude Gates (a welfare officer for UNRRA). In direct contrast to his colleague Gibbons, Alexejev reported to Jacobson that he was prepared to "negotiate immediately with Czechoslovak government officials to ask them to continue their cooperative participation in providing food and transport." Furthermore, Alexejev hoped that the JDC would provide food and staff as needed. On that note of cooperation, the meeting adjourned. Apparently, Gibbons's reluctance to provide UNRRA funds for the Náchod operation had been an aberration.

Back in sync with UNRRA, Jacobson moved to schedule more meetings with high-ranking Czechoslovak government officials in a two-pronged strategy to secure national and international assurances for the Polish Jews passing through Náchod. A few days later on July 23, Jacobson convened with Zdeněk Nejedlý, the minister of social welfare and labor, for a three-hour meeting that included officials from the repatriation department. It soon became clear that the "Minister had not been aware of the full implications of the problem."

Unable to reach his colleagues in the Ministry of Foreign Affairs, the Ministry of the Interior, and the prime minister's office, Nejedlý agreed that "de facto arrangements existing today, i.e. the installations at Náchod, Bratislava, Bloubetin and Prague would continue to serve the Polish refugees," and "transportation by Czech railroads" would proceed indefinitely.[179] Nejedlý hoped that his ministry could help streamline operations for these particular refugees. In a thank-you letter to the minister, Jacobson celebrated the "liberal and humane attitude of the Czechoslovak Government and the Czechoslovak people in the help they are giving to the terror stricken Polish Jews."[180] After meetings with the Ministries of Foreign Affairs and the Interior, Jacobson was confident that "necessary steps" would be taken.[181]

Only one day following the suggestion of Minister Nejedlý for his ministry to assume the administration of this movement, Jacobson met with three Social Welfare and Labor officials to work out financial and logistical specifics. At this meeting, Jacobson made fifty thousand crowns available to the ministry for "the repair of a reception center in Náchod," which would house a repatriation office and an office for the JDC.[182] Ministry officials complained that UNRRA had only given "verbal assurance" that they would subsidize food and transport.[183] Promises of intervention, however, did not always translate to financial responsibility. As it had throughout most of 1946, during the summer months as the exodus reached its height, funding from the Czechoslovak government eclipsed the contributions of the JDC, the Prague Jewish community, and even UNRRA for activities on the Czechoslovak-Polish border.

Other documentation besides Jacobson's report reveals the fiscal reality. In a letter written on July 22, 1946, Arnošt Frischer related which parties had shirked their financial obligations. The former Jewish representative of the Czech government-in-exile and postwar member of the Jewish National Council in Prague noted that UNRRA had failed to support upward of seven hundred Polish Jews who crossed the border daily. Frischer considered Gibbons's revocation of funds to be "a grievous fault."[184] Contrary to the promises offered by UNRRA official Alexejev, it remained clear that UNRRA's support was insufficient.[185] In contrast, Frischer declared, "the Czechoslovakian government's behavior in this matter is excellent and they are not only granting asylum but also financial support." With emphasis, Frischer closed his note by stating, "I think it would not serve our cause if there could arise the impression that the Czechoslovakian government is more interested in these refugees than the international UNRRA."[186]

Another entity also seemed more interested than UNRRA in the fate of Polish Jews uprooted once again from Poland: the World Jewish Congress. As

Fig. 5.6. A young Polish Jewish family waits to board a Czechoslovak repatriation train that will take them further away from Poland. Courtesy Photo Archive of the Jewish Joint Distribution Committee.

officials assembled in Prague to decide what to do about Náchod, the recently established WJC representative in the Czechoslovak capital, Samuel Sharp, was busy communicating with A. L. Kubowitzki back in New York. Sharp had arrived in Czechoslovakia in June 1946 on the heels of a democratic parliamentary election that swept the Communist Party into power with nearly 38 percent of the votes cast and amid the (parliament-controlled) reelection of President Edvard Beneš.[187] During that summer of prolonged movement, Sharp met with an array of people, from Arnošt Frischer and Gershom Scholem to the leaders of the "*bricha* from Poland" who, according to him, sought his advice.[188] When the flow of Polish Jews into Czechoslovakia increased in July and August 1946, Sharp and WJC took action to protect the migration route crossing Czechoslovak borders even if these activities were downplayed publicly.[189]

For example, one day after La Guardia's public promise to transfer one hundred thousand European Jews away from Europe, Sharp visited Stefan Wierbłowski, the Polish ambassador to Czechoslovakia, and collected sensitive information to share with the WJC Office Committee during their July 12, 1946, meeting. At this meeting, Wierbłowski dismissed plans for the establishment of a Jewish "yishuv in Poland."[190] Instead, he agreed with Sharp fully that "Jews must leave Poland" despite his reluctance to issue "Polish documents to people who crossed the border illegally." Polish authorities would issue passports only to people with a "final visa of a country willing to accept them." While Spychalski's directives would soon change this policy, the WJC took Wierbłowski at his word and planned accordingly. Sharp's instructions from the WJC Office Committee arrived in an urgent telegram from Kubowitzki on July 17, 1946. "Alarmed news mass flight Polish Jews to CZSK," it began. WJC leaders urged Sharp to "visit immediately reception centers" to clarify the present situation and instructed him "to intervene on behalf of the WJC and take steps to facilitate passage of these Jews through Czechoslovakia."[191]

Sharp did just that. Just five days later, on July 22, he cabled back to Kubowitzki a short burst of information. Along with Louis Levene, Sharp had visited Náchod and noted that an average flow of six to seven hundred Polish Jews crossed into Náchod daily. There were "no difficulties" at the reception centers on the Czechoslovak side. He noted that there were "poor facilities," which would, he understood, soon be improved by the JDC and the "community." He thought that it would be "unwise" to join the action at "this moment," and Sharp promised to personally explain why to WJC officials when he arrived in Paris on July 26. An undated memo with evidence of Sharp's hand was tucked inside a WJC archival folder with other Náchod-related documentation and most likely indicates what he preferred to say "in person" after his trip to the border. He criticized the JDC.[192] In his assessment, their help was "insufficient" and "badly organized." Furthermore, because the JDC would not meet the "huge expenditure" accumulating at the border, Sharp urged the WJC to get "UNRRA and other agencies to cooperate" lest the Czechoslovak government attempt to reclaim the substantial debt for train transportation. For these financial reasons, Sharp suggested that the WJC should avoid "responsibility for the *bricha* action" and hide even "indirect connections" so as not to become entangled "in the question of the transportation debt." Instead, the WJC should assume the "utmost discretion in our association with the *bricha* movement."[193]

Neither Sharp nor Jacobson necessarily knew how "the Polish government" felt about the *bricha*. Opinions, policies, and procedures remained in flux, as the simultaneity of Wierbłowski's declaration with Spychalski's decision indicates. Fatefully for Polish Jews who decided to leave Poland after the Kielce pogrom, semi-official Czechoslovak and Polish support for the movement of Polish Jews away from Poland coincided on shockingly similar timelines. And notably, JDC representatives and Czechoslovak officials continued to provide support when UNRRA did not. Two days after his meeting with Nejedlý on July 25, 1946, Jacobson had dinner at the house of Dr. Zdeněk Toman, who served under Nosek as vice minister of the interior.[194] The two men "discussed security arrangements and the use of JDC staff to buttress the effort of the Ministry of the Interior in checking the refugees coming through." Specifically, Toman asked Jacobson for "an assurance that the people coming into Czechoslovakia would continue to be moved out quickly" and "discussed a plan to direct some of the refugees from Polish border points through Prague to Aš on the American Zone Germany border line, so that they could from there be routed directly to UNRRA camps in Germany."[195] Toman asked Jacobson to "submit in writing an overall plan with responsibilities affixed for the movements of Polish Jewish refugees through Czechoslovakia." In contradiction, Toman and his associate also proposed "that arrangements be made for some of the Polish Jews to work in-country for a few weeks as there was a critical labour shortage due to the deportation of Germans."[196] The messy mixture of movements that underpinned the ethnic revolution had unleashed severe economic repercussions across Czechoslovakia and in fact all of east central Europe. For this particular component of that revolution, fiscal responsibilities and future plans were further clarified in a meeting on July 26, 1946.

On that day, representatives from the Czechoslovak Ministries of the Interior, Foreign Affairs, and Social Welfare and Labor as well as the JDC discussed the plan that Nejedlý had proposed to Jacobson and "agreed that immediate steps would be taken to establish at least quasi-legal machinery to deal with the problem" of the uprooted Polish Jewish diaspora. Moreover, "the officials decided that it was necessary to get clear understanding from UNRRA regarding its supplementary allocation for coping with this situation" and that a bill of twenty-one million crowns would be submitted to UNRRA for "food advanced from January 5 to the present in order that a definite decision be given by UNRRA."[197] When asked what alternative existed if UNRRA denied the funding, Jacobson promised that the JDC would cooperate with the Czechoslovak government to ensure that the allocation was delivered.[198] Impressively, despite the chaotic governmental shuffle that followed in the wake of liberation and the reestablishment of agencies throughout Prague, the "problem" of sixty thousand Polish Jews passing and pooling near Náchod involved personnel at international, state, and local levels.[199]

A focus on Náchod citizen Rudolf Beck reveals a different type of tension between these three levels. Incarcerated as a "Jew" during the occupation, Beck returned to his home in Náchod soon after liberation in 1945. From his airy two-story house atop a hill less than a quarter mile from the main square, Beck worked to establish an infrastructure to support the Polish Jewish refugees who appeared in Náchod. He worked with health officials in Náchod, secured space in a convalescent home perched in the hills south of the city center for exhausted refugees, and pooled the resources of Náchod's Jewish community. As the flow of Polish Jews intensified by mid-July, however, the Prague Jewish Community decided that Beck needed more oversight. In mid-July, a letter traveled from the Jewish Community building on Maiselova Street in Prague to Náchod, where Beck received it. The situation on the border "in recent weeks" had become "so big" that it extended "beyond the capacity of [Náchod's] community."[200] Specifically, the letter asked Beck to cease his own negotiations with UNRRA and allow the Prague representative to take over in his stead.[201]

This letter, like other documents assembled thus far, demonstrates that the humanitarian crisis initiated by the exodus of Polish Jews increasingly fell under the purview of centralized bodies as it continued unabated by the end of July when upward of seven hundred refugees made the "green border" their exit point.[202] On July 31, 1946, the Jewish Telegraphic Agency reported that the Czechoslovak government had set up a "refugee camp housing 4,000 people" at Náchod.[203] Officials in the Prague Jewish Community wrote to the chief rabbi in London around this time asking for a mobile synagogue in order to serve the religious needs of the pooling refugees.[204] And, of course, as Polish Jews crossed into the northeast corner of Bohemia, authorities on Bohemia's western border and beyond prepared for this unabated influx. Some of those decision-makers, it turns out, made decisions about the uprooted Polish Jewish diaspora thousands of miles away from the Bohemian-Bavarian border.

Summer 1946: American Spaces

Six time zones away from Náchod, WJC officials Ignacy Schwarzbart and Charles Irwing Dwork sat down in the District of Columbia alongside Undersecretary of State Dean Acheson, Secretary of War Robert Patterson, their subordinates, and representatives from the JDC, the American Jewish Conference, and the American Jewish Committee to discuss Czechoslovakia's hemorrhaging border. Acheson called the meeting on July 22, 1946, to sift through the available intelligence and make recommendations to President Harry S. Truman about the path forward. It was obvious to Dwork, who had worked at the so-called "Jewish desk" of the Office of Strategic Services during the war, that the meeting had been "painstakingly prepared."[205] Acheson quoted a report by General McNarney that discussed the increased difficulties in the American zone since the publication of the Anglo-American Committee of Inquiry report in April. McNarney predicted that by September 1, 1946, 110,000 refugees would be in the American zone. This number represented the "greatest number that the American military authorities could accommodate."[206] And so, McNarney recommended that American authorities close the border between the US zone of occupied Germany and Czechoslovakia to head off the Jews leaving Poland on the first day of September and close the internal borders within occupied Germany immediately.

From this proposal the conversation spun outward. Was it antisemitism propelling the Jews away from Poland? What about the Jews crossing between the occupation zones? Could the border be kept open longer? Schwarzbart pleaded that the border be kept open for humanitarian reasons. Dwork offered a much more specific recommendation. He asked that the border be kept open for six more months, until one hundred thousand Jews could emigrate to Palestine, until a significant number of non-Jews could leave the American zone, and until "conditions in eastern Europe could be ameliorated."[207] After more discussion, Acheson promised that President Truman would have the final decision and that the internal borders within occupied Germany would be closed. Schwarzbart left the meeting steeped in doubt. The periodic silence that hung over the table made Schwarzbart question whether there would be "an immediate departure of the 100,000."[208] His intuition was correct. Such a transfer would not occur in 1946.

In the wake of this meeting, a handful of personalities urged President Truman to keep the border open past September 1. The majority leader of the House of Representatives, John McCormack; Senators James M. Mead and Joseph F. Guffy; Henry Wallace; and David Niles all intervened.[209] All of these interlocutors agreed that the border between Bavaria and Bohemia had to be kept open until at least December. Truman did not permanently close the border to fleeing Polish Jews in September 1946, nor did it close in December 1946.[210] This resulted in an unsustainable situation: Polish Jews could get into the US zones, but there was no systematic strategy to move them elsewhere.[211] The WJC Office Committee decided to "renew [their] efforts to get as many Jews out of Poland as possible."[212] They called a special meeting with the delegation of Polish Jews belonging to the Central Committee of Polish Jews. Nearly ten months after they had their first postwar meeting in September 1945, Tartakower and Sommerstein sat around the same conference table once again.

The notes left behind from this meeting exude anxiousness. WJC officials wanted to promote migration away from east central Europe to Palestine, but they had to balance that desire with the political situation at hand and the point of view offered by their guests from Poland, who were due to return to Poland imminently.[213] Just a week before this meeting, Samuel Sharp, the WJC official based in Prague, had recommended that the WJC avoid entangling itself in the situation unfolding around Náchod. But the current status quo presented a golden opportunity. As Tartakower stated near the beginning of the hour that he felt it was their collective "duty to take as many Jews from Poland as possible, probably thousands and even tens of thousands."[214] He continued that it would be "most desirable to get them to Palestine, but we all know that is impossible at the present time." And so, as "long as Jews do not have the possibility of getting to Palestine we must get them into other countries where their life and safety are assured," as in occupied Germany. Referencing the meeting Schwarzbart had attended with representatives from the Department of State and the Department of War on July 22, Tartakower reported on the "danger" that might ensue if the borders between the American zone in Germany of occupation and Poland "would close."[215] Sommerstein and his colleagues listened as the clocks ticked toward the time of their departure. He turned to Schwarzbart to ask him for his opinion on the recent meetings that he had attended.

Unlike almost all the other Office Committee minutes saved in the WJC archive, the minutes of this particular meeting suggest a strong editorial hand, and it is unclear to whom that hand belonged. Schwarzbart's answer to

Sommerstein was somewhat redacted. Allow me to cite the relevant portion in full, including crossed-out portions:

> [Schwarzbart] had the impression that both Departments feel that the closing of the borders are necessary because of administrative reasons and not because of any political reasons . . . Dr. Schwarzbart did not have the feeling that there is a tendency on the part of the authorities to struggle with the Jews who want to enter illegally. ~~The exodus from Poland has no legal support, not ever from us~~. We did not organize the exodus from Poland. ~~Our political line is not for exodus from Poland~~. That is what we stressed in our conference. We also emphasized that there is an emigration from the American Zone because the people want to go to Palestine . . . we saw that the attitude of both departments is humane and friendly. They wanted to discuss the whole problem with us. Their object was not to discuss the political line of taking Jews out of Poland but to cope with the real facts of the situation.[216]

Unlike Tartakower, who had proclaimed it a duty to take tens of thousands of Jews out of Poland, Schwarzbart wanted to distance the WJC from the activities unfolding across the Polish-Czechoslovak border. But Schwarzbart seemed to have gone too far in his distancing, and in the official minutes of the meeting, someone had crossed out statements indicating that WJC policy was legally and politically against the *bricha* or the *odsun* of Polish Jews. Much to the contrary, the WJC had dedicated funding, time, and their political network to ensure that the movement of Polish Jews away from Poland could continue despite threats of border closures and the impossibility of mass transfer plans away from Germany. Despite some investment in the Polish Central Committee and vague statements of support directed toward Jews who wanted to remain in the country of their citizenship, the WJC's "political line" had been for an exodus from Poland with only slight deviation since the spring and summer of 1944.

After letting Tartakower and Schwarzbart speak, two delegates from the Central Committee of Polish Jews, Sommerstein and Józef Sack, offered their opinions. Sommerstein observed "that it is not a question of an exodus from Poland but a question of doing everything necessary for the Jews of Poland."[217] And so the Polish delegation wanted the WJC "to persuade other countries and especially England and America to help with the situation in Poland." Sommerstein's colleague Józef Sack, a member of the Central Committee of Jews who would in 1947 be elected to Polish parliament, confronted the movement of Jews away from Poland more directly. The question of emigration, Sack noted, was "an internal problem for the Jews in Poland." Noting his own

Zionist leanings, he "would have said sometime ago that he was interested only in *aliyah* from Poland." But now he agreed with the direction the WJC was taking with regard to the finding of other migratory outlets. He noted that perhaps the WJC could "politically" influence countries in Scandinavia or France. Schwarzbart did not directly disregard Sack's suggestions, but he was quite pessimistic about quickly securing permanent homes for the Jewish DPs. Before the delegation from Poland left the meeting, Schwarzbart admitted, "The tide is against us."[218]

Summer 1946: A Different Antisemitism in Postwar Poland

Joel Cang was also pessimistic, but for a more precise reason. His reporting in postwar Poland indicates that the contours and qualities of antisemitism had changed. The pogrom in Kielce, he wrote, was "a tragic illustration of the state of insecurity in which the Jewish of Poland live today." Furthermore, "Hitler's racial propaganda fell" on "fertile ground" in Poland, and many remained committed to the "killing of Jews" well after the Führer's death."[219] Of course, Cang's reporting demonstrates that some tactics employed by anti-Semites remained the same. Cang observed that all three major postwar pogroms, first at Kraków, then at Radom, and finally at Kielce, involved a "ritual murder accusation."[220] Cang was surprised, for example, that the father of Henryk Błaszczyk believed his son when the young man declared that he had been kept by Jews and saw the bodies of other little children. He reported that in the wake of Kielce, rumors of ritual murder continued to spread and were effective.[221] Although people in the so-called crowd had believed in ritual murder for centuries, the constituents in this crowd had changed over time and, in particular, since the occupation.

Unlike when Cang wrote his article in *Jewish Social Studies* in 1939, members of the Peasant Party had become increasingly outspoken against Jews in the postwar period. Cang noted that all antisemites, those in the Catholic Church hierarchy as well as those speaking from more secular pedestals, used the same accusation: the "Jews" occupied a disproportionate number of leading positions in the postwar Polish government. Voices in the Peasant Party, Cang observed, used this accusation the most frequently. "Members of this party," Cang reported, "often say that the presences of Jews in the government is one of the chief causes of anti-Jewish feeling although they can point only to one Jew of cabinet rank, Mr. Hilary Minc." Less than a decade earlier, Cang had been impressed by the average member of the peasantry who did not, by and large, believe the antisemitic propaganda spread by parties such as the National

Democrats. This status quo had changed. So too had the degree and scale of antisemitic violence deemed societally permissive.

Unlike in the 1930s, when he reported on anti-Jewish riots in Grodno, Suwałki, and Raciąż, as well as the 1936 pogrom in Przytyk, the scale and the intensity of violence against Jews had increased astronomically by the mid-1940s.[222] The killing of Jews, Cang noted, had "become a daily affair" and implicated "thousands" of Christian Poles. Cang heard that a crowd "of at least 5,000" had reportedly took part in the Kielce pogrom.[223] Even if this number was inflated, consider the scale. In July 1946, fifty thousand people lived in Kielce and within that number around eight hundred Jews. If forty Jews died during the pogrom and if a substantial number of Polish Christians participated, the violent event impacted a significant percentage of the town directly. Reflecting more on the Kielce pogrom after his investigative work there, Cang noted the "surprising fact" that "in spite of the presence of large numbers of troops in the town, the pogrom shouldn't have lasted such a long time," nearly five hours. In fact, even after the army had stopped the "main pogrom" the beating and killing continued.[224] Cang, like other careful observers before him and historians after him, recognized that antisemitism itself had changed.

Schachter, Warhaftig, Schwarzbart, and Tartakower also recognized this fact, as we learned in chapter 4. I would like to expand on this "new" antisemitism at this juncture as we reflect on the reasons Polish Jews traveled toward Náchod. New moral standards that matured during occupation, familiar charges of ritual murder, accusations of *Żydokomuna* reinforced by wartime encounters with Soviets, rumors more generally, and a specific postwar context that was dominated by rampant civil and political violence made excessively deadly pogroms like the one that occurred in Kielce possible. The "novel, virulent quality of postwar anti-semitism in Poland" grew out of "actual experience acquired during the war years."[225] Nazi-imposed laws, societal treatment, and the actions that added up to genocide seemed to demonstrate that Jewish lives had less value. John Connelly writes about how Nazi ideology seemed flexible regarding the position of "Slavs" and completely inflexible toward the position and ultimate threat of the Jews. For the Nazis, Connelly reminds us, "the Jews were not a race among races. They were the race that destroyed [*zersetzen*] race, the very substance of human existence. There was a uniquely metaphysical dimension in the Nazi hatred of Jews."[226] Nazi occupation drew on this ideology and sought to normalize the public mistreatment, humiliation, uprooting, physical violence, and outright murder of the Jews throughout Europe, but especially in Poland where millions of Jews lived and, gruesomely, died. One specific example will suffice.

Writing from his perch as head of the county hospital, Dr. Zygmunt Klukowski saw societal norms drastically changed during the years of Nazi occupation. Klukowski kept a secret diary during the war that could have cost him and his family their lives had it been discovered. With contacts throughout the town and the views afforded by his hospital, Klukowski uniquely witnessed how the presence of Nazi officials, the constant threat of deportation for all Szczebrzeszyn residents to make room for incoming Volksdeutsche settlers, and the overarching, tense climate of occupation dismantled his town's social fabric.[227] Klukowski's self-awareness is striking: "We are living during strange times," he wrote in May 1942. "Now when people meet on the street the normal way of greeting is, 'Who was arrested? How many Jews were killed last night? Who was robbed?' These events are so common," he continued, "that, really, no one seems to care." "Slowly," he observed, "you become accustomed to everything."[228]

As Szczebrzeszyn's community dissolved into "fear, hatred and recrimination,"[229] Klukowski watched as Jews were pushed from their houses, publicly humiliated, killed in broad daylight, put on trains to Bełżec, and finally marched to the Jewish cemetery outside of town, where they were shot in mass graves. Klukowski witnessed occupation authorities doing these things. He also witnessed Polish men in the so-called Blue Police and local Polish Christians aid these activities, aggressively search for Jews to kill on August 8, 1942, and eventually take control of the massive "hunt for" and mass murder of Szczebrzeszyn's Jews at the end of October 1942.[230] Soon after this tragedy, Klukowski recorded in his clandestine diary that "the attitude towards Jews [was] changing. There are many people who see the Jews not as human beings but as animals that must be destroyed."[231] Klukowski's chronicling reinforces Anna Cichopek-Gajraj's argument—namely, the "great damage the Nazi occupation did to Poles as a community of citizens" was to "completely undermine the notion of morality in daily life." This development "would have dire consequences after the end of the war."[232]

Postwar violence with antisemitic intent "occurred in waves that coincided with political upheaval and the intensification of the civil war" in Poland.[233] During this particularly unstable period, a new "social atmosphere" reigned that merged anti-Jewish elements of Christianity, historical antisemitism that predated 1939, and the "wartime isolation of Jews" while also drawing on a novel irrational fear called *Żydokomuna*. This racist way of explaining the world built on a stereotype from the nineteenth century linking Jews to the spread of communist thinking and played out during the war at first (there were elements of *Żydokomuna* present in the Jedwabne pogrom) and even more pervasively after it as communism more generally and Soviet-style communism particularly spread throughout Polish spaces.[234] Since a majority of Polish Jews who survived World War II and the Holocaust did so in the Soviet Union, fears about *Żydokomuna* took on an air of plausibility for a traumatized, brain-drained, and economically weakened Polish society.[235] And while, as David Engel argues, "the bands that were most heavily responsible for killing Jews would not have existed except for the circumstances of the communist takeover," context alone "does not provide a sufficient explanation for this phenomenon."[236]

The violence directed toward Polish Jews after the Holocaust must be embedded within the fragile political context of the mid-1940s, distrust cultivated by Catholic officials that cast Jews as "others," and the personal experience of "surviving" and "watching" occupation, war, and genocide in this region.[237] It follows that an "increase in the level of aggression in interpersonal relations was one of the most important consequences of the war, which created a huge potential for violence and a readiness to use violence in situations of the slightest conflict."[238] Firearms were readily available, and the "experience of observing hatred and German atrocities simply removed all obstacles to further violence."[239] That violence (tinged with antisemitism or not) and rumors of it explicitly threatened the bodies of the Polish Jews and their children who returned from the Soviet Union. The collision of context with lived experience was extremely deadly for Polish Jews in the summer of 1946.

Summer 1946: Náchod and the World

On the eleventh day of August while in attendance at the Paris Peace Conference, UNRRA officials and WJC leaders such as Wise and Goldmann learned that Czechoslovakia's border with Poland had been closed following a British request.[240] General McNarney wanted to discourage "organized movements" of Jews into the US zone.[241] A few days after the closing of Bohemia's eastern border, US president Truman proposed that a special quota of fifty thousand refugees be admitted to the United States to alleviate the problems multiplying in the US occupation zones. Truman was not the only high-profile American leader concerned with events developing in DP camps.

The recently appointed director general of UNRRA, La Guardia, had arrived in Europe earlier that August to lead the Fifth General Council Meeting of UNRRA in Geneva. Speaking from the building that had housed the League of Nations and the first meeting of the WJC in 1936, La Guardia contested Britain's request to close Bohemia's border as well as McNarney's desire to ease DP problems by cutting off emigration. On the contrary, he declared that "'a persecuted people leaving a country'—and that is the case of Jews leaving Poland—are entitled to benefit from all the help and assistance that UNRRA is permitted to give displaced people."[242] UNRRA as a humanitarian organization would not ignore the sixty to seventy thousand Jews estimated to be leaving Poland. He urged the US to lobby those in control of Palestine to permit the admission of one hundred thousand DPs immediately. On the heels of La Guardia's statement, Prague Radio reported that the Czechoslovak-Polish border had been reopened on August 15 after a three-day closure. Around three thousand Jews were now crossing the border daily.

Finally, on the same day that the border reopened, General Czerwinski (whom Spychalski had called in front of Zuckerman about one month earlier) issued a memo to his border guards reminding them of the Polish-Czechoslovak Convention from May 30, 1925, which included rules and procedures for crossing the border between those two states. It is possible the memo is not linked to the reopening of the border. Czerwinski surmised that "Czech border guards wanted to talk about the matter of the border with their Polish counterparts," and the interwar convention served as an important reference point. He asked his guards to "organize the issue in a centralized way."[243] This was not the first time that this particular convention had been disseminated to Polish border guards.[244] Other remnants of memos and papers marked with his signature and sent to border stations along the "green border" corroborate Zuckerman's memory that Czerwinski possessed a high degree of power over border-related circumstances. His endorsement of this movement at this time was not, however, exceptional. Polish leaders assembling in Geneva agreed with the push to keep the border open and rejected the British request to halt the "exodus of the Jews."[245]

Near the end of UNRRA's Fifth General Assembly, Lt. Gen. Morgan, who had already been dismissed and reinstated in January, was dismissed again.[246] In his wake, General McNarney promised that "fleeing Polish Jews" would not only be admitted to the US zone, they would be assisted, even though they had "entered the US Zone illegally."[247] "We will give them haven, house them and feed them, as we have done in the past," he said. McNarney estimated that one hundred thousand Polish Jews might still leave Poland and that British requests to tighten east central European borders would fall on deaf ears. The UNRRA meeting in Geneva included a plan to continue help for the DPs up to six months after UNRRA's official liquidation at the end of 1946 as well as promises to "assist all those classified as refugees in the draft constitution of the IRO. This would include native Jews from Germany and Austria."[248] Words emanating from this UNRRA meeting in mid-August 1946 assured observers at the WJC and elsewhere that Polish Jews could access both the US zone in occupied Germany and UNRRA's financial support. Note that negotiations over the fate of these "displaced people unsuccessfully repatriated" coincided with the height of the so-called exodus of Polish Jews from Poland.[249] When La Guardia was faced with a question presuming that UNRRA's activities were helping underground immigration out of Poland, he denied such an effect. UNRRA officials could, La Guardia claimed, distinguish between refugees and the Polish underground by using "God-given intelligence and common sense."[250]

While a few non-Jewish Poles inevitably crossed the border near Náchod, authorities at the border in the late summer and early fall of 1946 worked to ensure that La Guardia's promise would be fulfilled. According to reporter Ladislav Khan, the "condition of transfer" across the border was "Jewish identity," which was "ascertained by verification of the doctor or the religious community."[251] There remained, however, some reports of non-Jewish migrants. Helena Szulcova, a twenty-three-year-old single woman, had heard that employment was more readily available in Czechoslovakia, and she had, allegedly, an uncle in Prague. She joined a group of Jews who "advised her to travel with them" and was caught at the border.[252] Another Polish Christian, Zbigniew Hartwig from Gomnici, "confessed during interrogation that he [was not] a Jew," that he was instead a "member of the illegal organization *Wolność i Niezawisłość* (WiN)," and that he had "snuck onto the transport for Jewish refugees from Náchod using a false document under the name Viliam Sempek."[253] If these cases were rare, they still commanded the attention of high-ranking members in the Czechoslovak Interior Ministry.

As Polish Jews streamed across the Polish-Czechoslovak border in the wake of the three-day closure in August 1946, Zdeněk Toman, who had met with Israel Jacobson in July, harbored deep concerns about the authenticity of the transmigrants entering his country from Poland. The Ministry of the Interior, Toman stated in an internal memorandum, had received word that sometimes non-Jews sneaked into "transports of Jewish refugees from Poland who flee . . . for political reasons and try to get from our country further west."[254] To correct this situation, Toman and the Ministry of the Interior asked that "transports of Jewish refugees [be] given more attention and [that] every suspicious person . . . [be] investigated with the participation of reliable Jewish representatives" before traveling further into the country.[255] In this way, the stream of displaced persons unsuccessfully repatriated had quite frequent and personal interactions with the JDC, local religious leaders, and, of course, Czechoslovak authorities.

Like so many Polish Jews, UNRRA officials, state workers, and international caretakers, Reverend Robert Smith traveled to Náchod in the summer of 1946. He arrived from Prague with his pen in the last week of August, when few obstacles impeded the daily flow of Polish Jews. He wanted to know how this town responded to the humanitarian crisis that had arrived at its threshold. Smith learned that "at first [Polish Jews] were billeted in private homes or in a hotel, but soon the barracks were taken over and the American JDC undertook the relief organization." Despite the leadership of the JDC, Smith noted that there was "a representative of the Czechoslovak Ministry of Social Welfare who looks after official contacts and a Czech Jewish doctor whom we saw at work." He estimated that "since the beginning of July over 32,000 people have passed through this camp" and a neighboring camp.[256] Furthermore, "the records of Náchod camp show that 1,765 refugees arrived on the first of August and during the peak period of the next few days the figures averaged over a thousand daily." In the eyes of world Zionists, Smith concluded, "Náchod [was] the most significant spot in Europe."[257]

Soon after Smith's provocative declaration, in September 1946, the stream of Polish Jewish transmigrants lessened considerably. This lessening coincided with a substantial drop in violence against Jews on Polish territory. By the fall of 1946, most repatriated Polish Jews who wanted to leave Poland had left already. By October 8, 1946, reports compiled by town officials estimated that no more than eleven thousand Jews remained in Szczecin.[258] The United Nations closed the border at Náchod in November 1946. The border was opened once again soon after and remained so for about three more months. A few thousand people crossed the border in the early winter of 1947, but new emigration policies in Poland made travel away from Poland much more difficult beginning in February 1947. In that month, roughly eighty thousand Polish Jews, just over one-third of all the Jews who had survived the Second World War or around 3 percent of the number that had held Polish citizenship in 1939, remained in Poland.[259]

CONCLUSION

Foundation tales simplify what is complex and contested. Journalistic coverage, precious oral testimonies, and canonical histories about the uprooted Polish Jewish diaspora, its return from the Soviet Union, and its pooling in displaced persons camps in 1946 utilize the same "larger-than-life" language invoked by Smith in his reportage. Overall, to cite a point made by David Engel, Israeli national consciousness has "gravitated" toward one telling of postwar Jewish history in Poland.[260] This chapter problematizes this telling, this language, and this foundation story by situating Náchod within a transatlantic and trans-European causal chain of personalities, places, and intellectual currents.

I have shown how the flow of Polish Jews outside of Poland began ("unofficially" in the fall of 1945 and then "officially" in the winter of 1946), quickened, lessened, stopped, and restarted across nearly a yearlong period. Like the broader narrative of this book, this chapter about Náchod and those who passed through it requires attention to contingency. Nothing about this movement from the Soviet Union, back to Poland, across the Czechoslovak border, and into the US zones of Germany and Austria was guaranteed. The resulting narrative imbricates what contemporary observers and subsequent historians have called the *bricha* within a broader story that at once depends on and transcends the confines of Jewish, Polish, Czechoslovak, and American military narratives.[261] From Zuckerman, Alexejev, and Spychalski to Jacobson, Beck, and Toman and then Truman, McNarney, and La Guardia, the contingent story of Náchod in 1946 is one of shifting dynamics, the power of personalities, and the result of shifting norms.

Within this transnational story, a special place in this long causal chain belongs to an array of Czechoslovaks.[262] Administrators in Náchod, security officers at the border, and government officials back in Prague made a series of decisions allowing the movement of these former Polish citizens away from Poland. Confronted with Polish Jews and non-Jews assembling at the border, ministers in high-level talks and civil servants working on the ground decided at a number of key moments in the spring and summer of 1946 to let only Polish citizens of Jewish descent into Czechoslovakia. Those Czechoslovak facilitators of the ethnic revolution crafted policies, upheld precedents encouraging movement, and ignored others that would have stifled the flow of these refugees while also financing a large part of this movement.

While the Czechoslovak involvement in this broader event is notable, Masaryk, Beck, Toman, and others did not work alone. Over nineteen months after V-E day, various circumstances and the work of numerous actors collided to permit more than one hundred thousand Polish Jews to leave the Soviet Union, return to Poland, leave Poland, and, eventually, arrive in DP camps in occupied Germany and Austria. As we have seen, the flow of Polish Jews into a new diaspora was highly contingent and predicated on more than just secret operatives. Like other uprootings underpinning the "ethnic revolution," the uprooting of Polish Jews from Poland required an intellectual revolution in thinking about the east central European body politic, a concomitant change in thinking about the rootedness of Jewish populations, and copious, intentional work by an unlikely group of actors.

CONCLUSION

Postwar Life Is Elsewhere: The Consequences of the "Ethnic" Revolution in East Central Europe

AN OBLONG MAP HANGS ON the wall of my office, which overlooks a canal dappled with lily pads in the center of Leiden. The map extends from Bohemia in the west to the Volga River in the east, and its yellowed outline frames interwar borders, dots representing cities and different, pixelated hues indicating where the cartographers agreed that different "national" groups lived. Like Edvard Beneš did while receiving visitors in British exile during the Second World War, I sometimes gesture to this map while conversing with students or colleagues. Mostly, though, I look at it and think.

From a short distance, this map resembles an unbalanced kaleidoscope replete with colors that coagulate in unexpected patterns. In this way, it resembles the vivid map of Mitteleuropa at the turn of the 20th century on the cover of this book. A ruby shade fills a large part of the western portion and indicates the rootedness of millions of Czechs. And then, the same color appears again roughly one thousand kilometers to the east in the Polish province of Volhynia, where upward of twenty thousand so-called "ethnic Czechs" had lived for decades farming on marshlands that had belonged to the Russian Empire. This dispersion of ethnicities and their concomitant colors multiplies: Poles (a buttery yellow) and Ruthenians (an electric purple) who live in Czechoslovakia. Belarusians (blood orange) and Ukrainians (deep violet) who live in the Polish *kresy*. Slovaks (pale red) in Hungary. Hungarians (pine green) in Romania. And, on this map produced by the Czechoslovak State Statistical Office in the 1930s, two groups are dispersed throughout this region: Germans (dark blue) and Jews (light blue). The "ethnic revolution" quickly and drastically changed this cartography. Some "minorities" and infrastructures supporting them did remain, of course. For the most part, however, ethnographic maps of states in east central Europe produced by the late 1940s reveal political entities that are much less ethnically heterogenous, much less nationally complex.

Some events cleave time and the way we talk about it. In the 1940s, there were many such "cleaving" events that are relevant to the narrative I have written here: the Second World War, the Holocaust, the birth of the United Nations, and the signing of a document declaring the independence of a new state, the state of Israel. Each of these events generated a "before" and an "after" that are simultaneously temporal, historical, and emotional. Stefan Zweig understood this cleaving and rendered it in the most exquisite prose shortly before he committed suicide with his wife in Brazil, uprooted across hemispheres from the region of his birth. "My feeling is," he told us in 1942, "that the world in which I grew up, and the world of today, and the world between the two are entirely separate worlds."[1] One of the events that swallowed Zweig and deracinated him from his home, his books, his culture, and his ancestry was the "ethnic revolution." Of course, this revolution was inextricably tied to total war, genocide, changing international norms, and the unexpected transcendence of monoethnic nation-states in Europe, in the Middle East, and around the world.[2] Still, this ethnic revolution needs to be understood on its own terms, as an east central European event that continues to cleave time and the way we talk about it.

Uprooting the Diaspora has charted the shape, speed, timeline, and participants of this ethnic revolution through conversations, letters, newspaper articles, annotated memoranda, documents filled with plans for the postwar world, memoirs, and policies that took shape on the ground in the region in the wake of war and the Holocaust. This book shows how (some) options narrowed, how (some) ideas about territorial and ethnic belonging became increasingly less elastic, and how accepting the transfer of surviving east central European Jews to an "ethnic" polity of their own in Palestine helped east central Europeans and other decision makers justify other population transfers, thus remaking postwar Poland and Czechoslovakia as (almost) ethnically homogenous polities. As Tara Zahra explains, the expulsions, transfers, and revisions of citizenship laws that collided in postwar east central Europe provided a "radical solution to national conflict in Europe" as well as "a final solution to the persistent problem of national hermaphroditism and ambivalence."[3]

I gently employ this quote and the words "final solution" within it as I speak about the Jewish component of this ethnic revolution. The Holocaust decimated the Jewish populations of this region, uprooted Jews from their homes, and nearly extinguished the Jewish culture unique to these lands. Yet the Holocaust did not definitively negate the east central Jewish diaspora. And while this genocide created the catastrophic preconditions for such an uprooting, this book shows that something else happened as well. Decision makers, many of them identified in the previous chapters, debated and eventually concluded that a quick turn toward ethnicized political belonging and the concomitant endorsement of population transfers for those who did not "belong" were necessary, and in doing so, they increasingly imagined themselves as providing solutions to a modern problem by seizing an unprecedented political opportunity. In the process, they unleashed severe and tragic consequences that become increasingly evident as we reflect backward. In what remains of this conclusion, I would like to briefly consider what I usually think about when I gaze at the interwar map above my office desk: namely, some of the broader consequences of this ethnic revolution.

I'll begin with the cultural consequences. Like many students of east central Europe without ancestral roots in the region, emotional words, exotic smells, unparalleled art, and a particular culture beckoned me to the study of this complex historical past. The more I read, ate, saw, and experienced, the more I realized that the convergence of peoples, the liminal voices that hinged between languages, and the entanglement of modern experiences fascinated me most. It became impossible for me to ignore the specific Jewish experience that matured in places such as Prague, Mikulov, Kraków, Warsaw, and the lesser known settlements in between and left an indelible imprint on the broader local, regional, and national cultures that emerged over generations and centuries. Milan Kundera noticed as much and bemoaned the loss of a context that had produced his own literary ancestry in his heartbreaking article "The Tragedy of Central Europe," which was published in the *New York Review of Books* in 1984. "No other part of the world," Kundera observed in this printed ode to a region dominated by Soviet power, "has been so deeply marked by the influence of Jewish genius."[4] Recalling Jews such as Sigmund Freud, Gustav Mahler, Joseph Roth, and, of course, Franz Kafka, Kundera envisioned these men as "the principal cosmopolitan, integrating element in Central Europe: they were its intellectual cement, a condensed version of its spirit, creators of its spiritual unity."[5]

My list extends beyond the one offered by Kundera. Franz Werfel, Julian Tuwim, Heda Margolius Kovály, Antoni Słonimski, Otto Dov Kulka, Zofia Grzesiak, and Stefan Zweig deserve particular mention. I even find that many non-Jewish cultural figures writing in Czech or Polish, such as Czesław Miłosz, Wisława Szymborska, Olga Tokarczuk, and Milan Kundera himself utilize Jewish themes in their most memorable works. These voices, on Kundera's list and my own, often emerge from or describe points of complex coexistence, from multiethnic and multireligious communities that mostly vanished in the wake of the ethnic revolution. Diversity did not always provide preconditions for peace and harmony, of course. But it did encourage generations of "fruitful cross-pollination" and the cultural production of a reality that was complicated and genuine.[6]

When I first traveled to Poland as an undergraduate at the turn of the twenty-first century, I encountered the exoticization of the now-vanished world that predated the ethnic revolution firsthand. I was part of a student-faculty research team that arrived in Kraków to create a collection of oral history interviews and material culture related to (what was then termed) the contemporary "renaissance of Jewish culture." There, we spent long almost-summer days in Kazimierz, the historical Jewish quarter in the city, and interviewed hoteliers, tour guides, bookstore owners, and galleristas catering to so-called heritage travelers. Wooden folk art, hovering odors of schmaltz, klezmer clarinets, and grainy black-and-white pictures cast me back to a prewar era marked by stereotypes instead of complexity.[7]

Forsaking any more direct judgment toward the purveyors of this "cultural past" in Kraków and toward those genealogically driven tourists seeking to "reclaim" something (and not usually something complex) from the past, there is an unmistakably bittersweet aspect of this reality, which has improved in the generation since but still continues. It shocks me to concede that this bittersweetness extends from the ethnic revolution as well as the Holocaust. Changing ideas about Jewish belonging, about a presumed gulf between Polishness and Jewishness, and about the untenable rootedness of the east central European Jewish diaspora contributed to the near extinction of a unique and multivalent Jewish civilization, partially differentiated from religion, infused by a diverse culture, and rooted, for better or for worse, in this particular soil. As late as October 1944, Arieh Tartakower affirmed the strength of "the Polish-Jewish idea."[8] This hybrid idea connected, Tartakower noticed at that tragic moment, "to the heart" and even had the potential to "connect Jewish and Polish hearts." As Tartakower wrote these poetic words, however, he and so many others were working to further corrode the strength of this (already diminished) concept. As a result, Polish Jewishness in its pre–World War II form barely, just barely, survived.

Now, some words about "belonging" and how it has been oversimplified by the ethnic revolution. The possibility of a specific type of east central European rootedness that transcended "ethnic" belonging nearly came to an end after World War II. This revolution in understanding of who belonged to a

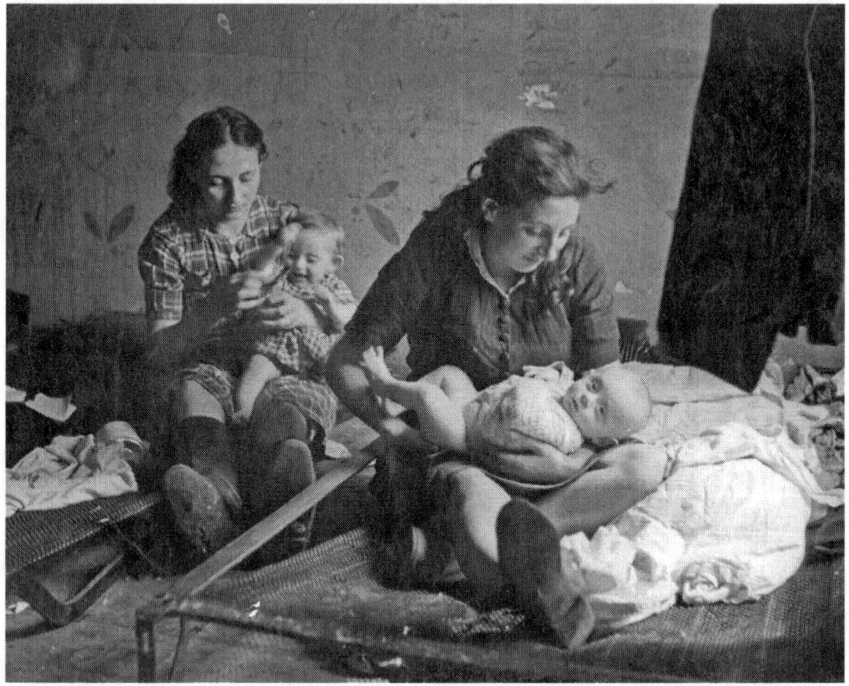

Fig. concl.01. Two Polish Jewish mothers and their children at an emergency reception center in Bratislava, Czechoslovakia. Courtesy Photo Archive of the Jewish Joint Distribution Committee.

Czechoslovak, a Polish, or a Jewish (or a German or a Hungarian) citizenry unleashed massive demographic changes in a region historically known for its ethnic coexistence. As a consequence, millions of people left their homes, fields, villages, neighbors, and former lives to live in a presumed ethnic homeland elsewhere. For more than one hundred thousand surviving "ethnic" Jews from this region, their ethnic homeland was presumed to be far away and across the Mediterranean Sea in Palestine. Not all of them got there (more than half of all Jews who passed through postwar DP camps were destined eventually for the United States), but the presumption enabled them to prolong an uprooting and uncertainty that began in the 1930s. A few hundred of the surviving Polish Jewish diaspora gathered for a meeting on May 6, 1946, at the displaced persons camp in Fritzlar, a small town in the American zone of occupied Germany. That day, the UNRRA director of the camp, Paul Jokelson, spoke to these "displaced people unsuccessfully repatriated" about their future plans and, possibly, their future regrets. After promising to answer questions from the crowd, Jokelson posed some questions himself.

Jokelson wanted to understand the thought process of the remnant of the Polish Jewish diaspora assembled before him. What, he questioned, "do the people who tell you not to go home have to offer to you?"[9] Jokelson promised that crowd that they would "inevitably be home-sick one day" and "irresistibly want to go home, to see again the country where you were born, to which you belong, to meet your friends, your relatives, to smell the odor of your native land." On that hypothetical day, however, "it will be too late because your comrades who have gone home, your government who [have asked] to go home will tell you: 'we needed your help to rebuild our country [and] you refused to come, you wanted to wait until the task was over: now it is too late, we don't need you anymore, you are now strangers.'" Jokelson prodded the displaced persons and asked in summation, "Is that what you want? Be one amongst these stateless people who are moved from one country to the other without being able to settle down, without being sure of what will happen the next day?" He then prompted his audience to volunteer for (another) repatriation back to Poland. If he collected at least three hundred names of those willing to return, he could obtain a direct train from Fritzlar to the Polish border.

His speech suggests that Jokelson could not understand why these Polish Jews, after so much displacement and tragedy, had opted for more displacement and uncertainty.[10] Perhaps his words here reflected a more general viewpoint espoused by his employer, the United Nations Relief and Rehabilitation Administration. Perhaps his words delivered on this particular day registered his disappointment with his camp's capacity for refugees, and so he wanted some to leave so as to alleviate his burden. I did not find a list of three hundred names willing to return to Poland attached to this speech in the archive, nor did I find evidence of the audience's response. What Jokelson misunderstood in this moment was something that these displaced persons of Polish Jewish inheritance already knew: their homelands, their postwar roots, and their "belonging" would be elsewhere because it had to be ethnicized in an explicit way. These three hundred were not alone. Almost all of the east central European Jewish characters in *Uprooting the Diaspora,* including those who vigorously supported the right of Jews to be rooted and rebuild in the region, opted for territorial and political belonging elsewhere very soon after the war ended. Their collective decision to forgo the return they had labored to protect even as they prioritized plans for a Jewish polity in Palestine illustrate just how powerful the ethnic revolution was.

Arieh Tartakower assumed his position as a professor of sociology at Hebrew University in fall 1946 but continued to work for the World Jewish Congress in various capacities after he left New York City. He died in his nineties, in 1982.[11] Nahum Goldmann died in 1982 as well, but in West Germany. He became an Israeli citizen in 1962 but did not live there permanently. A man of many passports, he acquired Swiss citizenship in the 1960s as well. Goldmann worked for the World Jewish Congress after the Second World War and became instrumental in brokering reparations and diplomatic agreements between West Germany and Israel. Maurice Perlzweig also continued in service to the WJC and died in New York City in 1985. He left behind an oral history memoir recorded under the auspices of Columbia University in the early 1980s. Joel Cang left behind more reporting and a book entitled *The Silent Millions: A History of Jews in the Soviet Union*. Cang became a naturalized British citizen in May 1947. In that same year, Zorach Warhaftig arrived in Palestine. A few months later, he became one of the signatories of the Israeli Declaration of Independence, despite not attending the official reading of the document due to fighting that interfered with his travel from Jerusalem. Warhaftig served in the Knesset (he was elected nine times between 1949 and 1981), "used precedents taken from Polish constitutional history in his work as one of the central architects of the Israeli constitutional regime in the period immediately after Israeli independence," and helped draft the 1950 Law of Return.[12] He died in Israel in 2002 after living ninety-six years.

Anselm Reiss lived even longer. In 1984, he died in Kfar Saba two years shy of his one hundredth birthday. The years of his life were divided almost equally between the Middle East and east central Europe. A. L. Kubowitzki also died in Israel. He moved there in 1948 when he left his job as the secretary general of the World Jewish Congress. After making aliyah, he changed his name (many others did so as well in Europe and beyond to indicate new forms of belonging) to Aryeh Leon Kubovy and joined the Israeli Foreign Ministry. He returned to east central Europe as ambassador to both Poland and Czechoslovakia. Later, he served as the chairman of Yad Vashem until his death in 1966. Ignacy Schwarzbart's diary ended up at Yad Vashem, but he never became an Israeli citizen. He held positions in the World Jewish Congress in New York after leaving the Polish government-in-exile, and he died there in 1961. Schwarzbart's colleague from the Czechoslovak government-in-exile Arnošt Frischer returned to Czechoslovakia after the war. He subsequently left for London in 1948 and died there in 1954. By 1954, Yitzchak Zuckerman had lived outside of Poland for eight years, and for five of them he had lived on the Ghetto Fighter's Kibbutz (Lohamei HaGeta'ot), which he had founded alongside his wife, Zivia

Lubetkin, and other surviving east central European Jews. He died in 1981. Jakob Apenszlak did not enjoy such a long life; nor did he, as far as the archival records reveal, return to Poland or build a new postwar home elsewhere.[13] In the fall of 1946, Tartakower's departure left Apenszlak alone at the helm of *NT*.

The ethnic revolution backed Apenszlak and others into a corner from where they tried to justify their connective tissue to east central Europe. An *NT* article written in October 1946 reveals as much. Despite the memory of how "significant numbers of Poles" had behaved toward Jews during the occupation, despite the antisemitism that stimulated "resignation from everything that connects one to Poland," and despite the "bitterness of those who left," Apenszlak and the scattered Polish Jewish diaspora were still connected to their former homeland.[14] "Jewish life in Poland" and "our heritage" would, according to Apenszlak, "remain, even after a majority of the survivors had left." Julian Tuwim imagined survivors returning. He saw a future when "we ghosts" would traverse seas and oceans to "return to the homeland and haunt the ruins in our unscared bodies and our wretched presumably spared souls."[15] Tuwim did return to Poland after his wartime exile abroad. His dual identification with Polishness (because he wanted to be Polish) and Jewishness (because of martyr's blood) remained, but the sizeable community that he invoked with the pronoun *we* in his visceral essay "We Polish Jews" did not. And even though Polish speakers encircled Basia Berman in early 1950s Tel Aviv, she still "clung to her ties with Poland." As historian Marci Shore describes, Berman wrote to the Polish Consulate proposing the creation of a Polish Center for Culture and Propaganda for Polish speakers in Israel, who at that time represented half of the country's population. The plans never materialized, and, according to her son, medical problems coupled with depression to bring Basia quite low. In her diary from the time, she wrote that she did not "exist here at all."[16] The "here" in her sentence, Israel, did not become a promised land for her. Even as a youngster, her son Emanuel (born in Poland in 1946) could recognize his mother's longing for a life, a culture, and the roots she had left behind.[17] These consequences of the ethnic revolution were not universal, of course. But scholars have more work to do if we want to understand how representative these voices are and how the ethnic revolution drowned out the chorus of these voices.

The ethnic revolution greatly contributed to a more severe lobotomization of belonging, especially in the generation or two that followed it. *Uprooting the Diaspora* communicates the "story of people living at a time when nationality mattered more than ever before" and when Jewish belonging in particular took on a more exclusive territorial, ethnic, and historical meaning.[18] It reified distinctions between Poles and Jews, Czechs and Jews, Jews and . . . others. It generated failed returns leading to new homelands and, sometimes, leading to alienation. And while I have sensed a softening of these feelings, especially as the communist period recedes further into memory, as Jewish life in the region has become more visible amid younger generations, and as scholars tied to the region have focused on the study of the pre–ethnic revolution past, gaps in the nomenclature, gaps in generations, and gaps in language perpetuate gaps in thinking about both the present and the past among descendants of this diaspora and, at times, some of those scholars who study it.[19] To draw on William Sebald's haunting novel *Austerlitz*, history remains more frequently than I would like "a concern with preformed images already imprinted on our brains, images at which we keep staring while the truth lies elsewhere, away from it all, somewhere as yet undiscovered."[20]

And finally, this quote brings me face-to-face with history and how the ethnic revolution impacts the writing of it. I came to this topic as a historian first of east central Europe and second of the modern Jewish experience therein. As a historian, I struggle to define the collective importance of the past. Contemporary sources from that past, from the decade (1936–1946) that spans the development and initiation of the ethnic revolution, use familiar words but impart vastly different meanings than sources that appear subsequently. This, of course, is why historians prioritize contingency. But contingency is more complicated when the histories we write strike deep chords within us. Of course, the ethnic revolution that unfolded here intersects with perhaps the most emotionally charged events in the entire Jewish experience, and certainly in the east central European or modern Jewish experience. Perhaps this is why one reader of an earlier draft of *Uprooting the Diaspora* congratulated me on writing "an entire book" in response to a question that, at least for him, had a "self-evident answer." In the struggle to the define the collective importance of this past or any past, historians must question that which appears to be self-evident or obvious, especially if their questioning probes ancestral inheritance, sensitive emotions, and collective memories that organize how we see history and position our own sense of belonging within it. As Wisława Szymborska elegantly reminds us, "there is no such obvious world."[21]

NOTES

INTRODUCTION

1. Appointed in December 1939, Schwarzbart worked first in Paris and then in Angers before relocating with the rest of the Polish government-in-exile to the United Kingdom after the fall of France. He was paid intermittently for contract work during the war. The definitive biography on Schwarzbart is Stola, *Nadzieja i Zagłada*.

2. Ignacy Schwarzbart, "Report Number 4: A General Outline Concerning the Polish Jewish Question," November 20, 1940, file no. A 20/7, Archive of the World Jewish Congress, American Jewish Archives, Cincinnati, OH, USA (hereafter WJC).

3. In Yiddish, the word for "diaspora" can be rendered as both *goles* and *golus*. I have kept the original spelling in quotations throughout but use *goles* in my own narrative.

4. "Memorandum to UN Special Committee on Palestine, 1947," file no. B 140/4, WJC.

5. Avinoam J. Patt argues that "Zionism was not a foregone conclusion for Holocaust survivors after the war." "Stateless Citizens of Israel," 165.

6. On the historical study of "international norms," see Pedersen, "Back to the League"; Pedersen, *Guardians*; Cramsey et al., "Timing Is Everything."

7. Sorkin, *Transformation of German Jewry*; Porter, *When Nationalism Began to Hate*; Rozenblit, *Reconstructing a National Identity*; Endelman, *Jews of Britain*; Schechter, *Obstinate Hebrews*; Slezkine, *Jewish Century*.

8. Case, *The Age of Questions*, 115–123.

9. Connelly discusses the term *ethnic revolution* and this process that unfolded during the 1940s in *From Peoples into Nations*, 512–21. He also notes that the "most avid ethnic cleansers" (17) were the Polish and Czech communists.

10. Zweig, *World of Yesterday*, 271.

11. In writing a history of a conversation, I am indebted to Marci Shore, who writes the "biography of a milieu" in *Caviar and Ashes*, 5.

12. In recent years, a handful of scholars have used the rich archive of the WJC to explore actors within this organization dedicated in principle to representing the diversity of Jewish voices across the world. See Lewis, *Birth of the New Justice*, 150–80; Z. Segev, *World Jewish Congress*; Loeffler, *Rooted Cosmopolitans*; Kurz, *Jewish Internationalism*; Rubin, "Future of the Jews." Overall, my intervention separates from others with my emphasis on east central European members of the WJC and the rich interactions they had with other east central Europeans and Allied power brokers throughout the 1940s and especially after the end of World War II.

13. Bryant, *Prague in Black*; Zahra, *Kidnapped Souls*; King, *Budweisers into Czechs and Germans*; Case, *Between States*; Lumans, *Himmler's Auxiliaries*; Weinberg, *The Foreign Policy of Hitler's Germany*; Thum, *Uprooted*; Douglas, *Orderly and Humane*; Gerlach, *Economy of Ethnic Cleansing*; Frommer, *National Cleansing*.

14. Bauer, *Flight and Rescue*; Engel, *Between Liberation and Flight*; Aleksiun, *Dokąd dalej?*; Kochavi, *Post-Holocaust Politics*, particularly 157–82; Patt, *Finding Home and Homeland*; G. Cohen, *In War's Wake*; Cichopek-Gajraj, *Beyond Violence*; Person, *Dipisi*.

15. Zahra, "Zionism, Emigration and East European Colonialism"; Levene, *War, Jews, and New Europe*; Zipperstein, *Elusive Prophet*; Smith, "Zionism and Diaspora Nationalism"; Hroch, "Zionism as European National Movement"; Penslar, "Narratives of Nation Building"; Stanislawski, *Zionism*; Čapková, *Češi, Němci, Židé?*; Morris, "Explaining Transfer"; Pianko, *Zionism and Roads Not Taken*; Loeffler, "Between Zionism and Liberalism"; Dubnov, "Zionism on the Diasporic Front"; Shanes, *Diaspora Nationalism*; Rabinovitch, *Jews and Diaspora Nationalism* and *Jewish Rights, National Rites*; Karlip, *Tragedy of a Generation*; Lichtenstein, *Zionists in Interwar Czechoslovakia*; Shumsky, *Beyond the Nation-State*; Almagor, "Fitting the Zeitgeist."

16. Bauer, *Jewish Emergence from Powerlessness*; Bauer, *From Diplomacy to Resistance*; Fink, *Defending the Rights of Others*; Mendelsohn, *On Modern Jewish Politics*.

17. By 1942, eight governments and a handful of "free movements" had assembled in England and purported to represent political entities based in occupied and Axis Europe. On the exiled government universe and the Jews more generally, see Láníček and Jordan, *Governments-in-Exile*. On the Polish and Czech governments-in-exile specifically, see Engel, *Facing a Holocaust*; Engel, *In the Shadow of Auschwitz*; Stola, *Nadzieja i Zagłada*; Livia Rothkirchen, "The Czechoslovak Government-in-Exile," and most recently, Láníček, *Czechs,*

Slovaks and the Jews. The exchange between Stola, "In the Shadow of the Facts," and Engel "Reading and Misreadings: A Reply to Dariusz Stola" is helpful as well. On the idea of population transfers within the exiled universe and among Poles and Czechs specifically, see Brandes, *Grossbritannien und seine osteuropäische Alliierten*; Brandes, *Der Weg zur Vertreibung*.

18. Almog, "Galut Nationalism"; Moss, "Thinking with Restriction"; Horowitz, "Muse and Muscle"; D. Heller, *Jabotinsky's Children*; Loeffler, *Rooted Cosmopolitans*; Rubin, "Future of the Jews"; Kurz, *Jewish Internationalism*; Shumsky, *Beyond the Nation-State*.

19. Brubaker, *Ethnicity without Groups*.

20. Zahra, *Kidnapped Souls*; Bryant, *Prague in Black*; King, *Budweisers into Czechs and Germans*; Judson, *Guardians of the Nation*; Lichtenstein, *Zionists in Interwar Czechoslovakia*; J. Beneš, *Workers and Nationalism*; Čapková, *Češi, Němci, Židé?*

21. Zahra, "Imagined Non-communities."

22. Engel, "Palestine in the Mind."

23. Stola has argued that the ruthless uprooting of Polish Jews during German and Soviet occupations provided necessary contexts for postwar conflict between Polish Jews and Polish Christians as well as the broad migration of Polish Jews. Personal correspondence with the author. On the trope of uprootedness in Jewish history, see G. Cohen, *In War's Wake*, 156–57.

24. Schechter, *Obstinate Hebrews*.

25. Shore, "Conversing with Ghosts"; Zaremba, *Wielka trwoga*; Connelly, *Captive University*; Service, *Germans to Poles*.

26. A. Dirk Moses has shown how the "ethnic revolution" unleashed in east central Europe had global repercussions. Moses, "Epilogue."

27. Connelly, *From Peoples into Nations*, 22.

28. On this point, I follow the lead of Dubnov, who problematizes the assumption of a Zionist "idea," "doctrine," or "ideology" in the singular. "Zionism on the Diasporic Front," 220.

29. Dubnov, "Between Liberalism and Jewish Nationalism."

30. Rozenblit, *Reconstructing a National Identity*; Rechter, *Jews of Vienna*.

31. Shanes, *Diaspora Nationalism*, 10.

32. Lichtenstein, *Zionists in Interwar Czechoslovakia*, 329. On the period during and after World War I, see Rybak, *Everyday Zionism*.

33. Lichtenstein, *Zionists in Interwar Czechoslovakia*, 329. On Zionism in Czechoslovakia, see also Čapková, "Specific Features of Zionism in the Czech Lands."

34. To consider this issue from two political vantage points, see Kijek, "Was It Possible"; D. Heller, *Jabotinsky's Children*.

35. Oz, "Meaning of Homeland," 250.

36. Codified in the 1906 Russian Zionists Helsingfors Program, this idea advocated work toward building a Jewish home as well as engagement in the diaspora.

37. Kubowitzki cites the urging of Simon Dubnow after the 1903 Kishinev Pogrom as an important moment in the formation of the WJC. Kubowitzki, *Unity in Dispersion. A History of the World Jewish Congress,* 30.

38. Shanes, *Diaspora Nationalism,* 11.

39. Shumsky, *Beyond the Nation-State,* 23.

40. Shanes, *Diaspora Nationalism,* 11.

41. Gruen, *Diaspora,* 232. Brubaker defines diaspora in three ways: "The first is dispersion in space; the second, orientation to a 'homeland'; and the third, boundary-maintenance." Brubaker, "'Diaspora' Diaspora," 5.

42. Boyarin, *Traveling Homeland,* 25.

43. Bourdieu, *Language and Symbolic Power,* 220.

44. Brubaker, "'Diaspora' Diaspora," 10.

45. Discussions of diaspora are often informed by a "strikingly idealist, teleological understanding of the nation-state, which is seen as the unfolding of an idea, the idea of nationalizing and homogenizing the population." Brubaker, "'Diaspora' Diaspora," 10. See also Brubaker, "Revisiting 'The "Diaspora" Diaspora.'"

46. *Diaspora* appears twice in the Deuteronomy (28:25 and 30:4), once in Nehemiah (1:9), once in Judith (5:19), twice in the Psalms (138/139 and 146/147:2), once in Isaiah (49:6), twice in Jeremiah (15:7 and 41/34:17), once in Daniel (12:2), once in Maccabees 2 (1:27), and twice in Solomon's Psalms (8:28 and 9:2). Dufoix, "Diaspora," 51. On one occasion, it appears in plural in the Psalms (#146). Hadas-Lebel, *Philo of Alexandria,* 31. The noun form *diaspora* comes from the Greek verb *diaspeiro,* which had been used since at least the fifth century BCE. *διασπείρω* is the verb, and *Διασπορά* is the noun.

47. תוּלָג and הָלוֹג, respectively. Dufoix, "Diaspora," 51.

48. Ibid., 52. Both nouns derive from the verb *galah,* which can mean "to be naked," "to make naked," or "to reveal what was hidden," more generally.

49. Hadas-Lebel, *Philo of Alexandria,* 32.

50. Dufoix, "Diaspora," 55.

51. In translation, this can be bluntly rendered "in the land of Israel" and "in the diaspora," or "קראל הצוחבו קראב." See *Makkot,* 7a: 3, and *The William Davidson Talmud* translation, accessed April 20, 2021, https://www.sefaria.org/william-davidson-talmud.

52. Scholem, *Major Trends in Jewish Mysticism,* 244–86, particularly 249.

53. Of course, other non-Jewish forms of nationalism embraced similar dreams. See Michael Dean, "What the Heart Unites"; Jacobson, *Special Sorrows;* and, more generally, Barton, *Folk Divided* and Tölölyan, "Beyond the Homeland."

We should note that nationalists more generally and Jewish nationalists therein "make new words but build on existing syntaxes," interpreting but not inventing "existing national chronicles and tales." Connelly, *From Peoples into Nations*, 21.

54. In his 1931 definition of *diaspora*, Simon Dubnow references the Armenians. "Diaspora," in *Encyclopedia of the Social Sciences*, 126–27. On diasporas and homelands more generally, see Robson, *States of Separation*, 141–68.

55. Frankel, *Prophecy and Politics*.

56. Gruen, *Diaspora*, 233.

57. Dubnow, "Eighth Letter," 185. For Ahad Ha'am's article, see "Negation of the Diaspora."

58. Dubnow, "Eighth Letter," 185.

59. Ibid., 188.

60. Rawidowicz, *State of Israel*, 150.

61. Dufoix, "Diaspora," 59.

62. Yitzhak Baer interpreted *galuth* as the "abolition of God's order." See Baer, *Galut*.

63. "Prozatimní pasové instrukce," fund no. 302-576-1, Archiv bezpečnostních složek ministerstva vnitra, Prague, Czech Republic (hereafter ABS). For the temporary passport and travel identity card for stateless people, see ABS no. 302-576-8.

1. ROOTED

1. On the World Jewish Congress, see Kubowitzki, *Unity in Dispersion*, and more recently, Z. Segev, *World Jewish Congress*.

2. *Protocole du premier Congrès juif*, 182.

3. Ibid. Of course, this was neither the first attempt nor the last to "unite" Polish Jewry into a discernible bloc. See Silber, *Different Nationality/Equal Citizenship*.

4. *Protocole du premier Congrés juif*, 182.

5. N.S. was most likely N. Szwalbe, one of the three standing editors of *Nasz Przegląd* at this time alongside Jakob Apenszlak and S. Wagman. N.S., "Kongres Genewski, Deklaracja żydowstwa polskiego," *Nasz Przegląd*, August 13, 1936, 3.

6. Marcus, *Social and Political History*, 408. The press conference took place on July 2, 1936.

7. Reinharz and Shavit, *Road to September 1939*, 51. Jabotinsky first used the words "Evacuation Plan" on June 13, 1936. Reinharz and Shavit, *Road to September 1939*, 55. Jabotinsky wrote then that "evacuation would turn Zionism 'from an amusement to a rescue plan' and that the country that would take it upon itself to carry it out 'would be walking on a magic carpet.'" Ibid., 51.

Inclusive of the 700,000 Polish Jews, he imagined that 1.5 million European Jews would move overall.

8. Broader international and colonial contexts inhibited movement away from Poland, of course. But migration toward Palestine failed, notably, on both registers.

9. Moss, "Thinking with Restriction"; Trębacz, *Nie tylko Palestyna*. On the WJC's policies in Europe more broadly, see Z. Segev, "Immigration, Politics and Democracy."

10. As Gershon David Hundert observes regarding the medieval and early modern Jewish community in the Polish lands, "More than security there was a sense of rootedness and permanence about this community. These qualities were attributed to the Jewish community by Poles as well." Hundert, "Some Basic Characteristics," 29.

11. Words such as *indigenous, integrated,* or *autochthonous* could be used in place of *rooted,* but the meaning of the sentence would change. Rootedness, it seems to me, operates on a more neutral level than these other words, but all three of these words were used in the 1930s and 1940s to describe the reality of Polish Jews in Poland. Consider the following, for example: "In 1935 Izaak Rubinstein, Chief Rabbi of Wilno and a chair of the Zionist religious Mizrachi in the eastern borderlands (*kresy*), reminded the *Sejm* that forced emigration would not solve the so-called Jewish question in Poland . . . 'we are autochthons in Poland and this land must feed us just like all its other inhabitants.'" Aleksiun, *Conscious History,* 165.

12. On the experience of Polish Jews within Poland in the 1920s and 1930s more generally, see Marcus, *Social and Political History;* Martin, *Jewish Life in Cracow;* Mendelsohn, *Jews of East Central Europe,* 11–84; Mendelsohn, *On Modern Jewish Politics,* 61–75; Mendelsohn, *Zionism in Poland;* C. Heller, *On the Edge of Destruction;* Miron, *Image of the Shtetl;* Polonsky, *Politics in Independent Poland;* Rothschild, *East Central Europe;* Wojtas, *Learning to Become Polish;* Cała, *Syn będzie Lech;* Landau-Czajka, *Polska-to nie oni;* Bacon, *Politics of Tradition;* Steffen, *Jüdische Polonität.* Also see the following collected volumes: Gutman et al., *Jews of Poland;* Katz, ed., *The Shtetl.* On Hebrew language historiography, see Engel, "Writing Polish Jewish History."

13. Melchior, *Społeczna Tożsamość Jednostki,* 27; Melchior, "Rootedness in Place," 71.

14. Weil, *Need for Roots,* 40.

15. On these twinned types of rootedness, see Melchior, "Rootedness in Place," 71–80. On the "acculturating youth," see Kijek, "Was It Possible," 128. On political debates about Jewish rootedness among politicians in the Sejm, see Aleksiun, *Conscious History,* 165–67, and on the work of historians at the end of the 1930s, see 216–57. On the Polish Jewish press, see White, *Jewish Lives;* Steffen,

"Polska—to także my!"; Jamiński, *Prasa żydowska w Polsce*; Fuks, *Prasa żydowska w Warszawie*.

16. Kijek, "Was It Possible," 121; Mendelsohn, *On Modern Jewish Politics*, 62. For her discussion on the Polish language as a medium of assimilation, see Steffen, *Jüdische Polonität*, 83–91.

17. According to Bernard Wasserstein, "although deeply attached to the country, which most of them regarded unquestionably as their home, Polish Jews were to a considerable degree isolated from the rest of the population, religiously, socio-economically, and politically. They had their own residential areas, political parties, newspapers, theaters, labor unions and professional organizations, often operating in their own language, Yiddish. Together these formed the scaffolding of a largely self-contained world within which it was possible, if one chose, to live almost without venturing into broader society." Wasserstein, *On the Eve*, 6.

18. Aleksiun, *Conscious History*, 262.

19. Mendelsohn notes that while Polonization came to pass, it was not accompanied by "a widespread acceptance of the integrationist ideology—Polish anti-semitism saw to that." Mendelsohn, *On Modern Jewish Politics*, 62. For an evaluation of the Polish-language press among Orthodox Jewish readers, see Steffen, *Jüdische Polonität*, 172–83. On the tourism of Polish Jews during the interwar period, see Madej-Krupitski, "Mapping Jewish Poland," and on Warsaw coffeehouses and Jewish members of the Polish intelligentsia, see Shore's exceptional book *Caviar and Ashes*, 1–152.

20. Slezkine, *Jewish Century*, 9.

21. Gutman, "Polish Anti-Semitism," 107; Hagen, "Before the 'Final Solution,'" 360. On the coverage of antisemitism in the Polish Jewish press, see Steffen, *Jüdische Polonität*, 242–312.

22. Aleksiun, *Conscious History*, 104. On language, see Schmeruk, "Hebrew-Yiddish-Polish," 290.

23. Biale et al., *Hasidism*, 610.

24. See Shandler, *Awakening Lives*; Cała, *Ostatnie Pokolenie*.

25. Biale et al., *Hasidism*, 597.

26. Shore, "Children of the Revolution," 29.

27. On Janusz Korczak's visits to Palestine, see Ketko, "Janusz Korczak's Visits," 359–72. Stefania Wilczyńska traveled to Palestine three times as well. More than 110,000 Polish Jews emigrated to France in the interwar period. Green, "Jewish Migrations to France," 146. Roughly 127,200 Polish Jews came to the United States from 1920 to 1924 and then 37,700 more from 1924 to 1939. After 1924, US immigration policies made emigration to America much more difficult. Most likely because of this, in 1925, more Polish Jews went to Palestine than to other locations. A total of 138,900 Polish Jews emigrated to Palestine

between 1920 and 1939 (and 91,100 from 1932 to 1938), but these numbers do not take "return migration" into account. Sizable numbers of Polish Jews also moved to Argentina, Brazil, and Canada (in that order). Unless cited otherwise, all numbers come from Tolts, "Population and Migration." This *YIVO Encyclopedia* article draws on statistics from the *American Jewish Year Book* (1921–1922); Tartakower, *Emigracja żydowska z Polski*; and Lestschinsky, "National Groups in Polish Emigration." Of course, not all Polish Jews were in an economic position to travel internationally.

28. Kijek, "Was It Possible," 130.

29. Aleksiun, *Conscious History*, 8.

30. Schorr, quoted in Aleksiun, *Conscious History*, 90.

31. D. Heller, *Jabotinsky's Children*.

32. I. Krakówski, "The Favorable Storm," *Czas*, September 9, 1936. Zahra, *The Great Departure*, 156.

33. According to Mendelsohn, "The relatively low level of *Aliyah* was not exclusively the fault of the British. The fact is that most European Jews did not want to go to Palestine, even most East European Jews." *On Modern Jewish Politics*, 114.

34. For this number on the Polish Census, see *Drugi Powszechny Spis Ludności z DN. 9.XII 1931*, 21.

35. That's about 13 percent of all Jews. Joseph Marcus reminds us that the number was twice as high in 1921 (*Social and Political History*, 17).

36. Schmeruk, "Hebrew-Yiddish-Polish," 290.

37. "Letter from Baruch Zuckerman to Stephen Wise," January 24, 1938, folder no. A 20/4, Archive of the World Jewish Congress, American Jewish Archives, Cincinnati, OH, USA (hereafter WJC).

38. See Kijek, *Dzieci modernizmu*; Kijek, "Between a Love of Poland"; D. Heller, *Jabotinsky's Children*, 6; Mendelsohn, *On Modern Jewish Politics*, 117–24.

39. Ninety percent of the Second Republic had been touched by war, and 20 percent of the territory saw heavy fighting. Polonsky, *Politics in Independent Poland*, 9. On the aftermath of World War I in the region more generally, see Connelly, *From Peoples into Nations*, 350–61. The Great War, the Russian Revolution, and the erosion of the Russian Empire in the wake of both produced the displacement of seven million inhabitants of the western Russian Empire into the Russian interior and an unmixing of populations as the war ended. See Lohr, *Nationalizing the Russian Empire* and "The Russian Army and the Jews"; Gatrell, *Whole Empire Walking*; Baron and Gatrell, "Population Displacement," 61. On Polish Jews and refugees in Vienna, see Rechter, "Galicia in Vienna." Despite these population movements, however, a large number of Poles (782,300) remained in the Soviet Union. Wróbel, "Class War or Ethnic Cleansing?," 33n61.

40. "Six times between 1914 and 1917, the Russian armies swept over territories and six times were beaten back by Austrian forces." Hyman, "Twenty-Five Years," 13. For the broader picture, see Rozenblit and Karp, *World War I*; N. Stone, *Eastern Front*.

41. Loeffler, "'The Famous Trinity of 1917.'"

42. Roth, *Wandering Jews*, 57. Related to this topic, see David Engel's article on Salo Baron and how his citizenship became precarious in Vienna during and after the Great War, "Crisis and Lachrymosity." Katrin Steffen explores how Polish Jews who spoke Polish well divided themselves from "Ostjuden" or "Eastern Jews" in racial, social, and linguistic ways, "Connotations of Exclusion."

43. On the dissolution of the Habsburg Empire specifically, consider Wheatley, "Central Europe as Ground Zero."

44. Pogroms broke out during the Ukrainian Civil War between 1917 and 1921. Tens of thousands of Jews (if not more) were killed during this period. For higher estimates, see Veidlinger, *In the Midst*.

45. Mendelsohn, *On Modern Jewish Politics*, 15. On the extent of physical violence and how it was linked to antisemitism, see Brykczyński, *Primed for Violence*.

46. Biale et al., *Hasidism*, 597–621.

47. Gershon Bacon notes that it took one decade for the legal system in the Polish state to unify. "One Jewish Street?," 325.

48. "Zionists" constituted those Jewish nationalists who believed that Palestine would be the (or a) significant center of future Jewish life. "Zionism and Zionist Parties," YIVO Encyclopedia of Jews in Eastern Europe, accessed March 14, 2021, https://yivoencyclopedia.org/article.aspx/Zionism_and_Zionist_Parties. "Bundists" belonged to Der Algemeyner Yidisher Arbeter Bund in Lite, Poyln, un Rusland (the General Union of Jewish Workers in Lithuania, Poland and Russia), which was founded in Vilna in 1897 to represent Jews drawn to establishing socialist or Marxist conditions where they currently lived. By the 1930s, the Bund had become the "dominant Jewish organization" in Poland. Blatman, "Bund." The two groups are often cast in opposition to each other, but as we will see, they are not necessarily oppositional.

49. Kopstein and Wittenberg, "Between State Loyalty," 184.

50. Seidman, *Sarah Schenirer*. Like Schwarzbart, Schenirer also had Galician roots.

51. Daniel Kupfert Heller writes, "The steady rise of ethnic nationalism among Catholic Poles and Jews alike" was accompanied by "an unprecedented acceleration of acculturation among Poland's Jews." *Jabotinsky's Children*, 16.

52. Cramsey et al., "Timing Is Everything"; Stach, *Nationalitätenpolitik aus der zweiten Reihe*.

53. On the eastern borderlands and the concept of *tutejsi*, see Ciancia, *On Civilization's Edge*; Brown, *Biography of No Place*. On the German minority in Poland, see Chu, *The German Minority in Interwar Poland*.

54. Marcus, *Social and Political History*, 25.

55. On interwar plans to rid Poland of "excess" Jews, see Zahra, *The Great Departure*, 143–144 and 155–158. On the limits of "Jewishness" and "Polishness," see Steffen, "Contested Jewish Polishness."

56. Roth, Wandering Jews, 95. Tobias Brinkman notes that in 1926, 13,000 Jews from Europe immigrated to Palestine during the Fourth Aliyah, but 7,300 went the other direction. In 1928, the "official net immigration was a mere 10"; see Brinkman, "Permanent Transit," 67. Zahra covers the concept of return migration more generally in *The Great Departure*, 105–141 and the topic of Poles and Czechoslovaks returning from the United States and France in the 1930s specifically, ibid., 136–141. On return migration from Palestine, see Ori Yehudai, "Displaced in the National Home" and *Leaving Zion*. Between 4,000–6,000 Jews left Czechoslovakia for Palestine, and most of those appeared to be transmigrants or stateless. So the number from Czechoslovakia was even lower, 1,500 at most. See Láníček, *Arnošt Frischer*, 22.

57. To quote Mendelsohn, the principle of "*doykayt*, a Yiddish word meaning (literally) 'hereness,' as opposed to the 'thereness' of Zionism and other forms of Jewish nationalism . . . did not necessarily imply hostility to emigration, which was sometimes necessary, but it did imply a strong attachment to the land in which the Jews resided along with an even stronger objection to the idea that Jews should establish an autonomous or sovereign territorial unit somewhere else in the world." Mendelsohn, *On Modern Jewish Politics*, 7. Samuel D. Kassow offers an explication of "hereness" in *Who Will Write Our History?*, 28.

58. Alroey, *Unpromising Land*, 12. Once in Mandate Palestine, the twenty-three-year-old worked on road construction, drained marshes, and battled with mosquitos. Anselm Reiss also left Palestine to return to Poland.

59. "Aryeh Tartakower Dead at 85," Jewish Telegraphic Agency (JTA), November 30, 1982.

60. In his analysis of Tartakower, which diverges from mine, Kenneth Moss notes that Tartakower "distinguished himself with several books in 1938–9 on the problem of Jewish emigration." "Thinking with Restriction," 213. Moss does not cite Tartakower's writings in Polish.

61. It was published as *Żydzi w Polsce odrodzonej: Działalność społeczna, gospodarcza, oświatowa i kulturalna*. It remains "the fullest expression of the history of Jews in Poland published before the Second World War," according to Jolanta Żyndul, review of *Żydzi w Polsce odrodzonej*.

62. Roth, *Wandering Jews*, 136.

63. *Protocole du premier Congrès juif*, 74.

64. "Organized Jewry Urged at Geneva," *New York Times*, August 10, 1936, 2.

65. The United States was asked to contribute a delegate to this initiative at the end of October 1933. "U.S. to Aid Reich Refugee Relief," *New York Times*, October 27, 1933.

66. Joel Cang, "League of Nations, Mr. McDonald in Warsaw," *Jewish Chronicle*, April 27, 1934, 33.

67. Besides his diary, see McDonald, "Letter of Resignation," for a brief overview of the work his commission attempted during its two-year existence.

68. Cang, "League of Nations," 33.

69. Böhler, *Civil War in Central Europe*, 30. This exchange of populations unfolded as a result of the brutality of the Greek-Turkish War and because it took place in the orientalized Balkans. Ther, "Pre-negotiated Violence."

70. Stola, "Migrations."

71. MacMillan, *Paris 1919*. Böhler, *Civil War in Central Europe*, 29–32.

72. Karch, "A Jewish 'Nature Preserve'" and chapter 2.

73. McDonald, *Advocate for the Doomed*, viii.

74. Holborn, "League of Nations," 124.

75. Holborn, "League of Nations," 125.

76. Ibid., 126.

77. In 1924, the passport was offered to stateless Armenians; in 1928, the "provisions were extended to Assyrian, Assyro-Chaldean, Turkish (friends of the Allies) and assimilated Refugees"; and on May 24, 1935, they were extended to refugees from the Saar Valley. "The Nansen Office attempted to send a group of Saarlanders to Paraguay after the 1935 plebiscite. The French Government was ready to pay for transport, and in 1937 about 150 people emigrated to Paraguay." Muhlen, "1930s," 106.

78. On the topic of "eastern" Jews applying for passports away from places of birth, see Roth, *Wandering Jews*, 57–59. On their expulsion from Vienna, see ibid., 67.

79. Holborn, "The League of Nations and the Refugee Problem," 124.

80. Tartakower, *Jewish Emigration Problem* [in Yiddish], 41–42. I thank Miriam Schulz for her help with this translation.

81. Tartakower, *Jewish Emigration Problem*, 44. Specifically, smaller organizations could not negotiate with governments to create new emigration routes and could not oversee an emigration bank that would offer fair exchange rates and reasonable money transfers.

82. Ibid., 46.

83. Ibid., 46.

84. Ibid., 43.

85. Tartakower, "Stan liczebny i rozwój naturalny ludności żydowskiej w Polsce." On Jewish political parties, see Haftka, "Żydowskie stronnictwa polityczne w Polsce Odrodzonej," 249–85.

86. In the 1921 Polish Census, of the 25,694,700 people in Poland, there were 2,048,878 Jews (7.97%), while in 1931 Jews had an almost 10 percent share in the Polish population, which they held until 1939 (when there were about 3.3 million Jews among 35-plus million citizens of Poland).

87. Tartakower, "Stan liczebny i rozwój naturalny ludności żydowskiej w Polsce," 224.

88. Tartakower, *Zarys socjologii żydostwa*, 213.

89. Ibid., 216.

90. Ibid., 236.

91. Zionism, Tartakower suggested, was "not synonymous with the creation of asylum in Palestine, it is not even synonymous with a complete disagreement over the future of Jews in the countries of the *golus*." Ibid, 238. Tartakower recalled that "in the first years of Zionism, this very popular idea of the 'negation of the *golus*' (or negation of the diaspora) that led to the practical consequences of abandoning all work to maintain and strengthen Jewish positions in those countries where the Jewish nation is concentrated, has long past." Ibid, 238.

92. Cang, "League of Nations," 33.

93. Ibid.

94. McDonald, *Advocate for the Doomed*, 363.

95. The cooperative banks often had connections to the JDC and functioned thanks to donations from American Jews. By 1938, the JDC supported 915 loan *kasses* (small-scale credit unions). See Polonsky, *Politics in Independent Poland*, 470; Hyman, "Twenty-Five Years"; Bauer, *My Brother's Keeper*, 36–37; Kassow, *Who Will Write Our History?*, 95–100, on Ringelblum; Marcus, *Social and Political History*, 138–40.

96. McDonald, *Advocate for the Doomed*, 364.

97. Ibid., 371.

98. Ibid., 792. On the so-called Haavara agreement, signed in 1933 and allowing German Jews to transfer some of their assets to Mandate Palestine, see Weiss, "Transfer Agreement."

99. McDonald, *Advocate for the Doomed*, 796.

100. At many times in his diary, McDonald had discussions about the international nature of the Jewish problem. Ibid., 81.

101. According to Moss, "by the end of the 1930s some 180,000 individuals had registered with Poland's Jewish Central Emigrant Society (JEAS) and the Palestine office in Warsaw that handled enquiries by Polish Jews wishing to leave for Palestine had some 200,000 names." Moss, "Thinking with Restriction," 206. Of course, this is a small percentage of the more than 3.3 million Jews living in Poland by the end of that decade. Moss does not include a discussion of return migration in his analysis. As Brinkman notes above, in 1928 the net migration from Europe to Palestine was ten (not ten thousand, ten!). "Permanent Transit," 67.

102. All quotes from Tartakower in this paragraph are from Tartakower, "Życie Żydowskie w Polsce Odrodzonej," 262. I thank Natalia Aleksiun, Ula Madej-Krupitski, and Michał Grochowski for their help in translating this passage. I include the original here, as the degree of Tartakower's conditional optimism depends a bit on translation: "Ale o ile minie koniec końców koszmar dzisiejszy politycznych i społecznych stosunków, o ile Państwo Polskie przezwyciężyć zdoła piętrzące się obecnie trudności gospodarcze i opanuje hydrę antysemitzymu, która zagraża nie tylko Żydom, lecz podrywa również podstawy bytu całego społeczeństwa, to nadejdą i dla ludności żydowskiej lepsze czasy." For a slightly different interpretation of Tartakower's perspective in 1938, see Żyndul, review of *Żydzi w Polsce odrodzonej*, 121–22.

103. McDonald, *Advocate for the Doomed*, 788.

104. Falek, "Multifaceted Image of Jewish Women."

105. McDonald met with Brandeis once on October 16, 1933. McDonald, *Advocate for the Doomed*, 129. He met with Weizmann several times. Ibid., 151–52.

106. "Sir Neill Malcolm Aids Reich Refugees," *New York Times*, February 19, 1936, 13.

107. Kubowitzki, *Unity in Dispersion*, 73.

108. Bacon, "One Jewish Street?," 327.

109. Kubowitzki, *Unity in Dispersion*, 58. Neither the Agudah, the Polish Bnai Brith, nor the Bund accepted the invitation to the congress.

110. Ibid., 58.

111. Ibid., 70–71.

112. The general histories cited above include discussions of these issues. For more specific evaluations, see Trębacz, "'Ghetto Benches' at Polish Universities"; Aleksiun, "Christian Corpses for Christians"; Plach, "Ritual Slaughter." On economic antisemitism, see Hagen, "Before the 'Final Solution.'"

113. Polonsky, *Politics in Independent Poland*, 467.

114. Ibid., 468.

115. Emmanuel Melzer covers emigration in one complete chapter; see *No Way Out*, 131–53. Marcus estimates that about five percent of the Jews in Poland voted for the Revisionists in the late 1930s (*Social and Political History*, 271).

116. Furthermore, the word *congress* enjoyed "high esteem among Polish Jews, holding out a dim promise of elevation, as it was somehow associated with the ancient parliament of Polish Jews, and had the prestige of contemporary Zionist ones." Marcus, *Social and Political History*, 372. On the Jewish national councils, see Mendelsohn, *On Modern Jewish Politics*, 64–65 (for those set up during and after the German occupation of Congress Poland); Kieval, *Languages of Community*, 211–16.

117. Zuckerman's attempt to organize "Polish Jewry" into an official Congress failed, in Kubowitzki's assessment, for "internal political reasons." Kubowitzki, *Unity in Dispersion*, 82. Kubowitzki estimates that eight hundred local organizations

were founded in Poland and six hundred thousand people were registered to the congress. Zuckerman offers other estimates in his February 1938 report: committees were organized in roughly 280 towns, and five hundred thousand Polish Jews bought registration cards at ten grosz apiece. According to his report, the Polish government began limiting his work after the publication of the WJC book *The Economic Situation of World Jewry*. Zuckerman was even called before a local governor himself and forced to sign away his right to an extension of his visa.

118. Mendelsohn, *On Modern Jewish Politics*, 55.

119. According to Marcus, "the World Zionist Organization was composed of federations set up on a territorial basis. As a heritage from the past partition of the country, there were three Zionist Federations (or organizations as they were called) in Poland: the Zionist Organizations of Central and Eastern Poland (ZOCEP), the Zionist Organization of Eastern Lesser Poland (ZOREG) and the Zionist Organization of Western Lesser Poland and Silesia (ZOSEG)." *Social and Political History*, 269.

120. Gutman et al., *Jews of Poland*, 5.

121. Marcus discusses this briefly; see *Social and Political History*, 372–74.

122. Baruch Zuckerman, "Report to the WJC, Filed on Feb. 25, 1938," folder no. A 20/4, WJC.

123. Ibid.

124. Ibid.

125. Ibid.

126. Ibid.

127. It eventually included "small traders, Revisionists, the Jewish Women's association, the General Zionists Group A, General Zionists Group B (which joined after lengthy negotiations), Poale Zion, Mizrachi, Histadrut and other small groups." Ibid.

128. Ibid.

129. Ibid.

130. Ibid.

131. For more about the campaign's focus on women, see the advertisement "For our equality! . . . Every Jew (regardless of sex) aged 18 or over can buy a vote, get the right to vote!," *Nowy Dziennik*, January 22, 1938, 4; "Women and the Self-Help Congress," *Nowy Dziennik*, February 22, 1938, 11.

132. On the censorship of the Polish Jewish press, see Steffen, *Jüdische Polonität*, 73–82.

133. For a reference to Anselm Reiss as participating in the organization, see "More about the Congress of Polish Jewry," *Nowy Dziennik*, January 3, 1938, 4. Ignacy Schwarzbart served on the committee drawn from eight political parties selected in Tarnow. See "Wybór komitetu dla kongresu samopomocy żydowskiej w Tarnowie," *Chwila*, January 7, 1938, 10.

134. "Rozpoczęła pracę dla Kongresu Samopomocy Żydowskiej w Polsce," *Chwila*, January 4, 1938 (morning ed.), 2.

135. "Konferencje Rejonów Kongresu Żydostwa Polskiego," *Nasz Przegląd*, November 10, 1937, 12.

136. "Zadania Komitetu Łódzkiego Dla Spraw Kongresu Żydowskiego w Polsce," *Nasz Przegląd*, November 6, 1937, 13. Arieh Tartakower made this announcement. On the Jewish Economic Committee, see Marcus, *Social and Political History*, 337–38.

137. "Okręgowa konferencja dla spraw żydowskiego kongresu w Polsce," *Nasz Przegląd*, December 20, 1937, 9.

138. Mizrachi leader Rabbi Isaac Nisenbaum stated that the "main goal of the Jewish Congress in Poland is to create the widest possible representation of Polish Jewry." "The Congress for Polish Jews" [in Yiddish], *Der Moment*, November 14, 1937, 3.

139. "Advertisement," *Nasz Przegląd*, December 26, 1937, 8.

140. "Dokoła kongresu żydowskiego w Polsce," *Nasz Przegląd*, January 5, 1938.

141. "Żydostwo religijnie za kongresem żydostwa polskiego," *Nowy Dziennik*, January 5, 1938, 11.

142. "Dokoła kongresu żydowskiego w Polsce Konferencja rejonowa meeting," *Nasz Przegląd*, January 5, 1938.

143. *Nasz Przegląd*, January 9, 1938, 12.

144. "Kronika Katowice," *Nowy Dziennik*, January 13, 1938.

145. "Utrudnianie akcji na rzecz kongresu Żydow polskich na Wołyniu," *Nasz Przegląd*, January 14, 1938, 11.

146. On the opening in Warsaw, see *Nasz Przegląd*, January 16, 1938, 9. On the event in Buczacz, see "Buczacz," *Chwila*, January 27, 1938, 10.

147. "Czy chcecie silnej reprezentacji na Kongresie Samopomocy Żydowskiej w Polsce?," *Nowy Dziennik*, January 21, 1938, 14.

148. This advertisement and two others appear on January 30, 1938, in *Chwila*, 10, 11, 12. See also *Chwila*, January 31, 1938, 8; February 1, 1938, 4; February 3, 1938, 5, 7; February 5, 1938 (morning ed.), 13.

149. *Nasz Przegląd*, January 28, 1938, 12. Another meeting in academic circles earlier in January discussed the Congress of Polish Jews as well. See "From Jewish Academic Life," *Nasz Przegląd*, January 19, 1938, 12.

150. Both also spoke before their colleagues at the Union of Engineers and Doctors. *Nasz Przegląd*, February 9, 1938, 10.

151. Eliasz Markus, "Kongres samopomocy Żydów przyjdzie," *Nowy Dziennik*, February 3, 1938, 5.

152. The same advertisement appeared on February 5 and 6, 1938. "SUNDAY! February 7 is the last day of the sale of election cards . . . Take part in a collective effort! Help create an instrument of Jewish defense and self-help! Elect delegates

for the first democratic Congress of Jews from Poland!," *Nasz Przegląd,* February 5, 1938, and February 6, 1938.

153. *Nasz Przegląd,* February 11, 1938, 11.

154. *Nasz Przegląd,* February 10, 1938, 6.

155. In Warsaw 61,891 cards were filled, in Łódź 42,450, in Białystok 10,302, in Brześć 6,399, in Równo 5,188, in Pińsk 3,712, in Wieluń 1,929, and in Zdunska Wola 1,846. See "In an Impressive Result of the Jewish Congress in Poland," *Nasz Przegląd,* March 17, 1938, 12.

156. "15 maja r.b. kongres żydostwa polskiego wybory dnia 24 kwietna," *Nasz Przegląd,* February 28, 1938, 3.

157. Under pressure from these threats of economic and political groups to withdraw from the initiative, the Organizing Committee decided to postpone the publication of the electoral calendar. See *Nasz Przegląd,* April 13, 1938, 5, 12.

158. "Data przełożonana kongresie Żydów polskich," *Nowy Dziennik,* April 10, 1938, 15.

159. Marcus, *Social and Political History,* 373.

160. Hillel Zeitlin, "On the Planned Jewish Congress" [in Yiddish], *Der Moment,* November 12, 1937, 3.

161. "Sprawozdanie z sesji rady partyjnej or. Ogólnych Syjonistów w Polsce," *Nasz Przegląd,* November 15, 1937, 10.

162. Jakob Apenszlak, "Plan na rok bieżący," *Nasz Przegląd,* January 1, 1938, 4.

163. On Pryłucki, see Weiser, *Jewish People, Yiddish Nation,* especially 31–72.

164. See coverage of Pryłucki's statements in "Dokoła kongresu żydowskiego w Polsce," *Nasz Przegląd,* January 25, 1938, 6. A discussion between opposing opinion writers was published in *Hajnt* (*Today*) and *Naye folks-tsaytung* (*New People's Newspaper*) in early January 1938. "Dokoła kongresu żydowskiego Dr. M. Kleinbaum w Hajncie, artykuł 'U Progu Nowej Ery,'" *Nasz Przegląd,* January 2, 1938.

165. On the Camp of National Unity and their policies in the late 1930s, see Rudnicki, "Anti-Jewish Legislation."

166. *Nasz Przegląd* covered these comments and published Sommerstein's response to them. See "Kwestia żydowska głównym tematem dyskusji budżetowych," *Nasz Przegląd,* January 19, 1938.

167. Baruch Zuckerman, "Report to the WJC, Filed on Feb. 25, 1938," folder no. A 20/4, WJC.

168. Cang worked as the editor of the *Foreign Correspondents Bulletin* in Warsaw and had spent four years at the London School of Economics. See "Letter from Joel Cang to the Foreign Editor of the Manchester Guardian," September 10, 1932, Joel Cang, 1932–1951 (B/C23/1-177), Guardian Newspaper European Foreign Correspondence, Archive of the *Manchester Guardian,* Manchester University Library, Manchester, United Kingdom. Cang published

more than one hundred articles for the *Manchester Guardian* between 1920 and 1947, usually under the bylines of "Special Correspondent" or "Warsaw Correspondent."

169. Cang, "Opposition Parties in Poland," 248. On peasant parties and land reform, see Connelly, *From Peoples into Nations*, 386–89.

170. Cang, "Opposition Parties in Poland," 245.

171. "Ukrainian Discontent," *Manchester Guardian*, February 3, 1938; "Polish Ukrainian Relations," *Manchester Guardian*, October 13, 1936.

172. To see this transformation of norms related to the Ukrainian question in Poland, see Cramsey et al., "Timing Is Everything."

173. Joel Cang, "The Endeks: Polish Antisemitic Party," *Manchester Guardian*, August 14, 1935. The Endeks used anti-Jewish violence as a means for undermining the authority of the government; see Melzer, "Anti-Semitism," 129.

174. On the Peasant Party, see Wynot, "Polish Peasant Movement."

175. Cang, "Opposition Parties in Poland," 249.

176. Ibid.

177. Ibid., 251. Note that Cang reported on the rise in antisemitic acts in the second half of 1935 as well. "Antisemitism in Poland—Rioting in Grodno," *Manchester Guardian*, July 2, 1935; "Boycott Week: Antisemitic Activity in Poland," *Manchester Guardian*, September 11, 1935; "Jews in the Polish Universities: Organized Assaults," *Manchester Guardian*, December 14, 1935.

178. Cang cited the Peasant Party weekly, *Zielony Sztandar*, from January 1937 on this point. Cang, "Opposition Parties in Poland," 250. Marcus discusses Madagascar in *Social and Political History*, 392–395. See also Trębacz, *Nie tylko Palestyna*, 194–272. Madagascar, it seems, was the favored hypothetical destination for at least two unsavory groups in the minds of antisemitic Polish elites who wanted to maintain the economic and political status quo during the 1920s and 1930s. The "idea of settling Madagascar with Polish citizens was first raised in 1926," and "at that time the idea was the migration of Polish peasants from the overpopulated countryside." Snyder, *Black Earth*, 60. See Zahra, *The Great Departure*, 105–141 and 156–157 for her coverage of the Madagascar Plan as one of many such plans to resettle Jewish populations from Europe elsewhere during the interwar period; Polonsky estimates that the surplus rural population in interwar Poland was as high as 4.5 million, *The Jews in Poland and Russia*, 69. From a broader colonial perspective, Robson (*States of Separation*, 65) suggests that "prewar negotiations between the British government and Zionist territorialists over Jewish settlement in Africa, in particular, had provided an early venue for articulating how ethnically based relocation could be presented to the international community as a mode of minority national empowerment while in practice serving to advance the imperial interests of its sponsors." For more on settler colonialism, see Pedersen, "Settler Colonialism."

179. Cang, "Opposition Parties in Poland," 51.

180. Ibid., 253.

181. The plebiscite included a second question as well: "Will a Jewish free state be beneficial to Jews at large?" In total, 16,543 Poles and 124 Jews replied yes, and 336 Poles and 1,049 Jews said no. See Cang, "The Jewish State—Views of Poland and of Poland's Jews," *Manchester Guardian*, August 24, 1937.

182. M. Kaplan, "When the Ordinary Became Extraordinary," 81. She also covers this in her book *Between Dignity and Despair*, 129–43. For a statistical discussion of German Jewish emigration, see Strauss, "Jewish Emigration from Germany," 313, 343.

183. For the so-called Czech Transfer, see Láníček, *Arnošt Frischer*, 58–64. Czechoslovak Jewish leader Arnošt Frischer left Prague at the end of 1939 as part of this transfer.

184. During a reporting trip to Danzig to study the outcome of the parliamentary elections there, Joel Cang was arrested. *Jewish Chronicle*, April 12, 1935, 9.

185. Kaplan provides the following numbers of German Jewish refugees by year: 37,000 in 1933, 23,000 in 1934, 21,000 in 1935 (10,000 returned during 1935), 25,000 in 1936, 23,000 in 1937, and 40,000 in 1938. See M. Kaplan, "When the Ordinary Became Extraordinary," 85.

186. Ibid., 84.

187. They arrived "shocked and confused, having been uprooted from a country they had loved as their own." T. Segev, *Seventh Million*, 35. See also Halamish, "Palestine as a Destination."

188. On this action more generally, see Jońca, "Expulsion of Polish Jews"; Weiss, *Deutsche und polnische Juden vor dem Holocaust*; Harris, "German Jews to Polish Refugees."

189. WJC members and head of the WJC British Section, Maurice Perlzweig, visited Poland to help resolve the Zbąszyń situation. *The Reminiscences of Maurice Perlzweig*, 531–36.

190. "Letter of WPC to Joel Cang," November 16, 1938, and "Letter from WPC alerting anonymous recipient to Cang's foreign credentials," November 20, 1938, Joel Cang, 1932–1951 (B/C23/1-177), Guardian Newspaper European Foreign Correspondence, Archive of the *Manchester Guardian*, Manchester University Library, Manchester, United Kingdom.

191. For a broad view on refugee policies at the end of the 1930s, see Frankl and Čapková, *Nejisté útočiště*.

192. *Sprawy Narodowościowe: czasopismo poświęcone badaniu spraw narodowościowych* 1938/3, 314.

193. Fishman-Tamir, "Mikhtaw l'Arnon Fishman Tarmi." See Ringelblum's letter from May 5, 1939, in Kassow, *Who Will Write Our History?*, 422n39.

194. Marcus, *Social and Political History*, 398.
195. Ibid., 247 (for the economic changes), 381 (for the political changes).
196. Ibid., 410.
197. Warhaftig, *Refugee and Survivor*, 18.

2. IN EXILE

1. The United Kingdom would only recognize the coterie of people around Beneš as the "provisional" Czechoslovak government four months later in July 1940.

2. Gerlach, *Economy of Ethnic Cleansing*, 2–10.

3. On the German minority in interwar Czechoslovakia more broadly, see Novotný, *British Legation in Prague*, 113–42, and the first third of Luža, *Transfer of the Sudeten Germans*.

4. Many German Social Democrats in Czechoslovakia tried to save the state. I thank Chad Bryant for bringing this to my attention.

5. Abraham Abrahams, "When Beneš Met Jabotinsky," 1948, p. 3, no. JIA P2/4/3, Jabotinsky Institute, Tel Aviv, Israel.

6. Ibid.

7. Lichtenstein, *Zionists in Interwar Czechoslovakia*, 71; Fink, *Defending the Rights of Others*, 126.

8. Abrahams, "When Beneš Met Jabotinsky." Jabotinsky justified his use of the term *evacuation*: "In modern times and under decent governments [evacuation] has always been associated with forethought, careful planning and decent accommodation at the of the journey prepared beforehand. Mass evacuation is the only remedy for the cancer of the Jewish distress." Jabotinsky, *Jewish War Front*, 2. This should be balanced by Dmitry Shumsky's observation that in this book Jabotinsky favored "multinational democracy in Palestine over the transfer scenario." *Beyond the Nation-State*, 258.

9. Lichtenstein, *Zionists in Interwar Czechoslovakia*, 87.

10. Unlike Poland, Czechoslovakia did not sign (nor did the Allied powers require them to sign) the Treaty of St. Germain, which contained minority protections in 1919. Notably, the 1920 Czechoslovak constitution granted equality to the country's minorities (German, Hungarian, Jewish, Rusyn, and Polish) but did not award rights to specific minorities. Lichtenstein, *Zionists in Interwar Czechoslovakia*, 87–88.

11. Abrahams, "When Beneš met Jabotinsky," 5. Note that Abrahams recorded his reflections about the 1940 conversation on the occasion of Beneš's death eight years later.

12. Jabotinsky also applied his theory of population transfers to the Arab populations in Palestine around the same time as this particular meeting. Rubin,

"Vladimir Jabotinsky and Population Transfers." Consider Jabotinsky and the Revisionist Movement's relationship with the Polish government-in-exile: Engel, "The Frustrated Alliance."

13. During the Great War, Beneš had approached foreign ministers and presidents of another allied coalition in the hope of creating a new state out of the territory of the Habsburg Empire. On the inner Czechoslovak leadership circle during the Second World War, see Beneš's three volumes of memoirs, Hauner, *Edvard Beneš*; Zeman, *The Life of Edvard Beneš*; a volume from the head of Beneš's presidential chancellery, Smutný, *Dokumenty z historie čsl. politiky*; an account from Beneš's personal secretary and legal advisor, Táborský, *President Edvard Beneš*; and writings from his personal archivist, Opočenský, *Formování československého zahraničního odboje*.

14. See Maisky, *Maisky Diaries*, 137, on Jan Masaryk's initial response to the Munich Agreement. For Maisky's coverage of Munich overall, see 130–44. On the Munich Agreement, see Lukes, *Czechoslovakia between Stalin and Hitler*; Steiner, "Soviet Commissariat of Foreign Affairs"; Smetana, *In the Shadow of Munich*.

15. For a brief outline of Jabotinsky's life see Horowitz "Muse and Muscle." On Revisionism in Czechoslovakia more generally see Čapková, "Piłsudski or Masaryk?"

16. Klein-Pejšová notes that Jewish entry into Czechoslovakia after World War I was "bitter" even if the state eventually became hospitable toward Jews. *Mapping Jewish Loyalties*, 22.

17. "Report of Ignacy Schwarzbart Filed on November 20, 1940," folder no. A 20/7, WJC.

18. Ibid.

19. Lichtenstein, *Zionists in Interwar Czechoslovakia*, 11.

20. Ibid., 55. On the myth of Czechoslovakia, see Orzoff, *Battle for the Castle*.

21. "Lev Zelmanovits' Visit to Beneš on March 28, 1941," file no. H 97/11, WJC. On Lev Zelmanovits and the so-called National Jewish Council, see Láníček, *Arnošt Frischer*, 70–71. Láníček also discusses the strained relationship between Zelmanovits and Beneš and the reason why Beneš did not choose him as a delegate on the Czechoslovak State Council. Ibid., 72–76. See Gil S. Rubin's interpretation of this meeting and the consequent memo prepared by Tartakower in "Future of the Jews," 50–55.

22. Ibid.

23. Letter from Lev Zelmanovits to Arieh Tartakower, March 8, 1941, file no. H 102/2, WJC.

24. Ibid.

25. Tartakower drafted an (unsent?) letter to Beneš a few weeks later. In it, he noted that "there might be some countries not so eager to assimilate their

Jewish citizens which might accept the slogan enforcing their emigration from the respective countries on the basis of principle formulated by Beneš." Láníček, *Czechs, Slovaks and the Jews*, 71. Láníček notes that the letter was most likely an unsent draft.

26. "Report on Meeting between Beneš, Silverman, Barou and Perlzweig on April 17, 1941," file no. H 97/11, WJC. Láníček discusses this in *Czechs, Slovaks and the Jews*, 55.

27. "Report on Meeting."

28. Ibid.

29. Ibid. The perception of Beneš as a fighter for Jewish rights is unnuanced at best and incorrect at worst.

30. Ibid.

31. Ibid.

32. Ibid.

33. Ibid.

34. Klein-Pejšová, *Mapping Jewish Loyalties*, 52. See her discussion of the 1919 Slovak census, the 1921 Czechoslovak census, and the discussions of national and linguistic belonging that accompanied both of these events, 47–84. On the interwar censuses, see Čapková, *Češi, Němci, Židé?*; Lichtenstein, *Zionists in Interwar Czechoslovakia*, 88–89; Zahra, *Kidnapped Souls*, 106–41.

35. Contrast this with the official definition of nationality crafted by the census preparers: "Nationality is understood as ethnic belonging, whose main external marker is as a rule mother tongue," quoted in Klein-Pejšová, *Mapping Jewish Loyalties*, 74.

36. Lichtenstein, *Zionists in Interwar Czechoslovakia*, 6. More specifically, "the Czechoslovak Constitution of February 29, 1920, did grant equality to the country's minorities, as had been agreed in Paris. It did not award rights to specific minorities. Jews' rights were included under the general provision securing equality before the law for the country's religious, racial, and linguistic minorities." Lichtenstein, *Zionists in Interwar Czechoslovakia*, 87–88. Also, "corporate minority rights required proof that the national, religious, or linguistic group in question comprised a considerable fraction (*značný zlomek*) of the population of a town or district, where a considerable fraction was defined as 20%." Klein-Pejšová, *Mapping Jewish Loyalties*, 99.

37. Zahra, *Kidnapped Souls*, 272.

38. Kuklík, *Czech Law in Historical Contexts*, 125.

39. Recently, two important studies of Jacob Robinson have been published: Rubin, "End of Minority Rights," and Loeffler, *Rooted Cosmopolitans*, 32–57.

40. "Memo from Dr. Jacob Robinson regarding 'Beneš's Ideas on the Jewish Problem, on September 25, 1941,'" file no. H 279/1, WJC.

41. Ibid. Robinson noted that the "formula" proposed by Napoleon's so-called *Sanhedrin* in the early 1800s was "much milder" in comparison.

42. Ibid.

43. Malvina Tartakower, "Uchodźtwo w Rosji, Persii i Palestynie," *NT*, April 12, 1943. Malvina Tartakower left Poland in September 1939; she went through eastern Małopolska, the Urals (where she chopped down trees), Persia, and Palestine before reuniting with her husband in New York City by April 1943.

44. "Minutes of the Meeting of the Representatives of Czech Jews and Polish Jews in the United States, Sept 25, 1941," file no. A 24/1, WJC.

45. Ibid.

46. Ibid.

47. Ibid.

48. "Draft of a Polish-Jewish Declaration on September 9, 1940," file no. A 24/1, WJC. "Loyal" was, according to Dariusz Stola, a key word to differentiate between Jews and so-called "ethnic" Germans in Poland. *Nadzieja i Zagłada*.

49. On Tartakower's objections, see Engel, *In the Shadow of Auschwitz*, 247.

50. "Minutes of the Committee on Polish Affairs," file no. A 24/1, WJC.

51. This statement materialized in the first half of June 1941 while Sikorski was in the United States. See "Polish Council Backs Sikorski's Statement on the Jewish Question," JTA, June 13, 1941. Engel observes that "the import of such proclamations, however, was nil." *In the Shadow of Auschwitz*, 109.

52. "Memo from Schwarzbart to Tartakower regarding His Meeting with Ambassador Ciechanowski, January 2, 1941," file no. H 278/15, WJC. Note that chap. 2, "Misja," in Stola's *Nadzieja i Zagłada* focuses on demands for a Polish government declaration in Jewish matters and fights against "emigracjonizm."

53. "Letter from Arieh Tartakower to Ignacy Schwarzbart on January 15, 1941," file no. A 20/7, WJC.

54. Ibid.

55. Of course, the concept of population transfers or population deportations is arguably as old as war itself. In the modern period, consider events during the Russo-Turkish War of 1877–1878 and the Balkan Wars of 1912–1913. Before and after World War I, several populations, including Jewish populations in the Russian Empire, were expelled and moved elsewhere within the empire. Lohr, *Nationalizing the Russian Empire*; Sanborn, "Unsettling the Empire"; Gerlach, *Economy of Ethnic Cleansing*, 19–21.

56. Bryant, *Prague in Black*, 97.

57. E. Beneš, "Central Europe after Ten Years," 249.

58. Ibid.

59. Ibid.

60. Ibid., 250.

61. Ibid.

62. Ibid.

63. Ibid., 251.

64. Ibid. "In the aftermath of the war, the new question was how Jewish individual and communal rights would be protected in the new east central European state system. Czechoslovakia was considered the linchpin of that system." Klein-Pejšová, *Mapping Jewish Loyalties*, 23.

65. This Beneš quote comes from 1932. See Wheatley, "Spectral Legal Personality," 276.

66. E. Beneš, "Little Entente," 67, 70, 72, respectively.

67. E. Beneš, "League of Nations," 70.

68. Ibid., 68.

69. Ibid., 68.

70. Ibid., 75.

71. E. Beneš, "Ten Years of the League," 212.

72. See T. Masaryk, "Reflections on the Question," 530; Macartney, "Minorities," 683; Osusky, "Why Czechoslovakia?," 469; Temperley, "Hungarian Frontiers," 445.

73. Jászi, "Dismembered Hungary," 276–77.

74. This type of decision, Temperley noted, was "clearly far beyond the powers" of this committee and, it turned out, the parties within the League in general. "Hungarian Frontiers," 443.

75. Armstrong, "Hitler's Reich," 602.

76. Consider Miller, "Nationality and Other Problems"; Vollmer, "New Polish Corridor"; Wiskemann, "'Drang Nach Osten' Continues." Laura Robson shows how a discourse about transfers especially in colonial contexts infused the League's discussions. She also identifies extraterritorial transfers within the Zionist movement as providing a precedent, say, for plans to transfer the Assyrians to a "far-flung territory like Brazil or British Guiana." *States of Separation*, 66.

77. Toynbee, "East after Lausanne," 86.

78. Waldeck, "Great New Migration."

79. Klaus Dietmar Hencke explains that Lausanne became an "idée fixe" for Churchill and others by 1944, quoted in Naimark, *Fires of Hatred*, 110.

80. After the division of this area into Jewish, Arab, and "neutral" entities, the Peel Commission championed the uprooting of some 1,300,000 Greeks and some 400,000 Turks as a task "vigorously and effectively" accomplished in the span of just eighteen months (which contradicts Waldeck's description above). Only as a "last resort" should the exchange be "compulsory." *Palestine Royal Commission Report*, 389. On the Jewish Agency's promotion of transfer plans to the Peel Commission, see Masalha, *Politics of Denial*, 24–26; Moses, "Epilogue," 284.

81. Samuel, "Palestine Report," 152.

82. Wasserstein, "Herbert Samuel."

83. *Final Report of the Palestine Partition Commission*, 53.

84. Armstrong, "Hitler's Reich," 598.

85. Ibid., 600.

86. Seton-Watson, "German Minority in Czechoslovakia," 651. After the Ukrainians, Seton-Watson noted, Germans were the largest "race" governed by "foreigners."

87. Bryant, *Prague in Black*, 25. In an effort to avert war in August 1939, the Polish proposed sixteen points to Ribbentrop, which included plans for an "exchange of populations" in the so-called Polish Corridor depending on plebiscite results. Von Wegerer, "Origins of this War," 715. Ribbentrop ultimately rejected this plan.

88. Aly, *Final Solution*, 19.

89. Adolf Hitler, quoted in Schechtmann, "Option Clause," 356.

90. See the drafts submitted by Joseph Schechtmann as he prepared his manuscript *Transfer of Populations*, which eventually was published as *European Population Transfers, 1939–1945* (Oxford: Oxford University Press, 1946), file no. C 117/8, WJC; Rubin, "Future of the Jews," 128–34.

91. Eberhardt, *Political Migrations*, 46. Himmler oversaw the removal of 12,271 Poles from Gdynia by October 26, 1939.

92. Bryant, *Prague in Black*, 112.

93. Lumans, *Himmler's Auxiliaries*, 1.

94. Frank, *Making Minorities History*, 162. Frank observes that Politis implied that population transfers on a massive scale could "engineer a new European order." This lineage is complicated. For Krystyna Kersten, the writings of French anthropologist and ethnographer George Montadon harbingered this revolution as early as 1916 when he published a memorandum for the first conference on nationalities. In it, he supported the "transfer of minorities and the application of ethnic criteria for the determination of future borders." Kersten, "International Migrations in Poland," 53. Also see Henckaerts, *Mass Expulsion*.

95. Frank, *Making Minorities History*, 162.

96. Ther and Hughes-Kreutzmuller, *Dark Side*, 102–3.

97. Bryant, *Prague in Black*, 9. From 1943 to 1948, another twenty-one million were on the move.

98. Weizmann, "Palestine's Role."

99. Consider that, according to Jabotinsky's *Jewish War Front*, Weizmann gave a speech in New York shortly before the book's publication in 1940 stating that Palestine had the capacity for fifty thousand immigrants annually. See chap. 29.

100. Maisky, *Maisky Diaries*, 330.

101. Weizmann, "Palestine's Role," 329–30.

102. Ibid., 337–38. Note that David Ben-Gurion observed in October 1941 that "the idea of transferring a population is gaining more sympathy as a practical and

the most secure means of solving the dangerous and painful problem of national minorities" because of resettlement schemes during the war. Ben-Gurion, "Lines for Zionist Policy," October 15, 1941, quoted in Masalha, *Expulsion of the Palestinians*, 128–29, 166n9. Shumsky zeroes in on a July 1943 speech and a March 1944 speech as instances when Ben-Gurion shifted his support toward a mononational iteration of a Jewish state. Shumsky, *Beyond the Nation-State*, 213.

103. Weizmann's January 1942 article "Palestine's Role" did not detail where funding for these transfers would originate either. On the transfer of Arab populations, see T. Segev, *One Palestine*, 403–8.

104. E. Beneš, "Organization of Postwar Europe," 235.

105. Ibid., 226.

106. On the meaning of "human rights" in the 1940s, see J. Robinson, *Human Rights and Fundamental Freedoms*, Moyn, *Last Utopia* and *Not Enough*, as well as Kurz, "Hide a Fact Rather Than State It" and *Jewish Internationalism*. Consider also G. Cohen on displaced people during the "Human Rights Revolution," *In War's Wake*, 79–99 and Loeffler, "Particularist Pursuit of American Universalism."

107. E. Beneš, "Organization of Postwar Europe," 237–238.

108. Frank, *Making Minorities History*, 173n106.

109. In February 1940, Beneš wrote to Sumner Welles that "we shall have to consider transfers of population and the creations of districts which would be, as far as possible, nationally homogenous in many cases." Frank, *Making Minorities History*, 151. As early as October 1940, Robert Bruce Lockhart, British liaison to the Czechoslovak government-in-exile and Beneš's "confidant," publicly declared, "'Beneš has found his own solution. He has borrowed it from Hitler.'" Ibid., 204.

110. Bryant, *Prague in Black*, 67. See also how the "prevailing opinion in Czech society" leaned toward expulsion for all the Germans, despite Beneš's claim that "loyal" Germans could remain. Zahra, *Kidnapped Souls*, 253–54.

111. Bryant, *Prague in Black*, 99.

112. Douglas mentions that Beneš had his last documented meeting with Jaksch at the end of 1942. That seems to contradict his statement that Beneš had ceased working with the Sudeten German Social Democratic party in 1941. Douglas, *Orderly and Humane*, 20 and 33, respectively. Láníček cites a letter from Beneš to the ÚVOD on September 6, 1941. *Czechs, Slovaks and the Jews*, 40.

113. Naimark, *Fires of Hatred*, 114; Mastný, "Beneš-Stalin-Molotov Conversations."

114. Seton-Watson, "German Minority in Czechoslovakia," 665.

115. Láníček extrapolates (correctly, I think) from the 1942 article as well. He writes that Beneš "didn't mention the Jews but the theory it presented entirely

matched his remarks on Zionism made privately during 1940 and 1941." *Czechs, Slovaks and the Jews*, 50. For Láníček's coverage of this article, see 47–51.

116. Bryant, *Prague in Black*, 210. Notably, these discussions about ending minority rights often complemented emerging discussions about war guilt and future postwar trials.

117. Arieh Tartakower, "For Our Freedom and Yours," *NT*, November 10, 1940, 2–3.

118. Ibid. The proper form would be *Polscy Żydzi*—but *Polscy Żydy* could be a deliberate usage of the term mostly used by antisemites, *Żydy*. I thank Michał Grochowski for making this explicit to me. Ignacy Schwarzbart utilized similar language during this period. See Stola, "Misja," in *Nadzieja i Zagłada*, chap. 2.

119. Arieh Tartakower, "A Neglected Case," *NT*, December 3, 1940, 7.

120. Arieh Tartakower, "Dream of Evacuation," *NT*, April 21, 1941, 2.

121. Ibid.

122. Arieh Tartakower, "Fine Reflection," *NT*, June 21, 1941, 4.

123. Ibid.

124. Arieh Tartakower, "On the Margins of the Discussion," *NT*, July 27, 1942, 2.

125. Jakob Apenszlak, "Not the Theme to Discuss," *NT*, June 21, 1941, 3.

126. Ibid.

127. Ibid.

128. "Minutes of the Meeting of the Joint Committee on Polish Jewish Affairs," file no. A 20/7, WJC.

129. Ibid.

130. Ibid.

131. Arieh Tartakower, "Misunderstanding or Blindness," *NT*, January 31, 1941, 3.

132. Jakob Apenszlak, "On the Way to a Polish-Jewish Understanding," *NT*, February 19, 1941, 1.

133. The word *minority* resonated differently in America than in Europe. See Kurz, *Jewish Internationalism*, 21–22.

134. Jakob Apenszlak, "Interview with Julian Tuwim," *NT*, May 31, 1941, 3.

135. Dawidowicz, *Holocaust Reader*, 72–73.

136. According to Christopher Browning, it was in late summer or early fall 1941 that Nazi officials ordered the mass murder of European Jewry. "Nazi Decision."

137. Notably, practically all non-Jewish groups in the region helped kill Jews, but the scale of involvement (measured by the number or percentage of Jews killed by locals rather than German troops) differed greatly. On local violence during this particular summer, see Kopstein and Wittenberg, *Intimate Violence*.

138. Arad, *Bełżec, Sobibór, Treblinka*.

139. Jakob Apenszlak, "Polish Soviet Agreement," *NT*, August 16, 1941, 1.

140. Arieh Tartakower, "The Near East and the Jewish National Headquarters," *NT*, August 16, 1941, 3.

141. Tartakower, "Looking to the Future," *NT*, September 20, 1941.

142. For the quote, see "Meeting of the Representatives of Czechoslovak and Polish Jews in the United States," file no. A 24/1, WJC.

143. Ibid.

144. Ibid.

145. Ibid.

146. See Wandycz, *Czechoslovak-Polish Confederation*. This proposed economic and military union would create a multistate buffer between Germany and the Soviet Union. This was the federation Beneš referred to in his 1942 *Foreign Affairs* article ("Organization of Postwar Europe").

147. On the Soviets' disapproval of this confederation and consequent dismissal of it, see Táborský, "Polish-Czechoslovak Confederation."

148. "Minutes of the Committee on Relief for Polish Jewish Refugees in Soviet Russia," file no. A 20/7, WJC.

149. Maurice Perlzweig, "Memo," January 23, 1942, file no. H 278/16, WJC.

150. Ibid.

151. Arieh Tartakower, "WJC Council on European Affairs," April 17, 1942, file no. A 1/8, WJC. The WJC aided Polish Jewish refugees as they escaped Europe, processed upward of ten thousand letters from Switzerland within the first year of operation, shipped medicine and food into Poland, and dispatched over fifty thousand parcels up to March 1941. Frischer was involved in a parcel scheme from the second half of 1943 through February 1945, when he decided the project was hopeless. See Láníček, *Arnošt Frischer*, 119–23. Some of the parcels did reach their destinations, like some to Terezin.

152. Tartakower, "WJC Council on European Affairs."

153. Ibid.

154. Ibid.

155. Jakob Apenszlak, "Thoughts about Tomorrow," *NT*, May 30, 1942, 1.

156. Arieh Tartakower, "Memo to the Office Committee," May 21, 1942, file no. H 278/15, WJC.

157. Ibid.

158. Ibid.

159. Arieh Tartakower, "Imposed Polemic," *NT*, February 6, 1921, 2.

160. Ibid.

161. Arieh Tartakower, "The Jewish Army," *NT*, March 17, 1941, 1.

162. Arieh Tartakower, "On the Building of a Jewish State," *NT*, March 31, 1941, 1.

163. Arieh Tartakower, "Under the Sign of Exile," *NT*, April 30, 1941, 1.

164. Ibid.

165. Ibid.

166. Ibid.

167. Ibid.

168. Arieh Tartakower, "Bad Results," *NT*, March 23, 1942, 2.

169. Jakob Apenszlak, "Project: Congress of Polish Jews," *NT*, November 20, 1943, 2, 7.

170. Ibid.

171. Arieh Tartakower, "The Day Tomorrow," *NT*, December 31, 1942, 1–2.

172. Arieh Tartakower, "We Will Not Give Up," *NT*, August 20, 1943, 2.

173. Historians continue to ask this difficult question. Láníček seems to have three different ideas. First, he writes that mid-1944 marks the time when most in exile realized "the true extent of the Holocaust." Láníček, *Czechs, Slovaks and the Jews*, 12. Later, he says, "The extent of the final solution was not comprehending in London until the last months of the war." Ibid., 117. Either way, he writes that it took a "long time" for people to realize the extent of the Jewish destruction. Ibid., 12. Engel seems to think that actors "knew" what was happening to Europe's Jews much earlier, perhaps as early as December 1942. *Facing a Holocaust*, 2. In sum, I agree with Dariusz Stola that we must distinguish between knowledge and understanding when considering the question "When did news of the Holocaust emerge?" My aim here is to show how reports of the great tragedy coexisted with optimism well into 1944.

174. "Letter from Maurice Perlzweig to Peter Jessup," in the "Annex" to *Reminiscences of Maurice Perlzweig*.

175. Fleming, *Auschwitz, the Allies and Censorship*, 108; Laqueur, *Terrible Secret*; Riegner, *Never Despair*.

176. Perlzweig, quoted in Fleming, *Auschwitz, the Allies and Censorship*, 107.

177. "Interview between Maurice Perlzweig and Peter Jessup, June 15, 1982," Oral History Research Office (New York: Columbia University, 1982).

178. Arieh Tartakower, "In the Scent of My Brother's Blood," *NT*, September 24, 1942.

179. Stola, "Early News of the Holocaust," 14. Engel uses documents from the Reprezentacja Żydostwa Polskiego. Reiss represented the Reprezentacja in Palestine, and Tartakower represented the Reprezentacja in the United States.

180. Ibid., 15–16.

181. Ministerstwo Spraw Zagranicznych, *Mass Extermination*, 3. On November 27, 1942, at a special meeting of the Polish National Council, Deputy Prime Minister Stanislaw Mikołajczyk offered a speech, which eventually became a resolution adopted by the council and the foundation of the December

10 pamphlet/statement. The resolution passed on November 27, 1942, indicated that one million Polish Jews had been killed (p. 13). On the early flow of information between occupied Poland and London, see Puławski, *Wobliczu Zagłady*.

182. Ministerstwo Spraw Zagranicznych, *Mass Extermination*, 8. For more context, see Adam Puławski's study of the communications to London on the fate of Jews from Poland, *Wobec "niespotykanego w dziejach mordu."*

183. Ministerstwo Spraw Zagranicznych, *Mass Extermination*, 9; "1,000,000 Polish Jews Killed by Electrocution and Gas, 250,000 from Warsaw," *NT*, December 10, 1942, 5.

184. Engel, *Facing a Holocaust*, 15. Engel's companion book, *In the Shadow of Auschwitz*, also covers the incoming intelligence up to the December 1942 declaration. He does not cite *NT* in either book.

185. Arieh Tartakower, "Kontrapropaganda," *NT*, December 31, 1942, 2.

186. Many Jews in Warsaw did not believe what was happening to them or their families and went to the Umschlagplatz by themselves. See Ferenc-Piotrowska, "All Those Rumors."

187. Fenyvesi, "The Nazi Secret No One Believed," *The Washington Post*, February 5, 1983, C1.

188. Engel, *Facing a Holocaust*, 46. He cites Reiss, *Besa'arot Hatekufah*, 235–36, and Ignacy Schwarzbart's diary.

189. Tenebaum, "My Heart Is in the Ghetto," *NT*, March 11, 1943, 3.

190. "The Polish Jewish Representative in Palestine as the Guests of Minister Kot," *NT* March 11, 1943, 3.

191. "Through the Red Cross, a Swiss Letter Demands the Investigation of Nazi Persecution," *NT*, March 11, 1943, 3.

192. Warhaftig, *Refugee and Survivor*, 253.

193. Arieh Tartakower, "The Ghetto Fights," *NT*, June 11, 1943, 2.

194. "Ignacy Schwarzbart Diary," May 18, 1943, M2/770, Yad Vashem Archive, Jerusalem, Israel. See Stola, *Nadzieja i Zagłada*, 238.

195. Arieh Tartakower, "Memo to the Office Committee," June 24, 1943, file no. H 278/15, WJC.

196. Ibid.

197. Engel argues that this was not a "serious attempt" at rescue and instead was designed to bolster public opinion about Poland and to "prevent the Katyń affair from turning into a diplomatic fiasco." *Facing a Holocaust*, 72. See 68–74 for his entire description. Engel argues that by May 1943 the Polish government "appears to have effectively abandoned any notion that a Polish Jewish community of interest might ever be found" in the wake of the so-called Erlich-Alter affair.

198. Arieh Tartakower, "Memo to the WJC Office Committee," July 12, 1943, file no. D 2/12, WJC.

199. Arieh Tartakower, "Confidential Letter to the WJC Office Committee," file no. D 2/12, WJC. On Jan Karski, see his memoir *Story of a Secret State*; Lanzmann, *Karski Report*; Engel "Western Allies and the Holocaust"; Engel, *Facing a Holocaust*, 90; Rappak, "'Raport Karskiego'-kontrowersje i interpretacje."

200. Arieh Tartakower, "Death of Sikorski," *NT*, July 16, 1943, 1. Sikorski died alongside his daughter when his plane crashed off the coast of Gibraltar. See Wandycz, *Price of Freedom*, 228–30.

201. "Report of the Jewish National Committee in Poland," May 24, 1944, received on September 1, 1944, by the Representation of Polish Jewry, file no. H 274/11, WJC.

202. Ibid.

203. Ibid.

204. Ignacy Schwarzbart, "Statement before the Council of the Anglo-Jewish Association," file no. H 91/1, WJC.

205. Ignacy Schwarzbart, "Telegraph to Tartakower on October 25, 1943," file no. H 291/6, WJC.

206. "Ignacy Schwarzbart Diary," December 1, 1943.

207. Reflecting on his visit to Winston Churchill on Good Friday, April 23, 1941 (four days into the Warsaw Ghetto Uprising), Soviet ambassador to the UK Ivan Maisky noted that the broader Soviet "objective . . . (was) to explode Sikorski's government and clear the way for the creation of a more democratic and friendly Polish Government by the time or at the time when the Red Army enters Polish territory." Maisky, *Maisky Diaries*, 511. On the Katyń situation in general, see 505–11.

208. The Soviet Union gave support to the Związek Patriotów Polskich (Union of Polish Patriots or ZPP) in the USSR and the Polska Partia Robotnicza (Polish Worker's Party or PPR) in occupied Poland. The British and the Americans continued to back the so-called London Poles. Both ZPP and PPR joined the Polish Committee of National Liberation proclaimed in July 22, 1944. Shore, *Caviar and Ashes*, 153–94.

209. Frank, *Making Minorities History*, 208; Hauner, "We Must Push Eastwards."

210. A. Leon Kubowitzki, "Letter to Arnošt Frischer," May 24, 1943, file no. H 97/11, WJC.

211. Ibid.

212. Ibid. Note that Goldmann attributes "liberal ideals" to Beneš. The extent of Beneš's "liberalism" is a point of debate.

213. Ibid.

214. Ibid.

215. Ibid.

216. Arnošt Frischer, "Letter to A. Leon Kubowitzski," June 21, 1943, file no. H 97/11, WJC.

217. Ibid. See Sands, *East West Street*, for more conversations between Raphael Lemkin and Hersch Lauterpracht, two eminent Jewish lawyers who contemplated the complexities of group rights versus individual rights.

218. Frischer, "Letter to A. Leon Kubowitzski."

219. Ibid.

220. The Hebrew magazine *Palcor* reported that Beneš made this comment in New York on October 3, 1943. Ing. Ivan Novák, the Czechoslovak consul in Jerusalem, informed a representative in the London government of this report in *Palcor* three days after the supposed statement on October 6, 1943. "Report of Novák to Dr. Kraus," in Archiv No. 1613, Londýnsky Archiv Důvěrný [Confidential London Archive], Signatura No. 511, Židovká Otázka [The Jewish Question], Archiv Ministerstva Zahraničních Věcí České Republiky [Archive of the Foreign Ministry of the Czech Republic], Prague, Czech Republic (hereafter AMZV).

221. Chaim Weizmann, "Letter to Edvard Beneš," November 12, 1943, Edvard Beneš L 26, in Signatura No. 264 Korrespondence Židovské Spolky [Correspondence with Jewish Groups] Inventary No. 1659, Archiv Ústavu Tomáše Garrigue Masarykův a Archiv [Archive of the Tomáš Garrigue Masaryk Institute], Prague, Czech Republic (hereafter ÚTGM). Weizmann had recently obtained support for the idea of a Jewish commonwealth in Palestine from Ivan Maisky. According to Maisky's diary, Maisky met Weizmann in England on February 3, 1941.

3. NEGATING THIS DIASPORA

1. Jakob Apenszlak, "Facing Palestine," *NT*, December 21, 1944, 1.

2. Ibid. Schwarzbart offers a similar view in his diary after Zygielbojm's suicide. See Stola, *Nadzieja i Zagłada*, 239.

3. Apenszlak, "Facing Palestine."

4. On Nahum Goldmann, see Goldmann, *Autobiography of Nahum Goldmann*; Goldmann, *Mein Leben*; Patai, *Nahum Goldmann*; Raider, *Nahum Goldmann*; Dranger, *Nahum Goldmann.*

5. "Address delivered by Dr. Nahum Goldmann," in WJC, *War Emergency Conference*, 11.

6. Ibid. This argument does not represent an awareness of the settlement capacity of Mandate Palestine in the 1920s and 1930s or the logistics of transfer between these two regions.

7. Ibid., 11.
8. Ibid.
9. Ibid.
10. Ibid.
11. "Dr Nahum Goldmann speaks about rights of Jews in War Emergency Conference of World Jewish Congress," CriticalPast video, November 1944, 8:52, https://www.criticalpast.com/video/65675039008_Dr-Nahum-Goldmann_Emergency-Conference-of-Jewish-Congress_suggestions-by-Dr-N-Goldmann. See specifically from 6:00–6:40.
12. WJC, *War Emergency Conference*, 27.
13. Ibid., 28.
14. Ibid., 31.
15. Ibid.
16. This amendment was issued to reporters and promptly reproduced in pamphlet form alongside declarations detailing the punishment of war criminals, indemnification, the treatment of Jews from Axis countries, statelessness, and the future of Germany.
17. Notably, similar language was used to describe "ethnic" Poles leaving Lwów (ceded to the Ukrainian Soviet Socialist Republic) for Wrocław (ceded to Poland) after 1945. I thank Dariusz Stola for this reference.
18. The Emergency Committee for Zionist Affairs became the "American" Emergency Committee for Zionist Affairs after the United States declared war in December 1941.
19. "Meeting of the Office Committee of the AECZA," June 3, 1942, file no. C 5/3, WJC. On the American Jewish Committee, see Marshall, *American Jewish Committee*; Sanua, *Let Us Prove Strong*; N. Cohen, *Not Free to Desist*; Robin, *Pursuit of Equality*. On the Jewish Agency, see Kats, *Partner to Partition*. For a recent evaluation of Ben-Gurion's thoughts, see Shumsky, *Beyond the Nation-State*, 172–219.
20. "Meeting of the Office Committee of the AECZA," June 3, 1942.
21. Kolsky, *Jews against Zionism*; Kaufman, *Ambiguous Partnership*.
22. "Meeting of the Office Committee of the AECZA," June 5, 1942.
23. Ibid.
24. Goldmann, *Autobiography of Nahum Goldmann*, 221.
25. Ibid.
26. Ibid., 12.
27. Ibid., 20, 23.
28. Ibid., 78.
29. Ibid., 79.
30. Halpern, *Idea of the Jewish State*, 39–40.
31. On the American Jewish Committee, see N. Cohen, *Not Free to Desist*.

32. Bauer, *From Diplomacy to Resistance*, 241.

33. Hannah Arendt considers how "non-Zionists" in the American context had a "pronounced tendency towards [the] pro-Palestine view" by 1944. "Zionism Reconsidered," 368. For Arendt, American Jews had changed the course of pro-Palestine Zionism overall.

34. "Meeting of the Office Committee of the AECZA," December 25, 1942.

35. Ibid.

36. Ibid.

37. The rift that developed between Ben-Gurion and Weizmann between 1940 and 1942 stemmed, in part, from a demographic disagreement. Ben-Gurion wanted immediate emigration of the largest possible number of European Jews.

38. "Meeting of the Office Committee of the AECZA," December 25, 1942.

39. Ibid.

40. Ibid.

41. Ibid. I should also note the numerical difference from what Weizmann had enunciated a year prior in *Foreign Affairs* when he suggested that nearly two million Jews could be brought to Palestine from Europe after the war.

42. Adler-Rudel, "Chronicle of Rescue Efforts"; Bermuda Conference on Refugees, *Report of Proceedings*; Tartakower and Grossmann, *Jewish Refugee*.

43. In attendance were Harold Willis Dodds, a professor of politics and university president at Princeton, who chaired the American delegation, and Richard Law, the parliamentary undersecretary of state for foreign affairs, who served as his British counterpart. See the "Appendix" in *Reports of the World Jewish Congress*; Marrus, *Unwanted*, 284–86.

44. "The British Embassy to the Department of State," January 20, 1943, in United States Department of State, *Foreign Relations of the United States* (hereafter *FRUS*), no. 103.

45. In February 1943, a similar situation played out with regard to promises from the Mexican government. In principle, officials in Mexico City agreed to accept upward of "28,000 Polish refugees from the Middle Eastern Region." The United States government was "willing to make an order to facilitate the transportation and care of these Polish nationals" as well as offering money to the Polish government to help care for these refugees. "The Ambassador in the United Kingdom (Winant) to the Secretary of State," April 15, 1943, *FRUS*, no. 116.

46. "The Consul General at Hamilton (Beck) to the Secretary of State," April 21, 1943, *FRUS*, no. 124.

47. Ibid.

48. Accordingly, a colleague replied "that the area did not seem climatically well suited, that it was planned to send other refugee groups there, if possible, and that transport presented outstanding difficulties." "The Chargé in the United

Kingdom (Matthews) to the Secretary of State," February 20, 1943, *FRUS*, no. 104.

49. Engel, *Facing a Holocaust*, 71.

50. "The Consul General at Hamilton (Beck) to the Secretary of State," April 20, 1943, *FRUS*, no. 121.

51. "The Chargé in the United Kingdom (Bucknell) to the Secretary of State London," December 5, 1943, *FRUS*, no. 200.

52. Some decisions positively impacted refugees, such as the decision to create a fund for Spanish refugees, but the majority of decisions and indecisions negatively impacted the millions of displaced people in Europe and beyond.

53. Despite the intentions of one US congressman who believed "that the question of Polish-Jewish refugees in Russia should be brought up but not determined," a resolution did not ensue. "The Consul General at Hamilton (Beck) to the Secretary of State," *FRUS*, no. 117.

54. "Memorandum by President Roosevelt to the Secretary of State," May 14, 1943, *FRUS*, document no. 143. Roosevelt's reaction is even more revealing in light of research linking him to the so-called M-Project (M is thought to stand for migration), which began in July 1942 and studied options for postwar Jewish migration. On the M-Project, see Mazower, *No Enchanted Palace*, 104–49.

55. The Belgian, Czechoslovak, Greek, Luxemburg, Netherlands, Norwegian, Polish, Soviet, United Kingdom, United States, and Yugoslav governments wrote the declaration.

56. Significantly, no allowance was made for future border changes that could render, by way of example, a formerly Polish city as part of a shifting Ukraine.

57. For new data on the speed of the Jewish genocide, especially in Poland, see Stone, "Quantifying the Holocaust," who draws heavily on the careful research of Arad, *Bełżec, Sobibór, Treblinka*. In contrast, consider Christopher Browning's estimate that in March 1943, "about three quarters of all the Jews whom the Nazis and their accomplices would murder were still alive." Only eleven months later, "three fourths of the roughly six million victims of the Holocaust were dead." Browning, *Path to Genocide*, 169.

58. *Reports of the World Jewish Congress*.

59. On the IGCR, see Marrus, *Unwanted*, 285–86; Sjoberg, *Powers and the Persecuted*. On Leith Ross, see Marrus, *Unwanted*, 298–99.

60. Jessup, "UNRRA."

61. Stroop and Wirth, *Es gibt keinen jüdischen Wohnbezirk in Warschau mehr!*

62. In chap. 1, James McDonald noted in his diary how Weizmann's desire for emigrants to Palestine often trumped his concerns for the Jews of Europe.

63. "Meeting of the Office Committee of the AECZA," June 1, 1943. In April 1943, Weizmann thought that "two million Jews might survive when the fighting had ceased." Marrus, *Unwanted*, 290.

64. "Meeting of the Office Committee of the AECZA," June 1, 1943.

65. Ibid.
66. Ibid.
67. Ibid.
68. Ibid.
69. "The Secretary of State to the Ambassador in the United Kingdom (Winant)," June 25, 1943, *FRUS*, no. 155.
70. Less than one month before the agreement for UNRRA was signed by forty-four member countries, Winant cabled Hull to suggest on behalf of the Executive Committee of UNRRA that "in order to avoid overlapping with the IGCR, the proposed UNRRA should be responsible for maintenance of refugees in areas where it is operating, if it is prepared to undertake this task." "The Ambassador in the United Kingdom (Winant) to the Secretary of State," October 14, 1943, *FRUS*, no. 179. Once the UNRRA Conference got underway in Atlantic City in November 1943, Hull thought it "unadvisable for IGCR representatives to attend the Atlantic City Conference at this time." So, Myron Taylor of the IGCR did not.
71. For an overview of the foundations of UNRRA and the first meeting, see Shephard, *Long Road Home*, 50–55; Reinisch, "'Auntie UNRRA' at the Crossroads"; Reinisch, "Internationalism in Relief"; Reinisch, "We Shall Rebuild." For the official institutional history, see Woodbridge, *UNRRA*. Other helpful books include G. Cohen, *In War's Wake*; Humbert et al., *Outcast Europe*; Armstrong-Reid and Murray, *Armies of Peace*. For an overview of the International Refugee Organization, see Holborn, *International Refugee Organization*.
72. "Jewish Postwar Program Adopted by the Executive Committee," file no. A 1/8, WJC.
73. Ibid.
74. Ibid.
75. Ibid.
76. "Letter from Tartakower to Stańczyk," July 18, 1943, file no. H 272/10, WJC.
77. Ibid.
78. "Telegram from Tartakower to Kwapiński," October 1943, file no. H 291/6, WJC.
79. Frederick Fried and Hugo Perutz, "Aide Memoire of the WJC on the Occasion of the UNRRA Meeting in Atlantic City," November 5, 1943, file no. H 98/3, WJC.
80. Ibid.
81. "Jewish Postwar Program."
82. Ibid.
83. Ibid. Additionally, "it [was] clearly understood that the religious and the cultural rights of the Arab population in the Jewish commonwealth should be respected and guaranteed."

84. "United Nations Asked to Recognize Central Jewish Relief Body for Post War Aid," JTA, November 17, 1943.

85. Tartakower met with two members of the Polish delegation and with Jan Masaryk to persuade him to speak about the Jewish tragedy in his conference-wide remarks. Arieh Tartakower, "UNRRA and the Jewish Cause," file no. D 2/10, WJC.

86. Ibid.

87. "UNRRA Will Not Make Special Provisions for Treatment of Jewish War Victims," JTA, November 22, 1943.

88. "UNRRA Expected to Coordinate Work of Jewish Relief Agencies in Liberated Europe," JTA, November 28, 1943.

89. "UNRRA Will Do Everything Possible to Return Displaced Jews to Homelands," JTA, November 26, 1943.

90. Ibid.

91. Ibid.

92. "According to Article 10 of the Recommendations of the UNRRA Subcommittee on DPs, UNRRA will assist in the care of DPs who cannot or who are not willing to be repatriated until the IGCR is prepared to remove them to new places of settlement." See "Memo from Dr. Kubowitzski," December 21, 1943, file no. D 4/3, WJC.

93. Ibid.

94. "The Importance of the UNRRA," 1944, file no. B 139/4, WJC.

95. According to Ben Shephard, by 1943 the term *displaced person* was "now firmly established in the official lexicon." Shephard, *Long Road Home*, 52.

96. Arieh Tartakower, "Pod znakiem pomocy," *NT*, November 20, 1943, 1.

97. Jakob Apenszlak, "Projekt Kongresu," *NT*, November 20, 1943, 2, 7.

98. Jakob Apenszlak, "Sprawa Kongresu," *NT*, December 28, 1943.

99. Jakob Apenszlak, "Program of the World Conference of Polish Jewry," *NT*, January 23, 1945. He predicted that five hundred thousand could return.

100. Maurice Perlzweig, "Memo to the Office Committee," January 4, 1944, file no. A 71/2. It was unclear if Arieh Tartakower would be able to depart on time.

101. The American and World Jewish Congresses established the Institute of Jewish Affairs in February 1941 to study past and current Jewish experiences and make suggestions for the future of Jewry after World War II.

102. During committee deliberations, IGCR chair Sir George Rendel and UNRRA director-general Herbert Lehman disagreed over the administration of refugee relief and repatriation.

103. See Engel's coverage of Tartakower's time in London in early 1944, *Facing a Holocaust*, 103–39.

104. Arieh Tartakower, "Report on the Work Done during My Visit to Great Britain: January 6, 1944–March 15, 1944," file no. A1/4, WJC.

105. Ibid.

106. Ibid.

107. "Arieh Tartakower to the Executive Committee," February 14, 1944, file no. A 1/4, WJC.

108. At the same time that he met with ministry-level officials in the Polish government, Tartakower also worked with Nahum Goldmann (who by accident remained in England during the same term as Tartakower), Anselm Reiss (who worked as a representative of Polish Jewry in Palestine), and Ignacy Schwarzbart. See Engel on the establishment of Żegota and the foundation laid by Reiss and Tartakower, who were a "catalyst for the decision," *Facing a Holocaust*, 139.

109. "Arieh Tartakower to the Executive Committee," February 14, 1944.

110. "Arieh Tartakower to the Executive Committee," January 22, 1944, file no. A1 1/4, WJC.

111. Tartakower, "Report on the Work Done."

112. Ibid.

113. Ibid.

114. Ibid.

115. Arieh Tartakower, "W atmosferze londyńskiej," *NT*, March 30, 1944.

116. Ibid.

117. "Arieh Tartakower to the Executive Committee," February 14, 1944.

118. According to the "Office Committee Minutes" from February 1, 1944, Baruch Zuckerman had booked a meeting hall for May 7–11, 1944, for the War Emergency Conference. By March 8, the Office Committee was considering postponement. On March 21, Goldmann reported that the War Emergency Congress was set for May 20. On April 22, the conference was delayed indefinitely because the Palestinian delegation could not arrive on time. On August 7, the date of the Emergency Conference was set for November 11, 1944.

119. Arieh Tartakower, "Na froncie pomocy i odbudowy," *NT*, May 20, 1944, 4.

120. Malvina Tartakower, "Uchodźtwo w Rosji, Persii I Palestynie," *NT*, April 12, 1943.

121. Ibid.

122. "Address by Dr. Jacob Robinson," May 18, 1942, file no. A 67/1, WJC.

123. Arieh Tartakower, "Memorandum to the Office Committee," May 1, 1944, file no. D 2/9, WJC. At this meeting, Tartakower also handed over forty applications for UNRRA jobs.

124. Arieh Tartakower, "Letter to Major General GH Hilldring," November 13, 1944, file no. D 2/2, "Arieh Tartakower Correspondence and Memos, 1942–1946," WJC.

125. Arieh Tartakower, "Report on Conference with Mr. Earl Harrison," March 20, 1945, file no. D 11/2, WJC.

126. Arieh Tartakower, "Report on Conferences Held in London, July 26–Sept 2, 1945," file no. D 2/13, WJC.

127. "Memo Submitted to the First Session of the General Assembly of the United Nations, Nov 46," file no. B 139/19, WJC.

128. See Weissmann's "Suggested Draft for Memorandum to 'UNRRA'" dating from January 25, 1944, and arriving to Tartakower sometime in May 1944, file no. A 71/5, WJC.

129. Arieh Tartakower, "W dziejowej chwili," *Nasza Trybuna*, June 27, 1944, p. 1.

130. On refugees in Portugal more generally, see M. Kaplan, *Hitler's Jewish Refugees*.

131. Z. Segev, *The World Jewish Congress during the Holocaust*,146.

132. Ibid., 149.

133. Ibid., 152.

134. On children who were displaced or orphaned by war and their belonging, see Zahra, *Lost Children*; Taylor, *In the Children's Best Interests*; Grossmann, "Trauma, Memory, and Motherhood"; Baumel, "DPs, Mothers and Pioneers"; Douglas, *Orderly and Humane*, 229–53; Kadosh, "Heroic Acts and Missed Opportunities"; Kirsh, "Lost Children of Europe."

135. A. L. Kubowitzki, "Memo to the Office Committee," May 13, 1944, file no. A 71/5, WJC.

136. The number of Jewish refugees involved in this operation is unclear.

137. Ibid.

138. Ibid.

139. See the Office Committee Minutes from August 4, 1944, file no. A 71/2, for the accusation that the Jewish Joint Distribution Committee (JDC) "kidnapped" some of the children that the WJC moved from France to Lisbon.

140. Zohar Segev agrees that the JDC refused to participate in this operation because of the WJC's emphasis on Palestine. *The World Jewish Congress during the Holocaust*, 152. Segev cites another letter between Weissmann and Wise dating from April 22, 1944; see file no. H 293/3, WJC. Regardless, the WJC Office Committee did not issue their decision on Kubowitzki's initiative until May.

141. The reason for the delay is unclear. See "Office Committee Meeting," May 23, 1944, file no. A 71/2.

142. "Minutes of Office Committee Meeting," May 14, 1944, file no. A 71/2, WJC.

143. Z. Segev, 152.

144. "Minutes of Office Committee Meeting," July 6, 1944, file no. A 71/3, WJC.

145. "Minutes of Office Committee Meeting," May 30, 1944, file no. A 71/2, WJC.

146. John W. Pehle was named executive director of the War Refugee Board in February 1944. For more on Pehle, see his interview with Claude Lanzmann in the film *Shoah*. See also Penkower, "Jewish Organizations."

147. Arieh Tartakower, "Memo to the Office Committee," July 10, 1944, file no. H 272/10, WJC.

148. Ibid.

149. "Minutes of Office Committee Meeting," April 22, 1944, file no. A 71/2, WJC. All quotes in the next two paragraphs stem from this committee meeting as well.

150. "Minutes of Office Committee Meeting," May 30, 1944, file no. A 71/2, WJC.

151. "Minutes of Office Committee Meeting," June 30, 1944, file no. A 71/2, WJC.

152. "Meeting with Mikołajczyk on June 14, 1944," file no. A 71/2, WJC. According to figures assembled by Polish intelligence associations in London, ninety thousand Polish Jews remained in ghettos, hundreds of thousands of Jews were living in small towns and villages, and between eight hundred thousand and one million Polish Jews remained in Poland overall. Finally, the four men considered the Polish Jewish refugees in the Soviet Union.

153. Ibid.

154. "Executive Committee Discussion on the Policy Statement of the German Jewish Representative Committee," June 8, 1944, File #A 71/3, WJC.

155. Executive Committee Discussion on the Policy Statement.

156. For the postponement of the original meeting, see "Minutes of Office Committee Meeting," April 25, 1944, file no. A 71/2, WJC.

157. Ibid.

158. "Executive Committee Discussion on the Policy Statement of the German Jewish Representative Committee," June 8, 1944, file no. A 71/3, WJC.

159. It is possible that Perlzweig had the Versailles Treaty in mind. Jews in Germany would have to share any reparations burden after the Second World War. I thank Dariusz Stola for raising this possibility.

160. Ibid.

161. Ibid.

162. Ibid.

163. Ibid.

164. Ibid.

165. Goldmann, *Autobiography of Nahum Goldmann*, 215.

166. "Executive Committee Discussion on the Policy Statement." Notably, Zygielbojm used the word *współmierny* in his suicide letter when he criticized the Polish government-in-exile for responding in a "commensurate" way to the Jewish tragedy. I thank Dariusz Stola for this reference.

167. Ibid.

168. Ibid.

169. Ibid.
170. Ibid.
171. Ibid.
172. Ibid.
173. "Special Office Committee Meeting on June 30, 1944," file no. A 71/2, WJC. See Robinson et al., *Minorities Treaties.*
174. "Special Office Committee Meeting on June 30, 1944."
175. Ibid.
176. Ibid.
177. Ibid.
178. Ibid.
179. Ibid.
180. For background on this second meeting and Canada's role in UNRRA, see Armstrong-Reid and Murray, *Armies of Peace.*
181. G. Cohen briefly covers Warhaftig's activities and cites this book. *In War's Wake,* 197.
182. Warhaftig, *Refugee and Survivor,* 289.
183. *Reminiscences of Maurice Perlzweig,* 536. He continued, "We don't believe in reality unless it hits us in the face."
184. Warhaftig, *Refugee and Survivor,* 19.
185. On the initial weeks of flight, see Adler and Aleksiun, "Seeking Relative Safety."
186. His family's journey across the Pacific began on June 4, 1941, just a few weeks before Hitler's invasion of the Soviet Union. Unable to secure a visa to the United States like her husband, Naomi settled for a Canadian visa and spent eight months between 1941 and 1942 living alone in Montreal with their young son before moving to the United States.
187. "Minutes of Office Committee Meeting," April 18, 1944, file no. A 71/2, WJC.
188. Warhaftig and Fischoff, *Relief and Rehabilitation,* 64. Warhaftig suggested that UNRRA codes adopt the year 1933 as the beginning of the "war" so that Jews who had experienced discrimination or expulsion from Germany, Austria, and even Czechoslovakia before September 1, 1939, could qualify for UNRRA aid. Ibid., 110. Warhaftig was also concerned about stateless Jews or Jews with domiciles that did not match their official citizenship. Ibid., 125.
189. Ibid., 116. Quoting letters exchanged between Kubowitzki and Tartakower and between Sir George Rendel and Director-General Lehman—both members of the Subcommittee on Policies with Respect to DPs—Warhaftig recounted how WJC officials worked to clarify the position of those stateless and enemy-national Jews scattered throughout Europe.
190. Ibid., 129.

191. Ibid., 116.
192. Ibid., 147.
193. Ibid., 135.
194. Ibid., 153.
195. Ibid., 154.
196. Ibid.
197. Ibid., 140.
198. "WJC Office Committee Meeting," August 24, 1944, file no. A 72/3, WJC; "Jews for UNRRA Sought," *New York Times,* September 9, 1944. This article quoted an announcement saying that the book would be sent to all delegates on September 15, the day the meetings were supposed to begin. On September 16, 1944, the *Washington Post* reported that the meeting had been delayed because of an East Coast hurricane.
199. "WJC Office Committee Meeting," August 24, 1944, file no. A 72/3, WJC.
200. Warhaftig and Fischoff, *Relief and Rehabilitation,* 255.
201. Porter, "Dutch Oppose Aid to Italy by UNRRA," *New York Times,* September 22, 1944.
202. Porter, "Aid to Expatriates by UNRRA Is Voted," *New York Times,* September 24, 1944.
203. "The Jewish Groups Voice Hope over UNRRA Activities," *New York Times,* September 30, 1944.
204. Arieh Tartakower et al., "Report on the Activities of the WJC Delegation on the Second Session of the Council of UNRRA in Montreal," file no. A 71/2, WJC.
205. Ibid.
206. Porter, "UNRRA Will Spend a Billion in 1945," *New York Times,* September 21, 1944.
207. Ibid.
208. Porter, "Help for Jews Proposes Acheson," *New York Times,* September 28, 1944.
209. Tartakower et al., "Report on the Activities."
210. Ibid.
211. Ibid.
212. Ibid.
213. Ibid.
214. "War Emergency Congress Proceedings," file no. A 67/2, WJC, 462–67, especially 466. An interesting discussion ensued when this language was proposed. A few debated whether Palestine should be referred to as the "only place" where children would be sent. The "ideal place" was Palestine, but the delegates left out the words "only place" to ensure that children would be rehabilitated even if they could not get to Palestine.

215. Ibid., 32.

216. Ibid., 28.

217. Ibid., 31.

218. It would also support the Jewish Agency for Palestine, help reestablish in liberated countries "organized Jewish communit[ies] on democratic lines and affiliated with the WJC," and work with the United Nations to provide evidence of Nazi atrocities and guidance on Jewish themes. Ibid.

219. "Schwarzbart and Reiss at the Meeting of Polish Jews in New York," *NT,* December 21, 1944, 8.

220. "Jochanan Tartakower Fell in Battle," *NT,* October 23, 1944.

221. Arieh Tartakower, "The Conference of World Jewry," *NT,* November 18, 1944, 1.

222. "HaTikvah," or "The Hope," was a song strongly affiliated with the World Zionist Organization and the Zionist movement.

223. World Jewish Congress, "War Emergency Congress," 123.

224. Ibid., 497.

4. UNCERTAIN CITIZENSHIP

1. Wisława Szymborska, "The End and the Beginning."

2. Besides millions of Germans, consider that 1,500,000 Poles lived in areas annexed to the Soviet Union in 1939, roughly 500,000 Ukrainians lived in postwar Polish territory, and 140,000 Ukrainians were resettled in Poland in 1947, along with almost 90,000 Slovaks and 70,000 Hungarians. See Zahra, *Lost Children,* 175.

3. For Jews who wanted to stay (and did stay) in Poland, see Auerbach, *House at Ujazdowskie 16;* Shore, *Caviar and Ashes;* Schatz, *Generation;* Kijek, "Aliens"; Kijek, "Reichenbach/Rychbach/Dzierżoniów." For a comparison with Slovakia, see Cichopek-Gajraj, *Beyond Violence.* For Jews who did not necessarily want to go to or stay in Palestine after World War II, see Yehudai, *Leaving Zion;* Patt, *Finding Home and Homeland;* Grodzinsky, *In the Shadow.*

4. Jan Tomasz Gross notes that "we must seek the reasons for the novel, virulent quality of postwar anti-semitism in Poland not in collective hallucinations nor in prewar attitudes, but in actual experiences acquired during the war years." *Fear,* 246. Bryant quotes reports stating that postwar antisemitism was stronger than in interwar Czechoslovakia as well. *Prague in Black,* 225. For a comparative look at violence and the antisemitic overtones it did or did not have, see Cichopek-Gajraj, *Beyond Violence,* 114–45. More on antisemitism, violence, and postwar pograms will be said in the next chapter.

5. Cichopek-Gajraj, *Beyond Violence,* 145.

6. On the process by which displaced persons and Jews in particular gathered in camps throughout Germany and Austria, see Person, "I Am a Jewish

DP"; Person, *Dipisi*; Grossmann, *Jews, Germans, and Allies*; G. Cohen, *In War's Wake*, 126–50; Kochavi, *Post-Holocaust Politics*, 157–93; Grodzinsky, *In the Shadow*; Patt, *Finding Home and Homeland*; Mankowitz, *Life between Memory and Hope*; Crago-Schneider, "Jewish 'Shtetls' in Postwar Germany." Recall that expelled Germans from Poland, Czechoslovakia, Hungary, and elsewhere were also filtering into occupied Germany and made up 16.5 percent of the West German population in 1950. See Bryant, *Prague in Black*, 207.

7. "Document #8386/III/2/45, Letter to the Soviet Ambassador to the Czechoslovak Republic," Londýnský Archiv-Důvěrný, Karton No. 185, AMZV. Some of his luggage was (at least temporarily) lost.

8. The current and former president was not, however, the first government official to reach his liberated state. For instance, the official Czechoslovak government delegate on liberated territory, František Němec (1898–1963), spent a handful of months in Subcarpathian Rus', the easternmost part of the First Czechoslovak Republic, beginning in 1944. By returning with two well-known communist politicians, Beneš sent an explicit message about the postwar Czechoslovak government.

9. "Návrat pana presidenta republiky do Prahy středu 16. Května 1945," Oddíl III, KPR/1, P1/1, "Navrat do Prahy," ÚTGM. According to the same source, the Ministry of Information announced the train route in advance on the radio and in newspapers so citizens along the route could decorate their homes.

10. Prague's streets had been cleaned in preparation for this parade. Remnants of the Prague Uprising, a three-day urban battle to rid the city of her Nazi occupiers, were removed by city officials. This was no small task, as nearly seventeen hundred Czech urban combatants and almost one thousand German soldiers fell on the city streets during the fighting from May 5 to 8, 1945.

11. On Beneš's arrival and for useful background on the so-called Košice Program that followed him, see Bryant, *Prague in Black*, 254–56.

12. *United Nations Conference on International Organization* and Janowsky, "The Human Rights Issue at the San Francisco Conference."

13. This rift between the Polish government-in-exile (the London Poles) and the Soviet Union began in earnest with the discovery (by Nazi forces) of a mass grave of Polish military officers near Katyń in April 1943. This finding led to an international investigation, Polish accusations toward the Soviets for the crime, and, eventually, the severing of diplomatic ties between the Polish government-in-exile and the Soviet Union. Lukas, *Strange Allies*. Most importantly, this point marked the beginning of political preparations for the establishment of the Soviet-backed Polish governmental apparatus under the guise of the State National Council (Krajowa Rada Narodowa) in Warsaw in 1943. In July 1944, the Krajowa Rada Narodowa established the Polish Committee of National Liberation, which, later that year, was transformed into a provisional government

of the Republic of Poland. In January 1945, Czechoslovakia quickly recognized this government as the "official" government of Poland. The Americans and the British supported the London Poles a few more months until summer 1945. At that point, the prime-minister-in-exile, Stanisław Mikołajczyk, joined a "new" government, called the Provisional Government of National Unity (Tymczasowy Rząd Jedności Narodowej), alongside communist and socialist members (many of whom spent the war in the Soviet Union) of the former provisional government. The British and the Americans revoked their recognition of the Polish government-in-exile at that time. For a short overview of diplomatic consequences of the existence of divided Polish governments, see Polonsky, *Great Powers*; Karski, *Great Powers and Poland*; Harper and Parlin, *Polish Question*; Kersten, Micgiel, and Bernhard, *Establishment of Communist Rule*; Porter, *Poland in the Modern World*, 144–86; Applebaum, *Iron Curtain*, chaps. 4 and 6. In works already cited in this book, see coverage of the topic in Shore, *Caviar and Ashes*, 194–257; Wandycz, *Czechoslovak-Polish Confederation*; Engel, *Facing a Holocaust*.

14. "Report of the Czechoslovak Press Bureau," October 23, 1942, file no. H 29/2, WJC. See chap. 1 of Láníček, *Czechs, Slovaks and the Jews*, for more on the Czech government-in-exile, radio broadcasts, and the BBC. Láníček mentioned this broadcast but dated it to 1943, not 1942.

15. "Masaryk's Speech at Royal Albert Hall, London," October 29, 1942, file no. H 98/5, WJC.

16. J. Masaryk, *Minorities and the Democratic State*, 7.

17. Ibid., 7.

18. Masaryk referred to the support directed toward Henlein's party in the Sudetenland.

19. J. Masaryk, *Minorities and the Democratic State*, 19.

20. Thus, those who opted for German citizenship in the Reich "ceased to be citizens of their former states," and "governments of the liberated countries are, therefore, entitled to decide for themselves whom among the Germans they will restore citizenship." Those German nationals who wished to prove themselves good citizens of Czechoslovakia could apply for their citizenship to be reinstated. Ibid.

21. Ibid., 20.

22. "The Atlantic City Conference of UNRRA," original pamphlet produced by the British Section of the WJC with editing, Londýnský Archiv-Důvěrný, box no. 33, AMZV.

23. Ibid.

24. Ibid.

25. Josef Hanc, "Report on UNRRA Meeting in Atlantic City," Londýnský Archiv-Důvěrný, box no. 33, AMZV. Hanc served as a diplomat in the Czechoslovak Foreign Service and as a lecturer at the Fletcher School of Law and

Diplomacy at Tufts University during the war, and he wrote in journals and the *New York Times* on Czechoslovak themes. For his published wartime writings see, *Tornado across Europe, Eastern Europe and the United States* and "Czechs and Slovaks since Munich."

26. Hanc, "Report on UNRRA Meeting."

27. "Letter from Ripka to Procházka," January 25, 1944, Londýnský Archiv-Důvěrný, box no. 33, AMZV.

28. Ibid.

29. "Letter from Procházka to Ripka," January 26, 1944, Londýnský Archiv-Důvěrný, box no. 33, AMZV.

30. Wachsman, *Jan Masaryk*, 16.

31. Ibid., 15.

32. "Memo to the Office Committee from Dr. Perlzweig," May 16, 1944, file no. H 98/3, WJC. Additionally, Perlzweig noted that "it would be impossible for Masaryk to say anything of value if more than two of us were present." Láníček references this meeting in *Czechs, Slovaks and the Jews*, 116–37.

33. "Memo to the Office Committee from Dr. Perlzweig."

34. Ibid.

35. J. Masaryk, *Volá Londýn*, 261.

36. Ibid., 261.

37. Ibid., 262. See also Láníček, *Czechs, Slovaks and the Jews*, 31.

38. J. Masaryk, *Volá Londýn*, 262.

39. Ibid., 263.

40. Čapková, "Between Expulsion and Rescue"; Bryant, *Prague in Black*, 248–49; Staněk, "Němečtí židé v Československu," 42–46. On German(-speaking Jews) in Poland, see Cichopek-Gajraj, *Beyond Violence*, 152–65.

41. Weis, *Problem of Statelessness*, 3.

42. Ibid. Weis offered a clarification in terminology: "In this paper nationality is used in the Anglo-American sense to denote membership in a state and not in the sense used in Central Europe, where it denotes belonging to a nation."

43. Ibid., 36.

44. Ibid.

45. For biographical information, see Jackson, "Editorial Paul Weis." For a broader postwar overview of the issues in this pamphlet, see Weis, *Nationality and Statelessness*. Weis was connected to the International Refugee Organization and was a legal advisor to the United Nations High Commissioner for Refugees in Geneva. He also wrote as "Paul Weis."

46. Weis, *Problem of Statelessness*, pamphlet published by the British Section of the WJC: 1945, pp 3, Box 440, Londýnský Archiv [London Archive], Archive of the Ministry of Foreign Affairs, Czech Republic, 4.

47. Ibid., 19.

48. Ibid., 21–22.

49. Ibid., 22.
50. Ibid., 23.
51. Ibid.
52. Ibid.
53. Ibid., 24.
54. Letter from Maurice Perlzweig to Jan Masaryk, July 12, 1945, file no. H 98/3, WJC.
55. "Memorandum from M. L. Perlzweig to Jan Masaryk," July 13, 1945, file no. H 98/3, WJC.
56. Ibid.
57. Marrus, *Unwanted*, 311. At this time, nearly 2.75 million Soviet nationals were transferred according to a separate agreement.
58. Ibid.
59. See also a contemporary article, Pinson, "Jewish Life in Liberated Germany."
60. Arieh Tartakower, "San Francisco and Polish Jewry," *NT*, March 28, 1946. "A community of three and a quarter million persons, eight or nine tenths of which were starved to death or killed by the Germans, this is a unique event in the history of Jewish martyrology."
61. Arieh Tartakower, "A Great Challenge," *NT*, May 30, 1945.
62. Arieh Tartakower, "Report on Conference with Mr. Earl Harrison," file no. D 11/2, WJC.
63. Ibid. Reflecting on this meeting, Tartakower exuded positivity. The impression Harrison made on both parties was "favorable." In fact, Tartakower concluded with an optimistic statement: "Much can be expected from him in the future, if our contact with him will remain close enough."
64. Kochavi, *Post-Holocaust Politics*, 134–56.
65. Gerard Cohen states that following the Harrison Report, the "statelessness of Jews was finally recognized by Allied relief policies and United Nations agencies." *In War's Wake*, 129.
66. "Report of Earl G. Harrison," United States National Archive, August 3, 1945, https://www.docsteach.org/documents/document/harrison-report-concerning-conditions-displaced-persons-post-ww2.
67. Harry S Truman, *Public Papers of the Presidents of the United States*, 153.
68. "Fraternity Honors Dean," *New York Times*, May 3, 1946.
69. Hoffmann, "Germans into Allies," 66.
70. Zaremba, "'War' Syndrome," 61. For an expansion of the ideas in this article, see Zaremba, *Wielka trwoga*.
71. Tartakower, "Great Challenge."
72. Arieh Tartakower, "International Relief," *NT*, June 30, 1945.
73. Ibid.

74. Ibid.

75. "Minutes of Office Committee Meeting," September 25, 1945, file no. A 73/2, WJC.

76. G. Cohen, *In War's Wake*, 132–34.

77. Arieh Tartakower, "The Problem of Displaced Jews," *NT*, August 31, 1945.

78. S. Cohen, "Choosing a Heim"; Bockley, "Historical Overview of Refugee Legislation"; Kochavi, "Britain and the Illegal Immigration."

79. Arieh Tartakower, "Pierwsze spotkanie z przybyłymi z Polski wysłannicy Żydów," *NT*, August 31, 1945.

80. Ibid. See Aleksiun, *Dokąd dalej?*, 142–67, on this meeting and the organizational efforts related to *bricha* that stemmed from it.

81. Tartakower, "Pierwsze spotkanie."

82. Ibid. The language is "Tu uwewnętrznia się przekonanie, że najlepszym i najdogodniejszym rozwiązaniem kwestji Żydów polskich byłoby rychłe przeniesienie ich, możliwie wszystkich, do Palestyny."

83. Pinson writes that "the fiercest and most fanatical demonstration of the denial of the diaspora was the refusal of the camp committees to allow orphaned Jewish children to be evacuated to more adequately equipped homes in Britain and France." "Jewish Life in Liberated Germany," 116.

84. Warhaftig's appointed job was to distribute relief in any way possible and make connections between this American Jewish organization and the survivors remaining in occupied Germany.

85. Zorach Warhaftig, "'Jews in the Camps in Germany and Austria': Reports Based on Observations Made during a Trip, October 12–November 27, 1945," file no. C 129, WJC.

86. The only major voice to oppose this trend, Warhaftig noted, was Dr. Schwartz of the JDC, who wanted Jews to remain in German camps because then they would fall under UNRRA's purview financially.

87. When Warhaftig spoke with him, "Ben-Gurion stated that he would oppose any movement of Jews from the camps for temporary stays in any country. The concentration of Jewish DPs in Germany, especially in the American zone of occupation creates a difficult and pressing problem for the U.S. and this may be used in the fight for the opening of the gates of Palestine," Warhaftig, "'Jews in the Camps in Germany and Austria.'"

88. Ibid.

89. The American zone in Germany hosted the highest number of Jewish DPs at forty-five thousand. Roughly one-third of the DPs were prewar refugees from Germany and Austria.

90. Note that upward of fifty thousand Jews were in France by 1947, and thirty thousand Jews were in Belgium. Most of them were of Polish origin. Weinberg, *Recovering a Voice*.

91. One Polish man whom Warhaftig met had already changed homes five or six times since the war ended. This man identified threats from the local population, overall insecurity, and psychological reasons behind his drifting. Warhaftig, "Jews in the Camps."

92. Bryant notes the degree of "unprecedented violence" used during the "wild" expulsion of the Germans in Czechoslovakia. *Prague in Black*, 211. This was especially notable because occupied Bohemia and Moravia had been relatively peaceful compared to Poland.

93. David Gerlach pushes against the usage of the word *wild* to explain this part of the expulsion, as he sees it as sporadic yet specific instead. *Economy of Ethnic Cleansing*, 27–65.

94. Warhaftig, "Jews in the Camps."

95. Alternatively, Warhaftig notes that the higher authorities in Poland had some "negative" views, but Warhaftig could not envision them stopping this movement before the planned upcoming elections—notably, these elections were eventually delayed until January 1947, with a three-question referendum proceeding them by six months in July 1946. The three-question referendum (notably) coincided with the Kielce pogrom. Ibid.

96. Warhaftig, "Jews in the Camps."

97. Arieh Tartakower to Jacob Robinson, "Jewish Stateless Aliens," April 1945, file no. C 92/9, WJC.

98. "Nine Months of the WJC Actvities (Oct 1, 1945–June 30, 1946)," F 5/7, WJC.

99. Ignacy Schwarzbart, "Report on the Visit to the American Zone in Germany/Diary of the Trip," file no. H 276/1, WJC.

100. "Did the Anglo-American Commission promise the immigration of hundreds of thousands of Jews to Palestine? What will happen to the Polish Jews who were sent to Russia? What is the attitude of the members of the former Polish London government to the anti-Jewish pogroms in Poland and what did the Jewish Congress do in this respect? Does the Jewish Congress know that several thousand Jews have been arrested in Berlin? What did the Jewish Congress do to give the people here professional training?" Ibid.

101. Ibid.

102. Ibid.

103. Pinson, "Jewish Life in Liberated Germany," 115.

104. "Conversation between Rosenberg and Easterman," July 3, 1945, file no. H 98/3, WJC. Láníček references this conversation in *Arnošt Frischer*, 162. For a more theoretical discussion of loyalty among Czechoslovak Jews, see Láníček, "What Did It Mean?"

105. Zahra, *Lost Children*, 148. Zahra cites Marrus, *Unwanted*, 313–17, and Judt, *Postwar*, 22.

106. On the "wild expulsion," which was "wildest" from mid-May to late July, see Glassheim, *Cleansing the Czechoslovak Borderlands*, 42–66; Bryant, *Prague in Black*, 230–40; Douglas, *Orderly and Humane*, 93–129.

107. On the council or the Rada židovských náboženských obcí v zemích české a moravskoslezské, see Láníček, *Arnošt Frischer*, 147–50.

108. For background on the Jews who lived in Subcarpathian Rus', see Segal, *Genocide in the Carpathians*.

109. Personal correspondence and conversations between the author and Martin Weiss.

110. I found a document bearing his name in the files of the Czechoslovak Repatriation Commission, but the dates did not make sense. Marty smiled when I told him this and explained why: At some point, a few years after the war, another brother who survived the war in the Soviet labor-camp system returned to Czechoslovakia in the 1950s. Since his brother had a criminal record for illegal political activity in the 1930s, he had used Marty's name on all official documentation.

111. In May 1945, for instance, those remaining in Terezín concentration camp were quarantined for typhus, and yet a steady stream of survivors trickled back to Prague while exit was "officially" denied. I thank Lisa Peschel for clarifying this for me.

112. Yehudai, "Displaced in the National Home," 77. Yehudai counts four hundred returning to Greece, six hundred returning to Poland, one thousand returning to Czechoslovakia (mostly in April 1946), and five hundred returning to Austria. This is much lower than perceived estimates in British circles of thirty-five thousand that wanted to be repatriated.

113. Arthur Opsal, "Report from the Czechoslovak Repatriation Mission in Katowice," October 25, 1945, file no. 304–215-13, ABS.

114. Zahra reminds us the *odsun* required a concomitant campaign to resettle at least two million Czechs in the homes and businesses that Germans had once occupied. *Lost Children*, 174–75. Some of those Czechs came from within interwar Czechoslovak territory, some were "ethnic" Czechs living elsewhere as far away as Volhynia, and some were displaced themselves. Gerlach notes that forced population transfers coexisted with smaller groups of new settlers who sometimes left for new homes on their own volition. See Gerlach, *Economy of Ethnic Cleansing*, 1–2.

115. Opsal, "Report."

116. On the Košice government, see Vartíková, *Košický vládny program*. On the National Front, see K. Kaplan, *Národní fronta, 1948–1960*; Vošahlíková, *Československá sociální demokracie a Národní fronta*; Frommer, "Retribution as Legitimation." For coverage of the "Action Committees" of the National Front, which emerged after February 1948, see Connelly, *Captive University*.

117. For minutes of the meetings, see the Klement Gottwald Archive 1261/3, Karton No. 137, Národní Archiv, Prague, Czech Republic. Some of the meeting minutes are hard to decipher, and at least one meeting is not accounted for in the preserved materials. The parties included (in English) the Communist Party of Czechoslovakia (KSČ), the Communist Party of Slovakia (KSS; formed in 1939), the Czechoslovak Social Democratic Party (CSDP), the Czechoslovak National Socialist Party (CNSP; national-liberal, petty bourgeoisie, no connection to the German Nazis), the Czechoslovak People's Party (CPP; a Catholic group) and the (Slovak) Democratic Party.

118. Glassheim, *Cleansing the Czechoslovak Borderlands*, 44. See also Glassheim, "National Mythologies and Ethnic Cleansing." The Ministry of the Interior was controlled by the Communist Party.

119. "Meeting Minutes from the 22nd Meeting of the Government on May 25, 1945," 1261/3, Karton No. 137, Národní Archiv.

120. Bryant, "Either German or Czech," 698.

121. "Meeting Minutes from the 38th Meeting of the Government on July 10, 1945," 1261/3, Karton No. 137, Národní Archiv.

122. On this decree, see Zahra, *Lost Children*, 182.

123. On the Czechoslovak plans to expel the Hungarian minority, see Stola, "Forced Migrations."

124. On Magyar(-speaking) Jews in Slovakia, see Cichopek-Gajraj, *Beyond Violence*, 165–78.

125. On national committees in Czechoslovakia after World War I, see Connelly, *From Peoples into Nations*, 338.

126. Eagle Glassheim notes that in some towns a "wild west atmosphere reigned." The "national committees were the only authority locally" and "relied on self-proclaimed former partisans to maintain order," *Cleansing the Czechoslovak Borderlands*, 44. On the role that national committees played in postwar trials and retribution, see Frommer, *National Cleansing*, 46–49.

127. "The Agreement between Czechoslovakia and the Soviet Union Regarding Subcarpathian Rus," file no. 425–233-6, ABS. Fierlinger had also received confirmation from Stalin that the Soviets would interfere if the Czechoslovaks expelled Sudeten Germans. Frank, "Reconstructing the Nation-State," 32.

128. "Úprava československého státního občanství podle dekretu č. 33/145," Mězinárodní Odbory, 1945–1949, box no. 158, AMZV.

129. Ibid.

130. Láníček (*Arnošt Frischer*, 153) writes about the August legislation as well.

131. There is a possibility that the George Weiss quoted here and later in this chapter was also known as Jiří Weiss. Jiří Weiss was the well-known filmmaker of the movie about Subcarpathian Rus described at the beginning of this section. He was born in Prague, lived in England during the Second World War, made

films there on behalf of the Czechoslovak government-in-exile, returned to Czechoslovak territory in 1945, and came from (at least partially) a German-speaking, Czechoslovak family.

132. Láníček, *Arnošt Frischer*, 85.

133. "Letter from Weiss to Frischer," November 28, 1945, file no. 425–230-7, ABS.

134. Ibid.

135. Ibid.

136. Ibid. Recall that in chap. 2, World Jewish Congress officials raised this issue with Beneš in the early 1940s.

137. Ibid.

138. Arnošt Frischer, "The Jewish Position in Czechoslovakia," file no. H 100/2, WJC.

139. Ibid. One significant injustice detailed in Frischer's report occurred in Ústí Nad Labem when German-speaking Jews (presumably identified as German nationals on the 1930 census) had to wear a "white armlet."

140. Ibid.

141. Ibid.

142. Ibid.

143. Ibid.

144. Paul Reiner, "Memo: Re: Confirmation of Czechoslovakian Citizenship to Jewish Persons," 1945, file no. H 100/7, WJC.

145. Ibid.

146. Ibid.

147. On the chaotic postwar conditions in Liberec, see Frommer, *National Cleansing*, 49–52. Regarding postwar Jewish life in Czechoslovakia more generally, see Brod, "Židé v poválečném Československu"; Cramsey, "Saying Kaddish in Czechoslovakia."

148. "Memo on the Conversation with Councilor Werner," February 4, 1946, file no. 425–192-75, ABS.

149. Gerlach, *Economy of Ethnic Cleansing*, 10–18.

150. See Glassheim, *Cleansing the Czechoslovak Borderlands*, 60–66, on the organization of the *odsun* from the standpoint of the Allied Military Authorities and the national committees. Taking a broader look, Zahra reads the *odsun* as the "final and most decisive battle in a war that dragged on for more than 50 years" between nationalists and those who felt "nationally indifferent." *Kidnapped Souls*, 258. On the organized part of the *odsun*, as opposed to the "wild" part, see Bryant, *Prague in Black*, 240–52.

151. Glassheim, *Cleansing the Czechoslovak Borderlands*, 62.

152. "Memo on the Conversation with Councilor Werner." On the interplay between local government officials on national committees, local economic influencers, and expulsion policies, see Gerlach, *Economy of Ethnic Cleansing*, 65–103. He covers events in Liberec at multiple junctures.

153. "Memo on the Conversation with Councilor Werner." See Gerlach, "Beyond Expulsion," on language casting Jews as unproductive in the postwar borderlands; Gerlach, "Working with the Enemy," for more on economic tensions during the expulsion; and Frommer, "Expulsion or Integration," on romantic and personal tensions during the expulsion.

154. "Memo on the Conversation with Councilor Werner."

155. In addition to granting citizenship, these committees had the purview to allocate apartments to, in Macháček's determination, "nationally reliable persons of Slav nationality" ibid.

156. Ibid. Zahra, *The Great Departure*, 233. Some German-speaking Czechoslovak Jews were forcibly expelled as Germans from May 1945 to September 1946, ibid.

157. "Informace o opčním právu obyvatelů Zakarüatské (sic) Ukrajiny," March 11, 1946, file no. 425–233-02, ABS.

158. Ibid. The Interior Ministry also issued vague instructions regarding the status of "nationally entangled families." See Zahra, *Lost Children*, 188.

159. Arnošt Frischer, "Report on Meeting with Jan Masaryk," March 18, 1946, file no. 425–231-1, ABS.

160. Ibid.

161. Ibid.

162. Ibid.

163. Ibid.

164. "Letter from Tartakower to Irwing Dwork, in response to your inquiry of March 15, 1946," file no. H 99/17, WJC.

165. Ibid.

166. Francis T. Williamson, "Undated Letter," file no. H 99/17, WJC.

167. "Zápis o schůzi představenstva Rady židovských náboženských obcí v zemích České a Moravskoležské (RZNO)," March 24, 1946, file no. 425–233-6, ABS.

168. Ibid.

169. Ibid.

170. "Zápis o schůzi představenstva RZNO," April 10, 1946, file no. 425–233-6, ABS.

171. On the difficulty that Jews, especially German-speaking Jews, had in restituting their property, see Gerlach, *Economy of Ethnic Cleansing*, 214–22. For coverage on property issues in Slovakia, see Cichopek-Gajraj, *Beyond Violence*, 90–113. For a broader look at Jewish property issues, see Martin Dean, Goschler, and Ther, *Robbery and Restitution*; Robinson, "Report on Stolen Jewish Property by the Chairman of the WJC Department of Compensations," file no. 303/XIII/190, Centralny Komitet Żydow w Polsce: Wydział Repatriacji, Archiwum Żydowskiego Instytutu Historycznego, Warsaw, Poland (hereafter CKŻP: WR).

172. "Memo Dated March 26, 1946," file no. H 99/17, WJC.

173. Ibid.

174. "Memo to Wise and Perlzweig Dated from April 2, 1946," file no. H 99/17, WJC.

175. "Anonymous Memo Dating from May 12, 1946," file no. H 100/7, WJC.

176. Ibid.

177. Frommer, *National Cleansing*, 32. On the events that brought the Communists to power in Czechoslovakia, see Bryant, *Prague in Black*, 259–65; Connelly, *Captive University*; K. Kaplan, *Short March*; Kovály, *Under a Cruel Star*.

178. Interior Minister Nosek declared the organized *odsun* complete on October 24, 1946. See Frommer, *National Cleansing*, 264.

179. Decree S-3559/89-17/9-46, file no. 425–192-74, ABS. Zahra (*Kidnapped Souls*, 257), Gerlach (*Economy of Ethnic Cleansing*, 217–18), and Cichopek-Gajraj (*Beyond Violence*, 168–69) cover this decree as well.

180. Decree S-3559/89-17/9-46, file no. 425–192-74, ABS.

181. Ibid. Láníček, *Arnošt Frischer*, 156.

182. Decree S-3559/89-17/9-46. Moreover, "the results of these investigations should be submitted referring to this decree to the Ministry of the Interior which reserves the right to decide the individual cases whether the person of Jewish origin or German or Hungarian nationality were Germanizing or Hungarianizing in sense of this decree."

183. Jacobmeyer, "Displaced Persons Problem."

184. Weis, "International Protection of Refugees," 196.

185. "Memo Submitted to the First Session of the General Assembly of the United Nations, November 1946," file no. B 139/19, WJC. We learn that Kubowitzki wrote this memo because on December 9, 1946, he received a letter from the secretary-general of the United Nations in response to this memo; see "Letter from U.N. Secretary General to Kubowitzski," file no. B 139/19, WJC.

186. UN General Assembly, Resolution 62 (1).

187. Weis, "International Protection of Refugees," 221. Weis went on to help Jacob and Nehemiah Robinson and Louis Henkin formulate the terms of the 1951 Refugee Convention. Kurz, *Jewish Internationalism*, 2.

188. In March 1946, for instance, Warhaftig observed that the recently established Anglo-American Committee of Inquiry on Palestine reported that the current repatriation of 391,000 Jewish refugees and DPs was of a "provisional character only" and a larger number "hope they may be able to quit Europe forever." Warhaftig, "Where Shall They Go?" file no. C129/7, WJC.

189. Warhaftig, "Where Shall They Go?"

190. Ibid.

191. The positive discrimination could materialize in various forms: more calories, separate camps, more protection under UN law, and so on.

192. "Resolution on Refugees and DPs," MO #205, Archiv MZV.

193. Consider that on April 15, 1946, Czechoslovak delegate Karel Lisický stated that his government "was not greatly concerned with the refugee problem. It was, however, extremely interested in ensuring that no assistance be given to persons of German origin who had been or would be transferred to Germany." "Resolution on Refugees and DPs," MO no. 205, AMZV.

194. "Matters of Jewish Interest at the First Meeting of the UNO in London (January–February 1946)," in "Problems of Refugees and Displaced Persons, April 1946," file no. B 139/19, WJC.

195. Ibid.

196. Ibid.

197. G. Cohen draws extensively on the archives of the IRO his book on DPs who remained displaced from late 1946 onward, whom he terms the "last million." *In War's Wake*, 8–9, 143–47.

198. *Constitution of the International Refugee Organization*, art. 2, sec. 1, b. iii, and annex II, 1, respectively.

5. UPROOTED

1. Zuckerman, *Surplus of Memory*, 676.

2. Ibid., 676.

3. On the Central Committee of Polish Jews as well as other Jewish institutions in postwar Poland, see Engel, "Reconstruction of Jewish Communal Institutions"; Dobroszycki, "Restoring Jewish Life."

4. Aleksiun, "Situation of Jews in Poland."

5. Zuckerman, *Surplus of Memory*, 678.

6. Ibid., 655.

7. Ibid., 656.

8. As opposed to the Ukrainian and Belarusian nationals who possessed interwar Polish citizenship and survived the war on Soviet territory (including the part of interwar Poland annexed by the Soviet Union as part of the Molotov-Ribbentrop Pact in 1939), Polish Jews and Polish Christians across Soviet spaces were classified as "Polish citizens" and entitled to sponsored repatriation. For more on numbers, consider Stankowski and Weiser, "Demograficzne skutki Holokaustu"; Edele et al., "Saved by Stalin?." As Dariusz Stola has argued, we still do not know how many Polish citizens survived World War II and the Holocaust in the Soviet Union. Not all of them registered with authorities or repatriated officially in 1946, and we can assume that a significant number settled in the USSR for good. Some returned in later repatriations between 1956 and 1958.

9. On the complicated and contingent process by which repatriation plans materialized and then unfolded, see Litvak, "Polish-Jewish Refugees," 230–34; Nesselrodt, *Dem Holocaust entkommen*, 246–58; Kaganovitch, "Stalin's Great Power Politics"; Shlomi, "Jewish Organizing Committee in Moscow"; Sula,

"Z ZSRR na Dolny Śląsk," 580–82. On the repatriation of Polish citizens more generally, see Jolluck, *Exile and Identity*, 279–86; Sword, *Deportation and Exile*, 174–99; Kersten, *Repatriacja ludności polskiej*; Bugaj, *Dzieci polskie w ZSRR i ich repatriacja*; Głowacki, *Ocalić i repatriować*; Engel, *Between Liberation and Flight*, 120–24, 156–57.

10. Meng, *Shattered Spaces*, 60–110, on Warsaw particularly.

11. On the "early" *bricha* movements, consider Zuckerman, *Surplus of Memory*, 654–59; Bauer, *Flight and Rescue*, 3–111.

12. See Bauer, *Flight and Rescue*, 113–51 for Poland and 152–90 in "transit countries." He covers this movement, the so-called Great Exodus, in *Flight and Rescue*, 206–40.

13. Bauer covers the *shlihim* and their organization and work extensively in *Flight and Rescue*.

14. Redlich, *Life in Transit*; Kenney, *Rebuilding Poland*; Kaminski, *Polacy wobec nowej rzeczywistosci*; Kersten, *Establishment of Communist Rule*; Shore, *Caviar and Ashes*; Shore, "Children of the Revolution."

15. For more on British lobbying, responses, and opinions regarding the emigration of Jews away from Poland and east central Europe more generally, see Kochavi, *Post-Holocaust Politics*, 157–74.

16. Especially in the past decade, rich contributions have profiled this group from a variety of vantage points. See Zessin-Jurek and Friedla, *Syberiada Żydów polskich*, which includes more than six hundred pages of original articles and translated articles into Polish; Edele, Fitzpatrick, and Grossmann, *Shelter from the Holocaust*; Nesselrodt, *Dem Holocaust entkommen*; Adler, *Survival on the Margins*; Belsky, "Encounters in the East"; Jockusch and Lewinsky, "Paradise Lost?"; Grossmann, "Remapping Relief and Rescue." An older work to consider is Litvak, *Jewish Refugees from Poland*. Besides Jolluck and Sword in an earlier footnote, see Żaroń, *Ludność polska w związku radzieckim*, for the experience of Polish citizens more generally. For the evacuation of Soviet citizens, including some Polish Jews who took Soviet citizenship, see Manley, *To the Tashkent Station*. According to numbers provided by Laura Jockusch and Tamar Lewinsky, "only about 350,000 of the prewar Polish Jewish population of 3.3 million survived the Second World War. Thirty to fifty thousand of these were liberated in the territory of the prewar Polish state, and an additional seventy to eighty thousand were freed from camps in Germany and Austria. Some 230,000 or more Polish Jews survived in the Soviet Union, and of these an estimated 180,000 opted for repatriation immediately after the war's end—possibly some 200,000 by late 1946." Jockusch and Lewinsky, "Paradise Lost?," 374.

17. Between 720,000 and 780,000 Polish citizens were forcibly resettled by the Soviets between 1939 and 1941. See Gurjanow, "Cztery deportacje 1940–41;" Siemaszko, "Mass Deportations." Eliyana R. Adler and Natalia Aleksiun estimate that "300,000 Jews fled the areas recently occupied by the Germans for those now under

Soviet control" in 1939. "Seeking Relative Safety," 41. See also Adler, "Hrubieszów at the Crossroads." On refugees to the newly occupied territories more generally, see Gross, "Sovietization of Western Ukraine"; Gross, "Jewish Community"; Jolluck, *Exile and Identity*, 1–36; Levin, "Fateful Decision"; Litvak, "Plight of Refugees"; Siekierski, "Jews in Soviet-Occupied Eastern Poland," 110–13. On the children's experience in the Soviet-occupied parts of Poland, see Grudzińska-Gross and Gross, *War through Children's Eyes*; Michlic, "What Does a Child Remember?"

18. See Sword, *Deportation and Exile*, 28–60, on the Sikorski-Maisky Pact of 1941 and the "Amnesty" for Poles.

19. See the "Registry of the Union of Warsaw Jews in Szczecin" from 1946 in "Sprawozdania sytuacyjne miasto Szczecin 1946–1947," Nr. Wol No. 915, Karton 2, Wydzial repatriacji, State Archives in Szczecin, Szczecin, Poland (hereafter SAS). Oral testimonies are housed at the Shoah Foundation, the Fortunoff Video Archive, the Jewish Holocaust Center in Melbourne, Yad Vashem, the United States Holocaust Memorial Museum, and the Jewish Historical Institute in Warsaw. Published testimonies from this group of children include those in *Fun letstn khurbn (From the Latest Destruction)*; *Dzieci oskarżają (The Children Accuse)*; Tenenbaum, *'Ehad me-'ir u-shenayim mi-mishpahah (One from a City and Two from a Family)*; Grynberg, *Children of Zion*. On Polish deportees in Osz and Kyrgyzstan more generally, see Głowacki, *Obywatele polscy w Kirgizji*.

20. Seventy-seven thousand children under eighteen, or nearly one-third of all the Polish repatriates, returned to Polish soil by mid-1946. Boćkowski, "Repatriacja dzieci polskich," 102. See Korzon, "Przesiedlona ludność polska w ZSRR," 4–7, for his numbers regarding the 202,332 Polish repatriates (Jews and non-Jews) and the 52,332 children up to the age of sixteen that constituted 26 percent of this group.

21. The families that were created during this time and place were not necessarily biological. For more on this point, see Aleksiun, "On Jews in Hiding."

22. Notably, Adler and Aleksiun explore how family relations impacted "the decision to flee and early experiences under Soviet occupation." "Seeking Relative Safety," 42. See Redlich, *Life in Transit*, on the ideological differences between Zionists (151–80) and "Others" (181–202).

23. I thank Dariusz Stola for this clarification. The Union of Polish Patriots (Związek Patriotów Polskich or ZPP) purported to represent "all" Polish citizens in the Soviet Union after the breakdown of relations between the Soviet Union and the Polish government-in-exile in the spring of 1943. Led by communist-leaning Poles (of both Jewish and non-Jewish backgrounds), it was allied with the Soviet government, distributed aid, collected information from more than a hundred individual ZPP branches, and, later, helped organize the mass repatriation in 1946. See Nesselrodt, *Dem Holocaust entkommen*, 229–70; Sword, *Deportation and Exile*, 113–42.

24. Jakob Apenszlak coined the term *Jewish Polishness* in early July 1946 to represent a unique aspect of the intellectual milieu in the interwar Second Polish Republic, an aspect that was Polish in a decidedly Jewish way. Steffen, *Jüdische Polonität*. I return to this concept of Jewish Polishness later in this chapter.

25. On average, Jews tended to represent around 40 percent of each branch of the ZPP, but this percentage could vary widely. According to the ZPP central records, by the fall of 1943 there were 223,806 formerly Polish citizens registered with the ZPP; 51 percent considered themselves to be ethnically Polish, 44 percent ethnically Jewish, and 5 percent ethnically Ukrainian or Belarusian.

26. "Sprawozdanie," Sygnatura No. 80, "Położenie ludności polskiej i działalność ZPP w obwodzie Czekałowie, 1944–1946," The Union of Polish Patriots Collection (Związek Patriotów Polskich or ZPP) at the Archiwum Akt Nowych, Warsaw, Poland (hereafter AAN).

27. "Sprawozdanie," Sygnatura No. 174, "Położenie ludności polskiej i działalność ZPP w Turkiestanie, 1945–1946," ZPP.

28. The publicity for the event was published in Russian. "Wstrząsająca tragedja Żydowstwa Polskiego," Sygnatura No. 172, ZPP.

29. Libionka and Weinbaum, "Deconstructing Memory and History"; Slucki, "Struggle Unparalleled in Human History." On this type of national narrative building more generally, see Corney, *Telling October*.

30. For more on the socialist dynamic, consider Bolesław Drobner's plans for Jews in postwar Poland. In an article entitled "A Serious Problem" that he submitted to the ZPP's newspaper *Wolna Polska* in November 1943, Drobner hoped that those who looked for work would be helped and the "returning Polish Jews" would be seen as "workers rather than apprentices." "Sprawa żydowska: Notatki historyczne. Poz. 634/e1.SP," Sygn. No. 421/II-2, Bolesław Drobner Collection, AAN. I thank Laurie Koloski for this reference. On Drobner, see Kunakhovich, "Kultury powojenne"; Koloski, "Painting Kraków Red."

31. When her subjective interviewer asked why she went back to Poland, Jenny Balsam repeated, "Why?" with a slight look of disbelief. "Why I was born there! I wanted to go back and find my family!" The videotaped testimony of Jenny Balsam, USC Shoah Foundation Institute, file no. 16041, June 5, 1996.

32. Arieh Tartakower, "A Great Challenge," *NT*, May 30, 1945.

33. Anglo-American Committee of Inquiry, "Anglo-American Committee of Inquiry Report," April 1946, app. 2, point no. 21. On the work of this committee and their report, see Kochavi, *Post-Holocaust Politics*, 170–74; Moses, "Epilogue," 260.

34. For an excavation of individual agency during this period, see Krzyżanowski, *Ghost Citizens*.

35. "Repatriacja," Sygn. No. 303/VII/5, CKŻP: WR.

36. Ibid.

37. Ibid.

38. On the civil power struggle in postwar Poland, see Polonsky and Drukier, *Beginnings of Communist Rule*; Naimark and Gibianskiĭ, *Establishment of Communist Regimes*; Thum, *Uprooted*; Brzezinski, *Soviet Bloc*; Shore, *Caviar and Ashes*; Engel, "Patterns of Anti-Jewish Violence"; Schatz, *Generation*, especially 209–18. On the role of the Secret Police in consolidating control (Soviet and otherwise) in the region, see Applebaum, *Iron Curtain* and Pucci, "A Revolution in a Revolution."

39. When dealing with displaced person populations and (largely) undocumented movement such as this, accurate numbers prove difficult to determine. The highest estimates count that 170,000 Polish Jews passed through Czechoslovakia on their way to the US zones in Germany and Austria and that 130,000 Polish Jewish transmigrants traveled through Náchod or its vicinity in 1946 alone. Numbers preserved in Czechoslovakian Interior Ministry archives are a bit more judicious. The numbers of Polish Jews who registered at Náchod's Repatriation Office are 4,037 in June, 8,079 in July, 13,290 in August, and 11,935 from September to December. Not all Polish Jews who passed through Náchod registered with the repatriation department there.

40. Gerard Cohen offers a precise evaluation of the word *refugee* overall and how its meaning changed especially in 1946. *In War's Wake*, 35–57.

41. Count František Schönborn, "Report of September 1945," file no. 425-230-8, ABS.

42. Ibid. See also: Friedl, "'Palestine Must Be the Ultimate Goal.'"

43. Cichopek-Gajraj, *Beyond Violence*, 146.

44. Ibid., 147.

45. "Repatriation Report," P44/8, Edvard Beneš, Collection II (EBII), ÚTGM. Good general overviews of Polish repatriation remains Kersten, *Repatriacja ludności polskiej*; Czerniakiewicz, *Repatriacja ludności polskiej z ZSRR*.

46. Schönborn, "Report of September 1945."

47. Ibid.

48. Ibid.

49. "Conversation with Jan Masaryk on July 3, 1945," file no. H 98/3, WJC.

50. "Letter from Wolski to Keith," October 11, 1945, Sygnatura No. 456, Generalny Pełnomocnik Rządu do Spraw Repatriacji, AAN (hereafter GPRSR). At this point, the US Embassy in Warsaw was housed at Hotel Polonia.

51. "Statement of Plans for the Care of Polish Children in Allied or Neutral Countries," undated (before October 1945), Sygnatura No. 456, GPRSR. According to a report sent from Poland to Palestine in March 1946, "1,200 children live with non-Jewish families; between 1,500–2,000 children live in various convents." Redlich, *Life in Transit*, 62.

52. "Meeting to Discuss the Return of Polish DPs from the British, American and French Zones," September 10, 1945, Sygnatura No. 456, GPRSR. By this time, 282,000 displaced people with pre–World War II Polish citizenship had pooled into the US zone in Germany. For a contemporary description of this see Proudfoot, "The Anglo-American Displaced Persons Program for Germany and Austria."

53. Redlich, *Life in Transit*, 229. Violence against Jews also peaked in February and July 1946. Engel, "Patterns of Anti-Jewish Violence," 2. In contrast, Engel notices "peaks" in deaths of "government officials and supporters killed by illegal organizations" between February and May 1945, between February and May 1946, and between September and October 1946. Ibid., 21. Helpful on the immediate return of Polish Jews are Aleksiun, "Returning from the Land"; Aleksiun, "Where Was There a Future?"; Szaynok, "Bund i Komuniści żydowscy"; Stefaniak, "Nielegalna emigracja Żydów."

54. McDonald, *Refugees and Rescue*, and McDonald, *To the Gates of Jerusalem*, cover this period in his career.

55. "UNRRA Chief in Germany Slurs Polish Jews," JTA, January 3, 1946.

56. Ibid.

57. Shlomi, "Jewish Organizing Committee in Moscow."

58. "Report of 'Grajscomorska' to Chief of the Department of the Border," January 23, 1946, Meldunek Międzylesie, NR. 48/47II 274/47, Archiwum Straży Granicznej [Archive of Border Guard], Szczecin, Poland. The name "Grajscomorska" could also refer to a place and not a person. It does not necessarily sound like a Polish name. I thank Dariusz Stola and Michał Grochowski for noticing this.

59. Benedikt Stein, "Proceeding of the Meeting Which Took Place on Feb. 1 at 11 AM, Office of the Government Committee on Matters Related to the Polish Citizens of Jewish Background (Vyzn.n. Židovsk.ho)," February 2, 1946, file no. 425–231-2, ABS. In Czech, the ministries are as follows: Ministerstvo Zahraničních Věcí, Ministerstvo Vnitra, and Ministerstvo Zdravotnictví. The Jewish Joint Distribution Committee is a worldwide Jewish relief organization founded in 1914.

60. Ibid.

61. Ibid.

62. Ibid.

63. Note that this new category was slightly different from the UN classification pertaining to "displaced people who do not want to return to their prewar homes and thus desired to be settled elsewhere."

64. File no. 302–163-5, ABS. Elfan Rees did not spell his last name "Riese." For a postwar discussion of his views, see Rees, *Century of the Homeless Man*.

65. Letter "To the Kierownika Sekcji Operacyjnej" (Head of Sectional Operations), February 18, 1946, Meldunek Międzylesie, nr 48/47, II 274/47, Archiwum Straży Granicznej.

66. "Wewelsburg Camp Opens on January 25," January 12, 1946, Sygnatura No. 339, GPRSR.

67. "Order/Memorandum Displaced Person to Military Government 1 Corps District to . . . UNRRA District Headquarters and Polish Liaison Mission," January 25, 1946, Sygnatura No. 339, GPRSR.

68. Person, "'I Am a Jewish DP"; Person, *Dipisi*.

69. "Crum Recommends Immediate Evacuation," JTA, February 12, 1946.

70. Ibid.

71. "Mrs. Roosevelt Reports on Tragedy of Displaced Jews," JTA, February 21, 1946.

72. Ibid.

73. "Central Jewish Bodies Submit Joint Memorandum to UNRRA," JTA, March 20, 1946.

74. "The Central Committee of the UNRRA Will Act Friday," JTA, March 14, 1946. The JTA reported that Lehman had not been well since the death of his son, Lt. Peter Lehman, in a plane crash over England in 1944.

75. Arieh Tartakower, "Memorandum to the Office Committee," March 21, 1946, file no. H 273/13, WJC.

76. Dr. Ludwik Rajchman served as the second leading officer of the Polish delegation and did not necessarily agree with Stańczyk. Rajchman would later be instrumental in the creation of UNICEF.

77. Tartakower, "Memorandum to the Office Committee." On the category of converted Jews and the "remainder" that conversion leaves behind, see Seidman, *Faithful Renderings*, 143.

78. Tartakower, "Memorandum to the Office Committee."

79. Rajchmann, "Letter on the Fourth Session of UNRRA," April 12, 1946, Sygnatura No. 425, GPRSR.

80. "German Operations Report for April, Part 1, Appendix B," June 1, 1946, Sygnatura No. 425, GPRSR.

81. Report, "Informace pro pane minister," March 1, 1946, file no. 304–257-6, ABS.

82. Ibid.

83. Ibid. Eleven Jewish refugees from Poland were detained in Náchod during the week prior to this report.

84. Recall that the mass resettlement of the Poles (and other non-Ukrainian, non-Belarusian, non-Russian people) from the territories ceded to the USSR started in the second half of 1944 and reached its peak in the second half of 1945.

85. "List of Transports to Tarnów," undated (must be at least the end of 1946), Sygn. No. 303/V/54, CKŻP: WR.

86. "Wykaz transportów przybyłych za czas repatriacji (in Katowice)," August 31, 1946, Sygn. No. 303/V/34, CKŻP: WR.

87. "Un-named report," undated (must be from after June 26, 1945), Sygn. No. 303/V/6, CKŻP: WR.

88. Jewish Community of Chełm, "Telegram to the Central Jewish Committee of Poland," and "Reply of the Central Jewish Committee to Chełm" (only the second document has a semilegible date), March 2, 1946, Sygn. No. 303/V/29, CKŻP: WR.

89. "Protokól from the Head of the Jewish Committee in Kraków," March 28, 1946, Sygn. No. 303/V/37, CKŻP: WR.

90. "Protokól walnego zebrania dla spraw repatriacji z dn. 31.3.1946," April 1, 1946, Sygn. No. 303/V/27, CKŻP: WR.

91. Berman and Zelicki, "Cable to WJC," May 14, 1946, file no. H 276/13, WJC. The Polish Jewish authorities requested "immediate help, money, clothes and food" from the WJC Executive Committee.

92. Zelicki and Falk, "Letter to Head of the Jewish Committee in Wrocław," August 9, 1946, Sygn. No. 303/V/63 CKŻP: WR.

93. "Sprawozdania sytuacyjne miasto Szczecin 1946–1947," Nr. Wol No. 915, Karton 2, Wydział Repatriacji, SAS. See Musekamp, *Zwischen Stettin und Szczecin*; Service, *Germans to Poles*; Karch, *Nation and Loyalty* on Silesis and Stettin/Szczecin more generally.

94. Cichopek-Gajraj, *Beyond Violence*, 147. On German Jews on Polish territory, see ibid., 152–65. See also Čapková, "Germans or Jews?"

95. Kersten, "Kształtowanie stosunków ludnościowych," 104.

96. Wörn, "Jews in Szczecin." Wörn discusses the insufficient preparations for Jewish return to the Recovered Territories on 61–63, work on 70–76, and emigration away from Poland (where he quotes mainly from Bauer) on 81–83.

97. "Sprawozdania sytuacyjne miasto Szczecin 1946–1947," Nr. Wol No. 915, Karton 2, Wydział Repatriacji, SAS.

98. *Tygodnik Informacyjny*, July 10, 1946, 1.

99. Engel discusses this in *Between Liberation and Flight*, 124–25, as does Aleksiun in *Dokąd dalej?*, 107–27. More recently, Redlich has synthesized these three scholars and provided his own gloss in *Life in Transit*, 151–77.

100. Bauer seems to think it happened quickly, even instantaneously. "There was a basic readiness to leave the country," he writes, and "the majority of repatriants [*sic*] were content to sit on their suitcases waiting for a legal way to leave Poland." Bauer, *Flight and Rescue*, 126. Redlich is more cautious: "There was a tendency among Polish Jews, both those returning to their prewar locales and those settling in other towns and cities, to try to rebuild their lives in Poland." *Life in Transit*, 152. As Aleksiun shows, Zionist-leaning groups provided more than infrastructure and financial help; the party experience and the kibbutz

provided familial-like structures. *Dokąd dalej?*, 125–42. Finally, Engel suggests that anti-Jewish violence influenced the timing of departure. *Between Liberation and Flight*, 148–50.

101. According to Engel, "The attraction of the Palestinian option appears to have lain most likely not in any *a priori* conception of Palestine as the Jewish national homeland or outright rejection of continued Jewish existence in the diaspora, nor does it seem to have been located in the intrinsic appeal of life in that country." Instead, "Palestine represented for them an alternative, a possibility for escape from a present that they perceived as immediately threatening." "Palestine in the Mind," 234.

102. Datner-Śpiewak,"Instytucje opieki nad dzieckiem i szkoły."

103. Jakub Schwalbendorf, "Notes from the Repatriation Clerk," *Tygodnik Informacyjny*, July 10, 1946, 12.

104. Ibid.

105. *Tygodnik Informacyjny*, July 10, 1946, 13.

106. Jan Kaniewski, "Letter to Mr. Wolski in the Ministry of the Recovered Territories," May 1946, "Ref Ogólny: Korespondencje w sprawie osadnictwa Żydów, 1946," in "Żydowska Kongregacja Wyznaniowa 1946–48," SAS.

107. A. Chorzewski, "Letter to Wydział społeczno-politycznego," July 1946, "Ref Ogólny: Korespondencje w sprawie osadnictwa Żydów, 1946," in "Żydowska Kongregacja Wyznaniowa 1946–48," SAS.

108. On Bein, see Schneider, "Behind the Iron Curtain."

109. *Tygodnik Informacyjny*, July 28, 1946, 2.

110. "Chorzewski to Minister of Recovered Territories," June 17, 1946, "Żydowska Kongregacja Wyznaniowa 1946–48," SAS.

111. "Memo Re: *Odsun* of People of Jewish Descent, Who Were Also Polish State Citizens," April 18, 1946, file no. 304–257-1, ABS.

112. "Rifkind Report Recommending Transfer of Jewish DPs to Palestine," JTA, April 8, 1946, 2–3.

113. "Lehman Wants Immediate Transfer of 100,000 Jews to Palestine Says Situation Is Tense," JTA, May 15, 1946.

114. "General Morgan Says 100,000 Displaced Jews Could Be Transported to Palestine in One Month," JTA, April 10, 1946. Kochavi covers this in *Post-Holocaust Politics*, 163–64.

115. Ibid.

116. Patt, "Stateless Citizens of Israel," 169.

117. "James McDonald Calls for Prompt Admission of 100,000 Displaced Jews to Palestine," JTA, May 15, 1946.

118. "Crum Says Truman Should Order Army to Plan Transfer of 100,000 Jews to Palestine," JTA, May 17, 1946.

119. Arieh Tartakower, "The Report of the Palestine Inquiry Commission," *NT*, April 30, 1946.

120. "Jewish Agency Memorandum Says $45,000,000 May Be Needed to Transport, Resettle 100,000," JTA, July 5, 1946. About $8 million to $10 million would be needed for transportation; $15 million to $20 million for maintenance, medical care, rehabilitation, and training; and $12 million to $15 million for immediate clothing and minimum household utensils and furniture.

121. "1,000 Palestine Visas Assigned to Children in Germany, Austria, Czechoslovakia and France," JTA, April 9, 1946.

122. "Office Committee Index Jan–June 1946," file no. A 73/6, WJC. See in this index "Reports, correspondence regarding Poland."

123. "Army Will Leave Borders of US Zone in Germany Open to Jewish Refugees from East," JTA, June 14, 1946.

124. Around this time, June 1946, the American journalist I. F. Stone traveled to Europe and "joined" the *bricha*. In the book that details his journey to postwar Europe, his journey within Europe, and his journey from Europe toward Palestine, he often masks the names of geographic locations and important people. It seems that he was in Náchod (what he calls "Anton") before moving toward Slovakia, *Underground to Palestine:* 25–46.

125. Arieh Tartakower, "Pod adresem angielsko amerykanskiej komisji," *NT,* January 31, 1946.

126. Jakob Apenszlak, "Będą w Polsce," *NT,* January 31, 1946.

127. Ibid.

128. Jakob Apenszlak, "A Link with Polish Jewry," *NT,* June 30, 1946.

129. Ibid.

130. Arieh Tartakower, "Pomozmy repatriantom!," *NT,* May 31, 1946. For an exception to this line of argumentation, see Arieh Tartakower, "Bilans Polsko-Żydowski w Londynie," *NT,* September 29, 1945.

131. Samuel Margoshes, "What I Saw in Poland," *NT,* April 30, 1946.

132. Ibid.

133. Jakob Apenszlak, "The Gates of Palestine," *NT,* July 31, 1945.

134. Apenszlak, cited in Steffen, "'Żydowska polskość' jako koncepcja tożsamości," 141.

135. "Short Minutes of the Office Committee Meeting," September 17, 1946, file no. A 74/1, "Office Committee, Minutes with Index Jul–Dec 1944," WJC.

136. On the June Referendum, see Mikołajczyk, *Rape of Poland,* 167–185; Applebaum, *Iron Curtain,* 311–317 covers the Referendum as well as the six months between it and the parliamentary elections in January 1947, and Paczkowski, Andrzej, *Referendum Z 30 Czerwca, 1946 R.*

137. The Kielce pogrom occurred on the heels of a controversial referendum and should be linked to this moment in Polish postwar political history. Michlic, *Poland's Threatening Other,* 227. Also helpful on this point are Cała, *Image of the Jew*; Tokarska-Bakir, "'Classmates; in Klimontów."

138. Zuckerman, *Surplus of Memory,* 660. Bauer cites Zuckerman's telling in *Flight and Rescue,* 208–9.

139. Zuckerman, *Surplus of Memory,* 660.

140. Ibid.

141. Ibid, 661.

142. Ibid.

143. Ibid.

144. On the Kielce pogrom itself, see Meducki and Wrona, *Antyżydowskie wydarzenia kieleckie*; Szaynok and Kersten, *Pogrom Żydów w Kielcach.*

145. Joel Cang, "Pogrom Begun by Rumour, Kielce," *Manchester Guardian,* July 6, 1946.

146. Redlich talks about rumors in Łódź in *Life in Transit,* 79, 80. See also Cichopek-Gajraj, *Beyond Violence,* 114–46.

147. Cang, "Pogrom Begun by Rumour."

148. Ibid.

149. Ibid.

150. Zuckerman, *Surplus of Memory,* 663.

151. Ibid., 662.

152. Ibid., 663.

153. Joel Cang, "Danger to Jews Still Growing in Poland," *Manchester Guardian,* July 17, 1946.

154. Redlich, *Life in Transit,* 62. See also Engel, "Patterns of Anti-Jewish Violence," 35; Gross, "In the Aftermath."

155. Zuckerman, *Surplus of Memory,* 670.

156. Ibid. On anti-Jewish violence after Kielce, see Gross, *Fear,* 81–166; Gutman, *Jews in Poland,* 34–39; Gross, *Upiorna dekada,* 94–95; Chodakiewicz, *After the Holocaust,* 221.

157. "A Message from the Central Committee of Polish Jews," *Tygodnik Informacyjny,* August 20, 1946, 1.

158. Ibid.

159. Zuckerman, *Surplus of Memory,* 664.

160. Ibid., 665.

161. Ibid., 667.

162. Ibid.

163. Zuckerman and his team designed this "repatriation" stamp, and he claims to have brought one of these stamps to Israel and left it in his museum at the Ghetto Fighter's Kibbutz. Zuckerman, *Surplus of Memory,* 669.

164. Rudawski, *Mój obcy kraj?*

165. Zuckerman, *Surplus of Memory,* 672.

166. Ibid.

167. In Bauer's assessment, the complicated situation in Poland by August 1946 "points to a definite Russian policy." *Flight and Rescue,* 223. Zuckerman references a "long conversation" he had with Bauer about the beginnings of the *bricha,* but Bauer ignored Zuckerman's thoughts. *Surplus of Memory,* 654.

168. Ibid., 671.

169. Cang, "Danger to Jews Still Growing."

170. Ibid.

171. Zuckerman, *Surplus of Memory,* 669; Litvak, "American Joint Distribution Committee," 285.

172. "La Guardia Hopes Britain Will Admit 100,000 to Palestine," JTA, July 11, 1946.

173. Bauer uses Jacobson's report extensively. See *Flight and Rescue,* 216–19. Bauer isolated Jacobson as "the person responsible" for "assuring the safe passage of Jewish refugees through Europe." *Out of the Ashes,* 107. For Israel Jacobson's full report, see Israel Jacobson, "Report," file no. 425–192-75, ABS.

174. Bauer, *Flight and Rescue,* 227–40, on Náchod in the summer of 1946.

175. The organized violence against Jews was partially fueled by the radio broadcasts of the recently appointed archbishop of Warsaw and Cardinal August Hlond. See Thum, *Uprooted,* 46–49.

176. Jacobson, "Report." Kochavi (*Post-Holocaust Politics,* 187–88) and Bauer (*Flight and Rescue,* 216–17) cover Gibbons's visit.

177. Jacobson, "Report."

178. Ibid.

179. Ibid.

180. Israel Jacobson, "Letter to Nejedlý," July 24, 1946, file no. 425–192-75, ABS.

181. Ibid.

182. Jacobson, "Report." A regularly scheduled train left Náchod with six hundred Jewish passengers each night. At 6:30 the next morning, the train arrived in Devínska Nová Ves, Slovakia, where children and luggage were loaded into automobiles and the adults walked on foot to Marchegg across the border in Austria. There, the group waited again for a train to Vienna and stayed in four buildings. Later, they left in the direction of Munich. The Repatriation Center in Náchod was in the hills just east of the town square where a senior citizen home remains today (the so-called Masarykův Dům). Ladislav Khan, "Z našeho Náchoda do zaslíbené země" [From our Náchod to the beloved land], *Svet Práce,* November 26, 1946. On Vienna, see Anthony, "Return of Concentration Camp Survivors."

183. Jacobson, "Report."

184. Arnošt Frischer, "Letter to Allan Strock," July 22, 1946, file no. 425–233-04, ABS.

185. Náchod resident Rudolf Beck, who helped organize the relief on the ground, writes on the back of a picture in his personal archive that the Czechoslovak government "financed this effort with the agreement of the Soviet Union, namely by providing vehicles and issuing travel documents." See Personal Archive of Rudolf Beck, Náchod, Czech Republic.

186. Frischer, "Letter to Allan Strock."

187. During his time in Prague, Sharp also traveled to the Zionist regional conference in Luhacovice and represented the WJC at the reopening of the Jewish Museum in Prague. Sharp was moved to the Paris office in September 1946. "Short Minutes of the Office Committee, Wednesday September 11, 1946," file no. A 74/1, "Office Committee, Minutes with Index Jul–Dec 1944," WJC. For more on Kubowitzki's disappointment with Sharp's attitude, see "Kubowitzski Letter to Sharp," November 14, 1946, file no. H 97/12, WJC.

188. Samuel Sharp, "Letter to Kubowitzski," July 12, 1946, file no. H 274/3, WJC.

189. In advance of a meeting convened to unify "American Jewry for a common action concerning the Jews in Poland," the Office Committee decided that the WJC delegation to the event would "act in the role of observer" and not make any firm commitments. "Short Minutes of Office Committee Meeting, Monday July 15, 1946," in "Office Committee, Minutes with Index, July–Sep 1946," file no. A 74/1, WJC.

190. Sharp, "Letter to Kubowitzski."

191. "Short Minutes of Office Committee Meeting, Monday July 15, 1946," in "Office Committee, Minutes with Index, July–Sep 1946," file no. A 74/1, WJC.

192. Samuel Sharp, "Undated Report," probably before August 15, 1946, file no. H 97/12, WJC. In the report, Sharp notes that his friend is scheduled to come to Prague on August 15, 1946, so the report must have been written before that. One thousand Czech korona equals twenty dollars in mid-1946.

193. Ibid.

194. Jacobson, "Report." In interviews included in the 2003 documentary *Between a Star and Crescent: Bricha (Mezi hvězdou a půlměsícem: Bricha)*, Jacobson and his wife note Toman's instrumental role in the Náchod operation.

195. Jacobson, "Report."

196. Ibid. These refugees "would be paid prevailing wage rates," and a plan to employ Polish workers in the former Sudetenland would be "considered."

197. Ibid.

198. Ibid. According to Bauer, *Flight and Rescue*, 219, "In the end, UNRRA paid only $250,000 for the expenses borne by the Czechs. This sum was apparently paid at the end of September 1946, while the actual expenses came to

52,406,750 crowns up to that date (or about $1,048,000). As far as is known the Czechs were never reimbursed for the rest of the sums expended."

199. On September 13, 1946, Edward M. Warburg, chairman of the American JDC, stated that sixty thousand Polish Jews had taken to the road during the last three months in flight from the antisemitic outbreaks in Poland: "The Czechoslovakian Government has provided generous aid, including reception centers and transportation through their country." "Statement by Edward M. Warburg," September 13, 1946, file no. 425–192-74, ABS. On July 19, a press conference was held in the JDC office at which the press of the United States, England, and a number of other countries were represented. Israel Jacobson issued a statement highly praising Czechoslovak ministries. "Press Conference at JDC Office," July 19, 1946, file no. 425–192-74, ABS.

200. "Letter from the Prague Jewish Community to Rudolf Beck," July 15, 1946, Personal Archive of Rudolf Beck, Náchod, Czech Republic.

201. Ibid.

202. Samuel Sharp, "Telegram to Kubowitzski," July 21, 1946, file no. H 274/3, WJC. Sharp visited Náchod in July 1946 and noted that the average flow of six to seven hundred Polish Jews met with no difficulties in Czechoslovakia. See Sharp's reports in file no. H 97/12, WJC.

203. "Czech Refugee Camp for 4,000 Set Up Near Polish Border," JTA, July 31, 1946.

204. Jewish Community in Prague, "Telegram Requesting Mobile Synagogues from the Chief Rabbis [*sic*] Council London," July 25, 1946, file no. 425–231-6-0011, ABS.

205. Memo from Dwork to Kubowitzki, July 22, 1946, file no. D 59/11, WJC. On Dwork's work during the war, see Aronson, "Preparations for the Nuremberg Trial."

206. Ibid.

207. Ignacy Schwarzbart, "Memo to Members of the Office Committee," July 26, 1946, file no. D 55/3, WJC.

208. Ibid.

209. Wahl, "Memo to Grossman," July 23, 1946, file no. D 59/11, WJC. On the influence that David Niles and others had on Truman's policy toward the Jewish DPs and Palestine/Israel, see Davidson, "Truman the Politician"; M. Cohen, *Truman and Israel*; Judis, *Genesis*.

210. On Truman, see Kochavi, *Post-Holocaust Politics*, 98–101, 121–24.

211. There was, of course, some movement away from DP camps. "555 Jewish Refugees Arrive (to Palestine)," JTA, July 29, 1946.

212 "Report of the Delegation of the Central Jewish Committee in Poland," file no. H 273/20 WJC.

213. Emil Sommerstein did not depart the United States in 1946. He had a stroke and stayed in the United States until his death in 1957.

214. "Report of the Delegation of the Central Jewish Committee."

215. Ibid.

216. Ibid.

217. Ibid.

218. Ibid.

219. Joel Cang, "Kielce Pogrom," *Manchester Guardian*, July 13, 1946.

220. It "may sound incredible," Cang wrote, "but it is a fact that in Poland there are large numbers, some venture to say millions who still believe that Jews use the blood of Christian children for ritual purposes." Cang even found this belief "amongst the Polish intelligentsia." Ibid. On the pogrom in Kraków, see Anna Cichopek-Gajraj, *Pogrom Żydów w Krakowie.*

221. Cang, "Danger to Jews Still Growing."

222. Violence occurred in Raciąż in 1945 as well. See Kotkiewicz, "Mord na Żydach w Raciążu."

223. Cang, "Pogrom Begun by Rumour."

224. Ibid.

225. Gross, *Fear*, 246.

226. Connelly, "Nazis and Slavs," 32–33.

227. Klukowski, *Diary from Occupation*, 209–10 for August 8, 1942, and p. 219 for October 21, 1942.

228. Ibid., 199.

229. Connelly, "Poles and Jews," 658. Connelly cites Klukowski's diary; ibid., 648–49.

230. On the phenomenon of the so-called *Judenjagd*, or "hunt for the Jews," see Grabowski, *Hunt for the Jews.*

231. Klukowski, *Diary from Occupation*, 227.

232. Cichopek-Gajraj, *Beyond Violence*, 142. For a close study of the impact of the war, displacement, and Nazi ideology in another societal context, see the excellent study by Redlich, *Together and Apart in Brzezany*. For more on the regulations and ensuing societal mechanisms that the Germans introduced to prevent assistance to Jews, see Frydel, "Devil in Microhistory"; Frydel, "*Judenjagd*."

233. Cichopek-Gajraj, *Beyond Violence*, 114. According to Cichopek-Gajraj, Szynok "was the first to point to the political aspect as critical for understanding anti-Jewish violence in postwar Poland" (ibid.).

234. On *Żydokomuna*, see Shore, "Conversing with Ghosts"; Gerrits, "Anti-Semitism and Anti-Communism"; Kopstein and Wittenberg, "Who Voted Communist?" On the communist elements of the Jedwabne pogrom, see Gross, *Neighbors*, 19. See Kopstein and Wittenberg, *Intimate Violence*, 64–65, for how the

political situation in Jedwabne differed from other nearby places where pogroms occurred.

235. Marcin Zaremba writes "that 37.5 percent of university-educated people and around 30 percent of secondary-educated people in the Polish Second Republic perished." Zaremba, "'War' Syndrome," 31. Furthermore, the "political, intellectual and cultural elite" was "decimated by the war and occupation." Left in their place was the "majority of the population––poor, uneducated, resentful, brimming over with anxiety and trauma, more closely connected to the Church, conservative, traditional, living mostly in villages and small towns."

236. Engel, "Patterns of Anti-Jewish Violence," 38.

237. See Kersten, *Polacy, Żydzi, komunizm*, for her concept of the "social atmosphere," which blended Christian-inspired anti-Judaism, political antisemitism, and the reality of Jewish wartime isolation. Michael Steinlauf uses the work of Robert Jay Lifton, who explores how "death imprint," "death guilt," and "psychic numbing" can consciously and unconsciously reduce one's ability to feel for "others." Steinlauf, *Bondage to the Dead*, 57. See also Stola's review of Steinlauf's book. Stola, "Review."

238. Zaremba, "'War' Syndrome," 42. Consider Cichopek-Gajraj's analysis of Zaremba, *Beyond Violence*, 145.

239. Zaremba, "'War' Syndrome," 43.

240. "McNarney Says He Is Trying to Discourage 'Organized Movements' of Jews into US Zone," JTA, August 11, 1946. On the Jewish question at the Paris Peace Talks in 1946, see Kurz, "In the Shadow of Versailles."

241. "McNarney Trying to Discourage."

242. "Laguardia Reports to UNRRA Council on Jews Fleeing from Poland," JTA, August 14, 1946.

243. Gwidon Czerwinski, "Letter to Border Guards," August 15, 1946, Sygnatura No. 217/154, Archiwum Straży Granicznej.

244. On July 5, 1946, one day after the Kielce pogrom, it was reissued as well. This sort of reissued memo most likely came from Czerwinski's hand, but it is unsigned.

245. "Poland and Rumanian [*sic*] Control Council Reject British Request to Halt Exodus of Jews," JTA, August 16, 1946.

246. "Chief of UNRRA DP Operations in Germany Dismissed," JTA, August 21, 1946.

247. "McNarney Says Fleeing Polish Jews Will Be Admitted to US Zone and Assisted," JTA, August 22, 1946. Wise and Goldmann attended a meeting with McNarney along with other Jewish leaders on August 25, 1946.

248. "UNRRA Votes to Continue Help to DPs until Six Months after Its Liquidation," JTA, August 19, 1946.

249. G. Cohen, *In War's Wake*, 139.

250. "La Guardia Says Some Refugees Fleeing Poland Entitled to UNRRA Aid as 'Persecuties,'" *Jewish Telegraphic Agency,* August 20, 1946.

251. Khan, "Z našeho Náchoda do zaslíbené země."

252. "Protokol, 25 October 1946," file no. 305–871-1, ABS.

253. "Protokol, 4 November 1946," file no. 305–871-1, ABS.

254. Zdeněk Toman, "Memo to Sebor," November 1946, file no. 305–871-1, ABS.

255. Ibid.

256. Robert Smith, "The Jewish Train from Náchod," *Scotsman,* September 4, 1946.

257. Ibid. Smith wrote, "Notably, other border areas might have been traversed more easily, such as the border pass near Międzylesie-Lichkov." I thank Michał Grochowski for bringing this to my attention.

258. "Sprawozdania sytuacyjne miasto Szczecin, 1946–1947," Nr. Wol No. 915, Karton 2, Wydział repatriacji, SAS.

259. Cichopek-Gajraj, *Beyond Violence,* 5.

260. Engel, "Palestine in the Mind."

261. G. Cohen continues the *bricha* story from 1947 to 1949 and situates the International Refugee Organization within it. *In War's Wake,* 143–47. In 1948, Cohen states, the IRO backed migration to Israel. Ibid., 129.

262. Bauer surmised that "quite simply, no Jews could have passed to Bratislava or Prague had it not been for the aid and sympathy extended by the Czechs." Bauer, *Flight and Rescue,* 182. Bauer also writes, "It must have cost the Czechs a very considerable sum of money for trains and food and they earned the sympathy and the gratitude of the Jews." Ibid., 184. For Kochavi's coverage of Czechoslovakia through 1948, see *Post-Holocaust Politics,* 185–93. The Czechoslovakian government spent eighty million crowns for 130,000 Polish Jewish transmigrants. See "Text of the Press Conference of Dr. Rudolf Kuraz . . . for the Jewish Press on Monday March 17, 1947," file no. H 101/2, WJC.

CONCLUSION

1. Zweig, *World of Yesterday,* 2.

2. Arguably, the "ethnic" revolution was the most complete revolution unleashed by the Second World War.

3. Zahra, *Kidnapped Souls,* 264.

4. Kundera, "Tragedy of Central Europe."

5. Ibid. Hannah Arendt lists her own litany of east central European Jewish personalities in her 1943 essay "We Refugees," 274.

6. Connelly, "Poles and Jews," 658.

7. On this phenomenon, especially in the early 2000s, see Gruber, *Virtually Jewish*; Lehrer, *Jewish Poland Revisited.*

8. Arieh Tartakower, "We Think about Poland," *NT,* October 23, 1944, 6.

9. "Speech of Paul Jokelson to DPs in Fritzlar," Sygnatura No. 460, Generalny Pełnomocnik Rządu RP Repatriacji w Warszawie, AAN.

10. Soon after he gave this speech, in 1948, Jokelson (1905–2002) left his home in France to join his new wife in America, where he lived for the rest of his life.

11. One of Tartakower's obituaries stated that "his major books were published" only after his "settlement in Israel." In this obituary, elsewhere becomes more than a place; it provides a perspective on a life, an academic oeuvre. Elazar, "In Memoriam," 11.

12. Likhovski, "Peripheral Vision," 245. On Warhaftig's later life, see Joffe, "Zerach Warhaftig," *Guardian*, October 9, 2002.

13. His wife, Paulina, settled in Palestine during the war, but he did not join her or his son, Henryk, there.

14. Jakob Apenszlak, "Resignation from Heritage," *NT*, October 31, 1946, 1.

15. Tuwim, *My Żydzi Polscy*, 43.

16. Berman, quoted in Shore, "Children of the Revolution," 44. According to Shore, "her son later wrote that 'her marginal and passive position after reaching her "promised land," standing in such contrast with her intense social involvement in Poland in the preceding years, must have hurt her tremendously.'" Berman even offered to serve as a professional librarian staffing the center.

17. I think of both mother and son when I think of William Sebald's hero Austerlitz, the fictional Czech Jewish man who had been whisked away to Wales as part of the *Kindertransport* when he was a boy. As far back as he could remember, Austerlitz felt as if he "had no place in reality," as if he "were not there at all." Sebald, *Austerlitz*, 185.

18. Bryant, *Prague in Black*, 268.

19. On the softening of this distinction from the 1970s onward, see Gebert, *Living in the Land*; Rothstein, "Am I Jewish?"

20. Sebald, *Austerlitz*, 69–70.

21. Szymborska, "The Poet and the World."

BIBLIOGRAPHY

ARCHIVES

Czech Republic

Archiv bezpečnostních složek ministerstva vnitra [Archive of the Security Services of the Ministry of the Interior], Prague (ABS).

Archiv Ministerstva Zahraničních Věcí České Republiky [Archive of the Foreign Ministry of the Czech Republic], Prague (AMZV).

Archiv Ústavu Tomáše Garrigue Masarykův a Archiv [Archive of the Tomáš Garrigue Masaryk Institute], Prague (ÚTGM).

Národní Archiv [National Archive], Prague.

Personal Archive of Rudolf Beck, Náchod.

Israel

Jabotinsky Institute, Tel Aviv.

Yad Vashem Archive, Jerusalem.

Poland

Archiwum Akt Nowych [Central Archive of Modern Records], Warsaw.

Archiwum Państwowe w Szczecinie [State Archives in Szczecin], Szczecin (SAS).

Archiwum Straży Granicznej [Archive of Border Guard], Szczecin.

Archiwum Żydowskiego Instytutu Historycznego [Archives of Jewish Historical Institute], Warsaw.

United Kingdom

Archive of the *Manchester Guardian*, Manchester University Library, Manchester.

United States

Archive of the United States Holocaust Memorial Museum, Washington, DC.
Archive of the World Jewish Congress, the American Jewish Archives, Cincinnati, OH (WJC).
Jewish Joint Distribution Archive, New York, NY.
YIVO Institute for Jewish Research, New York, NY.

NEWSPAPERS, JOURNALS, AND NEWS AGENCIES

Chwila
Czas
Der Moment
Gazeta Polska
The Jewish Chronicle
The Jewish Telegraphic Agency (JTA)
The Manchester Guardian
Nasz Przegląd
Nasza Trybuna (*NT*)
The New York Times
Nowy Dziennik
Palcor
The Scotsman
Sprawy Narodowościowe
Svet Práce
Tygodnik Informacyjny
The Washington Post

DOCUMENTARIES

Between a Star and Crescent: Bricha [*Mezi hvězdou a půlmě sícem: Bricha*], directed by Martin Šmok and Petr Bok (2003).
The Karski Report, directed by Claude Lanzmann (2010).
Shoah, directed by Claude Lanzmann (1985).

GOVERNMENT AND INSTITUTIONAL DOCUMENT COLLECTIONS

"Report of the Anglo-American Committee of Enquiry Regarding the Problems of European Jewry and Palestine." Lausanne, Switzerland: April 20, 1946.

Constitution of the International Refugee Organization, United Nations, 1946.
Drugi Powszechny Spis Ludności z DN. 9.XII 1931 R. Warsaw: Nakładem Głównego Urzędu Statystycznego, 1938.
Final Report of the Palestine Partition Commission. London: His Majesty's Stationery Office, November 9, 1938.
Foreign Relations of the United States: Diplomatic Papers, 1943, General: Volume 1. Edited by E. Ralph Perkins and N. O. Sappington. Washington DC: U.S. Government Printing Office, 1964.
Ministerstwo Spraw Zagranicznych, Poland. *The Mass Extermination of Jews in German Occupied Poland: Note Addressed to the Governments of the United Nations on December 10th, 1942, and Other Documents*. London: Hutchinson, 1942.
The Palestine Royal Commission Report. London: His Majesty's Stationery Office, July 7, 1937.
Protocole du premier Congrès juif, mondial, Genève, 8–15 aout 1936. Geneva: Edité par le Comité exécutif du Congrès juif mondial, 1936.
Reports of the World Jewish Congress (British Section). London: British Section of the World Jewish Congress, 1943.
United Nations Conference on International Organization. *The United Nations Conference on International Organization, San Francisco, California, April 25 to June 26, 1945: Selected Documents*. Department of State Publication 2490. Washington, DC: US Government Printing Office, 1946.
United Nations General Assembly. Resolution 62 (1), "Refugees and Displaced Persons: Constitution of the International Refugee Organization, Article 2, Section 1, b. iii." December 15, 1946.
United States Department of State. *Foreign Relations of the United States: Diplomatic Papers, 1943*. Department of State Publication. Washington, DC: US Government Printing Office, 1963.
World Jewish Congress (WJC). *War Emergency Conference of the World Jewish Congress, Atlantic City, November, 1944: Addresses and Resolutions*. British Section (Series) No. 14. London: World Jewish Congress, British Section, 1945.

ARTICLES IN JOURNALS

Adler, Eliyana R. "Hrubieszów at the Crossroads: Polish Jews Navigate the German and Soviet Occupations." *Holocaust and Genocide Studies* 28, no. 1 (2014): 1–30.
Adler, Eliyana R., and Natalia Aleksiun. "Seeking Relative Safety: The Flight of Polish Jews to the East in the Autumn of 1939." *Yad Vashem Studies* 46, no. 1 (2018): 41–71.
Adler-Rudel, S. "A Chronicle of Rescue Efforts." *Leo Baeck Institute Year Book* 11 (1966): 213.

Aleksiun, Natalia. "Christian Corpses for Christians: Dissecting the Anti-Semitism behind the Cadaver Affair of the Second Polish Republic." *East European Politics and Societies* 25, no. 3 (2011): 393–409.

———. "Returning from the Land of the Dead: Jews in Eastern Galicia in the Immediate Aftermath of the Holocaust." *Kwartalnik Historii Żydów*, no. 2 (2013): 257–71.

———. "The Situation of the Jews in Poland as Seen by Soviet Security Forces in 1945." *Jews in Eastern Europe* 3, no. 37 (1998): 52–68.

Almagor, Laura. "Fitting the Zeitgeist: Jewish Territorialism and Geopolitics, 1934–1960." *Contemporary European History* 27, no. 3 (2018): 351–69.

Anthony, Elizabeth. "The Return of Jewish Concentration Camp Survivors to Vienna in the Immediate Postwar Period." *Kwartalnik Historii Żydów*, no. 2 (2013): 286–92.

Armstrong, Hamilton Fish. "Hitler's Reich: The First Phase." *Foreign Affairs* 11, no. 4 (1933): 589–608.

Aronson, Shlomo. "Preparations for the Nuremberg Trial: The O.S.S., Charles Dwork, and the Holocaust." *Holocaust & Genocide Studies* 12, no. 2 (1998): 257–281.

Baron, Nick, and Peter Gatrell. "Population Displacement, State-Building, and Social Identity in the Lands of the Former Russian Empire, 1917–1923." *Kritika: Explorations in Russian and Eurasian History* 4, no. 1 (2003): 51–100.

Baumel, Judith Taylor. "DPs, Mothers and Pioneers: Women in the She'erit Hapletah." *Jewish History* 11, no. 2 (1997): 99–110.

Beneš, Edvard. "Central Europe after Ten Years." *Slavonic and East European Review* 7 (Jan. 1929): 245–260.

———. "The League of Nations: Successes and Failures." *Foreign Affairs* 11, no. 1 (1932): 66-80.

———. "The Little Entente." *Foreign Affairs* 1, no. 1 (1922): 66–72.

———. "The New Order in Europe." *Nineteenth Century and After*, 130 (1941): 150–155.

———. "The Organization of Postwar Europe." *Foreign Affairs* 20, no. 2 (1942): 226–42.

———. "Ten Years of the League." *Foreign Affairs* 8, no. 2 (1930): 212–24.

Blatman, Daniel. "Bund." YIVO Encyclopedia of Jews in Eastern Europe. Accessed March 14, 2021. https://yivoencyclopedia.org/article.aspx/Bund.

Bockley, Kathryn M. "A Historical Overview of Refugee Legislation: The Deception of Foreign Policy in the Land of Promise." *North Carolina Journal of International Law and Commercial Regulation* 21, no. 1 (1995): 253–92.

Boćkowski, Daniel. "Repatriacja dzieci polskich z głębi ZSRR w latach 1942–1952." In *Studia z Dziej.w Rosji i Europy Środkowo-Wschodniej 1994* (29): 99–108.

Browning, Christopher. "The Nazi Decision to Commit Mass Murder: Three Interpretations—the Euphoria of Victory and the Final Solution, Summer–Fall 1941." *German Studies Review* 17, no. 3 (1994): 473–81.

Brubaker, Rogers. "The 'Diaspora' Diaspora." *Ethnic and Racial Studies* 28, no. 1 (2005): 1–19.

———. "Revisiting 'The "Diaspora" Diaspora.'" *Ethnic and Racial Studies* 40, no. 9 (2017): 1556–61.

Bryant, Chad. "Either German or Czech: Fixing Nationality in Bohemia and Moravia, 1939–1946." *Slavic Review* 61, no. 4 (2002): 683–706.

Cang, Joel. "The Opposition Parties in Poland and Their Attitude towards the Jews and the Jewish Problem." *Jewish Social Studies* 1, no. 2 (1939): 241–56.

Čapková, Kateřina. "Between Expulsion and Rescue: The Transports for German-Speaking Jews of Czechoslovakia in 1946." *Holocaust and Genocide Studies* 32, no. 1 (2018): 66–92.

———. "Germans or Jews? German-Speaking Jews in Poland and Czechoslovakia after World War II." *Kwartalnik Historii Żydów*, no. 2 (2013): 348–62.

———. "Piłsudski or Masaryk? Zionist Revisionism in Czechoslovakia 1925–1940." *Judaica Bohemiae*, no. 35 (1999): 210–39.

———. "Specific Features of Zionism in the Czech Lands in the Interwar Period." *Judaica Bohemiae*, no. 38 (2002): 106–59.

Cohen, Sharon Kangisser. "Choosing a Heim: Survivors of the Holocaust and Post-war Immigration." *European Judaism: A Journal for the New Europe* 46, no. 2 (2013): 32–54.

Connelly, John. "Nazis and Slavs: From Racial Theory to Racist Practice." *Central European History* 32, no. 1 (1999): 1–33.

———. "Poles and Jews in the Second World War: The Revisions of Jan T. Gross." *Contemporary European History* 11, no. 4 (2002): 641–58.

Cramsey, Sarah. "Saying Kaddish in Czechoslovakia: Memorialization, the Jewish Tragedy and the 'Tryzna.'" *Journal of Modern Jewish Studies* 7, no. 1 (2008): 35–50.

Cramsey, Sarah, and Jason Wittenberg. "Timing Is Everything: Changing Norms of Minority Rights and the Making of a Polish Nation-State." *Comparative Political Studies* 49, no. 11 (2016): 1480–512.

Datner-Śpiewak, H. "Instytucje opieki nad dzieckiem i szkoły powszechne Centralnego Komitetu Żyd.w Polskich w latach 1945–1946." *Biuletyn Żydowskiego Instytutu Historycznego* 3 (1981): 37–51.

Davidson, Lawrence. "Truman the Politician and the Establishment of Israel." *Journal of Palestine Studies* 39, no. 4 (2010): 28–42.

Dobroszycki, Lucjan. "Restoring Jewish Life in Post-war Poland." *Soviet Jewish Affairs* 3, no. 2 (1973): 58–72.

Dubnov, Arie M. "Between Liberalism and Jewish Nationalism: Young Isaiah Berlin on the Road towards Diaspora Zionism." *Modern Intellectual History* 4, no. 2 (2007): 303–26.

———. "Zionism on the Diasporic Front." *Journal of Israeli History* 30, no. 2 (2011): 211–24.

Elazar, Daniel. "In Memoriam: Prof. Arieh Tartakower." *World Union of Jewish Studies Newsletter* 22 (1983): 11–13.

Engel, David. "Crisis and Lachrymosity: On Salo Baron, Neobaronianism, and the Study of Modern European Jewish History." *Jewish History* 20, no. 3 (2006): 243–64.

———. "An Early Account of Polish Jewry under Nazi and Soviet Occupation Presented to the Polish Government-in-Exile, February 1940." *Jewish Social Studies* 45, no. 1 (1983): 1–16.

———. "The Frustrated Alliance: The Revisionist Movement and the Polish Government-in-Exile, 1939–1945." *Studies in Zionism* 7, no. 1 (1986): 11–36.

———. "Palestine in the Mind of the Remnants of Polish Jewry." *Journal of Israeli History* 16, no. 3 (1995): 221–34.

———. "Patterns of Anti-Jewish Violence in Poland, 1944–1946." *Yad Vashem Studies* 26 (1998): 43–85.

———. "Reading and Misreadings: A Reply to Dariusz Stola." *Polin: Studies in Polish Jewry* 8 (1994): 345–81.

———. "The Reconstruction of Jewish Communal Institutions in Postwar Poland: The Origins of the Central Committee of Polish Jews, 1944–1945." *East European Politics and Societies* 10, no. 1 (1995): 85–107.

———. "'The Western Allies and the Holocaust': Jan Karski's Mission to the West, 1942–1944." *Holocaust and Genocide Studies* 5, no. 4 (1990): 363–80.

———. "Writing Polish Jewish History in Hebrew." *Gal-Ed: On the History of the Jews in Poland* 11 (1989): 15–29.

Falek, Pascale. "A Multifaceted Image of Jewish Women at Belgian Universities during the Interwar Period." *Journal of Jewish Identities* 3, no. 1 (2010): 25–40.

Ferenc-Piotrowska, Maria. "'All Those Rumors Occupy People's Thoughts . . .' On the Relationship between Rumors and Knowledge about the Holocaust in the Warsaw Ghetto." *Rocznik Antropologii Historii* 11 (2018): 139–58.

Fishman-Tamir, Arnon. "Mikhtaw l'Arnon Fishman Tarmi." *Yalkut Moreshet*, no. 2 (1964): 28–32.

Friedl, Jiří. "'Palestine Must Be the Ultimate Goal.' Count František Schönborn's Report of September 1945 on Jewish Refugees from Poland in Czechoslovakia." *Slovanský přehled* no. 1 (2018): 135–158.

Frommer, Benjamin. "Expulsion or Integration: Unmixing Interethnic Marriage in Postwar Czechoslovakia." *East European Politics and Societies* 14, no. 2 (2000): 381–410.

———. "Retribution as Legitimation: The Uses of Political Justice in Postwar Czechoslovakia." *Contemporary European History* 13, no. 4 (2004): 477–92.

Gerlach, David. "Beyond Expulsion: The Emergence of 'Unwanted Elements' in the Postwar Czech Borderlands, 1945–1950." *East European Politics and Societies* 24, no. 2 (2010): 269–93.

———. "Working with the Enemy: Labor Politics in the Czech Borderlands, 1945–48." *Austrian History Yearbook* 38 (2007): 179–207.

Gerrits, André. "Anti-Semitism and Anti-Communism: The Myth of 'Judeo-Communism' in Eastern Europe." *East European Jewish Affairs* 25, no. 1 (1995): 49–72.

Glassheim, Eagle. "National Mythologies and Ethnic Cleansing: The Expulsion of Czechoslovak Germans in 1945." *Central European History* 33, no. 4 (2000): 463–86.

Green, Nancy L. "Jewish Migrations to France in the Nineteenth and Twentieth Centuries: Community or Communities?" *Studia Rosenthaliana* 23 (1989): 135–53.

Gross, Jan Tomasz. "In the Aftermath of the Kielce Pogrom: The Special Commission of the Central Committee of Jews in Poland." *Gal-Ed: On the History of the Jews in Poland* 15 (1997): 119–36.

Grossmann, Atina. "Remapping Relief and Rescue: Flight, Displacement, and International Aid for Jewish Refugees during World War II." *New German Critique*, no. 117 (2012): 61–79.

———. "Trauma, Memory, and Motherhood: Germans and Jewish Displaced Persons in Post-Nazi Germany, 1945–1949." *Archive fur Sozialgeschichte* 38 (1998): 215–39.

Gurjanow, Aleksander. "Cztery deportacje 1940–1941." *Karta* 12 (1994): 114–136.

Hagen, William W. "Before the 'Final Solution': Toward a Comparative Analysis of Political Anti-Semitism in Interwar Germany and Poland." *Journal of Modern History* 68, no. 2 (1996): 351–81.

Hanc, Josef. "Czechs and Slovaks since Munich." *Foreign Affairs* 18, no. 1 (1939): 102.

Harris, Bonnie M. "From German Jews to Polish Refugees: Germany's Polenaktion and the Zbąszyn Deportations of October 1938." *Kwartalnik Historii żydów* 230, no. 2 (2009): 175–205.

Hauner, Milan. "'We Must Push Eastwards!' The Challenges and Dilemmas of President Beneš after Munich." *Journal of Contemporary History* 44, no. 4 (2009): 619–56.

Holborn, Louise W. "The League of Nations and the Refugee Problem." *Annals of the American Academy of Political and Social Science* 203 (1939): 124–35.

Hroch, Miroslav. "Zionism as European National Movement." *Jewish Studies* 38 (1998): 73–81.

Hyman, Joseph C. "Twenty-Five Years of American Aid to Jews Overseas: A Record of the Joint Distribution Committee." *American Jewish Yearbook* 41 (1939): 141–79.

Jackson, Ivor. "Editorial Paul Weis, 1907–1991." *International Journal of Refugee Law* 3, no. 2 (1991): 183–84.

Janowsky, Oscar. "The Human Rights Issue at the San Francisco Conference: Was It a Victory?" *Menorah Journal* 34 (1946): 29–55.

Jaszi, Oscar. "Dismembered Hungary and Peace in Central Europe." *Foreign Affairs* 2, no. 1 (1923): 270.

Jessup, Philip C. "UNRRA, Sample of World Organization." *Foreign Affairs* 22, no. 3 (1944): 362–73.

Jockusch, Laura, and Tamar Lewinsky. "Paradise Lost? Postwar Memory of Polish Jewish Survival in the Soviet Union." *Holocaust and Genocide Studies* 24, no. 3 (2010): 373–99.

Jońca, Karol. "The Expulsion of Polish Jews from the Third Reich in 1938." *Polin* 8 (1994): 255–81.

Kaganovitch, Albert. "Stalin's Great Power Politics, the Return of Jewish Refugees to Poland, and Continued Migration to Palestine, 1944–1946." *Holocaust and Genocide Studies* 26, no. 1 (2012): 59–94.

Kaplan, Israel, ed. *Fun letstn khurbn* (*From the Latest Destruction*). Munich: Central Historical Commission, 1946–1947.

Karch, Brendan. "A Jewish 'Nature Preserve': League of Nations Minority Protections in Nazi Upper Silesia, 1933–1937." *Central European History* 46, no. 1 (2013): 124–60.

Kersten, Krystyna. "International Migrations in Poland after World War II." *Acta Poloniae Historica* 19 (1968): 49.

Ketko, Tamar. "Janusz Korczak's Visits to Palestine in 1934 and 1936." *Jewish Culture and History* 21, no. 4 (2020): 359–72.

Kijek, Kamil. "Between a Love of Poland, Symbolic Violence, and Antisemitism. The Idiosyncratic Effects of the State Education System on Young Jews in Interwar Poland." *Polin: Studies in Polish Jewry* 30 (2018): 237–264.

Kijek, Kamil. "Was It Possible to Avoid 'Hebrew Assimilation'? Hebraism, Polonization, and Tarbut Schools in the Last Decade of Interwar Poland." *Jewish Social Studies: History, Culture, Society* 21, no. 2 (2016): 105–41.

Kochavi, Arieh. "Britain and the Illegal Immigration to Palestine from France following World War II." *Holocaust and Genocide Studies* 6, no. 4 (1992): 383–96.

Kopstein, Jeffrey, and Jason Wittenberg. "Between State Loyalty and National Identity: Electoral Behavior in Inter-war Poland." *Polin: Studies in Polish Jewry* 24 (2011): 171–86.

———. "Who Voted Communist? Reconsidering the Social Bases of Radicalism in Poland." *Slavic Review* 62, no. 1 (2003): 87–109.

Kotkiewicz, Adam Dariusz. "Mord na Żydach w Raciążu w sierpniu 1945 roku." *Notatki Płockie: Kwartalnik Towarzystwa Naukowego Płockiego* 56, no. 4 (2011): 38–43.

Kunakhovich, Kyrill. "Kultury powojenne: Sztuka i komunizm w Krakowie i Lipsku." *Pamięć i Sprawiedliwość* 25, no. 1 (2015): 163–84.

Kundera, Milan. "The Tragedy of Central Europe." Translated by Edmund White. *New York Review of Books* 31, no. 7 (1984): 33–38.

Kurz, Nathan. "'Hide a Fact Rather Than State It': The Holocaust, the 1940s Human Rights Surge, and the Cosmopolitan Imperative of International Law." *Journal of Genocide Research* 23, no. 1 (2021): 37–57.

Láníček, Jan. "What Did It Mean to Be Loyal? Jewish Survivors in Post-war Czechoslovakia in a Comparative Perspective." *Australian Journal of Politics and History* 60, no. 3 (2014): 384–404.

Lestschinsky, Jacob. "National Groups in Polish Emigration." *Jewish Social Studies* 5 (1943): 99–114.

Levene, Mark. "Nationalism and Its Alternatives in the International Arena: The Jewish Question at Paris, 1919." *Journal of Contemporary History* 28, no. 3 (1993): 511–31.

Levin, Dov. "The Fateful Decision: The Flight of the Jews into the Soviet Interior in the Summer of 1941." *Yad Vashem Studies* 20 (1990): 115–42.

Likhovski, Assaf. "Peripheral Vision: Polish-Jewish Lawyers and Early Israeli Law." *Law and History Review* 36, no. 2 (2018): 235–66.

Loeffler, James. "Between Zionism and Liberalism: Oscar Janowsky and Diaspora Nationalism in America." *AJS Review* 34, no. 2 (2010): 289–308.

———. "The Particularist Pursuit of American Universalism: The American Jewish Committee's 1944 'Declaration on Human Rights.' *Journal of Contemporary History* 50, no. 2 (2015): 274–295.

———. "'The Famous Trinity of 1917': Zionist Internationalism in Historical Perspective." *Simon Dubnow Yearbook* 15 (2016): 211–38.

Lohr, Eric. "The Russian Army and the Jews: Mass Deportation, Hostages, and Violence during World War I." *Russian Review* 60, no. 3 (2001): 404–19.

Macartney, C. A. "Minorities: A Problem of Eastern Europe." *Foreign Affairs* 9, no. 1 (1930): 674.

Masaryk, Thomas G. "Reflections on the Question of War Guilt." *Foreign Affairs* 3, no. 4 (1925): 529–40.

Mastný, Vojtěch. "The Beneš-Stalin-Molotov Conversations in December 1943: New Documents." *Jahrbücher Für Geschichte Osteuropas* 20, no. 3 (1972): 367–402.

McDonald, James G. "Letter of Resignation of James G. McDonald, High Commissioner for Refugees (Jewish and Other) Coming from Germany." US Library of Congress, World Digital Library. December 27, 1935. https://www.loc.gov/item/2021666891/.

Melchior, Małgorzata, "Rootedness in Place, Rootedness in Memory as Exemplified by Polish-Jewish Identity." *Sprawy Narodowościowe*, no. 31 (2007): 71–80.

Miller, David Hunter. "Nationality and Other Problems Discussed at the Hague." *Foreign Affairs* 8, no. 4 (1930): 632–40.

Moss, Kenneth B. "Thinking with Restriction: Immigration Restriction and Polish Jewish Accounts of the Post-liberal State, Empire, Race, and Political Reason, 1926–39." *East European Jewish Affairs* 44, no. 2–3 (2014): 205–24.

Osusky, Stefan. "Why Czechoslovakia?" *Foreign Affairs* 15, no. 1 (1936): 455.

Pedersen, Susan. "Back to the League of Nations." *American Historical Review* 112, no. 4 (2007): 1091–117.

Penkower, Monty N. "Jewish Organizations and the Creation of the U.S. War Refugee Board." *Annals of the American Academy of Political and Social Science* 450, no. 1 (1980): 122–39.

Person, Katarzyna. "'I Am a Jewish DP. A Jew from the Eternal Nowhere': Jews from Poland in Displaced Persons Camps in the Occupation Zones of West Germany." *Kwartalnik Historii Żydów* 246, no. 2 (2013): 312–18.

Pinson, Koppel S. "Jewish Life in Liberated Germany: A Study of the Jewish DP's." *Jewish Social Studies* 9, no. 2 (1947): 101–26.

Plach, Eva. "Ritual Slaughter and Animal Welfare in Interwar Poland." *East European Jewish Affairs* 45, no. 1 (2015): 1–25.

Proudfoot, Malcolm J. "The Anglo-American Displaced Persons Program for Germany and Austria." *American Journal of Economics and Sociology* 6, no. 1 (1946): 33–54.

Pucci, Molly. "A Revolution in a Revolution: The Secret Police and the Origins of Stalinism in Czechoslovakia." *East European Politics and Societies* 32, no. 1 (2018): 3–22.

Rappak, Wojtek. "'Raport Karskiego'—kontrowersje i interpretacje." *Zagłada Żydów Studia i Materiały* 10 (2014): 96–130.

Rechter, David. "Galicia in Vienna: Jewish Refugees in the First World War." *Austrian History Yearbook* 28 (1997): 113–30.

Reinisch, Jessica. "'Auntie UNRRA' at the Crossroads." *Past and Present* 218, no. 8 (2013): 70–97.

———. "Internationalism in Relief: The Birth (and Death) of UNRRA 1." *Past and Present* 210, no. 6 (2011): 258–89.

———. "'We Shall Rebuild Anew a Powerful Nation': UNRRA, Internationalism and National Reconstruction in Poland." *Journal of Contemporary History* 43, no. 3 (2008): 451–76.

Rothkirchen, Livia. "The Czechoslovak Government-in-Exile: Jewish and Palestinian Aspects in the Light of the Documents." *Yad Vashem Studies* 9 (1973): 157–99.

Rothstein, Rachel. "'Am I Jewish?' and 'What Does It Mean?': The Jewish Flying University and the Creation of a Polish-Jewish Counterculture in Late 1970s Warsaw." *Journal of Jewish Identities* 8, no. 2 (2015): 85–111.

Rubin, Gil S. "The End of Minority Rights: Jacob Robinson and the 'Jewish Question' in World War II." *Simon Dubnow Institute Yearbook* 11 (2012): 55–72.

———. "Vladimir Jabotinsky and Population Transfers between Eastern Europe and Palestine." *Historical Journal* 62, no. 2 (2018): 1–23.

Sanborn, Joshua. "Unsettling the Empire: Violent Migrations and Social Disaster in Russia during World War I." *Journal of Modern History* 77, no. 2 (2005): 290–324.

Schechtmann, Joseph B. "The Option Clause in the Reich's Treaties on the Transfer of Population." *American Journal of International Law* 38, no. 3 (1944): 356–74.

Segev, Zohar. "Immigration, Politics and Democracy: The World Jewish Congress in Europe, 1936–1939." *Studies in Ethnicity and Nationalism* 17, no. 2 (2017): 209–26.

Seton-Watson, R. W. "The German Minority in Czechoslovakia." *Foreign Affairs* 16, no. 4 (1938): 651–66.

Shore, Marci. "Children of the Revolution: Communism, Zionism, and the Berman Brothers." *Jewish Social Studies* 10, no. 3 (2004): 23–86.

———. "Conversing with Ghosts: Jedwabne, Zydokomuna, and Totalitarianism." *Kritika: Explorations in Russian and Eurasian History* 6, no. 2 (2005): 345–74.

Slucki, David. "'A Struggle Unparalleled in Human History': Survivors Remember the Warsaw Ghetto Uprising." *American Jewish History* 103, no. 2 (2019): 203–25.

Smith, Anthony D. "Zionism and Diaspora Nationalism." *Israel Affairs* 2, no. 2 (1995): 1–19.

Steffen, Katrin. "Connotations of Exclusion—'Ostjude,' 'Ghettos' and Other Markings." *Simon Dubnow Institute Yearbook* 4 (2005): 459–79.

Steiner, Zara. "The Soviet Commissariat of Foreign Affairs and the Czechoslovak Crisis in 1938: New Material from the Soviet Archives." *Historical Journal* 42, no. 3 (1999): 751–79.

Stola, Dariusz. "Early News of the Holocaust from Poland." *Holocaust and Genocide Studies* 11, no. 1 (1997): 1–27.

———. "Forced Migrations in Central European History." In "The New Europe and International Migration, Part I, Central and Eastern Europe: The Twin Specters of Mass Unwanted Migration and Mass Involuntary Migration." Special issue, *International Migration Review* 26, no. 2 (1992): 324–41.

———. "In the Shadow of the Facts." *Polin: Studies in Polish Jewry* 8 (1994): 330–44.

———. "Migrations in Central and Eastern Europe." *International Migration Review* 32, no. 4 (1998): 1069–72.

———. "Review of *Bondage to the Dead: Poland and the Memory of the Holocaust.*" *Holocaust and Genocide Studies* 11, no. 3 (1997): 426–31.

Stone, Lewi. "Quantifying the Holocaust: Hyperintense Kill Rates during the Nazi Genocide." *Science Advances* 5, no. 1 (2019): eaau7292. https://advances.sciencemag.org/content/5/1/eaau7292.

Strauss, Herbert A. "Jewish Emigration from Germany: Nazi Policies and Jewish Responses." *Leo Beck Institute Yearbooks* 25 (1980): 313–43.

Szymborska, Wisława. "The Poet and the World: Nobel Lecture on the Occasion of Winning the Nobel Prize for Literature." Nobel Lecture, December 7, 1996. Translated by Stanislaw Baranczak and Clare Cavanagh. https://www.nobelprize.org/prizes/literature/1996/szymborska/lecture/.

Táborský, Eduard. "A Polish-Czechoslovak Confederation: A Story of the Soviet Veto." *Journal of Central European Affairs* 9 (1950): 379–95.

Temperley, Harold. "How the Hungarian Frontiers Were Drawn." *Foreign Affairs* 6, no. 1 (1927): 432–447.

Tokarska-Bakir, Joanna. "Classmates: In Klimontów." *Kwartalnik Historii Żydów*, no. 2 (2013): 205–15.

Toynbee, Arnold J. "The East after Lausanne." *Foreign Affairs* 2, no. 1 (1923): 84–98.

Viscount, Samuel. "Alternatives to Partition." *Foreign Affairs* 16, no. 1 (1937): 143–55.

Vollmer, Clement. "A New Polish Corridor." *Foreign Affairs* 12, no. 1 (1933): 156–59.

Von Wegerer, Alfred. "The Origins of This War: A German View." *Foreign Affairs* 18, no. 4 (1940): 700–718.

Waldeck, Countess. "The Great New Migration." *Foreign Affairs* 15, no. 3 (1937): 537–46.

Wasserstein, Bernard. "Herbert Samuel and the Palestine Problem." *English Historical Review* 91, no. 361 (1976): 753–75.

Weis, Paul. "The International Protection of Refugees." *American Journal of International Law* 48, no. 2 (1954): 193–221.

Weiss, Yfaat. "The Transfer Agreement and the Boycott Movement: A Jewish Dilemma on the Eve of the Holocaust." *Yad Vashem Studies* 26 (1998): 129–72.

Weizmann, Chaim. "Palestine's Role in the Solution of the Jewish Problem." *Foreign Affairs* 20, no. 1 (1942): 324–338.

Wheatley, Natasha. "Central Europe as Ground Zero of the New International Order." *Slavic Review* 78, no. 4 (2019): 900–911.

———. "Spectral Legal Personality in Interwar International Law: On New Ways of Not Being a State." *Law and History Review* 35, no. 3 (2017): 753–87.

Wiskemann, Elizabeth. "The 'Drang Nach Osten' Continues." *Foreign Affairs (Pre-1986)* 17, no. 4 (1939): 764–773.

Wörn, Achim. "Jews in Szczecin, 1945–50: At the Crossroad between Emigration and Assimilation." *Region: Regional Studies of Russia, Eastern Europe, and Central Asia* 6, no. 1 (2017): 55–85.

Wróbel, Piotr J. "Class War or Ethnic Cleansing? Soviet Deportations of Polish Citizens from the Eastern Provinces of Poland, 1939–1941." *Polish Review* 59, no. 2 (2014): 19–42.

Yehudai, Ori. "Displaced in the National Home: Jewish Repatriation from Palestine to Europe, 1945–48." *Jewish Social Studies: History, Culture, Society* 20, no. 2 (2014): 69–110.

Zahra, Tara. "Imagined Non-communities: National Indifference as a Category of Analysis." *Slavic Review* 69, no. 1 (2010): 93–119.

Żyndul, Jolanta. Review of *Żydzi w Polsce odrodzonej* (*Jews in the Restored Poland*) and "Głos Gminy Żydowskiej" ("The Voice of the Jewish Community"). *Shofar: An Interdisciplinary Journal of Jewish Studies* 29, no. 3 (2011): 118–22.

ARTICLES IN EDITED VOLUMES

Aleksiun, Natalia. "Uneasy Bonds: On Jews in Hiding and the Making of Surrogate Families." In *Jewish and Romani Families in the Holocaust and Its Aftermath*, edited by Eliyana Adler and Kateřina Čapková, 85–99. New Brunswick, NJ: Rutgers University Press, 2020.

———. "Where Was There a Future for Polish Jewry? Bundist and Zionist Polemics in Post–World War II Poland." In *Jewish Politics in Eastern Europe: The Bund at 100*, edited by Jack Lester Jacobs, 227–242. Basingstoke: Macmillan, 2001.

Almog, Shmuel. "Galut Nationalism." In *The Jewish Point: Jews as Seen by Themselves and by Others* [in Hebrew], 33–40. Tel Aviv: Sifriyat Po'alim, 2002.

Arendt, Hannah. "We Refugees." In *The Jewish Writings*, edited by Jerome Kohn and Ron H. Feldman, 264–274. New York: Schocken Books, 2007.

———. "Zionism Reconsidered." In *The Jewish Writings*, edited by Jerome Kohn and Ron H. Feldman, 343–374. New York: Schocken Books, 2007.

Bacon, Gershon. "Agudat Israel in Interwar Poland." In *The Jews of Poland between the Two World Wars*, edited by Yisrael Gutman, Ezra Mendelsohn, Jehuda Reinharz, and Chone Schmeruk, 20–35. Hanover, NH: New England University Press, 1989.

———. "One Jewish Street? Reflections on Unity and Disunity in Interwar Polish Jewry." In *New Directions in the History of the Jews in the Polish Lands*, edited by Antony Polonsky et al., 324–337. Boston: Academic Studies, 2018.

Blatman, Daniel, and Renee Poznanski. "Jews and Their Social Environment: Perspectives from the Underground Press in France and Poland." In *Facing the Catastrophe: Jews and Non-Jews in Europe during World War II*, edited by Beate Kosmala and Georgi Verbeeck, 159–228. Occupation in Europe Series. Oxford: Berg, 2011.

Brinkman, Tobias. "Permanent Transit: Jewish Migration during the Interwar Period." In *1929: Mapping the Jewish World*, edited by Hasia R. Diner and Gennady Ėstraĭkh, 53–72. New York, New York University Press Scholarship Online, 2016).

Brod, Petr. "Židé v poválečném Československu." In *Židé v novodobých dějinách*, edited by Václav Veber, 147–162. Prague: Karolinum, 1997.

Browning, Christopher. "Hitler and the Euphoria of Victory." In *The Final Solution: Origins and Implementation,* edited by David Cesarani, 137–149. London: Routledge, 1994.

Brumberg, Abraham. "The Bund and the Polish Socialist Party in the Late 1930s." In *The Jews of Poland between the Two World Wars,* edited by Yisrael Gutman, Ezra Mendelsohn, Jehuda Reinharz, and Chone Schmeruk, 75–96. Hanover, NH: New England University Press, 1989.

Čapková, Kateřina. "Dilemmas of Minority Politics: Jewish Migrants in Postwar Czechoslovakia and Poland." In *Postwar Jewish Displacement and Rebirth, 1945–1967,* edited by Françoise Ouzan and Manfred Gerstenfeld, 63–75. Jewish Identities in a Changing World. Leiden: Brill, 2014.

Cohen, Boaz. "Dr. Jacob Robinson, the Institute of Jewish Affairs and the Elusive Jewish Voice in Nuremberg." In *Holocaust and Justice: Representation and Historiography of the Holocaust in Post-war Trials,* edited by David Bankier and Dan Michman, 81–100. Jerusalem: Yad Vashem, 2010.

Dubnow, Simon. "Eighth Letter [1909]: in *Nationalism and History: Essays on Old and New Judaism*. Edited by Koppel Pinson, 182–192. Cleveland: Meridian Books, 1961.

Dufoix, Stéphane. "'Diaspora': A Study in Socio-historical Semantics." In *Transnationalism: Diasporas and the Advent of a New (Dis)order,* edited by Eliezer Ben Rafael and Yitzak Sternberg, 47–74. Leiden: Brill, 2009.

Edele, Mark and Wanda Warlik, "Saved by Stalin? Trajectories of Polish Jews in Soviet Second World War. In *Shelter from the Holocaust: Rethinking Jewish Survival in the Soviet Union,* edited by A. Grossmann, S. Fitzpatrick, and M. Edele, 95–160. Detroit: Wayne State University Press, 2017.

Engel, David. "Jewish Diplomacy at a Crossroads." In *1929: Mapping the Jewish World,* edited by Hasia R. Diner and Gennady Ėstraĭkh, 27–35. New York: NYU Press Scholarship Online, 2016.

Frank, Matthew. "Reconstructing the Nation-State: Population Transfer in Central and Eastern Europe, 1944–1948." In *The Disentanglement of Populations: Migration, Expulsion and Displacement in Postwar Europe, 1944–1949,* edited by Jessica Reinisch and Elizabeth White, 36–42. London: Palgrave MacMillan, 2011.

Frydel, Tomasz. "The Devil in Microhistory: The 'Hunt for Jews' as a Social Process, 1942–1945." In *Microhistories of the Holocaust,* edited by Claire Zalc and Tal Bruttmann, 171–189. New York: Berghahn Books, 2017.

———. "*Judenjagd*: Reassessing the Role of Ordinary Poles in the Holocaust." In *Perpetrators: Dynamics, Motivations and Concepts for Participating in Mass Violence,* edited by Timothy Williams and Susanne Buckley-Zistel, 187–203. Centre for Conflict Studies, Marburg University, 2016.

Gross, Jan Tomasz. "The Jewish Community in the Soviet-Annexed Territories on the Eve of the Holocaust: A Social Scientist's View." In *The Holocaust in the Soviet Union: Studies and Sources on the Destruction of the Jews in the Nazi-Occupied Territories of the USSR, 1941–1945*, edited by Lucjan Dobroszycki and Jeffrey S. Gurock, 191–206. Armonk, NY: M. E. Sharpe, 1993.

———. "The Sovietization of Western Ukraine and Western Byelorussia." In *Jews in Eastern Poland and the USSR, 1939–1946*, edited by Norman Davies and Antony Polonsky, 60–77. London: Macmillan Academic and Professional, 1991.

Grynberg, Henryk. *Children of Zion: Jewish Lives.* Translated by Jacqueline Mitchell. Evanston, IL: Northwestern University Press, 1998.

Gutman, Yisrael. "Polish Anti-Semitism between the Wars: An Overview." In *The Jews of Poland between the Two World Wars*, edited by Yisrael Gutman, Ezra Mendelsohn, Jehuda Reinharz, and Chone Schmeruk, 97–108. Hanover, NH: New England University Press, 1989.

Ha'am, Ahad. "Negation of the Diaspora [1909]." In *The Zionist Idea: A Historical Analysis and Reader.* Edited by Arthur Hertzberg, 270–271. Philadelphia: Jewish Publication Society of America, 1997.

Haftka, Aleksander. "Żydowskie stronnictwa polityczne w Polsce Odrodzonej." In *The Jews in Renewed Poland: Activities, Society, Economy, Education and Culture*, vol. 2, edited by Aleksander Haftka, Ignacy Schiper, and Arieh Tartakower, 249–285. Warsaw: Warszawskie Zakłady Graficzne, 1933.

Halamish, Aviva. "Palestine as a Destination for Jewish Immigrants and Refugees from Nazi Germany." In *Refugees from Nazi Germany and the Liberal European States*, edited by Frank Caestecker and Bob Moore, 122–150. New York: Berghahn Books, 2010.

Hochberg-Mariańska, Maria, ed. *Dzieci oskarżają* (*The Children Accuse*). Kraków, Łódź, Warsaw: Wiedza Powszechna, 1947.

Hoffmann, Stefan-Ludwig. "Germans into Allies: Writing a Diary in 1945." In *Seeking Peace in the Wake of War: Europe, 1943–1947*, edited by Stefan-Ludwig Hoffmann, Sandrine Kott, Peter Romijn, and Olivier Wieviorka, 63–91. Studies of the NIOD Institute for War, Holocaust and Genocide Studies. Amsterdam: Amsterdam University Press, 2015.

Horowitz, Brian. "Muse and Muscle: Story of My Life and the Invention of Vladimir Jabotinsky." In *Story of My Life*, by Vladimir Jabotinsky. Edited by Brian Horowitz and Leonid Katsis, 1–32. Detroit, MI: Wayne State University Press, 2016.

Hundert, Gershon David. "Some Basic Characteristics of the Jewish Experience in Poland." In *From Shtetl to Socialism: Studies from Polin*, edited by Antony Polonsky, 19–25. Liverpool: Liverpool University Press, 1993.

Jacobmeyer, Wolfgang. "The Displaced Persons Problem: Repatriation and Resettlement." In *European Immigrants in Britain, 1933–1950*, edited by Johannes-Dieter Steinert and Inge Weber-Newth, 137–149. München: De Gruyter Suar, 2003.

Kaplan, Marion. "When the Ordinary Became Extraordinary: German Jews Reaction to Nazi Persecution, 1933–1939." In *Social Outsiders in Nazi Germany*, edited by Robert Gellately and Nathan Stoltzfus, 66–98. Princeton, NJ: Princeton University Press, 2001.

Kersten, Krystyna. "Kształtowanie stosunków ludnościowych." In *Polska Ludowa, 1944–1950: Przemiany Społeczne*, edited by Franciszek Ryszka and Hanna Jędruszczak, 74–176. Wrocław: Ossolineum, 1974.

Kijek, Kamil. "Aliens in the Lands of the Piasts: The Polonization of Lower Silesia and Its Jewish Community in the Years 1945–1950." In *Jews and Germans in Eastern Europe: Shared and Comparative Histories*, edited by Tobias Grill, 234–256. Oldenburg: De Gruyter, 2018.

———. "Reichenbach/Rychbach/Dzierżoniów: A Center for Jewish Life in Poland in the Period of Transition, 1945–1950." In *Our Courage—Jews in Europe, 1945–48*, edited by Kata Bohus, Atina Grossmann, Werner Hanak, and Mirjam Wenzel, 104–117. Oldenburg: De Gruyter, 2020.

Litvak, Yosef. "The American Joint Distribution Committee and Polish Jewry." In *Organizing Rescue: National Jewish Solidarity in the Modern Period*, edited by Selwyn Ilan Troen and Benjamin Pinkus, 269–315. London: Cass, 1992.

———. "The Plight of Refugees from the German-Occupied Territories." In *The Soviet Takeover of the Polish Eastern Provinces, 1939–1941*, edited by Keith Sword, 57–71. London: Palgrave Macmillan, 1991.

———. "Polish-Jewish Refugees Repatriated from the Soviet Union at the End of the Second World War and Afterwards." In *Jews in Eastern Poland and the USSR, 1939–46*, edited by Norman Davies and Antony Polonsky, 227–239. Studies in Russia and East Europe. Basingstoke: Macmillan, 1991.

Marrus, Michael Robert. "A Jewish Lobby at Nuremberg: Jacob Robinson and the Institute of Jewish Affairs, 1945–1946." In *The Nuremberg Trials: International Criminal Law since 1945*, edited by Walter R. Hippel, Lawrence Raful, Herbert R. Reginbogin, and Christoph Safferling, 63–72. Berlin: De Gruyter, 2011.

Melzer, Emmanuel. "Anti-Semitism in the Last Years of the Republic." In *The Jews of Poland between the Two World Wars*, edited by Yisrael Gutman, Ezra Mendelsohn, Jehuda Reinharz, and Chone Schmeruk, 126–137. Hanover, NH: New England University Press, 1989.

Michlic, Joanna Beata. "What Does a Child Remember? Recollections of the War and the Early Postwar Period among Child Survivors from Poland." In *Jewish Families in Europe, 1939–Present: History, Representation, and Memory*, edited by Joanna B. Michlic, 153–172. Waltham, MA: Brandeis University Press, 2017.

Morris, Benny. "Explaining Transfer: Zionist Thinking and the Creation of the Palestinian Refugee Problem." In *Removing Peoples: Forced Removal in the Modern World*, edited by Richard Bessell and Claudia B. Haake, 349–357. Oxford: Oxford University Press, 2009.

Moses, A. Dirk. "Epilogue: Partitions, Hostages, Transfer—Retributive Violence and National Security." *Partitions: A Transnational History of Twentieth-Century Territorial Separatism*, edited by Arie M. Dubnov and Laura Robson, 257–296. Stanford, CA: Stanford University Press, 2019.

Muhlen, Patrick von zur. "The 1930s: The End of the Latin American Open-Door Policy." In *Refugees from Nazi Germany and the Liberal European States*, edited by Frank Caestecker and Bob Moore, 103–108. New York: Berghahn Books, 2010.

Patt, Avinoam J. "Stateless Citizens of Israel." In *The Disentanglement of Populations: Migration, Expulsion and Displacement in Post-war Europe, 1944–9*, edited by Jessica Reinisch and Elizabeth White, 162–183. Basingstoke: Palgrave Macmillan, 2011.

Pedersen, Susan. "Settler Colonialism at the Bar of the League of Nations." In *Settler Colonialism in the Twentieth Century*, edited by Caroline Elkins and Susan Pedersen, 113–134. London: Routledge, 2005.

Penslar, Derek. "Narratives of Nation Building: Major Themes in Zionist Historiography." In *The Jewish Past Revisited: Reflections on Modern Jewish Historians*, edited by David Myers and David Ruderman, 104–127. Studies in Jewish Culture and Society. New Haven, CT: Yale University Press, 1998.

Oz, Amos, and Nitza Ben-Dov. "The Meaning of Homeland." In *The Amos Oz Reader*, 235–252. New York: Houghton Mifflin Harcourt, 2009.

Reinisch, Jessica. "Old Wine in New Bottles? UNRRA and the Mid-century World of Refugees." In *Refugees in Europe, 1919–1959: A Forty Years' Crisis?*, edited by Matthew Frank and Jessica Reinisch, 147–176. London: Bloomsbury, 2017.

Rudnicki, Szymon. "Anti-Jewish Legislation in Interwar Poland." In *Antisemitism and Its Opponents in Modern Poland*, edited by Robert Blobaum, 148–170. Ithaca, NY: Cornell University Press, 2005.

Schmeruk, Chone. "Hebrew-Yiddish-Polish: The Trilingual Structure of Jewish Culture in Poland." In *The Jews of Poland between the Two World Wars*, edited by Yisrael Gutman, Ezra Mendelsohn, Jehuda Reinharz, and Chone Schmeruk, 285–311. Hanover, NH: New England University Press, 1989.

Schneider, Sommer. "Behind the Iron Curtain." In *The JDC at 100: A Century of Humanitarianism*, edited by Mikhail Mitsel, Elissa Bemporad, Jaclyn Granick, Suzanne D. Rutland, Veerle Vanden Daelen, Laura Hobson Faure, Anna Sommer Schneider, et al., 315–360. Detroit, MI: Wayne State University Press, 2019.

Schulze, Rainer. "Forced Migration of German Populations during and after the Second World War: History and Memory." In *The Disentanglement of Populations: Migration, Expulsion and Displacement in Post-war Europe, 1944–9*, edited by Jessica Reinisch and Elizabeth White, 51–71. Basingstoke: Palgrave Macmillan, 2011.

Shlomi, Hana. "The Jewish Organizing Committee in Moscow and the Jewish Central Committee in Warsaw, June 1945–Feb 1946: Tackling Repatriation."

In *Jews in Eastern Poland and the USSR, 1939–46*, edited by Norman Davies and Antony Polonsky, 7-21. Studies in Russia and East Europe. Basingstoke: Macmillan, 1991.

Siekierski, Maciej. "The Jews in Soviet-Occupied Eastern Poland at the End of 1939: Numbers and Distribution." In *Jews in Eastern Poland and the USSR, 1939–46*, edited by Norman Davies and Antony Polonsky, 110–115. New York: St. Martin's, 1991.

Siemaszko, Zbigniew Sebastian. "The Mass Deportations of the Polish Population to the USSR, 1940–1941." In *The Soviet Takeover of the Polish Eastern Provinces, 1939–41*, edited by Keith Sword, 217–235. London: Palgrave Macmillan, 199.

Stankowski, Albert, and Piotr Weiser. "Demograficzne skutki Holokaustu." In *Następstwa zagłady Żydów: Polska 1944–2010*, edited by Feliks Tych and Monika Adamczyk-Garbowska, 15–38. Lublin: Wydawnictwo UMCS i Żydowski Instytut Historyczny im. Emanuela Ringelbluma, 2011.

Stefaniak, Marcin. "Nielegalna emigracja Żydów z Pomorza Zachodniego w latach 1945–1948." In *Żydzi i ich sąsiedzi na Pomorzu Zachodnim w XIX i XX wieku*, edited by Mieczysław Jaroszewicz and Włodzimierz Stępiński, 365–376. Warszawa: Wydawnictwo DiG, 2007.

Steffen, Katrin. "Contested Jewish Polishness: Language and Health as Markers for the Position of Jews in Polish Culture and Society in the Interwar Period." In *New Directions in the History of the Jews in the Polish Lands*, edited by Antony Polonsky, Hanna Węgrzynek, and Andrzej Żbikowski, 366–85. Boston: Academic Studies, 2018.

———. "'Polska—to także my!': Prasa polsko-żydowska (1918–1939)." In *Studia z dziejów trójjęzycznej prasy żydowskiej na ziemiach polskich (XIX–XX w.)*, edited by Joanna Nalewajko-Kulikov, 129–140. Warsaw: Neriton/Instytut Historii PAN, 2012.

———. "Żydowska polskość jako koncepcja tożsamości w polsko-żydowskiej prasu międzywojennego i jej dziedzictwo w 'Naszej Trybunie' w latach 1940–1952." In *Żydowski Polak, polski Żyd. Problem tożsamości w literaturze polsko-żydowskiej*, edited by Alina Molisak and Zuzanna Kołodziejska, 140–153. Warsaw: Elipsa, 2011.

Sula, Dorota. "Z ZSRR na Dolny Śląsk: Przesiedlenie i repatriacja polskich Żydów w latach 1945–1946." In *Syberiada Żydów polskich: Losy uchodźców z Zagłady*, edited by Lidia Zessin-Jurek and Katharina Friedla, 561–586. Warsaw: Żydowski Instytut Historyczny, 2020.

Szymborska, Wisława. "The End and the Beginning." In *Miracle Fair: Selected Poems of Wisława Szymborska*, translated by Joanna Trzeciak. New York: W.W. Norton, 2001: 48.

Tartakower, Arieh. "Stan liczebny i rozwój naturalny ludności żydowskiej w Polsce." In *The Jews in Renewed Poland: Activities, Society, Economy, Education and Culture*, vol. 2, edited by Aleksander Haftka, Ignacy Schiper, and Arieh Tartakower, 185–224. Warsaw: Warszawskie Zakłady Graficzne, 1933.

Ther, Phillip. "Pre-negotiated Violence: Ethnic Cleansing the Long First World War." In *Legacies of Violence: Eastern Europe's First World War*, edited by Jochen Böhler, Włodzimierz Borodziej, and Joachim Von Puttkamer, 258–84. München: Oldenbourg, De Gruyter, 2014.

Tölölyan, Khachig. "Beyond the Homeland: From Exilic Nationalism to Diasporic Transnationalism." In *The Call of the Homeland: Diaspora Nationalisms, Past and Present*, edited by Athena S. Leoussi, Allon Gal, and Anthony D. Smith, 27-45. Leiden: Brill, 2010.

Trębacz, Zofia. "'Ghetto Benches' at Polish Universities: Ideology and Practic." In *Alma mater antisemitica: Akademisches Milieu, Juden und Antisemitismus an den Universitäten Europas zwischen 1918 und 1939*, edited by Regina Fritz, Grzegorz Rossoliński-Liebe, and Jana Starek, 113–36. Vienna: New Academic, 2016.

Wynot, Edward. "The Polish Peasant Movement and the Jews, 1918–1939." In *The Jews of Poland between the Two World Wars*, edited by Yisrael Gutman, Ezra Mendelsohn, Jehuda Reinharz, and Chone Schmeruk, 36–55. Hanover, NH: New England University Press, 1989.

Zahra, Tara. "Zionism, Emigration and East European Colonialism." In *Colonialism and the Jews*, edited by Ethan B. Katz, Lisa Moses Leff, and Maud S. Maundel, 166–192. Bloomington: Indiana University Press, 2017.

Zaremba, Marcin. "The 'War' Syndrome: World War II and Polish Society." In *Seeking Peace in the Wake of War: Europe, 1943–1947*, edited by Stefan-Ludwig Hoffmann, Sandrine Kott, Peter Romijn, and Olivier Wieviorka, 27–62. Studies of the NIOD Institute for War, Holocaust and Genocide Studies. Amsterdam: Amsterdam University Press, 2015.

MONOGRAPHS

Adler, Eliyana. *Survival on the Margins: Polish Jewish Refugees in the Wartime Soviet Union*. Cambridge, MA: Harvard University Press, 2020.

Aleksiun, Natalia. *Conscious History: Polish Jewish Historians before the Holocaust*. Liverpool: Littman Library of Jewish Civilization, 2021.

———. *Dokąd dalej? Ruch syjonistyczny w Polsce, 1944–1950* [Where to? The Zionist movement in Poland, 1944–1950]. Warsaw: Trio, 2002.

Alroey, Gur. *An Unpromising Land: Jewish Migration to Palestine in the Early Twentieth Century*. Stanford, CA: Stanford University Press, 2014.

Aly, Götz. *Final Solution: Nazi Population Policy and the Murder of the European Jews*. Translated by Belinda Cooper and Allison Brown. London: Bloomsbury, 1999.

Applebaum, Anne. *Iron Curtain: The Crushing of Eastern Europe, 1944–56*. London: Allen Lane, 2012.

Arad, Yitzhak. *Bełżec, Sobibór, Treblinka: The Operation Reinhard Death Camps*. Bloomington: Indiana University Press, 1987.

Arendt, Hannah. *The Jewish Writings*. Edited by Jerome Kohn and Ron H. Feldman. New York: Schocken Books, 2007.

Armstrong-Reid, Susan, and David R. Murray. *Armies of Peace: Canada and the UNRRA Years*. Toronto: University of Toronto Press, 2008.

Auerbach, Karen. *The House at Ujazdowskie 16: Jewish Families in Warsaw after the Holocaust*. Modern Jewish Experience. Bloomington: Indiana University Press, 2013.

Bacon, Gershon. *The Politics of Tradition: The Agudat Yisrael in Poland, 1916–1939*. Jerusalem: Magnes, 1996.

Baer, Yitzhak. *Galut*. Bücherei Des Schocken Verlags 61. Berlin: Schocken, 1936.

Barton, Hildor Arnold. *A Folk Divided: Homeland Swedes and Swedish Americans, 1840–1940*. Carbondale: Southern Illinois University Press, 1994.

Bauer, Yehuda. *Flight and Rescue: Brichah*. Contemporary Jewish Civilization Series. New York: Random House, 1970.

———. *From Diplomacy to Resistance: A History of Jewish Palestine, 1930–1945*. Philadelphia: Jewish Publication Society of America, 1970.

———. *The Jewish Emergence from Powerlessness*. Toronto: University of Toronto Press, 1979.

———. *My Brother's Keeper: A History of the American Jewish Joint Distribution Committee, 1929–1939*. Philadelphia: Jewish Publication Society of America, 1974.

———. *Out of the Ashes: The Impact of American Jews on Post-Holocaust Jewish European Jewry*. Oxford: Pergamon, 1989.

Belsky, Natalie. "Encounters in the East: Evacuees in the Soviet Hinterland during the Second World War." PhD diss., University of Chicago, 2015.

Beneš, Jakub S. *Workers and Nationalism: Czech and German Social Democracy in Habsburg Austria, 1890–1918*. Oxford: Oxford University Press, 2017.

Biale, David, David Assaf, Benjamin Brown, Uriel Gellman, Samuel C. Heilman, and Marcin Wodziński. *Hasidism: A New History*. Princeton, NJ: Princeton University Press, 2018.

Böhler, Jochen. *Civil War in Central Europe, 1918–1921: The Reconstruction of Poland*. Oxford: Oxford University Press, 2018.

Bourdieu, Pierre. *Language and Symbolic Power*. Cambridge, MA: Harvard University Press, 1991.

Boyarin, Daniel. *A Traveling Homeland: The Babylonian Talmud as Diaspora*. Philadelphia: University of Pennsylvania Press, 2015.

Brandes, Detlef. *Der Weg zur Vertreibung, 1938–1945: Pläne und Entscheidungen zum "Transfer" der Deutschen aus der Tschechoslowakei und aus Polen*. Munich: Oldenbourg, 2001.

———. *Grossbritannien und seine osteuropäische Alliierten: Regierungen Polens, der Tschechoslowakei und Jugoslawiens im Londoner Exil vom Kriegsausbruch bis zur Konferenz von Teheran*. Munich: Oldenbourg, 1988.

Brown, Kate. *A Biography of No Place: From Ethnic Borderland to Soviet Heartland*. Cambridge, MA: Harvard University Press, 2004.

Browning, Christopher R. *The Path to Genocide: Essays on Launching the Final Solution*. Cambridge: Cambridge University Press, 1992.

Brubaker, Rogers. *Ethnicity without Groups*. Cambridge, MA: Harvard University Press, 2004.

Bryant, Chad Carl. *Prague in Black: Nazi Rule and Czech Nationalism*. Cambridge, MA: Harvard University Press, 2007.

Brykczyński, Paul. *Primed for Violence: Murder, Antisemitism, and Democratic Politics in Interwar Poland*. Madison: University of Wisconsin Press, 2016.

Brzezinski, Zbigniew. *The Soviet Bloc: Unity and Conflict*. Cambridge, MA: Harvard University Press, 1960.

Bugaj, Tadeusz. *Dzieci polskie w ZSRR i ich repatriacja 1939–1952* (Jelenia Góra: Prace Karkonoskiego Towarzystwa Naukowego, 1982).

Caestecker, Frank, and Bob Moore. *Refugees from Nazi Germany and the Liberal European States*. New York: Berghahn Books, 2010.

Cała, Alina. *The Image of the Jew in Polish Folk Culture*. Jerusalem: Magnes Press, Hebrew University, 1995.

———. *Ostatnie Pokolenie: Autobiografie polskiej mlodzieży żydowskiej okresu międzywojennego: ze zbiorów YIVO Institute for Jewish Research w Nowym Jorku*. Warsaw: Wydawnictwo Sic!, 2003.

———. *Syn będzie Lech . . . Asymilacja Żydów w Polsce międzywojennej*. Warsaw: Neriton, 2006.

Čapková, Kateřina. *Češi, Němci, Židé? Národní Identita Židů v Čechách, 1918–1938* [Czech, German, Jew? The nationality identity of Jews in Bohemia, 1918–1938]. Prague: Paseka, 2005.

Case, Holly. *Between States: The Transylvanian Question and the European Idea during World War II*. Palo Alto, CA: Stanford University Press, 2009.

———. *The Age of Questions; or, A First Attempt at an Aggregate History of the Eastern, Social, Woman, American, Jewish, Polish, Bullion, Tuberculosis, and Many Other Questions over the Nineteenth Century, and Beyond*. Princeton, NJ: Princeton University Press, 2018.

Chodakiewicz, Marek Jan. *After the Holocaust: Polish-Jewish Conflict in the Wake of World War II*. New York: East European Monographs, 2003.

Chu, Winson. *The German Minority in Interwar Poland*. Publications of the German Historical Institute. Cambridge: Cambridge University Press, 2012.

Ciancia, Kathryn. *On Civilization's Edge: A Polish Borderland in the Interwar World*. Oxford: Oxford University Press, 2020.

Cichopek-Gajraj, Anna. *Beyond Violence: Jewish Survivors in Poland and Slovakia, 1944–48*. New Studies in European History. Cambridge: Cambridge University Press, 2014.

———. *Pogrom Żydów w Krakowie 11 sierpnia 1945 r* [Pogrom of Jews in Kraków, August 11, 1945]. Warsaw: Jewish Historical Institute, 2000.

Cohen, Gerard Daniel. *In War's Wake: Europe's Displaced Persons in the Postwar Order*. Oxford Studies in International History. Oxford: Oxford University Press, 2012.

Cohen, Michael Joseph. *Truman and Israel*. Berkeley: University of California Press, 1990.

Cohen, Naomi. *Not Free to Desist: The American Jewish Committee, 1906–1966*. Philadelphia: Jewish Publication Society of America, 1972.

Connelly, John. *Captive University: The Sovietization of East German, Czech, and Polish Higher Education, 1945–1956*. Chapel Hill: University of North Carolina Press, 2000.

———. *From Peoples into Nations: A History of Eastern Europe*. Princeton, NJ: Princeton University Press, 2020.

Corney, Frederick C. *Telling October: Memory and the Making of the Bolshevik Revolution*. Ithaca, NY: Cornell University Press, 2004.

Crago-Schneider, Kierra Mikaila. "Jewish 'Shtetls' in Postwar Germany: An Analysis of Interactions among Jewish Displaced Persons, Germans, and Americans between 1945 and 1957 in Bavaria." PhD diss., University of California, Los Angeles, 2013.

Czerniakiewicz, Jan. *Repatriacja ludności polskiej z ZSRR 1944–1948*. Warszawa: PWN, 1987.

Dawidowicz, Lucy S. *A Holocaust Reader*. West Orange, NJ: Behrman, 1976.

Dean, Martin, Constantin Goschler, and Philipp Ther. *Robbery and Restitution: The Conflict over Jewish Property in Europe*. War and Genocide, vol. 9. New York: Berghahn Books, 2007.

Dean, Michael W. "What the Heart Unites, the Sea Shall Not Divide: Claiming Overseas Czechs for the Nation, 1848–1914." PhD diss., University of California, Berkeley, 2014.

Douglas, R. M. *Orderly and Humane: The Expulsion of the Germans after the Second World War*. New Haven, CT: Yale University Press, 2012.

Dranger, Jacob. *Nahum Goldmann: Ein Leben fur Israel*. Frankfurt: Europaische Verlagsanstalt, 1959.

Dubnow, Simon. *Encyclopedia of the Social Sciences*. Paris: Dubnow Fund, 1931. Originally published in Yiddish as *Algemeyne Entsiklopedye*.

Dufoix, Stéphane. *The Dispersion: A History of the Word Diaspora*. Leiden: Brill, 2017.

Eberhardt, Piotr. *Political Migrations on Polish Territories (1939–1950)*. Warsaw: Polska Akademia Nauk, 2011.

Edele, Mark, Sheila Fitzpatrick, and Atina Grossmann. *Shelter from the Holocaust: Rethinking Jewish Survival in the Soviet Union*. Detroit: Wayne State University Press, 2017.

Endelman, Todd. *The Jews of Britain, 1656 to 2000*. Berkeley: University of California Press, 2002.

Engel, David. *Between Liberation and Flight: Holocaust Survivors in Poland and the Struggle for Leadership* [in Hebrew]. Tel Aviv: ʻAm Oved, 1996.

———. *Facing a Holocaust: The Polish Government-in-Exile and the Jews, 1943–1945*. Chapel Hill: University of North Carolina Press, 1993.

———. *In the Shadow of Auschwitz: The Polish Government-in-Exile and the Jews, 1939–1942*. Chapel Hill: University of North Carolina Press, 1987.

Fink, Carole. *Defending the Rights of Others: The Great Powers, the Jews, and International Minority Protection, 1878–1938*. Cambridge: Cambridge University Press, 2004.

Fleming, Michael. *Auschwitz, the Allies and Censorship of the Holocaust*. Cambridge: Cambridge University Press, 2014.

Frank, Matthew James. *Making Minorities History: Population Transfer in Twentieth-Century Europe*. Oxford: Oxford University Press, 2017.

Frankel, Jonathan. *Prophecy and Politics: Socialism, Nationalism, and the Russian Jews, 1862–1917*. Cambridge: Cambridge University Press, 1981.

Frankl, Michal, and Kateřina Čapková. *Nejisté útočiště: Československo a uprchlíci před nacismem 1933–1938*. Prague: Paseka, 2008.

Frommer, Benjamin. *National Cleansing: Retribution against Nazi Collaborators in Postwar Czechoslovakia*. Studies in the Social and Cultural History of Modern Warfare. Cambridge: Cambridge University Press, 2005.

Fuks, Marian. *Prasa żydowska w Warszawie, 1823–1939*. Warsaw: Państwowe Wydawn. Nauk, 1979.

Gatrell, Peter. *A Whole Empire Walking: Refugees in Russia during World War I*. Bloomington: Indiana University Press, 1999.

Gebert, Konstanty. *Living in the Land of Ashes*. Kraków: Austeria, 2008.

Gerlach, David W. *The Economy of Ethnic Cleansing: The Transformation of the German-Czech Borderlands after World War II*. Cambridge: Cambridge University Press, 2017.

Glassheim, Eagle. *Cleansing the Czechoslovak Borderlands: Migration, Environment, and Health in the Former Sudetenland*. Pittsburgh: University of Pittsburgh Press, 2016.

———. *Obywatele polscy w Kirgizji: Wybór dokumentów (1941–1946)*. Warszawa: Naczelna Dyrekcja Archiwów Państwowych, 2010.

———. *Ocalić i repatriować: Opieka nad ludnością polską w głębi terytorium ZSRR (1943–1946)*. Łódź: Uniwersytetu Łódzkiego, 1994.

Goldmann, Nahum. *The Autobiography of Nahum Goldmann: Sixty Years of Jewish Life*. New York: Holt, Rinehart and Winston, 1969.

———. *Mein Leben: USA, Europa, Israel.* Munchen: Langen Muller, 1981.

Grabowski, Jan. *Hunt for the Jews: Betrayal and Murder in German-Occupied Poland.* Bloomington: Indiana University Press, 2013.

Grodzinsky, Yosef. *In the Shadow of the Holocaust: The Struggle between Jews and Zionists in the Aftermath of World War Two.* Monroe, ME: Common Courage, 2004.

Gross, Jan Tomasz. *Fear: Anti-semitism in Poland after Auschwitz—an Essay in Historical Interpretation.* Princeton, NJ: Princeton University Press, 2006.

———. *Neighbors: The Destruction of the Jewish Community in Jedwabne, Poland.* New York: Penguin Books, 2002.

———. *Upiorna dekada: Trzy Eseje O Stereotypach Na Temat Żydów, Polaków, Niemców i Komunistów 1939–1948.* [Ghastly decade, 1939–1948: Three essays on stereotypes about Jews, Poles, Germans and Communists]. Kraków: Tow. Autorów I Wydawców Prac Nauk. "Universitas," 1998.

Grossmann, Atina. *Jews, Germans, and Allies: Close Encounters in Occupied Germany.* Princeton, NJ: Princeton University Press, 2007.

Gruber, Ruth Ellen. *Virtually Jewish: Reinventing Jewish Culture in Europe.* Berkeley: University of California Press, 2002.

Grudzińska-Gross, Irena, and Jan Tomasz Gross. *War through Children's Eyes: The Soviet Occupation of Poland and the Deportations, 1939–1941.* Hoover Archival Documentaries. Stanford, CA: Hoover Institution Press, Stanford University, 1981.

Gruen, Erich S. *Diaspora: Jews amidst Greeks and Romans.* Cambridge, MA: Harvard University Press, 2002.

Gutman, Yisrael. *The Jews in Poland after World War II* [in Hebrew]. Jerusalem: Merkaz Zalman Shazar, 1985.

Gutman, Yisrael, Ezra Mendelsohn, Jehuda Reinharz, and Chone Schmeruk, eds. *The Jews of Poland between the Two World Wars.* Hanover, NH: New England University Press, 1989.

Hadas-Lebel, Mireille. *Philo of Alexandria: A Thinker in the Jewish Diaspora.* Translated by Robyn Fréchet. Leiden: Brill, 2012.

Haftka, Aleksander, Ignacy Schiper, and Arieh Tartakower. *The Jews in Renewed Poland: Activities, Society, Economy, Education and Culture.* Warsaw: Warszawskie Zakłady Graficzne, 1933.

Halpern, Ben. *The Idea of the Jewish State.* Harvard Middle Eastern Studies. Cambridge, MA: Harvard University Press, 1961.

Hanc, Josef. *Eastern Europe and the United States.* Boston: World Peace Foundation, 1942.

———. *Tornado across Europe: The Path of Nazi Destruction from Poland to Greece.* New York: Greystone, 1942.

Harper, John Lamberton, and Andrew Parlin. *The Polish Question during World War II.* Baltimore: Johns Hopkins University, 1990.

Hauner, Milan, ed. *Edvard Beneš: Paměti 1938–45: Paměti I—Mnichovské dny/ Paměti II—Od Mnichova k nové válce a k novému vítězství/ Paměti III—Dokumenty*. Prague: Academia, 2007.

Heller, Celia Stopnicka. *On the Edge of Destruction: Jews of Poland between the Two World Wars*. New York: Columbia University Press, 1977.

Heller, Daniel Kupfert. *Jabotinsky's Children: Polish Jews and the Rise of Right-Wing Zionism*. Princeton, NJ: Princeton University Press, 2017.

Henckaerts, Jean-Marie. *Mass Expulsion in Modern International Law and Practice*. Boston: Martinus Nijhoff, 1995.

Holborn, Louise W. *The International Refugee Organization: A Specialized Agency of the United Nations—Its History and Work, 1946–1952*. Oxford: Oxford University Press, 1956.

Humbert, Laure, Sharif Gemie, Fiona Reid, and Louise Ingram. *Outcast Europe: Refugees and Relief Workers in an Era of Total War, 1936–1948*. London: Continuum, 2011.

Jabotinsky, Vladimir. *The Jewish War Front*. London: George Allen and Unwin, 1940.

Jacobson, Matthew Frye. *Special Sorrows: The Diasporic Imagination of Irish, Polish and Jewish Immigrants in the United States*. Cambridge, MA: Harvard University Press, 1995.

Jamiński, Zygmunt. *Prasa żydowska w Polsce*. Lwów: Urzednicza, 1936.

Jolluck, Katherine R. *Exile and Identity: Polish Women in the Soviet Union during World War II*. Series in Russian and East European Studies. Pittsburgh: University of Pittsburgh Press, 2002.

Judis, John B. *Genesis: Truman, American Jews, and the Origins of the Arab/Israeli Conflict*. New York: Farrar, Straus and Giroux, 2014.

Judson, Pieter M. *Guardians of the Nation: Activists on the Language Frontiers of Imperial Austria*. Cambridge, MA: Harvard University Press, 2006.

Judt, Tony. *Postwar: A History of Europe since 1945*. New York: Penguin Group, 2005.

Kaminski, Lukasz. *Polacy wobec nowej rzeczywistosci, 1944–1948: Formy pozainstytucjalnego zywiolowego oporu spolecznego*. Torun: Wydawnictwo Adam Marszalek, 2000.

Kaplan, Karel. *Národní fronta, 1948–1960* [National Front, 1948–1960]. Prague: Academia, 2012.

———. *The Short March: The Communist Takeover in Czechoslovakia, 1945–1948*. London: C. Hurst, 1987.

Kaplan, Marion. *Between Dignity and Despair: Jewish Life in Nazi Germany*. Studies in Jewish History. Oxford: Oxford University Press, 1998.

———. *Hitler's Jewish Refugees: Hope and Anxiety in Portugal*. New Haven, CT: Yale University Press, 2020.

Karch, Brendan Jeffrey. *Nation and Loyalty in a German-Polish Borderland: Upper Silesia, 1848–1960*. Publications of the German Historical Institute. Cambridge: Cambridge University Press, 2018.

Karlip, Joshua. *The Tragedy of a Generation: The Rise and Fall of Jewish Nationalism in Eastern Europe*. Boston: Harvard University Press, 2013.

Karski, Jan. *Story of a Secret State*. Boston: Houghton Mifflin, 1944.

———. *The Great Powers and Poland, 1919–1945. From Versailles to Yalta*. Lanham, MD: University Press of America, 1985.

———. *Story of a Secret State: My Report to the World*. Washington, DC: Georgetown University Press, 2014.

Kassow, Samuel D. *Who Will Write Our History? Emanuel Ringelblum, the Warsaw Ghetto, and the Oyneg Shabes Archive*. Helen and Martin Schwartz Lectures in Jewish Studies. Bloomington: Indiana University Press, 2007.

Kats, Yosef. *Partner to Partition: The Jewish Agency's Partition Plan in the Mandate Era*. London: Frank Cass, 1998.

Katz, Steven. *The Shtetl: New Evaluations*. New York: New York University Press, 2007.

Kaufman, Menahem. *An Ambiguous Partnership: Non-Zionists and Zionists in America, 1939–1948*. Jerusalem: Magnes Press, Hebrew University, 1991.

Kenney, Padraic. *Rebuilding Poland: Workers and Communists, 1945–1950*. Ithaca, NY: Cornell University Press, 1997.

Kersten, Krystyna, John S. Micgiel, and Michael H. Bernhard. *The Establishment of Communist Rule in Poland, 1943–1948*. Societies and Culture in East-Central Europe. Berkeley: University of California Press, 1991.

Kersten, Krystyna. *Repatriacja ludności polskiej Po II Wojnie światowej: Studium Historyczne*. Wrocław: Zakład Narodowy Im. Ossolińskich, 1974.

———. *Polacy, Żydzi, komunizm: anatomia półprawd 1939–1968*. Warsaw: Niezależna oficyna wydawnicza, 1992.

Kieval, Hillel J. *Languages of Community: The Jewish Experience in the Czech Lands*. Berkeley: University of California Press, 2000.

Kijek, Kamil. *Dzieci modernizmu: Świadomość, kultura i socjalizacja polityczna młodzieży żydowskiej w II Rzeczypospolitej*. Wrocław: Wydawnictwo Uniwersytetu Wrocławskiego, 2017.

King, Jeremy. *Budweisers into Czechs and Germans: A Local History of Bohemian Politics, 1848–1948*. Princeton, NJ: Princeton University Press, 2002.

Kirsh, Mary Fraser. "The Lost Children of Europe: Narrating the Rehabilitation of Child Holocaust Survivors in Great Britain and Israel." PhD Diss., Univ. of Wisconsin, Madison, 2012.

Klein-Pejšová, Rebekah. *Mapping Jewish Loyalties in Interwar Slovakia*. Bloomington: Indiana University Press, 2015.

Klukowski, Zygmunt. *Diary from the Years of Occupation, 1939–1944*. Translated by George Klukowski. Urbana: University of Illinois Press, 1993.

Kochavi, Arieh J. *Post-Holocaust Politics: Britain, the United States, and Jewish Refugees, 1945–1948*. Chapel Hill: University of North Carolina Press, 2001.

Koloski, Laurie. "Painting Kraków Red: Politics and Culture in Poland, 1945–1950." PhD diss., Stanford University, 1998.

Kolsky, Thomas A. *Jews against Zionism: The American Council for Judaism, 1942–1948*. Philadelphia: Temple University Press, 1990.

Kopstein, Jeffrey, and Jason Wittenberg. *Intimate Violence: Anti-Jewish Pogroms on the Eve of the Holocaust*. Ithaca, NY: Cornell University Press, 2018.

Korzon, Andrzej. "Przesiedlona ludność polska w ZSRR." PhD diss., Instytut Historii PAN, Warszawa, 1967.

Kovály, Heda. *Under a Cruel Star: A Life in Prague, 1941–1968*. Cambridge, MA: Plunkett Lake, 1986.

Krzyżanowski, Łukasz. *Ghost Citizens: Jewish Return to a Postwar City*. Cambridge, MA: Harvard University Press, 2020.

Kubowitzki, Aryeh Leon. *Unity in Dispersion: A History of the World Jewish Congress*. New York: World Jewish Congress, 1948.

Kuklík, Jan. *Czech Law in Historical Contexts*. Prague: Karolinum, 2015.

Kurz, Nathan. *Jewish Internationalism and Human Rights after the Holocaust*. Cambridge: Cambridge University Press, 2020.

Landau-Czajka, Anna. *Polska-to nie oni: Polska i Polacy w polskojęzycznej prasie żydowskej II Rzeczypospolitej*. Warsaw: Żydowski Institut Historyczny, 2015.

Láníček, Jan. *Arnošt Frischer and the Jewish Politics of Early 20th-Century Europe*. London: Bloomsbury Academic, 2017.

———. *Czechs, Slovaks and the Jews, 1938–48: Beyond Idealization and Condemnation*. New York: Basingstoke, 2013.

Láníček, Jan, and James Jordan. *Governments-in-Exile and the Jews during the Second World War*. London: Valentine Mitchell, 2013.

Laqueur, Walter. *The Terrible Secret: Suppression of the Truth about Hitler's "Final Solution."* Boston: Little, Brown, 1981.

Lehrer, Erica. *Jewish Poland Revisited: Heritage Tourism in Unquiet Places*. Bloomington: University of Indiana Press, 2013.

Levene, Mark. *War, Jews, and the New Europe: The Diplomacy of Lucien Wolf, 1914–1919*. Littman Library of Jewish Civilization (Series). Oxford: published for the Littman Library by Oxford University Press, 1992.

Lewis, Mark. *The Birth of the New Justice: The Internationalization of Crime and Punishment, 1919–1950*. Oxford: Oxford University Press, 2014.

Lichtenstein, Tatjana. *Zionists in Interwar Czechoslovakia: Minority Nationalism and the Politics of Belonging*. Bloomington: Indiana University Press, 2016.

Litvak, Yosef. *Jewish Refugees from Poland in the Soviet Union, 1939–1946* [in Hebrew]. Jerusalem: Institute of Contemporary Jewry, Hebrew University of Jerusalem, 1988.

Loeffler, James. *Rooted Cosmopolitans: Jews and Human Rights in the Twentieth Century*. New Haven, CT: Yale University Press, 2018.

Lohr, Eric. *Nationalizing the Russian Empire: The Campaign against Enemy Aliens during World War I*. Cambridge, MA: Harvard University Press, 2003.

Lukas, Richard C. *The Strange Allies: The United States and Poland 1941–1945*. Knoxville: University of Tennessee Press, 1978.

Lukes, Igor. *Czechoslovakia between Stalin and Hitler: The Diplomacy of Edvard Benes in the 1930s*. Oxford: Oxford University Press, 1996.

Lumans, Valdis O. *Himmler's Auxiliaries: The Volksdeutsche Mittelstelle and the German National Minorities of Europe, 1933–1945*. Chapel Hill: University of North Carolina Press, 1993.

Luža, Radomír. *The Transfer of the Sudeten Germans: A Study of Czech-German Relations, 1933–1962*. London: Routledge and Kegan Paul, 1964.

MacMillan, Margaret. *Paris 1919: Six Months That Changed the World*. New York: Random House, 2003.

Madej-Krupitski, Urszula. "Mapping Jewish Poland: Leisure Travel and Identity in the Interwar Period." PhD diss., University of California, Berkeley, 2020.

Maisky, Ivan M. *The Maisky Diaries: The Wartime Revelations of Stalin's Ambassador in London*. Edited by Gabriel Gorodetsky. New Haven, CT: Yale University Press, 2016.

Mankowitz, Zeev W. *Life between Memory and Hope: The Survivors of the Holocaust in Occupied Germany*. Studies in the Social and Cultural History of Modern Warfare. Cambridge: Cambridge University Press, 2002.

Manley, Rebecca. *To the Tashkent Station: Evacuation and Survival in the Soviet Union at War*. Ithaca, NY: Cornell University Press, 2009.

Marcus, Joseph. *Social and Political History of the Jews in Poland, 1919–1939*. Berlin: Mouton, 1983.

Marrus, Michael Robert. *The Unwanted: European Refugees from the First World War through the Cold War*. Oxford: Oxford University Press, 1985.

Martin, Sean. *Jewish Life in Cracow, 1918–1939*. London: Vallentine Mitchell, 2004.

Masalha, Nur. *Expulsion of the Palestinians: The Concept of "Transfer" in Zionist Political Thought, 1882–1948*. Washington, DC: Institute for Palestine Studies, 1992.

———. *The Politics of Denial: Israel and the Palestinian Refugee Problem*. London: Pluto, 2003.

Masaryk, Jan. *Minorities and the Democratic State*. Lucien Wolf Memorial Lecture. London: Jewish Historical Society of England, 1943.

———. *Volá Londýn* [London calling]. Prague: Prace, 1946.

Mazower, Mark. *No Enchanted Palace: The End of Empire and the Ideological Origins of the United Nations*. Princeton, NJ: Princeton University Press, 2009.

McDonald, James G. *Advocate for the Doomed: The Diaries and Papers of James G. McDonald*. Edited by Richard Breitman, Barbara McDonald Stewart, and Severin Hochberg. Bloomington: Indiana University Press, 2007.

———. *Refugees and Rescue: The Diaries and Papers of James G. McDonald, 1935–1945*. Edited by Richard Breitman, Barbara McDonald Stewart, and Severin Hochberg. Bloomington: Indiana University Press, 2009.

———. *To the Gates of Jerusalem: The Diaries and Papers of James G. McDonald, 1945–1947*. Edited by Richard Breitman, Barbara McDonald Stewart, and Severin Hochberg. Bloomington: Indiana University Press, 2014.

Meducki, Stanisław, and Zenon Wrona. *Antyżydowskie wydarzenia kieleckie 4 lipca 1946 roku: Dokumenty i materiały*. Kielce: Urząd miasta Kielce, 1992.

Melchior, Małgorzata. *Społeczna Tożsamość Jednostki: (w świetle Wywiadów Z Polakami Pochodzenia żydowskiego Urodzonymi W Latach 1944–1955)* [The social identity of an individual: In the light of interviews with Poles of Jewish origin born in 1944–1955]. Warsaw: Uniwersytet Warszawski, Instytut Stosowanych Nauk Społecznych, 1990.

Melzer, Emmanuel. *No Way Out: The Politics of Polish Jewry, 1935–1939*. Cincinnati, OH: Hebrew Union College—Jewish Institute of Religion, 1997.

Mendelsohn, Ezra. *The Jews of East Central Europe between the World Wars*. Bloomington: Indiana University Press, 1983.

———. *On Modern Jewish Politics*. New York: Oxford University Press, 1993.

———. *Zionism in Poland: The Formative Years, 1913–1926*. New Haven, CT: Yale University Press, 1981.

Meng, Michael. *Shattered Spaces: Encountering Jewish Ruins in Postwar Germany and Poland*. Cambridge, MA: Harvard University Press, 2011.

Michlic, Joanna Beata. *Poland's Threatening Other: The Image of the Jew from 1880 to the Present*. Lincoln: University of Nebraska Press, 2006.

Mikołajczyk, Stanisław. *The Rape of Poland: Pattern of Soviet Aggression*. New York: Whittlesey House, 1948.

Miron, Dan. *The Image of the Shtetl and Other Studies of Modern Jewish Literary Imagination*. Syracuse, NY: Syracuse University Press, 2000.

Moyn, Samuel. *The Last Utopia: Human Rights in History*. Cambridge, MA: Harvard University Press, 2010.

———. *Not Enough: Human Rights in an Unequal World*. Cambridge, MA: Harvard University Press, 2018.

Musekamp, Jan. *Zwischen Stettin und Szczecin: Metamorphosen einer Stadt von 1945 bis 2005*. Wiesbaden: Harassowitz, 2010.

Naimark, Norman M. *Fires of Hatred: Ethnic Cleansing in Twentieth-Century Europe*. Cambridge, MA: Harvard University Press, 2001.

Naimark, Norman M., and L. I͡a. Gibianskiĭ. *The Establishment of Communist Regimes in Eastern Europe, 1944–1949*. Boulder, CO: Westview, 1997.

Nalewajko-Kulikov, Joanna, ed. *Studia z dziejów trójjęzycznej prasy żydowskiej na ziemiach polskich (XIX–XX)*. Warsaw: Neriton, 2012.

Nesselrodt, Markus. *Dem Holocaust entkommen: Polnische Juden in der Sowjetunion, 1939–1946*. Berlin: De Gru. Oldenbourg, 2019.

Novotný, Lukáš. *The British Legation in Prague: Perception of Czech-German Relations in Czechoslovakia between 1933 and 1938*. Berlin: De Gruyter Olderbourge, 2019.

Opočenský, Jan. *Formování československého zahraničního odboje v letech 1938–1939 ve světle svědectví Jana Opočenského*. Edited by Milan Hauner. Prague: Arenga, 2000.

Orzoff, Andrea. *Battle for the Castle: The Myth of Czechoslovakia in Europe, 1914–1948*. Oxford: Oxford University Press, 2009.

Paczkowski, Andrzej. *Referendum Z 30 Czerwca, 1946 R.: Przebieg I Wyniki*. Dokumenty Do Dziejów PRL, Zesz. 4. Warszawa: Polska Akademia Nauk, Instytut Studiów Politycznych, 1993.

Patai, Raphael. *Nahum Goldmann: His Missions to the Gentiles*. Judaic Studies Series. Tuscaloosa: University of Alabama Press, 1987.

Patt, Avinoam J. *Finding Home and Homeland: Jewish Youth and Zionism in the Aftermath of the Holocaust*. Detroit: Wayne State University Press, 2009.

Pedersen, Susan. *The Guardians: The League of Nations and the Crisis of Empire*. Oxford: Oxford University Press, 2015.

Person, Katarzyna. *Dipisi: Żydzi polscy w amerykańskiej i brytyjskiej strefach okupacyjnych Niemiec, 1945–1948*. Warsaw: Żydowski Instytut Historyczny, 2019.

Pianko, Noam. *Zionism and the Roads Not Taken: Rawidowicz, Kaplan, Kohn*. Modern Jewish Experience. Bloomington: Indiana University Press, 2010.

Polonsky, Antony, ed. *The Great Powers and the Polish Question, 1941–45: A Documentary Study in Cold War Origins*. London: London School of Economics and Political Science, 1976.

———. *Politics in Independent Poland, 1921–1939: The Crisis of Constitutional Government*. Oxford: Clarendon, 1972.

———. *The Jews in Poland and Russia: Volume III: 1914–2008*. Liverpool: The Littman Library of Jewish Civilization, 2012.

Polonsky, Antony, and Bolesław Drukier. *The Beginnings of Communist Rule in Poland*. London: Routledge and Kegan Paul, 1980.

Porter, Brian. *Poland in the Modern World: Beyond Martyrdom*. A New History of Modern Europe. Chichester: Wiley-Blackwell, 2014.

———. *When Nationalism Began to Hate: Imagining Modern Politics in Nineteenth Century Poland*. Oxford: Oxford University Press, 2002.

Puławski, Adam. *Wobec "niespotykanego w dziejach mordu": Rząd RP na uchodźstwie, Delegatura Rządu RP na Kraj, AK a eksterminacja ludności żydowskiej od "wielkiej akcji" do powstania w getcie*. Chełm: Stowarzyszenie Rocznik Chełmski, 2018.

———. *Wobliczu Zagłady: Rząd RP na Uchodźstwie, Delegatura Rządu RP na Kraj, ZWZ-AK wobec deportacji Żydów do obozów zagłady (1941–1942)*. Lublin: Instytut Pamięci Narodowej/Oddział w Lublinie, 2009.

Rabinovitch, Simon. *Jewish Rights, National Rites: Nationalism and Autonomy in Late Imperial and Revolutionary Russia*. Stanford Studies in Jewish History and Culture. Stanford, CA: Stanford University Press, 2014.

———. *Jews and Diaspora Nationalism: Writings on Jewish Peoplehood in Europe and the United States*. Waltham, MA: Brandeis University Press, 2012.

Raider, Mark, ed. *Nahum Goldmann: Statesman without a State*. SUNY Series in Israeli Studies. Albany: State University of New York Press, 2009.

Rawidowicz, Simon. *State of Israel, Diaspora, and Jewish Continuity: Essays on the "Ever-Dying People."* Edited by Benjamin C. I. Ravid. Tauber Institute for the Study of European Jewry Series 26. Hanover, NH: University Press of New England, 1998.

Rechter, David. *The Jews of Vienna and the First World War*. London: Littman Library of Jewish Civilization, 2001.

Redlich, Shimon. *Life in Transit: Jews in Postwar Lodz, 1945–1950*. Studies in Russian and Slavic Literatures, Cultures and History. Boston: Academic Studies, 2010.

———. *Together and Apart in Brzezany: Poles, Jews, and Ukrainians, 1919–1945*. Bloomington: Indiana University Press, 2002.

Rees, Elfan. *Century of the Homeless Man*. New York: Carnegie Endowment for International Peace, 1957.

Reinharz, Jehuda, and Yaacov Shavit. *The Road to September 1939: Polish Jews, Zionists, and the Yishuv on the Eve of World War II*. Waltham, MA: Brandeis University Press, 2018.

Reinisch, Jessica, and Elizabeth White. *The Disentanglement of Populations: Migration, Expulsion and Displacement in Post-war Europe, 1944–9*. Basingstoke: Palgrave Macmillan, 2011.

Reiss, Anselm. *Besa'arot Hatekufah* [In the storms of the era] [in Hebrew]. Tel Aviv: Am Oved, 1982.

The Reminiscences of Maurice Perlzweig. New York: Columbia University Oral Research Office, 1993.

Riegner, Gerhart. *Never Despair: Sixty Years in the Service of the Jewish People and the Cause of Human Rights*. Chicago: Ivan R. Dee, 2006.

Robin, Frederick. *The Pursuit of Equality: A Half Century with the American Jewish Committee*. New York: Crown, 1957.

Robinson, Jacob. *Human Rights and Fundamental Freedoms in the Charter of the United Nations: A Commentary*. From War to Peace, no. 4. New York: Institute of Jewish Affairs of the American Jewish Congress and the World Jewish Congress, 1946.

Robinson, Jacob, Oscar Karbach, Max M. Laserson, Nehemiah Robinson, and M. V. Vishniak. *Were the Minorities Treaties a Failure?* New York: Institute of Jewish Affairs of the American Jewish Congress and the World Jewish Congress, 1943.

Robson, Laura. *States of Separation: Transfer, Partition, and the Making of the Modern Middle East*. Berkeley: University of California Press, 2017.

Roth, Joseph. *The Wandering Jews*. Translated by Michael Hofmann. London: Granta, 2001.

Rothschild, Joseph. *East Central Europe between the Two World Wars*. Seattle: University of Washington Press, 1974.

Rozenblit, Marsha L. *Reconstructing a National Identity: The Jews of Habsburg Austria during World War I*. Studies in Jewish History. Oxford: Oxford University Press, 2001.

Rozenblit, Marsha L., and Jonathan Karp. *World War I and the Jews: Conflict and Transformation in Europe, the Middle East, and America*. New York: Berghahn Books, 2017.

Rubin, Gil S. "The Future of the Jews: Planning for the Postwar Jewish World, 1939–1946." PhD diss., Columbia University, 2017.

Rudawski, Michał. *Mój obcy kraj?* Warsaw: Agencja Wydawnicza Tu, 1996.

Rybak, Jan. *Everyday Zionism in East-Central Europe, 1914–1920: Nation-Building in War and Revolution*. Oxford: Oxford University Press, 2021.

Sands, Philippe. *East West Street: On the Origins of Genocide and Crimes against Humanity*. New York: Knopf, 2016.

Sanua, Marianne Rachel. *Let Us Prove Strong: The American Jewish Committee, 1945–2006*. Brandeis Series in American Jewish History, Culture, and Life. Waltham, MA: Brandeis University Press, 2007.

Schatz, Jaff. *The Generation: The Rise and Fall of the Generation of Jewish Communists of Poland*. Berkeley: University of California Press, 1991.

Schechter, Ronald. *Obstinate Hebrews: Representations of Jews in France, 1715–1815*. S. Mark Taper Foundation Imprint in Jewish Studies. Berkeley: University of California Press, 2003.

Schechtmann, Joseph B. *European Population Transfers, 1939–1945*. Studies of the Institute of World Affairs. Oxford: Oxford University Press, 1946.

Scholem, Gershon. *Major Trends in Jewish Mysticism*. Jerusalem: Schocken, 1941.

Sebald, William. *Austerlitz*. Translated by Anthea Bell. New York: Modern Library, 2001.

Segal, Raz. *Genocide in the Carpathians: War, Social Breakdown, and Mass Violence, 1914–1945*. Stanford Studies on Central and Eastern Europe. Stanford, CA: Stanford University Press, 2016.

Segev, Tom. *One Palestine, Complete: Jews and Arabs under the British Mandate*. Translated by Haim Watzman. New York: Metropolitan Books, 2000.

———. *The Seventh Million: Israelis and the Holocaust*. New York: Holt, 1991.

Segev, Zohar. *The World Jewish Congress during the Holocaust: Between Activism and Restraint*. Berlin: De Gruyter Oldenbourg, 2017.

Seidman, Naomi. *Faithful Renderings: Jewish-Christian Difference and the Politics of Translation*. Chicago: University of Chicago Press, 2006.

———. *Sarah Schenirer and the Bais Yaakov Movement: A Revolution in the Name of Tradition*. Liverpool: Littman Library of Jewish Civilization, 2019.

Service, Hugo. *Germans to Poles: Communism, Nationalism and Ethnic Cleansing after the Second World War*. New Studies in European History. Cambridge: Cambridge University Press, 2013.

Shandler, Jeffrey, ed. *Awakening Lives: Autobiographies of Jewish Youth in Poland before the Holocaust*. New Haven, CT: Yale University Press, 2002.

Shanes, Joshua. *Diaspora Nationalism and Jewish Identity in Habsburg Galicia*. Cambridge: Cambridge University Press, 2014.

Shaviṭ, Yaʻaḳov. *Jabotinsky and the Revisionist Movement, 1925–1948*. Right in Zionism and in Israel, 1925–1985, vol. 1. London: Cass, 1988.

Shephard, Ben. *The Long Road Home: The Aftermath of the Second World War*. London: Bodley Head, 2010.

Shore, Marci. *Caviar and Ashes: A Warsaw Generation's Life and Death in Marxism, 1918–1968*. New Haven, CT: Yale University Press, 2006.

Shumsky, Dmitry. *Beyond the Nation-State: The Zionist Political Imagination from Pinsker to Ben-Gurion*. New Haven, CT: Yale University Press, 2018.

Silber, Marcos. *Different Nationality/Equal Citizenship: Polish Jewry's Struggle for Autonomy during the First World War* [in Hebrew]. Tel Aviv: Merkaz Zalman Shazar, 2014.

Sjöberg, Tommie. *The Powers and the Persecuted: The Refugee Problem and the Intergovernmental Committee on Refugees (IGCR), 1938–1947*. Lund Studies in International History. Lund, Sweden: Lund University Press, 1991.

Slezkine, Yuri. *The Jewish Century*. Princeton, NJ: Princeton University Press, 2004.

Smetana, Vít. *In the Shadow of Munich: British Policy towards Czechoslovakia from the Endorsement to the Renunciation of the Munich Agreement (1938–1942)*. Prague: Karolinum, 2014.

Smutný, Jaromír. *Dokumenty z historie čsl. politiky 1939–1943*. Prague: Academia, 1966.

Snyder, Timothy. *Black Earth: The Holocaust as History and Warning*. New York: Penguin Random House, 2015.

Sorkin, David. *The Transformation of German Jewry, 1780–1840*. Oxford: Oxford University Press, 1987.

Stach, Stephan. *Nationalitätenpolitik aus der zweiten Reihe. Konzepte und Praktiken zur Einbindung nationaler Minderheiten in Piłsudskis Polen (1926–1939)*. Göttingen: Wallstein, 2021.

Stanislawski, Michael. *Zionism and the Fin de Siècle: Cosmopolitanism and Nationalism from Nordau to Jabotinsky*. Berkeley: University of California Press, 2001.

Steffen, Katrin. *Jüdische Polonität: Ethnizität und Nation im Spiegel der polnischsprachigen jüdischen Presse, 1918–1939*. Gottingen: Vanderhoeck and Ruprecht, 2004.

Steinlauf, Michael C. *Bondage to the Dead: Poland and the Memory of the Holocaust*. Modern Jewish History. Syracuse, NY: Syracuse University Press, 1997.

Stola, Dariusz. *Nadzieja i Zagłada: Ignacy Schwarzbart—żydowski Przedstawiciel W Radzie Narodowej RP, 1940–1945*. Wyd. Biblioteka Polonijna 31. Warszawa: Oficyna Naukowa, 1995.

Stone, I. F. *Underground to Palestine*. New York: Boni and Gaer, 1946.

Stone, Norman. *The Eastern Front, 1914–1917*. New York: Charles Scribner's Sons, 1975.

Stroop, Jürgen, and Andrzej Wirth. *Es Gibt Keinen Jüdischen Wohnbezirk in Warschau Mehr!* Warsaw: Instytut Pamięci Narodowej, Żydowski Instytut Historyczny, 2003.

Sword, Keith. *Deportation and Exile: Poles in the Soviet Union, 1939–48*. Studies in Russia and East Europe. London: Macmillan, 1994.

Szaynok, Bożena, and Krystyna Kersten. *Pogrom Żydów W Kielcach 4 Lipca 1946*. Warszawa: Wydawn Bellona, 1992.

Szymborska, Wisława. *Miracle Fair: Selected Poems of Wislawa Szymborska*. Translated by Joanna Trzeciak. New York: W. W. Norton, 2001.

Táborský, Eduard. *President Edvard Beneš: Between East and West, 1938–1948*. Stanford, CA: Stanford University Press, 1981.

Tartakower, Arieh. *Emigracja żydowska z Polski*. Warsaw: Instytut Badań Spraw Narodowościowych, 1939.

———. *The Jewish Emigration Problem and the Jewish World Congress*. Paris: Executive Committee for the Jewish World Congress, 1936.

———. *Zarys socjologii żydostwa*. Lwów: Nowa Drukarna Lwowska, 1938.

Tartakower, Arieh, and Kurt R. Grossmann. *The Jewish Refugee*. New York: Institute of Jewish Affairs of the American Jewish Congress and the World Jewish Congress, 1944.

Taylor, Lynne. *In the Children's Best Interests: Unaccompanied Children in American-Occupied Germany, 1945–1952*. German and European Studies. Toronto: University of Toronto Press, 2017.

Tenenbaum, Benjamin. *'Ehad me-'ir u-shenayim mi-mishpahah (One from a City and Two from a Family)*. Merhavia: Sifriat Poalim, 1947.

Ther, Philipp, and Charlotte Hughes-Kreutzmuller. *The Dark Side of Nation-States: Ethnic Cleansing in Modern Europe*. War and Genocide, vol. 19. New York: Berghahn Books, 2014.

Thum, Gregor. *Uprooted: How Breslau Became Wrocław during the Century of Expulsions*. Princeton, NJ: Princeton University Press, 2011.

Trębacz, Zofia. *Nie tylko Palestyna: Polskie plany emigracyjne wobec Żydów 1935–1939*. Warszawa: Żydowski Instytut Historyczny im. Emanuela Ringelbluma, 2018.

Tuwim, Julian. *My Żydzi Polscy . . .* [We Polish Jews . . .]. Warsaw: Fundacja Shalom, 1993.

Vartíková, Marta. *Košický vládny program* [Košice government program]. Bratislava: Nakladatel'stvo Pravda, 1978.

Veidlinger, Jeffrey. *In the Midst of Civilized Europe: The Pogroms of 1918–1921 and the Onset of the Holocaust*. New York: Metropolitan Books, 2021.

Vošahlíková, Pavla. *Československá sociální demokracie a Národní fronta* [Czechoslovakian social democracy and the National Front]. Prague: Academia, 1985.

Wachsman, Z. H. *Jan Masaryk, Friend of the Jewish People*. New York: Czechoslovak Information Service, 1943.

Wandycz, Piotr S. *Czechoslovak-Polish Confederation and the Great Powers: 1940–43*. Indiana University Publications, Slavic and East European Series. Bloomington: Indiana University Press, 1956.

———. *The Price of Freedom: A History of East Central Europe from the Middle Ages to the Present*. London: Routledge, 2017.

Warhaftig, Zorach. *Refugee and Survivor: Rescue Efforts during the Holocaust*. Jerusalem: Yad Vashem, 1988.

Warhaftig, Zorach, and Ephraim Fischoff. *Relief and Rehabilitation: Implications of the UNRRA Program for Jewish Needs*. From War to Peace, no. 1. New York: Institute of Jewish Affairs of the American Jewish Congress and the World Jewish Congress, 1944.

Wasserstein, Bernard. *On the Eve: The Jews of Europe before the Second World War*. New York: Simon and Schuster, 2012.

Weil, Simone. *The Need for Roots: Prelude to a Declaration of Duties towards Mankind*. Translated by Arthur Wills. London: Routledge Classics, 2002.

Weinberg, David H. *Recovering a Voice: West European Jewish Communities after the Holocaust*. Oxford: Littman Library of Jewish Civilization, 2015.

Weinberg, Gerhard L. *The Foreign Policy of Hitler's Germany: Diplomatic Revolution in Europe, 1933–36*. Chicago: University of Chicago Press, 1970.

Weis, Paul. *Nationality and Statelessness in International Law*. Library of World Affairs, no. 28. London: Stevens and Sons, 1956.

Weiser, Keith Ian. *Jewish People, Yiddish Nation: Noah Prylucki and the Folkists in Poland*. Toronto: University of Toronto Press, 2011.

Weiss, Yfatt. *Deutsche und polnische Juden vor dem Holocaust: Jüdische Identität zwischen Staatsbürgerschaft und Ethnizität 1933–1940*. Berlin: De Gruyter Oldenbourg, 2000.

White, Angela. *Jewish Lives in the Polish Language: The Polish-Jewish Press, 1918–1939*. Bloomington: Indiana University Press, 2007.

Wojtas, Dorota. *Learning to Become Polish: Education, National Identity and Citizenship in Interwar Poland, 1918–1939*. Leipzig: Lambert Academic, 2009.

Woodbridge, George. *UNRRA: The History of the United Nations Relief and Rehabilitation Administration*. New York: Columbia University Press, 1950.

Yehudai, Ori. *Leaving Zion: Jewish Emigration from Palestine and Israel after World War II*. Cambridge: Cambridge University Press, 2020.

Zahra, Tara. *The Great Departure: Mass Migration from Eastern Europe and the Making of the Free World*. New York: W. W. Norton, 2016.

———. *Kidnapped Souls: National Indifference and the Battle for Children in the Bohemian Lands, 1900–1948*. Ithaca, NY: Cornell University Press, 2008.

———. *The Lost Children: Reconstructing Europe's Families after World War II*. Cambridge, MA: Harvard University Press, 2012.

Zaremba, Marcin. *Wielka trwoga: Polska, 1944–1947—Ludowa reakcja na kryzys* [The great fear: Poland, 1944–1947—people's reaction to the crisis]. Warsaw: Wydawnictwo Znak, Instytut Studiów Politycznych PAN, 2012.

Żaroń, Piotr. *Ludność polska w związku radzieckim w czasie II wojny światowej*. Warszawa: PWN, 1990.

Zeman, Zbynek. *The Life of Edvard Beneš, 1884–1948: Czechoslovakia in Peace and War*. Oxford: Clarendon, 1997.

Zessin-Jurek, Lidia, and Katharina Friedla, eds. *Syberiada Żydów polskich: Losy uchodźców z Zagłady*. Warsaw: Żydowski Instytut Historyczny, 2020.

Zipperstein, Steven J. *Elusive Prophet: Ahad Ha'am and the Origins of Zionism*. Berkeley: University of California Press, 1993.

Zuckerman, Yitzhak. *A Surplus of Memory: Chronicle of the Warsaw Ghetto Uprising*. Edited by Barbara Harshav. Berkeley: University of California Press, 1993.

Zweig, Stefan. *The World of Yesterday: An Autobiography*. London: Cassell, 1947.

INDEX

SARAH A. CRAMSEY is a historian of east central Europe, the global Jewish experience throughout historical time, and the significant Jewish diasporas unleashed in the 1940s. She trained at the University of California, Berkeley; Oxford University; and the College of William & Mary in Virginia. She teaches at Leiden University, where she is an Assistant Professor of Judaism and Diaspora Studies and Special Chair for Central European Studies.